SUGAR: A BITTERSWEET HISTORY

ELIZABETH ABBOTT is the former Dean of Women at Trinity College, University of Toronto, and the bestselling author of *A History of Celibacy* and *A History of Mistresses*.

Also by Elizabeth Abbott

A History of Celibacy
A History of Mistresses

SUGAR

A BITTERSWEET HISTORY

Elizabeth Abbott

Duckworth Overlook

First paperback edition 2010
This edition first published in 2009 by
Duckworth Overlook, London and New York

LONDON
Duckworth Publishers
90-93 Cowcross Street, London EC1M 6BF
Tel: 020 7490 7300 Fax: 020 7490 0080
info@duckworth-publishers.co.uk
www.ducknet.co.uk

NEW YORK
The Overlook Press
141 Wooster Street
New York, NY 10012
for bulk or special sales contact sales@overlookny.com

First published in 2008 by Penguin Group (Canada)

A catalogue record for this book is available
from the British Library

Cataloging-in-Publication Data is available
from the Library of Congress

ISBN 978 0 7156 3975 7 (UK)
ISBN 978 1 59020 647 8 (US)

Printed in the United Kingdom by
JF Print, Sparkford, Somerset

For my beloved son, Ivan Gibbs:
Sugar *is especially for you.*
In it you'll glimpse your Antiguan and Grenadian ancestors.

Contents

～

Acknowledgments

Sugar was a difficult book to finish. In a way, I've been writing it all my life, and this is only one ending. During the last several years, many people have helped me through the process.

Andrea Magyar, editorial director of Penguin Canada, accepted my proposal and made my dreams come true. She and Tracy Bordian, my managing editor who took over the editorial reins, understood my need for images.

My agent, Heide Lange, has been a stalwart support in this book as in all the others. *Sugar* is the latest in twenty years of the best kind of collaboration.

My copy editor, Shaun Oakey, was endlessly helpful.

Stella Petrone has dedicated her life to the cane cutters of the Dominican Republic and, since we visited *bateys* there together, has been a constant source of encouragement and inspiration. Stella, here is my testament to the world of the cane cutters who are always foremost in your thoughts and prayers.

Rick Halpern, formerly Chair of American Studies and a professor in the Department of History and now Principal of New College at the University of Toronto, was generous in offering information and bibliographies, and welcomed me to a seminar of the "Documenting Louisiana Sugar, 1845–1917" project. He also took time to do a critical reading of chapters 9 and 10 of the manuscript.

I am grateful to Franziska Ohnsorge, as brilliant at friendship as she is at economics, for her detailed critique and enormously helpful suggestions.

Mille mercis to the cane cutters I met in the Dominican Republic. *Paské nou té bien résévwa-mwen é nou té rakonté moin istwa nou. M'pap jam blié moun batey-yo kom mwen té promèt nou.*

Yves Pierre-Louis, my brother of the heart, you've accompanied me through another few years and another book and I love you.

Louise Abbott, my flesh-and-blood sister, commiserated, shared laughter and offered technical advice.

Steve and Bill Abbott are my rock-solid brothers, always looking out for me.

Dina Dilaveris contributed by being the most wonderful daughter-in-law a mother could hope for, our family's very own Greek goddess.

My cousin Phillip Abbott provided family reminiscences and photos and information about Antigua's (now defunct) sugar industry.

Dr. Michael Brett-Crowther, editor of the *International Journal of Environmental Studies*, kindly read my entire manuscript, made helpful suggestions and understood my connections to the sugar people.

Heather Conway, my dog-park buddy and friend, was always ready to work technological magic with the images that speak their thousands of words throughout this book.

My nephew Greg Abbott fed me luscious veggie stir-fries and helped out during the final stages.

Brian McKenna and Stephen Phizicky, who directed and produced the fabulous documentary *Big Sugar*, shared information about the Fanjuls and their Dominican *bateys*.

As always, my friends have been beside me and I treasure them: Margaret Gundara, Dolores Cheeks, Claire Hicks, Nina Picton, Pegi Dover, Paulette Bourgeois, Anita Shir-Jacob, Harriet Morris, Sherrill Cheda, Cathy Dunphy and Iris Nowell.

Thank you as well to Nina and Terry Picton for bringing me a copy of *Suiker/Sugar* from the Amsterdam Historical Museum.

As my neighbor and kindred spirit Susan Roy's doctoral dissertation progressed in tandem with my book, we shared cooking duties, the stresses of deadlines and the joys of writing.

Danke to Paul Hopkirk for putting me up (and putting up with me) in Berlin when I was visiting the Zucker-Museum.

Thanks to Julia Langer, Director of the Global Threats Program, WWF, for the book on Celia Sanchez.

Thanks to Asim Ali, Anna Birnie-Lefcovitch and Edyta Rogowska for helping with research. Special thanks to Sophie Chung for those summer days hunched together over a table at Robarts Library with only sesame snaps and the joys of scholarship to sustain us.

Introduction

Once upon a time, sugarcane was known only in lands far away from the Western world. It originated in Polynesia and later spread to India, where adults and children chewed cane stalks to release their sweet sap. In China, sexually hopeful men munched it as an aphrodisiac. But in Europe, where sugarcane was unknown, people sweetened their food with the more expensive honey, which the privileged also consumed in the form of mead, an intoxicating fermented honey wine.

Centuries passed until, in the eighteenth century, an Englishwoman did something that transformed the world.[1] I'll call her Gladys Brown. She was a farm laborer's wife with a hacking cough, three rheumy children and a daily ritual. When she could snatch a few minutes from the grinding round of her daily chores, Gladys would slouch onto the bench beside her cook-fire and imbibe a soothing cup of tea. That heady brew had already addicted aristocratic Europe. But when Gladys, a woman of modest means like millions of other Europeans, popped a chunk of sugar into her cuppa, she redrew the demographic, economic, environmental, political, cultural and moral map of the world.

By sipping her sugared tea, Gladys wrenched generations of men and women from Africa and transported them across the Atlantic to slavery. She ordained the sugar agriculture of the fertile colonies of the Caribbean Sea. She rewrote the map of North America, ensuring that Dutch-held New York and French-held Canada were returned to Britain. She shaped the nature and predilections of Western cuisine, its sauces, candies, drinks, pastries and confections. She put a lollipop into the mouths of our children, and predisposed us to the obesity North Americans and Europeans now battle as an urgent health problem. She lured my ancestors from Northern Ireland's County Fermagh to Antigua, where they lived and planted sugar.

Antigua is a good place to take leave of Gladys and to fast-forward a few centuries to my own birth, when I was born with sugar in my blood. Early in the twentieth century, my then-teenaged grandfather, Stanley Abbott, shipped out of his economically depressed homeland and sailed away to Canada. There, in the privacy of his family, he talked about the

Like Gladys, these French farmwomen find solace in their cups of tea.

homeland he never returned to. To outsiders curious about his accent, he pretended that he had emigrated from Blackpool in England.

I inherited Grand-Dad Stanley's Bible, a farewell gift from the mother he would never see again, and two elaborately embossed sterling silver cups. Both were presented to his grandfather, Richard Abbott, by the Antigua Western Agricultural Society, for "Making the Largest Return of Sugar at the Smallest of Expense" in 1845, and the second one, also in 1845, for "Making the Best Quality of Sugar at the Least Expense." Richard was also listed as a subscriber to Mrs. Flannigan's chatty two-volume book *Antigua and the Antiguans,* first published in 1844.

I developed a fascination with my West Indian heritage. I made contact with lost relatives and, in the Antiguan capital of St. John's, slept in my late great-grandmother Mary Johnston Abbott's bed. I listened transfixed as my great-aunt Millicent Abbott Sutherland recounted her travails as a widow supporting her children out in the cane fields of the Antigua Sugar Factory at Gunthorpes, weighing cane for private cane growers. I listened to calypso and read Caribbean literature. In 1983, I moved to Haiti.

Haiti intensified my fascination with sugar, and I promised myself that, one day, I would write a book about it. When I began to work as a journalist, I often filed sugar-focused stories. I explored the lives and (mis)fortunes of the thousands of Haitians who cross the Dominican border to harvest that republic's sugarcane. I invaded cane fields and watched as men slick with sweat hacked down the towering stalks. I interviewed their wives, sometimes in outside courtyards, sometimes

The author's great-great-grandfather, Richard Abbott, treasured these cups.

The Antigua Sugar Factory at Gunthorpes, view from Mackay Hill. Now closed, it was once Antigua's largest sugar factory, producing sugarcane and molasses to make rum. Its large horizontal steam engines were used to cut cane, pump water into boilers and drive the conveyor belt systems.

in the dank interiors of their low-ceilinged, mud-floored huts. In the giant warehouse of the Haitian American Sugar Company, dwarfed by neat pyramids of refined sugar, I interviewed officials about the company's impending demise. I visited clandestine *guldives* whose *clairin*—rot-gut rum made from distilled sugarcane—was all most Haitians could afford. I toured the cool interior of the Barbancourt Rum Distillery and, back in my Port-au-Prince home, chased my coffee with Barbancourt three-star dark rum. I read books lent me by an expatriate HASCO official and learned about ratooning, soil erosion and the variability of sugar yields.

Years after leaving Haiti to return to Canada, I visited the West African homeland of millions of sugar slaves. In Abomey, Benin (formerly Dahomey), a princely museum curator walked with me through the ruins of his ancestors' pre-colonial palace life. In the slave-trading port of Whydah, I mourned at the site of the barracoons where newly captured slaves were held in the now-rusted iron restraints and chains that are still displayed there. On a clear sunlit June morning,

On April 10, 1987, the Haytian American Sugar Company (HASCO), Haiti's second largest employer, was forced to close because smuggled Dominican sugar sold more cheaply. Here workers stack some of the 445,000 bags of unsold HASCO sugar.

I traveled down the Route des Esclaves, the long and eerily verdant trail that was the shackled slaves' last sight of Africa as they shuffled along in coffles to the waiting slavers.

As my book began to take shape, I devoured sugar-related literature and, in Berlin's Zucker-Museum and Toronto's Redpath Sugar Museum, examined the artifacts of historical sugar production. I also went to the Dominican Republic and visited five bateys, the hamlets where Haitian sugarcane workers live, witnessing without suffering the cane workers' hungry lives and unspeakable privations. Unlike them, I did not cut cane—"It's too dangerous for you," they warned me—or feel the despair of knowing that I could never escape from that bleak, unsafe and uncomfortable world.

The book that emerged from this research and these experiences is about the changes sugar brought to the world that existed before millions of Gladyses were captivated by its sweetness. Cane cultivation destroyed the indigenous Arawaks and Caribs, degraded their environment and created a New World peopled by Europeans and enslaved Africans and later millions of indentured Indians, Chinese and Japanese. Racism developed to justify black slavery and "coolie" labor, a new kind of slavery.

The sugar trade created crucial economic, financial and social links with the industrial revolution that fueled the growth of factories as Europe exchanged manufactured goods and baubles for captured Africans destined for the sugar colonies; North America was part of this trade and supplied those colonies with foodstuffs and other goods. The sugar lobby was an integral part of the system, promoting protectionism through sugar-favoring tariffs and by persuading legislators to provide sugar and rum to the inmates of poorhouses and to sailors in the Royal Navy.

Sugar the commodity forged its own path, conquering taste buds and, despite its lack of nutritional value, establishing itself as a culinary necessity in millions of pantries. This led to the proletarianization of sugar, once a luxury reserved for the wealthy but afterward the crutch and delight of toiling millions. Social rituals developed around sugar: elaborately iced wedding cakes; chocolate bunnies at Easter; cornucopias of candy at Halloween; chocolates on Mother's Day; candy canes at

Christmas. Sugar changed the very concept of meals, what they contained and where and with whom they were eaten, which in turn caused major alterations to family life.

Cane sugar also developed its rivalrous doppelgangers. The first was the beet sugar beloved of Napoleon and later Hitler, both eager to find a substitute source for the cane sugar that England's superior navy would put out of their reach in wartime. Later, saccharin and a proliferation of other artificial products have challenged sugar by sweetening with few or no calories. High-fructose corn syrup, high in calories but cheap, is a newer threat to sugar's supremacy.

The book's final chapter surveys the state of sugar today. As the Western world fattens, the still-powerful sugar lobby challenges such organizations as the World Health Organization about how much sugar a healthy diet may include. Today, as in the past, sugar is a major component of fast food, with sugary soft drinks delivering more sugar to Westerners than any other food. In many places, the sugar industry is so exploitative that it closely resembles the slavery of past centuries.

During the lengthy process of writing this book, I was haunted by two incidents that occurred in the Dominican Republic. The first was when, despite my sturdily soled New Balance shoes, I slipped on my way down a hillside thick with post-harvest cane leavings. As I struggled to right myself only to fall again, the gang of *batey* youngsters accompanying me began to slide as well, their plastic flip-flops useless in the slippery foliage. By the time we reached the bottom on our bottoms, our shared mishap had become shared hilarity.

The second incident was when I visited Santo Domingo with two veteran Haitian cane cutters, fathers of some of those children, who usually never left their *batey*. As we picnicked on a public bench, a Creole-speaking street vendor approached us with his tray of cigarettes and candy and began to chat. As I paid for a handful of his giant pinwheel lollipops my guests could not afford, he confided that he had recently fled a sugar *batey* to make a better life for himself in the city. Afterward, my guests carefully packed the lollipops away for their children. Although they both suffered from "sugar," the diabetes that afflicts so many cane workers, and knew about the dangers of too much sugar consumption, they could not resist the pleasure their children would have in eating the garishly colored confections. In my memories, those oversized lollipops are metaphors for the contradictory meanings of sugar as it transformed the world.

In the very last stages of writing, I suddenly decided to contact a DNA testing company I had read several articles about. Weeks after I submitted two swab-sticks sodden with my DNA—to make sure it was sufficient, I scraped the insides of my cheeks raw—I received a thick envelope containing the results. The analysis revealed bloodlines of European, sub-Saharan African and East Asian origins, my West Indian heritage rooted in long-ago personal mysteries. Whether writing about sugar planters, slaves or indentured coolies, I had been writing about my ancestors.

Part 1

The Oriental Delight Conquers the West

Chapter 1

The Reign
of Sugar Begins

CANE OVERTAKES COMB

Before sugarcane began the peregrinations that would lead it from its South Pacific and Asian homelands across oceans and continents, the world already knew and indulged in the sweetness of honey. At first, the ancients merely filched the sticky syrup from wild bees' hives. But slowly, as they learned to domesticate the industrious little creatures, apiculture was born. The first-century Roman poet Virgil's description of beekeeping, in his *Fourth Georgic*, helped spread this Mediterranean art to other honey-loving regions.

Honey appealed to two growing religions, Christianity and Islam. Christians used it to sweeten their medicines and spice their food, and fermented it into intoxicating mead. In the Middle Ages, heavy-drinking Bavaria, Bohemia and Baltic Europe consumed it in "industrial proportions."[2] Virginity-obsessed Christian theologians pronounced honey and beeswax produced by non-swarming (hence still virgin) bees sacred, and used only virtuously pure beeswax candles in Christian liturgies. Monasteries took up apiculture and produced these candles, mead and other honied by-products. Beekeepers had their special saints, including the famed "Honey-Tongued Doctor" Ambrose of Milan, and Valentine, whose feast day is famously sweetened.

Unlike the wine-drinking Jesus of Nazareth and the Christian leaders who proselytized the new religion, the Prophet Mohammed forbade his followers to consume alcohol. Muslims, their numbers ever growing, had to rely on nonalcoholic beverages. The Koran commended honey for its medicinal benefits, and mint tea, served very hot and laden with honey, was a favorite.

Honey remains an important sweetener in the Middle East, which imports it from Pakistan and the United States. Curiously, a significant source of Saudi terrorist Osama bin Laden's fortune is a vast network of honey shops. He and his al-Qaeda associates have also concealed drugs, weapons and money in honey shipments. "Inspectors don't want to inspect that product. It's too messy," a U.S. administration official explained.[3]

In the South Pacific, where sugarcane likely originated, legends tell variations of a story about how cane sprouted a woman and a man who, through their offspring, founded the human race. In one story, two fishermen, To-Kabwana and To-Karvuvu, repeatedly catch a piece of sugarcane instead of fish. When they tire of tossing it away only to see it reappear in their net, they plant it. The cane roots and grows into a woman who marries one of the men and becomes the mother of humanity. A similar legend from the Solomon Islands describes how knots of cane sprout a man and a woman who found the human race.

Cane was first domesticated in New Guinea and, perhaps independently, in Indonesia. Over time, travelers carried varieties of cane to tropical climates around the globe. In India, Vedic-period hymns refer to sugarcane, and in about 325 BC Kautilya, a government official, referred to five kinds of sugar, including *khanda*, from which we derive the word *candy*. Indian knowledge of sugarcane spread to China, where references to manufacturing it date from 286 BC. As Buddhism spread, so did sugarcane, because Buddhism taught about its healing properties, already well known in India; Chinese Mahayana Buddhist literature even referred to the Buddha as "King of Sugarcane." Sugarcane also had religious uses; for example, it sweetened the Kitchen God's ascent to heaven on cane stalks to report each family's deeds.

By the sixth century, an Indian cane hybrid reached Persia and by the early seventh century was being manufactured there. Egypt was growing it from the mid-eighth century, and by the tenth century sugarcane was an important Middle Eastern crop. Subsequent Arab expansion and conquest spread it throughout the Mediterranean. By the fifteenth century, sugarcane grew in Madeira, the Canary and Cape Verde islands, São Tomé and West Africa.

Six species of sugarcane have been identified, with *Saccharum officinarum*, the "sugar of the apothecaries" or "the noble cane," the most widely grown. All sugarcane is from the Graminaea grass family. *Saccharum officinarum* is tall and strong, its stalks up to two inches thick and as tall as twelve to fifteen feet at maturity. It is jointed and quite soft; when cut, it releases a sweet and juicy sap. Depending on the nature of the soil and the climate, the stems may be yellow, green or reddish brown; in the sunlight, the grassy cane is glistening green.

Sugarcane is propagated asexually from stem cuttings that must include one of the nodes, bands that circle the stem. The cuttings are planted in soil, and the buds that appear begin to root and grow their own stems. Cane is a thirsty crop that requires continual watering; in dry Egypt, for instance, it was irrigated twenty-eight times a season. Cane thrives in heat but cannot tolerate frost.

From its first planting, cane matures in anywhere from twelve to eighteen months, depending on the cane variety, the soil, the climate, the amount of irrigation, the effectiveness of the fertilizer nourishing it, the severity of attacks by vermin or disease, and other environmental factors. However, cane grows again without replanting for several seasons; this "ratoon" cane (from the Spanish *retoñar*, to sprout) gives progressively less sugar until it becomes more economical to replant and begin the cycle anew.

Visitors are often struck by the beauty of undulating, uncut cane fields. A nineteenth-century Scotswoman described sailing Antigua's "carpet of luxuriant green, for a little rain ... had clothed the fields in a garb of lovely verdure."[4] Cane workers who spend their days tramping through cane fields, scorched by the glaring sun, do not see them as shimmering vistas of nature. These hungry and underpaid workers do, however, appreciate the availability, taste and effects of the blandly sweet

In this 1903 image, labeled "Picaninnies' Candy Store, St. Kitts, B.W.I.," children in a cane field solemnly suck cane stalks.

sap that trickles out as they chew through the spiky pulp of the raw cane, quenching their thirst, assuaging their hunger and energizing themselves with its precious calories.

Processed cane is quite different from a stalk hacked down in the field. It is liquefied and boiled down into honey-like molasses and more refined syrups and finally crystallized into a form and a concentrated sweetness that has almost universal appeal, induces strong cravings in many, and is much more versatile in its uses than cane juice. In its final form of whitened grains, sugar so closely resembles salt that culinary mishaps involving an inadvertent substitution of one of these two white grains for the other are all too common.

The first stages of processing cane into sugar almost certainly were developed at different times by different societies. In all of them, the sap is released by mechanical presses that are often quite simple; the sap is repeatedly boiled down and skimmed until it is transformed into a viscous and easily transportable substance suitable for use in cooking. It is likely, on the other hand, that the more complex techniques required to crystallize sugar originated from a single source but, as historical geographer Jock Galloway notes in *The Sugar Cane Industry*, evidence that might trace its history is lacking. What we do know is that these techniques developed in northern India, from where they were introduced throughout the trade routes to the Far East and, through Persia, to the West and ultimately to the New World.

Sugarcane spread steadily across continents and oceans and, over time, rivaled and often replaced honey as the sweetener of choice. Honey's distinctive taste may be too strong for some food and drink, and until improved refining processes developed in the nineteenth century, it usually contained discernible, and perhaps disagreeable, amounts of beeswax. Sugar is more "neutral," and enhances without affecting the taste of the tea, coffee, chocolate and other substances it sweetens. By 1633, James Hart's *Klinike, or, the Diet of the Diseased* noted: "Sugar hath now succeeded honie, and is become of farre higher esteem, and is far more pleasing to the palat, and therefore everywhere in frequent use, as well in sicknesse as in health … Sugar is neither so hot nor so dry as honie."[5] As well, allergic reactions to honey, which contains allergens, may have led some people to prefer sugar.

Over the centuries, a plethora of factors worked to promote sugar over honey. As refining techniques developed and created interest in and familiarity with sugar, artistic bakers demonstrated how they could transform it into elaborate confections impossible to craft with honey or molasses, sugar's cruder liquid. Quite apart from the intrinsically different qualities of honey and sugar, interconnected issues of usage, supply, technology, culture and cost would profoundly influence the results of their rivalry and give sugar the lead.

Historically, sugar has had many uses; in *Sweetness and Power: The Place of Sugar in Modern History*, anthropologist and sugar scholar Sidney Mintz discusses the six principal ones. Focusing on Europe, Mintz describes sugar as a medicine; as a spice and condiment; as a decorative material; as a preservative; as a sweetener; and as a foodstuff. Christian Daniels, a scholar of the history of Chinese technology, expands on Mintz's list in "Agro-Industries: Sugarcane Technology," noting that in regions where it grows, unrefined sugarcane has additional and important uses. Cane stalk is woven into a sturdy building material, and its leaves become roofing shingles or cattle fodder. In Fiji, warriors employ sharpened cane stalks as spears. The stalks are used as well to splint broken limbs and, in pulp form, to dress wounds. Sugarcane sap serves as a source of liquid in areas where drinking water is not widely available. It is a medicine and a refreshing drink offered to guests and on ceremonial occasions. In traditional societies, its powers chase away evil spirits and imbue love potions with magic. Lastly, throughout Asia, sugarcane has been grown alongside taro and rice as another calorie-rich foodstuff. For reasons that remain mysterious, many Asian peoples enjoy sugar without succumbing to its addictive properties. Asians also use sugar medicinally for complaints such as sore throats, colds and menstrual discomfort.

Sugarcane's spread throughout the world was a long and meandering march that proceeded with the speed of the proverbial molasses in winter. Supply was often sporadic, the quality uneven, and the technology to process and refine it unwieldy or lacking. But religions, specifically the rivalrous Islam and Christianity, proved to be the principal agents of propagating knowledge of and desire for sugarcane. "Sugar, we are told, followed the Koran," Mintz writes.[6]

For centuries after his death in 632, the Prophet Mohammed's vision of Islamic world conquest inspired the Arab military and economic expansion that included Syria, the present-day Iraq, Egypt and Morocco and in 711 extended into Europe. In Spain, Arabic power held sway until 1492. The Arabs also traded to Africa and China, and were in many ways true cosmopolitans who established a sort of "pax Islamica."[7] Wherever the Arabs went, sugar and its concomitants of essential technology and administration—sophisticated irrigation techniques, the capital to construct them, water-distribution and land-use policies, sugar-friendly state taxes—went with them. Crucially, even after their defeat and departure, the sugar industry they had implanted continued, its operation assured by the local people whom the Arabs had carefully trained.

The Arabs were particularly interested in irrigation, essential to ever-thirsty sugarcane, and adopted every watering device they came across in their conquests. These included the water wheel or *noria*, and Persia's *qanat*, an irrigation system that avoided wasting water that would evaporate in hot, parched soil by conveying it through a system of underground tunnels called *qanats*. These *qanats*, later used in Egypt and India, were built on an incline from the mountains and used gravity to deliver water down into the cane fields.

We know much less about Arabic refining techniques, other than that they were relatively unsophisticated, though on very special occasions, such as the celebration of the end of the Ramadan fast in 990, Egyptian confectioners fashioned figures of trees, animals and castles out of sugar. The sugar this required had been repeatedly processed and was very fine, whitened and easy to work with. But as in Europe for many centuries, sugar art was a luxury and a rarity. The kind of sugar that followed the Koran was best for masking the taste of bitter medicines, as a medicine itself and as a spice that enhanced cooked meat and other foodstuffs. The more complicated methods of milling cane that produced light crystals and an even texture came later, and may have had Chinese rather than European origins.

The nature of the sugarcane labor force is also unclear. Sugar historian Noel Deerr believed that "although Islam recognised the status of slavery, the Mediterranean industry is free from that ruthless and bloody reproach, the curse of organised slavery that for four hundred years tainted the New World production."[8] Sugar scholars challenge this assertion, citing evidence that sugar workers were enslaved in Morocco and elsewhere in Africa. What *is* true is that slavery was rare in the Muslim sugar-growing world. Most work was done by tenant farmers or hired hands on large estates, and by peasants on their own small plots.

By the middle of the eleventh century, Islamic rule was weakening, and western European Christians railed against some of its teachings, notably polygamy and concubinage, and against its stranglehold on the Holy Land, birthplace of Jesus Christ. The outcome of Christian resentment and restlessness was a series of Crusades that began in 1095 and continued in waves until the end of the thirteenth century, orgies of bloodletting and persecution, military successes and spectacular failures. As they advanced into Muslim territory, the Crusaders were introduced to sugarcane. During the First Crusade, besieged by their Muslim enemies and "tormented by fearsome hunger," Crusaders gnawed on sugarcane and survived on its sap.[9] In areas they overran, specifically Cyprus and Sicily, Crusaders acquired the skills to manage the sugar industry, both cultivation and production.

Whether defeated or victorious, Crusaders returned home with a taste for sugar as well as other spices and foodstuffs. The Crusades themselves gave birth to militant religious orders driven as much by an ambition to acquire estates and political power as by Christian fervor. The Knights of Malta was one of several military orders whose members took up sugar planting. The Crusades transformed Europeans into sugar producers; they also laid the foundation for global conquest that, when secularized, led them to the New World in their quest for new lands.

The Mediterranean sugar industry survived the Crusades, but the nature of landholding changed as feudal lords, religious military orders, the Catholic Church and even Italian cities took them over. To compensate for the capital expenses sugar culture incurred, these new landowners often planted their cane on the demesne land. Then they imposed a *corvée* obliging peasant tenants to perform unpaid compulsory labor, in this case, working in the cane fields and mills. In Crete and Cyprus, much of the land was held in demesne, and these "landlords" made extensive use of the *corvée* to cultivate sugar.

The Black Death of 1347–50 killed one out of three people, emptied towns, businesses, farms and plantations and changed the face and functioning of Europe. Quite apart from wrecked social institutions, and orphaned and widowed families, a severe shortage of laborers empowered survivors, who could now command better wages and conditions. Some employers, sugarcane growers included, preferred to buy slaves—Greek, Bulgarian, Turkish and Tartar, often prisoners of war.

Then, in 1441, Antam Gonçalvez, the very young captain of a very small ship sailing southward down the west coast of Africa, decided to curry favor with Prince Henry of Portugal by capturing some natives. The first victim was a naked camel herder, wounded as he tried to defend himself from the Portuguese. "Spear to spear: such is the first recorded skirmish of Europeans and Africans south of the Sahara," writes Africanist Basil Davidson.[10]

Another young Portuguese, Nuño Tristão, joined Gonçalvez in a slave raid. Shouting "Portugal!" at the top of their lungs, they attacked startled natives and carried twelve back to Portugal. Lisboners suddenly demanded more of these Africans. In the mid-1440s, 235 Africans were kidnapped to Portugal, and "with this pathetic triumph the oversea slave trade may really be said to have begun."[11] It got to the point that the Portuguese word for "work" became "to work like a Moor."

On São Tomé, off the Guinea coast, Portuguese planters grew sugarcane with slave labor. In 1493, Portugal even sent two thousand Jewish children, aged two to ten, to work as sugar slaves. Their parents had recently fled to Portugal from Spain, where the Inquisition was forcing Jews to convert to Roman Catholicism. Only six hundred of these children survived their first year and, contrary to expectation, refused to Christianize. The Inquisition soon drove many adult Jews to leave Portugal as well; some went to Brazil, where, though supposedly "New Christians," they could quietly observe their faith safe from church interference and earn their living in the sugar industry.

Mediterranean sugar, too, was now often slave grown, and its production generally organized in ways that, in Galloway's estimation, permit "the antecedents of plantation agriculture [to] be recognized."[12] Sugar refining, however, remained so basic that it has been equated with "technological retardation."[13] Efficient and powerful sugar mills required vast and readily accessible supplies of wood to fuel them. Deforestation in the Mediterranean had been a critical problem even before the Arab conquest. Lack of fuel is the likely explanation for the sugar industry's failure to develop more efficient refining processes.

As it was, a mill in common use was simply a pair of grindstones, the upper one grinding cane over the immobile lower one. Another was the edge-runner, a human- or animal-powered wheel-shaped grindstone standing in a shallow pit. Uncut cane pieces were unloaded into the pit, and a driveshaft turned the wheel and crushed them. Sometimes presses of the sort used to extract oil from olives or to crush grapes supplemented these mills by crushing out more cane juice.

Once the cane stalks had been crushed, the next stage was to repeatedly boil the juice over intense heat, skim off the impurities and boil it again. A sixteenth-century observer described this process: "There are ... buildings called trapetti, where the sugar is solidified. If one enters one of these it is like going into the forges of Vulcan, as there are to be seen great and continuous fires, by which the juice is solidified. The men who work are blackened with smoke, are dirty, sweaty, and scorched. They are more like demons than men."[14]

At the end of this torturous process, other demonized workmen poured the syrup into inverted conical earthenware vessels, where it cooled and crystallized in loaf form. Molasses dripped through a hole at the tip of the cone, leaving the loaf of sugar drier and purer. The molasses could then be used in syrup form or boiled again to make more sugar. In Morocco and other sugar-growing areas, a further refinement was "claying." Very wet clay was placed on the top of the earthenware cones. The water would slowly seep down through the sugar, cleansing the remnants of molasses. The final loaf was drained to whiteness at the top, becoming darker and darker at the bottom.

Sugar was sold in several forms: as powder, lumps and loaves, clayed or not. It was such a luxury item that, in the thirteenth century, when England's King Henry III ordered three pounds of it, he added, "if so much is to be had." But in the fourteenth century, Venetian traders began to export substantial amounts. In 1319, Nicoletto Basadona carried 100,000 pounds of sugar and 1,000 of candy sugar to London. The bulk sugar trade expanded to Denmark in 1374 and to Sweden in 1390.

This sugar was prohibitively expensive, and used primarily to make nasty-tasting medicine tolerable. Without sugar, most items in the European pharmacopoeia—with a range of ingredients that included animal feces or urine, minced worms, gall from a castrated boar, roasted viper's skin and poisons such as hemlock—tasted at least as awful as Buckley's proudly horrid cough syrup.

As exports increased, a major change in sugar refining drastically altered the relationship between producer and refiner. Until the fifteenth century sugar had been milled and refined as close to the fields as possible, because cane must be processed within a day or two of being harvested, and its bulk makes it awkward to transport. But ambitious

European sugar importers challenged this way of doing things. From about 1470, they imported only crude sugar and refined it in their own refineries in Venice, Antwerp and Bologna. Later, sugar refineries were established throughout northern Europe.

On the one hand, this change substantially reduced the losses incurred from water damage to refined sugar. Fuel in the less deforested north was also cheaper and more plentiful, making northern refining cheaper as well. But in this new system, sugar producers effectively lost control over their commodity and were forced into a relationship with their European commercial associates we would now describe as colonial dependency.

This changed relationship between sugar producer and refiner served as a model for sugar production elsewhere. As Galloway explains, "The organization of the Mediterranean industry, as it evolved during the fourteenth and fifteenth centuries, heralded the organization of the Atlantic and American colonial industries. Indeed, the Mediterranean sugar industry can be seen as a school for the colonizers of Madeira, the Canaries and tropical America.... An important link in the chain of diffusion and development that has taken sugar cane from indigenous garden plant in New Guinea to agro-industry in the tropical world of today."[15] And so the Mediterranean sugar industry set the infrastructural stage for New World sugar culture. Only one crucial element was missing: the urgent and proliferating demand for sugar that would create societies wholly subservient to sugar production, and transform much of the world into relentless and reckless consumers of its sweet delights.

Royal and noble courts were the first to indulge in excessive sugar consumption. A Persian visitor claimed that in 1040, the sultan's bakers transformed 162,000 pounds of sugar into a life-sized tree and other sweet replicas. By the eleventh century, sugar sculptures were common in Islamic North Africa, and that century's caliph, al-Zahir, kept *sukker nakkasarli*—sugar artists—busy for weeks before Islamic feasts, sculpting sugar "art works" for his guests. One such display featured 157 sugar statues and seven table-sized castles. In the early fifteenth century, another caliph added a religious theme and ordered construction of a sugar mosque; he later presented this unique confection to beggars, who gorged on its domes and minarets. The Sultan Murad III celebrated his son's circumcision by ordering the *sukker nakkasarli* to create a procession of enormous sugar giraffes, elephants, lions, fountains and castles.[16]

European court bakers, too, became sugar artists. They mixed sugar, oil, crushed almonds or other nuts and vegetable gums into a malleable clay, then sculpted or pressed it into molds in the shapes of "castles, towers, horses, bears and apes" that were then baked or dried.[17] These elaborate and ostentatious sugar pieces known as "soteltes"—subtleties—decorated and dominated feast tables where guests would admire and then devour them. On November 18, 1515, England's Cardinal Thomas Wolsey celebrated his installation at Westminster Abbey with extraordinarily lavish soteltes depicting castles and churches, beasts and birds, fighting knights and dancing ladies, even an exquisite chess set, all made of "spiced plate" or hardened sugar. A fad in England and France was to serve up male and female sexual organs rendered in sugar. Even the church was not immune to this risqué humor, and until the English church outlawed the practice in 1263, Communion wafers were commonly baked in the shape of testicles.[18]

Sweet virtuosity also evolved into edible political parables or "warners," icing texts or figurines that warned religious dissenters or knightly rivals. By eating their host's complicated yet delicious candied ornaments, "strange symbols of his power," guests also "validated that power," Mintz explains.[19]

By the sixteenth century, this connection between sugar and power was so clear to both hosts and guests that the tables of the burgeoning merchant class groaned under "sundry outlandish concoctions, altogether sweetened with sugar."[20] Royals, nobles, knights and church officials were no longer the only ones able to afford these soteltes. Between 1350 and 1500, the cost of ten pounds of sugar dropped from a very high 35 percent of an ounce of gold to a mere 8.7 percent. Classic cookbooks illustrate how, by the late sixteenth century, ambitious commercial families were demanding recipes for sugary cakes and decorations in the shape of fruits, and even hard sugar cutlery, glasses and plates their guests could eat and drink from and later break into chunks of after-dinner hard candy.

It took more than a century for the joys of sugar to percolate downward to the working classes, who were by then beginning to clamor for it. By the fifteenth century, sugar production had expanded, with Cyprus in particular becoming an important source for Venice. At least one plantation was so extensive that four hundred laborers were required to work it.[21] By the end of the fifteenth century, Spanish planters were also producing sugar in the Canary Island colonies.

In 1493, Cristoforo Colombo, the forty-year-old Genoese known to the English-speaking world as Christopher Columbus, returned to the New World he persisted in identifying as Asia or the Indies. On this second voyage his cargo included sugarcane from the Canary Islands along with a surreal directive to the indigenous people signed by King Ferdinand and Juana "the Mad," his demented daughter, Queen of Castile. This letter informed the indigenous Taino people that "the late Pope gave these islands and mainland of the ocean and the contents hereof to the above-mentioned King and Queen, as is certified in writing and you may see the documents if you should so desire." Should the Taino dispute the pope's authority to dispose of their homeland, the monarchs warned, "we shall enslave your persons, wives and sons, sell you or dispose of you as the King sees fit; we shall seize your possessions and harm you as much as we can as disobedient and resisting vassals. And we declare you guilty of resulting deaths and injuries, exempting Their Highnesses of such guilt as well as ourselves and the gentlemen who accompany us."[22] This menacing missive authorized Columbus to Christianize those natives who had welcomed him so courteously in 1492, and to install Europeans on their expropriated land to plant Europeans crops.

Columbus's second arrival was very different from his first. For one thing, he learned that the Taino had been so infuriated by the arrogance and demands of the Spaniards he had left behind in 1492 as advance guard settlers that they had murdered them all. But Columbus had brought a huge contingent of reinforcements, twelve thousand prospective settlers including officials, priests, soldiers, farmers, agricultural experts and "gentlemen," and a variety of domestic animals, seeds and plants, including the sugarcane he had become familiar with on his mother-in-law's Madeira sugar holdings, and which the Crown required all settlers to grow on their land grants.

In the new settlement he diplomatically called Isabella, Columbus supervised the cane's planting and marveled at how readily it rooted and grew. In a dispatch to his sponsors, Ferdinand and Isabella, he predicted, "It is to be expected from the speed of the growth of the vines, wheat and sugar-canes that have been planted, that the products of this place will not be behind those of Andalusia and Sicily," well known for the concentrated sweetness of their sugarcane.[23]

In the early years, however, the Spaniards were far more interested in Hispaniola's gold than in farming. Under Columbus's orders, they forced natives to provide gold nuggets and dust, and made strenuous efforts to operate mines. Chaos and misery ensued. In the maelstrom of treachery, bloodshed and terror wrought by Columbus's brutal leadership and religious fanaticism, the colony failed and so did the sugarcane.

The natives suffered and died. Many settlers starved on their land grants and, in desperation, rebelled against the despotic Columbus and his brother Diego. Rumblings of Hispaniola's dire situation reached Ferdinand and Isabella, who sent Francisco de Bobadilla, a knight-commander in the military order of Calatrava, to investigate. On August 23, 1500, Bobadilla sailed into the harbor of Santo Domingo to the sight of the swaying corpses of seven hanged Spanish rebels. After landing, Bobadilla learned that the Columbus brothers had seventeen more Spaniards under sentence of death. Bobadilla assumed control of the government and shipped the Columbuses back to Spain in chains.

Ferdinand and Isabella forgave Columbus, by then a severely arthritic, self-aggrandizing religious maniac who sported a Franciscan robe and rope belt. They even sponsored further voyages. But they appointed a knight-commander in the military order of Alcantara, a *real* Franciscan lay brother, to govern Hispaniola and most of Spain's other colonies.

Explorers from Spain and other European nations—Portugal, France, England, Denmark, Holland and Sweden—were already expanding on Columbus's "discoveries" and claiming them for their monarchs. The sordid and violent story of the conquests of the Caribbean islands and the South American mainland is well known. So is Pope Alexander VI's astonishing division of the "non-Christian world" by which he granted the entire New World to Spain, and Africa and India to Portugal. A year later, in 1494, Spain and Portugal modified this arrangement through the Treaty of Tordesillas, putting Brazil into Portugal's sphere of influence. Ironically, neither Portugal nor Spain truly comprehended the vastness of the territories and the nature of the peoples they so blithely divvied up.

Europe's assumption of ownership of the New World set the stage for the sugar culture that Columbus had attempted to introduce. Sugar planting began in earnest in the early sixteenth century in Hispaniola when colonists planted cane brought in from the Canaries. The first major sugar planter was a surgeon, Gonzalo de Velosa, who lured Canary Island sugar experts to Hispaniola and paid them from his own pocket. Then, in partnership with two brothers, Christoval and Francisco Tapia, he constructed a horse-powered mill. The colony's new administrators, friars of the Hieronymite order, successfully encouraged sugarcane production through 500-gold-peso loans for building mills. Within a decade, scores of mills were processing cane for export back to Spain. In 1516, Gonzalo Fernández de Oviedo y Valdés, the colony's official historian and, until the gold deposits ran out, its gold-smelting supervisor, had the distinction of bringing the first documented New World sugar to Europe and making a personal present of the six loaves to Charles V; in 1517, the Hieronymite Fathers sent their monarch several more.

Two other successful planters were Columbus's son Diego and his grandson, Luiz, whose properties were Hispaniola's finest, and perfectly situated for oceangoing shipping. In 1520, now strategically married to Maria de Toledo, King Ferdinand's grandniece, Diego was appointed governor of Hispaniola, where he presided over the gaiety of his colonial court as well as his flourishing sugar plantation. By 1546, according to Oviedo, Hispaniola boasted twenty "powerful mills and four horse mills, and ... ships come from Spain continuously and return with cargoes of

NIGRITÆ EXHAUSTIS VENIS METALLICIS
conficiendo saccharo operam dare debent.

In Hispaniola, naked and scantily clad African slaves manufacture sugar, cutting it in the fields, boiling then storing it in clay vessels. From a woodcut by one of the De Bry brothers, who never visited Hispaniola.

sugar and the skimmings and molasses that are lost would make a great province rich."[24]

As sugar production took root, it uprooted almost everything that had been there before: the peoples and their civilizations, and the agriculture and the very soil and topography of the New World. American environmentalist Kirkpatrick Sale rightly sees the nature of Columbus's encounters with the natives as instrumental in the development of "everything of importance in the succeeding 500 years": "the triumph of capitalism, ... the establishment of a global monoculture, the genocide of the indigenes, the slavery of people of color, the colonization of the world, the destruction of primal environments."[25] To this list should be added: the creation of major trade routes, notably the famous triangular trade between the sugar lands, Europe, Africa and North America; the creation of new Creole societies; the redefinition of taste standards and the addiction of millions of people to sweetness and to unhealthy, disease-causing diets; the development of the language of human rights; and fatal damage to the planet's flora and fauna. "Growing sugar cane may have done more damage to wildlife than any other single crop on the planet," the World Wildlife Fund reported in 2004.[26] The agency for most of these transformations would be sugarcane culture, European version.

TAINO SLAVERY AS THE BLUEPRINT FOR NEW WORLD LABOR

All that remains of millions of Arawak-speaking Tainos and their way of life are the memoirs of European witnesses and the narratives of historical and archeological detectives. The following is a brief account of what was lost. Columbus is our first observer. The Tainos "all go around as naked as their mothers bore them…. They are very well built, with very handsome bodies and very good faces; their hair coarse, almost like the silk of a horse's tail, and short. They wear their hair over their eyebrows, except for a little in the back that they wear long and never cut." They were keenly intelligent, he wrote, but so "wondrous timid" that fifty Spaniards could overpower and control them.[27]

The Tainos were agriculturalists who reaped abundant crops year-round, with most of the farm work relegated to women. They cultivated the soil without depleting the nutrients or the water supply, and protected their crops from erosion by planting them *conuco*-style, in high mounds covered by leaves. They ensured against crop failure by sowing a range of foodstuffs, including manioc, corn, sweet potato, yams, squash, peppers and peanuts, and the cassava from which they made flatbread. In their ample spare time, Taino men supplemented this cornucopia with game, seafood, and fish they caught in cotton nets.

The Tainos lived in round houses built around a common courtyard-cum-playground. They sat on wooden chairs and slept in cotton hammocks or on banana-leaf mats. Life was communal and polygamous; each man shared a single home with his several wives and his children. Taino society was patriarchal, led by *caciques* and village elders.

The Tainos carved stone replicas of their gods, the *zemi*, as toads, reptiles or grimacing humans, and appeased these otherworldly beings with gifts of bread and other ritual offerings. They painted their bodies, decorated themselves with feathers and tickled their throats with sticks so they could vomit up impurities. They enacted elaborate ceremonies that included rhythmic drumming. The *zemi* responded to human appeals, counseling and healing through the agency of shamans.

The Tainos preserved their knowledge of their village's history with the help of the tribal historian, who communicated it to them in an epic chant. Village history was a central feature of Taino life. Their ancestors' bones were interred in the village's soil, and their souls resided there. The people had no concept of private ownership; land, like the sky and the sea, was part of the sacred universe and belonged to everyone. "In a way that few Europeans could understand, the land *was* Indian culture: it provided Native Americans with their sense of a fixed place in the order of the world, with their religious observances, and with their lasting faith in the importance of the struggling but united community as opposed to the ambitious, acquisitive individual," a recent study explains.[28]

Until the Europeans arrived, the Taino population numbered anywhere from three million to just under eight million.[29] When Bartolomé de Las Casas arrived in 1502, their extermination was already foreseeable. In 1514, their Spanish conquerors counted only twenty thousand survivors. In 1542, Las Casas recorded only two hundred, and within two decades, the Tainos of Hispaniola died out.

Las Casas is the primary narrator of the Tainos' life and death. He was a Renaissance man, a deacon and later a priest, a sugar planter, administrator, historian and anthropologist whose experiences ultimately transformed him into a human rights advocate. Early in 1502, the eighteen-year-old set out for Hispaniola, where his father had been rewarded with an *encomienda*, a grant of land that included its indigenous inhabitants and any tribute that could be exacted from them, and required the colonist to do military service during emergencies and to seek diligently to Christianize his charges. Later, Diego Columbus granted the young Las Casas his own *encomienda* after he helped suppress a native uprising.

The Taino holocaust is a tragedy on several levels because it provided the blueprint for the slavery that destroyed the lives and culture of millions of the Africans and others imported to work sugar plantations. Producers of other commodities also adopted this new form of coerced labor, which spread throughout the Americas, including to what became the United States. "The significance of Spain's Indian policy lies in the fact that it provided an instruction for Spain's successors in the Caribbean which they were not slow to better. It marked an indelible stamp of degradation on labour in the Caribbean," Trinidadian historian Eric Williams concludes.[30]

Unlike the Africans who succeeded them, who were torn away from their homelands, the Taino lost their identities and their lives at home. Their European conquerors expropriated their lands and dismantled their agriculture, planting instead unfamiliar chickpeas, wheat, onions, lettuce, grapes, melons and barley. They dishonored Taino *caciques*, humiliated Taino men and raped Taino women. They scorned Taino religious beliefs and social values, their polygamous family structure and their political institutions, and dismissed their carefully preserved history as savage claptrap. They dumped shackled Tainos onto Europe-bound ships for delivery into slavery; Columbus himself shipped five hundred to a Seville slave market.

Those Taino who did not succumb to overwork, malnutrition, brutality and despair could not withstand European diseases. They had no immunity to the smallpox, bubonic plague, yellow fever, typhus, dysentery, cholera, measles and influenza that germinated aboard filthy ships laden with sick and sickening sailors and colonists, putrid, maggot-riddled food, ailing livestock, flea-ridden dogs and cats and legions of enterprising rats. A single epidemic could kill off more than half of any village. In 1518, smallpox wiped out 90 percent of Hispaniola's remaining Tainos. By mid-century, they were extinct. In other colonies, up to

90 percent of the native population would disappear well before the seventeenth century. By 1611, for example, only seventy-four natives had survived the Spanish colonization of Jamaica.[31]

What did survive was slavery's fundamental brutality. Las Casas believed that when Spaniards punished a Taino by hacking off his ears, their savagery "marked the beginning of the spilling of blood, later to become a river of blood, first on this island and then in every corner of these Indies."[32] For centuries after, slaveholders hacked off extremities and limbs as part of their arsenal of punishment.

Las Casas describes the first time dogs were used against rebellious slaves. As the Tainos tried to pull down an outsized crucifix that symbolized the horror of their lives under Spanish occupation, the Spaniards responded furiously by unleashing twenty mastiff-hound crossbreeds trained to kill. The massive animals hurled themselves at the natives and ripped out their throats or eviscerated them. The Spanish applauded the snarling canines and afterward imported hundreds more. Powerful trained dogs became standard weapons in the never-ending struggle to subdue enslaved workers.

Las Casas quoted the *cacique* Hatuey, who warned against accepting Christianity: "They tell us, these tyrants, that they adore a God of peace and equality, and yet they usurp our land and make us their slaves. They speak to us of an immortal soul and of their eternal rewards and punishments, and yet they rob our belongings, seduce our women, violate our daughters."[33]

Hatuey's rage about violated womanhood would echo through the centuries. From its very beginnings, the slaveholder's right to rape any enslaved woman was a cornerstone of the institution of New World slavery. The racial dimension of slavery, and hence of rape, was just as evident, even when colonial laws specifically banned interracial sex. The growing numbers of mixed-race children were living proof that it was a common occurrence. The name of the first of these children is unknowable, but Mexican tradition identifies him as Martin Cortés, born in 1522 to conquistador Hernán Cortés and his Indian mistress, Malinche, the native noblewoman who, as his adviser and translator, had played a crucial role in his military successes.

The little boy's birth was not a happy event for his parents. Cortés no longer needed Malinche's counsel and comfort, and he worried that their relationship would cost him the noble title he longed for. He sent her away, ensuring that she was taken care of by marrying her off to one of his captains, Juan Jaramillo, and granting her a large tract of land. But Malinche's new husband regretted their marriage and swore that he had been taken advantage of while he was in a drunken stupor. Malinche died a few years later; Juan Jaramillo waited only weeks before remarrying.

To this day conflicted Mexicans express much of their bitterness about the Spanish conquest by reviling Malinche and Martin, she as a traitor, he as a symbol of her racial and sexual treachery. They denounce other Mexicans they consider turncoats as *malinchistas*. When *New York Times* reporter Clifford Krauss located the house where Malinche once lived with Cortés, its current occupant told him that "for Mexico to make this house a museum, would be like the people of Hiroshima creating a monument for the man who dropped the atomic bomb."[34] Writer Octavio Paz calls Malinche "the cruel incarnation of the feminine condition. The strange permanence of Cortes and La Malinche in the Mexican's imagination and sensibilities reveals that they are ... the symbols of a secret conflict that we have still not resolved."[35] In the 1980s, furious demonstrators destroyed a Coyoacan monument depicting the famous family of Cortés, Malinche and Martin.

Other Amerindians, including the Aztecs, Incas and Mayans, survived European conquest and mistreatment. So, barely, did the Caribs, fierce warriors who inhabited the islands now known as Trinidad, Guadeloupe, Martinique and Dominica, where they lived in seaside villages in sturdy, leaf-roofed houses built around a central fireplace. Like the Tainos, the Caribs farmed and fished, and slept in hammocks. In fact, much of domestic Carib culture likely resembled the Tainos', thanks to the Caribs' habit of kidnapping brides from Taino communities. The Caribs contemptuously rejected the Christianity of the proselytizing Europeans in favor of their own animist beliefs.

In most other ways, the Caribs were warlike and unlike the peaceable Arawaks. They routinely raided neighboring tribes in their dugout canoes, terrorizing Arawaks and Europeans alike. In 1610, they raided

Antigua and, so the tale is told, made off with the governor's wife and two children. In 1666, they murdered Antigua's ex-governor, broiled his head and took it back with them to Dominica.

Their cannibalism further distinguished the Caribs from the Arawaks. Carib flesh-lust was legendary and spawned countless stories—one Carib warrior claimed that French "meat" was tender but Spanish "meat" was tough, while another boasted that he preferred Arawaks to Europeans, who gave him a bellyache. Carib cannibalism probably stemmed from the belief that in ingesting an enemy's body parts one also ingests his strength, courage or skills, which would explain why they took such risks to remove Carib corpses from battle-fields, presumably to prevent the enemy from eating them.

Even after Europeans had a firm foothold in the West Indies, they could not enslave the Caribs, who escaped, fought back or committed mass suicide rather than live in slavery. In Grenada, a band of forty leapt to collective death from the steep hill now known as Morne des Sauteurs (Leapers' Hill). As the cane fields advanced, the Caribs retreated. By the early seventeenth century they held only Guadeloupe, Dominica and Martinique. Sometimes they intermarried with black Maroons, or fugitive slaves; their offspring were known as Black Caribs. Caribs often withdrew to the mountains and from these fortified outposts attacked European settlements, burning plantations and killing whites. Some scholars believe that Man Friday in Daniel Defoe's 1719 classic, *Robinson Crusoe*, was modeled on an Arawak captured by a marauding band of Caribs.

European disease and persecution decimated the Caribs, but survivors eventually developed new ways of living, and many settled down on a 232-acre reserve allocated them by the British, who won Dominica from the French in 1763. Today, Caribs still live in Dominica and St. Vincent.

BARTOLOMÉ DE LAS CASAS, SUGAR PLANTER AND GUILTY WITNESS

The brutality of New World slavery was condemned even as it was being developed. Its first public critics were the Dominican friars who arrived in 1510 and lived apostolically, in huts, sleeping on beds of branches, eating plain cabbage broth and wearing coarse habits. These men possessed only two boxes among them, full of psalters and liturgical paraphernalia. On December 21, 1511, Friar Antón Montesino, "the voice in the desert of this island," denounced the *encomienda* system, which granted land or even entire villages, including their indigenous inhabitants, to Spaniards. Grantees could exact tribute of gold nuggets or other precious items from the villagers, whom they were required to Christianize. The *encomienda* system, Friar Montesino thundered, held the natives in "a cruel and horrible servitude" and destroyed "infinite numbers of them by homicides and slaughters never before heard of.... Why do you keep them so oppressed and exhausted, without giving them enough to eat or curing them of the sicknesses they incur from the excessive labor you give them, and they die, or rather, you kill them?" he demanded.[36]

Young Las Casas, who produced slave-grown sugar, was unmoved, and he continued to exploit his slaves, though he tried to be compassionate. But in 1514 Las Casas had an epiphany: everything done to the Indians was unjust and tyrannical. He surrendered his slaves to the governor and devoted his life to documenting, preaching and lobbying against the abuses of the *encomienda* system. Las Casas was named Protector of the Indians, but in 1522, deeply discouraged and frustrated at his failure to halt the genocide, he resigned and later joined the Dominican Order.

As a Dominican, Las Casas focused on researching and writing his *Historia General de las Indias* and other influential histories and treatises that stoked the flames of reform of colonial policy. He was a persuasive and learned writer, and he buttressed his arguments with dramatic detail from his personal observations of the bloody course of Spain's New World settlement.

Las Casas was instrumental in the pope's issuing of *Sublimis Deus*, the 1537 papal bull often referred to as the Magna Carta of Indian Rights, a powerful pro-Indian document though never formally promulgated in the colonies. Indians are "truly men," the bull declared, who can become real Christians and, whether pagan or Christian, have the right to liberty and property.

In 1550, Charles V decided that only a public debate in front of a jury of legal experts and theologians could resolve the central issue of forcible conversion of conquered peoples. This intellectual extravaganza was held in Valladolid, in central Spain, and pitted Las Casas against scholar and humanist Juan Ginés de Sepúlveda. De Sepúlveda argued that conversion by conquest was legitimate, and dismissed the natives as "slaves by nature, uncivilized, barbarian and inhuman."[37] Las Casas rejected this thesis with a scriptural reference, and argued for peaceful conversion because the natives "are our brothers, and Christ gave His life for them."[38] The jury could reach no consensus: neither de Sepúlveda nor Las Casas had been overarchingly convincing. The debate did, however, focus attention on the New World and the treatment of its natives there.

In 1552, in his sixties, Las Casas produced his sensational *Brevísima Relación de la Destrución de las Indias* (*Very Brief Account of the Destruction of the Indians*), his heartbreakingly personal witness to the annihilation of the natives, fifteen million of them by his count. He also wrote powerful books about the Incas of Peru and, until he died at age eighty-two, worked on his *Historia de las Indias*. He defied the Spanish Inquisition, publishing some books without its permission.

Las Casas preached what can only be regarded as sixteenth-century liberation theology, which considers activism in the cause of human rights and social justice integral to Christian faith. For Las Casas, human rights were indistinguishable from practical, lived Christianity. Notre Dame law professor Paolo Carrozza has described Las Casas as "the midwife of modern human rights talk."[39]

Las Casas also introduced the principle of restitution for human rights violations. His widely detested *Confesionario* of 1546 spelled out how this would work. When a conquistador or *encomendero* came to confess, the confessor would immediately summon a notary. The penitent would swear before both priest and notary that his sins had driven him to award a power of attorney to his confessor to do whatsoever was necessary to make amends on his behalf, including—and this was the main point—"to restore his entire estate to the Indians ... without anything remaining for his heirs."[40] The penitent would also free the natives on his *encomienda*, and would authorize the notary to revoke any previous will and testaments. Las Casas's justification for this total restitution of worldly goods was theological: Pope Eugenius III had decreed that "confessors cannot give absolution to robbers, which is what all the said conquistadors of the Indies are, unless they first return all they have stolen."

Although Las Casas's *Confesionario* provoked only fury, and no penitents lined up to sign away their worldly goods as restitution to their native victims, his introduction of the principle of restitution was a great contribution to the development of human rights. It was also an explicit acknowledgment of the great wrongs being perpetrated.

Only in his old age did Las Casas address another great wrong—the enslavement of Africans to replace the Tainos and other natives—and acknowledge his role in it. In Las Casas's version of the story, certain sugar planters requested permission to buy black slaves from Spain because "the Indians were becoming fewer." After all, African slaves worked many of Spain's other sugar holdings. Besides, some of these planters promised Las Casas that if he could arrange for them to import a dozen black slaves, "they would give up their Indians so these Indians could be free."

Las Casas had leapt at this offer, and lobbied successfully to bring it to fruition. In 1517, Spanish officials, the Hieryonymite Brothers among them, agreed that four thousand black slaves would be divided between Spain's four colonies of Hispaniola, Cuba, Jamaica and San Juan. This was the first asiento, the trade license system that instantly became what Basil Davidson calls "an absolutely essential aspect of the whole Spanish-American enterprise. The Kings of Spain lived off the trade."[41] In attempting to free the Indians, Las Casas had facilitated the enslavement of the Africans, giving to humanity with one hand what he took away with the other.

Decades later, having slowly come to realize that the Africans' captivity was as unjust as the Indians', Las Casas pleaded "guilty through carelessness." He had helped prepare the way for the beginning of one of the greatest demographic transformations in history: the forcible transport of millions of mostly young Africans to the New World to toil as slaves. The asiento opened the floodgates to African slavery: from ten or twelve blacks in the early 1500s to more than thirty thousand on Hispaniola and more than a hundred thousand on Spain's other islands. "And as the sugar mills increased every day," Las Casas recalled, "the need to place Negroes in them increased, for each sugar mill using water requires at least eighty Negroes, and the sugar-mills using horses, thirty or forty."[42]

The original plan to import only blacks enslaved on Spanish territory was quickly abandoned in favor of taking them from Africa itself. This decision was taken because at the same time as the mines and sugar plantations were expanding, the Africans were dying off just like the Indians. "We used to think in this island, that, if a Negro were not hanged, he would never die," Las Casas wrote, "because we had never seen one die of illness, and we were sure that, like oranges, they had found their habitat, this island being more natural to them than Guinea." But Africans succumbed to the island's sugarcane fields, mills and boiling houses. "The excessive labour they had to endure, and the drinks they take made from cane syrup, death and pestilence were the result," Las Casas admitted.[43]

The slave traders responded energetically to the upsurge in demand. Portuguese slave traders "hastened—and hasten every day—to abduct and capture them in as many wicked ways as they can," Las Casas wrote, and so did Africans who sold their enemies to Europeans. "Thus we are the cause of all the sins which they commit against each other, as well as our own in buying them," he concluded, sharing out the blame between greedy Portuguese and heartless Africans.[44] Eric Williams dismisses this apology as lame and late, and notes that Las Casas "never became Protector of the Negroes," who had no protector.[45]

KING SUGAR BEGINS HIS DEPREDATIONS

By 1566, when Las Casas died, black slaves were so numerous "as a result of the sugar factories [that] ... the land seems an effigy or an image of Ethiopia itself," a contemporary marveled.[46] Sugarcane cultivation spread swiftly throughout the New World as colonizers from other European nations came, saw, conquered and planted. Thanks to militant adventurers like Columbus and Cortés, the Spanish were the first to stake claims to Hispaniola, Jamaica, Cuba, Puerto Rico and Trinidad as well as a slice of the Americas stretching from Texas to Patagonia. And thanks to the Treaty of Tordesillas that so generously granted them the right to Brazil, the Portuguese were second only to the Spanish.

From 1630 to 1660, England, France and Holland eagerly joined in the frenzied New World land grab and founded their own sugar colonies, which, during these three decades, the Dutch dominated. As colonization proceeded and mother countries battled each other, colonies changed hands and nationalities, often several times. Dominica and Grenada bounced back and forth between England and France. Spanish Jamaica became British in 1655. France's St. Vincent was ceded to Britain in 1763, restored to France in 1779 and regained by England in 1783 under the Treaty of Versailles.

In the earliest days of colonization, only a portion of land had been planted with cane, with the rest given to pasture, forest, crops to provision the workforce or cash crops. But as knowledge of sugar culture spread, and its profitability increased, sugar literally took over the new lands and earned the Caribbean colonies their nickname: the sugar islands.

As already noted, the experience of growing sugar in Madeira, the Canary Islands and São Tomé in North Africa provided some answers and some models, as did Spain's pioneering New World sugarcane efforts. Other colonial models would be created in response to evolving needs and demands.

Labor was the most pressing issue, and, for nearly a century, natives and Africans were not the only victims. At first mother countries supplied laborers in the persons of men and a few women desperate for a decent livelihood and eager for the land grant or the £10 grant promised after they served their years, usually three to ten, as indentured servants or, in the French colonies, *engagés*.

The reality was quite different from recruiters' promises, and indentured servitude was "maintained by the systematic application of legally sanctioned force and violence."[47] The transatlantic voyage killed many of the emigrants, and it was common practice to throw the sick overboard so they would not contaminate their shipmates. Once in the colonies, they were set right to work without any time to recuperate or

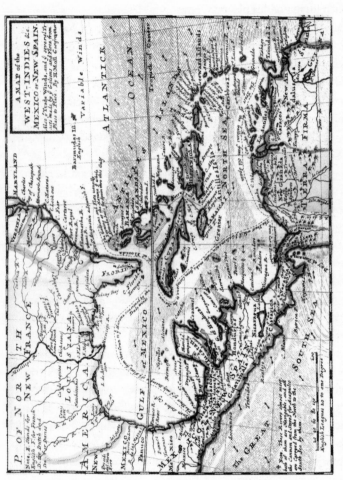

A Map of the West Indies & c. Mexico or New Spain. Also ye Trade Winds and ye several Tracts made by the Galeons and Flota from place to place. *From Atlas Minor, London, 1736, by influential Tory cartographer Herman Moll. This map, his masterpiece, portrayed the West Indies as a region with enormous commercial potential at the core of the developing British Empire. The map also assisted British buccaneers who preyed on Spanish shipping.*

become "seasoned." A seventeenth-century Catholic historian observed, "They are worked to excess; they are badly fed, and are often obliged to work in company with slaves, which is a greater affliction than the hard labour; ... and I know one [master] at Guadeloupe who had buried more than fifty upon his plantation, whom he had killed by hard work, and neglect when they were sick. This cruelty proceeded from their having them for three years only, which made them spare the Negroes rather than these poor creatures!"[48]

In Barbados, planter William Dickson recalled, the indentured servants were "stinted in their diet, and otherwise ill treated."[49] In a petition to Parliament in 1659, begging for relief, white servants indentured in Barbados described lives spent "grinding at the mills and attending the furnaces, or digging in this scorching island; having nothing to feed on (notwithstanding their hard labour) but potato roots, nor to drink, but water with such roots washed in it ... being bought and sold still from one planter to another, or attached as horses and beasts for the debts of their masters, being whipt at the whipping post (as rogues) for their masters' pleasure, and sleeping in sties worse than hogs in England." Decades later, nothing had changed. "They are domineered over and used like dogs," the governor of Barbados reported.[50]

Whenever they could, these white workers escaped, feigned sickness, attacked their masters or, most commonly, set fire to the hated cane fields. Those who did not rebel either died, often from yellow fever, or had to be released when their contracts or sentences expired, after which they demanded the plot of land promised them on expiration of their term of labor. Some became farmers themselves; few agreed to continue working on sugar plantations. Toward the end of the seventeenth century, sugar gobbled up all the available land on most of the islands, so even this incentive disappeared. The governor of Barbados worried that the poor whites would emigrate in droves, leaving the few who remained "to be murdered by Negroes."[51]

As well as indentured servants, Europe disgorged the inmates of its prisons onto New World sugar plantations, exporting felons as well as those convicted of such minor offenses as stealing the proverbial loaf of bread to feed a starving family. In Bristol, which by the seventeenth century had important sugar trade interests, judges and magistrates with interests in overseas plantations dealt with the shortage of sugarcane labor by adding years to prison sentences. Eight years' forced labor was thought quite suitable.

Religious nonconformists and political prisoners accused or suspected of disloyalty to their ruler were also transported to the cane fields. Oliver Cromwell sent Irish Catholic survivors of the 1649 massacre of Drogheda to Barbados and was so pleased with this policy that, whenever possible, he "barbadoed" his enemies, sending Scottish and Irish men and women to sugar plantations in Barbados, Jamaica and elsewhere, a policy some of his successors also adopted. "The lack of squeamishness shown in the forced labour of whites was a good training for the forced labour of blacks," writes Williams.[52]

By the end of the seventeenth century, as white forced labor was disappearing, the ratio of whites to blacks was one to two in St. Kitts, Montserrat and Grenada, one to three in Nevis, one to four in Antigua, one to six in Jamaica and one to eighteen in Barbados. Planters and resident officials understood that they could no longer attract significant numbers of whites to work the cane, and were increasingly concerned about the security implications of such enormous imbalances between white and black.

Sugar was the culprit in this imbalance: in colonies reliant on other crops, Cuba with its tobacco and Puerto Rico with its coffee, for example, whites outnumbered blacks. "Where sugar was king, the white man survived only as owner or overseer. Otherwise he was superfluous," Williams explains.[53]

By then sugarcane's environmental impact was also evident. Intensive cane cultivation depleted the soil and water tables and brought about the ruinous process of deforestation. European cattle overgrazed some native grasses and munched at least one species of thatch grass into extinction. Cattle, sheep and goats trampled grooves into their pastureland, packing down the soil so that rainfall slid over rather than into it. The channels this created caused erosion, which would not have happened "under the environmentally conservative indian *conuco* system of pre-Hispanic times," observes historical geographer David Watts.[54]

Another terrible change was the arrival of black, Norwegian and roof rats, harboring disease-bearing fleas and preying on native fauna and on the new crops. Sugarcane was particularly vulnerable, being plentiful, easily accessible and naturally appealing. The first rats that leapt from the *Niña, Pinta* and *Santa Maria* onto Hispaniola were the advance guard of an invading force that changed the face of native agriculture and crop yields. In today's famished Haiti, for example, rats eat up to 40 percent of the crops that farmers struggle to produce in the parched and eroded soil.

As Eric Williams lamented, "King Sugar had begun his depredations."[55]

Chapter 2

The Proletarianization of Sugar

THE NOBLE DELICACY

Sugar began life in Europe as an aristocrat, a luxury reserved for nobles who outdid each other with sugar-sculpted virtuosity. It was so highly valued that sycophantic officials curried favor with kings by offering them gifts of sugar loaves. Sugar symbolized wealth, and delighted those fortunate enough to have it available.

Let's peep in at a feast given by Mary of Hungary, regent of the Netherlands, in honor of Philip II, son and heir of Charles V. It's 1549, and Charles is under intense pressure to act decisively on the issue of New World Indian human rights. The highlight of the evening is the "sugar collation," a gastronomic orgy offered after both banquet and ball. Charles and Mary's other guests watch as each course is lowered to the ground on tables attached to massive pillars, followed by an outburst of thunder and lightning, with tiny pieces of candy simulating rain and hail. The tables are laden with sweets, including a hundred varieties of white conserves. The most impressive boasts sugar sculptures of a deer, boar, birds, fish, a rock and a sugar-fruit laurel tree. Does Charles feel the slightest twinge of conscience at the human cost of so much squandered sweetness? Does the spectacle remind him of the Valladolid debate, for which Bartolomé de Las Casas and Juan Ginés de Sepúlveda are even now preparing?

Whatever Charles might have thought that night, Mary of Hungary's party did not set the standard for sugary spectacles. In 1566, when Maria de Aviz married Alessandro Farnese, the Duke of Parma, the sugar platters at their wedding feast held a stunning array of sweets that guests devoured in sugar dishes and glasses, cutting larger *bonbons* with sugar knives and forks, mopping up syrupy ones with sugar bread. Even the candlesticks were sugar. But all that seemed quite modest when the city of Antwerp's wedding gift was revealed: more than three thousand sugar sculptures commemorating Maria's voyage from Lisbon to her new home in the Netherlands. Whales and sea serpents, storms and ships, then the cities that welcomed her en route, even Alessandro himself was replicated in stately sugar. As a parting token, each wedding guest took home a piece of the royal action.

Design for a sugar ornament of a muscular French poodle pulling a chariot driven by a triumphant winged figure holding a whip. Early 19th century.

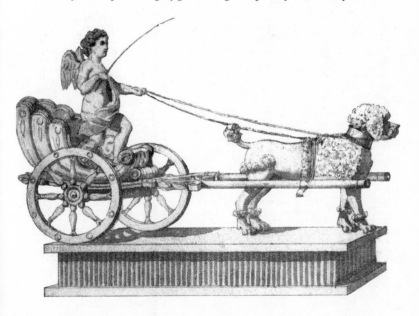

Even this was modest compared to a "sugar banquet" thrown in 1591 for England's sweet-toothed Virgin Queen, an event so spectacular that it likely inspired Shakespeare's *A Midsummer's Night Dream*. We'll peep in on it, too. This midsummer's night dream takes place in Elvetham, Hampshire, and will last four days. Edward, Earl of Hertford, who was once imprisoned in the Tower of London for bigamy, is its very motivated host. Edward is in perpetual political disgrace and needs royal favor to legitimize his children and generally feel secure. So he has built several pavilions to provide suitable accommodations for Elizabeth and her five hundred courtiers, and there's already a crescent-moon-shaped artificial lake lit with exploding fireworks. Elizabeth is now sitting in a hillside gallery, looking down as the evening begins.

The entertainment is centered on sugary representations of everything Hertford has thought will impress his scary royal guest, she of the passionate, unconsummated love affairs, who will never risk sharing her immense power with a husband. And so the parade of two hundred gentlemen and their hundred torchbearers are laden with confections of castles, soldiers and weaponry, followed by marzipan "beastes" and "all that can flie," "all kind of wormes" and "all sorts of fishes" and, because too modest a display might offend Her Majesty, a smorgasbord of candied delicacies including jellies and marmalades, fruits, nuts and seeds, sweetmeats, even—how daring in this fruit-fearing era—fresh fruit!

Elizabeth will nibble long and hard, for she has an insatiable sweet tooth. No wonder portraitists flatter her with closed-mouth images. Elizabeth is nearly sixty years old, attractive still and majestic. But, yes, her teeth *are* black, as at least one foreign courtier has reported, and yes, it likely *is* because she overindulges in sugar.

Sweet-toothed Elizabeth ruled over a sweet-toothed nation. Fittingly, sugar collations, as they were called, originated in England, famed for the awfulness of its cuisine, and they represent "one instance in dining history where something new and unique was devised in England for the first time," writes food historian Roy Strong.[56] By the seventeenth century, sugar collations led to the "void" that in turn evolved into dessert.

This wood engraving portrays sweets-loving Queen Elizabeth I smiling carefully, likely to conceal the blackened teeth that marred her appearance.

The "void" was the brief stretch between courses, or after a meal, when servants cleared, or "voided," the table, and enterprising hosts filled up that void with ornate sugar molds and flower, nut, spice and fruit confections, washed down by sweet wine. At first the void was taken standing up so the servants could do their work. Later it was moved into a separate area. The void was an entertainment centered on sugar rather than nutrition, and its originality and expense largely defined the host's status. Sugar courses were, writes Renaissance scholar Kim F. Hall, forms of "conspicuous consumption that trickled down from the courtly elite" to the merely very rich.[57]

By the mid-sixteenth century, sugar was trickling down to the middle classes, who were assisted by domestic manuals or cookbooks that promised culinary tips and the recipes of the envied upper classes. These cookbooks, a new phenomenon, were printed in large quantities and in vernacular languages and, Hall writes, they rivaled the Bible in popularity. In France between 1651 and 1789, for instance, 230 cookbook editions appeared. Continental cookbooks targeted male cooks, but England's male authors dedicated theirs to women. *The Queen-Like Closet, or Rich Cabinet* (1684), or *Rare and Excellent Receipts* (1690), for example, allowed a literate English woman to serve her family the same treats as any aristocrat, and favorite recipes revealed how to create sugar confections.

Lovely sugary desserts were also appearing on European tables. In France, two Italian-born Medici queens had a deep influence on French cooking. Queen Catherine, who in 1533 married the future Henri II when she was a tubby fourteen-year-old, imported Italian "virtuosi" to supervise the court's kitchens, and these men were especially adept at creating sugared desserts and treats. Catherine was both gluttonous and sugar-loving, and should be credited with popularizing the notion of climaxing meals with delightfully sweet confections.

In 1600, Marie de' Medici was married off to France's Henri IV, who hated his homely blond wife and presided over a court whose courtiers mocked her as "the fat banker." Marie escaped the tribulations of her hostile marriage and surroundings by comforting herself with food, especially sweets. She brought Giovanni Pastilla, the Medici clan's confectioner, to the French court, where his concoctions delighted the French as much as their queen. The term *bonbon*—good good—originated from the royal children's nickname for his wares, as did the word *pastille*, the small, sugared fruit tablets Pastilla specialized in.

As desserts spread, so did knowledge about varieties of sugar. Sugar usually came in loaf form and could be refined into the whitest granules. As Hall writes, "The categorization of the relative purity of sugars, combined with an emphasis on the site of production, existed to a degree rarely seen today—muscovado, clayed, refined, double refined, Madeiras, Barbados."[58] Brazilian sugar, for instance, was considered inferior to the whiter Barbadian and Jamaican imports. The housewife's treasured cookbook educated her and raised her standards by introducing her to aristocratic secrets.

The Accomplisht Cook, or the Art and Mystery of Cookery, published in 1678, is an extreme case in point. It gave complicated instructions for creating a sugar world of castles complete with turrets and moats, warships with cannons and flags, and forest animals roaming in parkland. This extravaganza was to be accompanied by pies with live frogs and birds sealed inside, so that when guests lifted off the crusts, "out skip some Frogs, which make the Ladies to skip and shriek; next ... out come the Birds, who by a natural instinct flying in the light, will put out the Candles; so that with the flying Birds and skipping Frogs, the one above, the other beneath, will cause much delight and pleasure to the whole company."[59] Too messy, unsanitary and inhumane for modern taste, but what an inspiration for the ambitious seventeenth-century matron stumped for unique dessert ideas!

Sugar was becoming a basic component of the English middle-class regimen. It sweetened rather than just spiced their food, and it was the raison d'être for their dessert. Unlike the French, who confined sugar to dessert and used it sparingly in main courses, the English loved sugar immoderately. In 1603, an Englishman reported, a delegation of Spaniards was astonished at "this fondness of our countrymen and countrywomen for sweets," and concluded that "they eat nothing but what is sweetened with sugar, drinking it commonly with their wine and mixing it with their meat."[60] Common sayings in many European languages held that "sugar never spoils a soup" and "no meat is ruined by sugar." Meat-loving England took this seriously.

Pudding was a major vehicle for sugar. "Blessed be he that invented pudding, for it is a Manna that hits the Palates of all Sortes of People," exclaimed M. Misson, surely one of the few French visitors to rave about English cooking.[61] Pudding was a direct response to sugar's new afford-ability, which sweetened the new century—the eighteenth—at about sixpence per pound, the price of a postage stamp. People accustomed to eking out their meager supplies by grating precious granules from a sugar loaf or from bits chopped from a loaf at the grocer's now dished it out with what seemed profligacy. They no longer reserved it as a deli-cacy to sprinkle on pie crusts but used it as an ingredient, and this was the origin of pudding.

Puddings did not begin life as dessert—they might be part of a second or third course that included fish, meat and vegetables, even pies, tarts or fruit. In the early eighteenth century, puddings combined flour and suet, the hard fatty tissue around sheep and cattle kidneys and loins; this heavy mixture was then sweetened with dried fruit and sugar and leavened and bound with eggs, small (weak) beer or yeast. This was the base for hundreds of pudding variations and, writes food historian Elisabeth Ayrton, "even the plainest dinner served above the poverty line was not complete without its pudding. Hot puddings, cold puddings, steamed puddings, baked puddings, pies, tarts, creams, moulds, charlottes and bettys, trifles and fools, syllabubs and tansys, junkets and ices, milk puddings, suet puddings: 'pudding' used as a generic term covers so many dishes traditional in English cookery that the mind reels."[62] Pudding also became a dessert dish, and was usually served at least once daily.

In 1747, housewife Hannah Glasse published what became her bestselling classic, *The Art of Cookery Made Plain and Easy*. Mrs. Glasse viewed her book as a money-making endeavor designed for "the lower sort," domestics whose employers would otherwise waste valuable time instructing them. She presented her 972 recipes,

342 copied wholesale from other books, clearly, even amusingly. One of her most interesting desserts is the very English Hedgehog, a little marzipan creature sculpted from a sugary, buttery dough, then stuck with sliced almonds to replicate hedgehog bristles. With more elaborate ingredients, Mrs. Glasse advised, Hedgehog could also be served as the first course.

In 1760, in *The Compleat Confectioner*, Mrs. Glasse responded to demand for dessert recipes. She even included instructions about the placement of dishes: "Every young lady ought to know both how to make all kind of confectionery and dress out a dessert.... But for country ladies it is a pretty amusement both to make the sweetmeats and dress out a dessert, as it depends wholly on fancy and but little expense."[63] She suggests an assortment of sweet goodies, including different-colored ice cream, "a thing us'd in all desserts."[64] As they instructed housewives in the confectionery arts, Mrs. Glasse and other cookbook writers taught and even proselytized the joys of sugar.

Ice cream was yet another way to deliver sugar—usually 12 to 16 percent of the total ingredients—and was gaining fans. Its European origins were likely seventeenth-century Italy and later France, from where it crossed over to England by 1671, when Charles II enjoyed ice cream on the Feast of St. George. In 1718, a recipe for ice cream was published, but it took Mrs. Glasse's immense readership (seventeen editions by the end of the century) to propel ice cream into the popular consciousness.

Ice cream had reached North America by the mid-eighteenth century. Thomas Bladen, governor of Maryland between 1742 and 1747, served "some fine Ice Cream which, with the Strawberries and Milk, eat most deliciously," reported an appreciative guest.[65] Ice cream was popular in New York City, where, in 1774, Philip Lenzi advised his customers that it was available at his confectionery shop almost every day. The Founding Fathers ate ice cream at George Washington's table; in the summer of 1790, his household and guests consumed $200 worth of the cold treat. The Washington variety, a frozen mixture of cream, eggs and sugar, may have been adapted from Mrs. Glasse's cookbook, which Martha Washington owned. Thomas Jefferson, on the other hand, learned his very complicated version of ice cream in France, and he liked to eat it wrapped in pastry.

Ice cream became much more widely known after President James Madison's wife, Dolley, served it at her husband's 1813 Inaugural Ball. Legend has it that Dolley first tasted ice cream in Wilmington, Delaware, at a tea room operated by Betty Jackson, a black woman whose daughter-in-law, Aunt Sallie Shadd, had purportedly invented it. In the late 1820s, African-American cook Augustus Jackson left his job at the White House and took up catering in Philadelphia, where he sold his ice cream to street vendors. In the late eighteenth century, a Frenchman who had fled Revolutionary France sold ice cream on the streets of New York, and a French traveler reported, "Nothing was more amusing than to watch [the ladies] smirk and simper as they tasted it. They could not understand how it could be kept so cold."[66] By 1837, reported English naval captain and novelist Frederick Marryat, "one great luxury in America ... even in the hottest seasons ... ice creams are universal and even cheap."[67] England warmed more slowly to ice cream that street vendors began to carry in the 1850s. In colder Canada, Thomas Webb first sold it in the mid-nineteenth century, in Toronto. In 1893, William Neilson began commercial production.[68]

Sugar's Bitter Mates: Tea, Coffee and Chocolate

Despite the enormous surge in desserts hot and cold, and in sweetening food generally, the true revolution in sugar consumption came after Europeans were introduced to three bitter but stimulating foreigners— tea, coffee and chocolate—and discovered that sugar transformed them into heavenly brews.

Europeans first encountered (mostly green) tea from China in the mid-seventeenth century. At first they drank it as the Chinese did, without sugar. Within decades, even before black tea had become popular, they began to add sugar, likely influenced by British sailors, who introduced their countrymen to Indian-style sugared tea, which prompted legions of others to take up tea drinking. In 1662, Charles II married Catherine of Braganza, who brought her Portuguese tea-drinking habit to England where she served tea at court instead of the alcohol that "heated or stupefied their brains morning, noon and night."[69] Tea drinking became popular among court ladies, and some courtiers took it up as well. Catherine became a well-loved queen whose subjects always identified her with her favorite beverage. Enthused poet-politician Edmund Waller,

Venus her Myrtle, Phoebus has his bays;
Tea both excels, which she vouchsafes to praise.
The best of Queens, the best of herbs, we owe
To that bold nation which the way did show.

We do not know exactly when people began to sweeten their tea, but tea expert Roy Moxham believes that in England they always did. By the end of the seventeenth century, adding sugar to tea was the fashion. Tea drinking quickly spread down through the social ranks. The advent of coffeehouses, which served both tea and coffee, popularized these beverages as nothing else had. (Teahouses came only in the late nineteenth century.) As with tea, clients sweetened their coffee with sugar. Diluting tea and coffee with milk took longer to catch on. Seventeenth-century France's trend-setting Marquise de Sévigné put milk in hers, but a century passed before the association of milk with tea and coffee became general.

The first coffeehouse opened in London in 1652, and by the end of the century there was one per thousand Londoners. Coffeehouses proliferated throughout England, and also on the Continent. A French visitor to London wrote approvingly, "You have all Manner of News there: You have a good Fire, which you may sit by as long as you please: You have a Dish of Coffee; you meet your Friends for the Transaction of Business, and all for a Penny, if you don't care to spend more."[70]

The coffeehouses became venues to conduct business and to debate political issues; Samuel Butler considered them "a kind of Athenian

Over tea in a coffeehouse, a swindler describes his latest stock market scam. "The other day, I pulled off another smart trick," he begins. The text alludes in part to LaFontaine's fable "The Fox and the Raven."

school." Politicians and the politically inclined flocked to them for the latest news, views and gossip. In eighteenth-century Paris, Voltaire, Diderot, Rousseau, Condorcet and other enlightened thinkers favored the Café Procope, which served Voltaire his favorite blend of coffee and chocolate.

Because tea and coffee were relatively cheap, modestly employed tradesmen could afford to frequent coffeehouses. This new inclusiveness displeased many of the elite clientele. One disgruntled observer commented, "As you have a hodge-podge of drinks, such too, is your company, for each man seems a leveler and ranks and files himself … without regard to degrees or order, so that often you may see a silly fop and a worshipful justice, a griping rook and a grave citizen, a worthy lawyer and an errant pickpocket, a reverend non-conformist and a canting mountebank, all blended together to compose a medley of impertinence."[71]

The beverages themselves also evoked strong reactions. Tea had the most vociferous detractors. Tea stripped away women's beauty, one critic warned, so that "your very chambermaids have lost their bloom by sipping tea." Tea drinking was also unsuitable for the warlike English, who risked becoming like "the most effeminate people on the face of the Earth—the Chinese, who are at the same time the greatest sippers of tea."[72]

On the other hand, those who promoted temperance lauded tea as "the cup that cheers but not inebriates." Tea and coffee created vital new overseas commercial ventures and increased joy and energy, argued their advocates; tea and coffee competed with existing agricultural and brewing concerns, rotted teeth and caused disease, charged their critics.

SUGAR AND SCIENCE

Until its metamorphosis as a sweetener and even a foodstuff, sugar had been used as a spice and as a medicine. Medical writers described how sugar could alter the body's humoral balance by generating choler, thereby heating it up, and how it could interact with other drugs, increasing their effectiveness. Many physicians believed that tea was healthful even when one sluiced oneself with it, and therefore sugar's role in making tea more palatable was equally positive.

By the late seventeenth century, professionals were more negative about sugar. Scaremongers claimed that sugar-loving West Indians and the grocery clerks who chopped off lumps of sugar from imported loaves seemed especially prone to scurvy. Physicians Thomas Tryon and Thomas Willis expressed other serious reservations. Tryon, a vegetarian whose popular how-to books urged moderate and compassionate consumption in general, argued that sugar was beneficial in small quantities and that people's delight in its was evidence of "the basically healthy and necessary character of sweetness." But Tryon cautioned that in excessive quantities, fermented or mixed with such fats as butter, sugar was dangerous. Tryon's most disturbing arguments against consuming sugar dealt with its production. He had visited a Barbadian sugar plantation and had seen for himself how sugar production affected the slaves there. Sugar slaves were brutalized and oppressed, he wrote, and that in itself was good enough reason to abstain from slave-produced sugar.

Dr. Thomas Willis, one of his century's great medical minds, artic-ulated what we now know to be incontrovertible arguments against excessive sugar consumption—sugar's connection with diabetes. In 1674, in *Phamaceutice rationalis*, Willis identified the sweetish flavor in the urine of those with diabetes mellitus, and his nickname for the disease, "the Pissing Evil," entered popular parlance in the English-speaking world. Though the illness had been known for centuries in the Middle East and Asia, it would be another century before the link between diabetics and sugar in the blood was clearly understood, but Willis intuited enough to sound the alarm against too much sugar.

Another physician, Dr. Frederick Slare, challenged Willis's views and likely swayed many people. *A Vindication of Sugars Against the Charge of Dr. Willis, Other Physicians, and Common Prejudices: Dedicated to the Ladies*, published in 1715, was an encomium to sugar as a tooth-cleaning powder, a hand lotion, a healing powder for minor wounds and, above all, an essential treat for babies and "the ladies" to whom his treatise was dedicated. Because their palates were more delicate than men's, being free of tobacco and other coarse substances, Willis applauded their growing use of sugar. He was particularly enthusiastic about breakfasts of sweetened tea, coffee or chocolate, each of them "endowed with uncommon virtues."[73]

As the debate over sugar raged, more Europeans consumed more sugar and tea, sugar and coffee, sugar and chocolate. In beer-loving Germany,

Johann Sebastian Bach's Coffee Cantata, performed at Leipzig's Zimmerman's Café, pitted a frustrated father against his coffee-addicted daughter Lieschen. "If I can't drink my bowl of coffee three times daily, then in my torment I will shrivel up like a piece of roast goat," Lieschen trilled. As Bach well knew, legions of people shared Lieschen's passion for coffee. The coffeehouses flourished, and ambitious merchants sought contracts for Caribbean sugar, Chinese and later Indian tea, African coffee and South American chocolate.

By the third quarter of the seventeenth century, chocolate, too, was a staple of coffeehouse offerings across Europe. The conquistador Cortés had introduced it to his Spanish homeland. *Chocolatl* was a bitter Aztec drink that the soon-to-be-defeated emperor Montezuma served in golden goblets; it was, after all, food for the gods. Until Cortés sweetened the acrid drink with sugar, the Spanish disliked it. But chocolate spiked with sugar and later vanilla, nutmeg, cinnamon and other spices, and served heated, became a much-loved beverage, reputed to have aphrodisiac and medicinal properties. Cortés could not be without a full chocolate pot on his desk.

Spaniards treasured their chocolate pots, in which they brewed an enchanting nectar of water with cocoa pods crushed into powder and flavored with sugar, cinnamon and vanilla. When Spanish women refused to sit through Sunday mass without a cup of chocolate, clerics had to pronounce on the nature of chocolate. Was it a food that Catholics had to abstain from during fasts, or was it a flavored liquid they could continue to enjoy because *liquidum non frangit jejuum*— liquid does not break the fast? Many priests declared that chocolate was mere liquid, and conveniently kept their churches full. This chocolate question echoed the sugar question of the thirteenth century, which Thomas Aquinas had resolved by pronouncing sugar a medicine, even if spiced: "Though nutritious in themselves, sugared spices are nonetheless not eaten with the end in mind of nourishment, but rather for ease in digestion; accordingly, they do not break the fast any more than the taking of any other medicine."[74]

The Spanish kept their delicious secret from the rest of the world. It got out a century later, after two Spanish infantas, Anne of Austria, married to Louis XIII, and Maria Theresa of Spain, married to Louis XIV, introduced it to France. (Courtiers who knew too much about the latter royal marriage snickered that chocolate was Maria Theresa's *only* passion.) Chocolate seduced the French as it had the Spanish. Like coffee and tea, it spread quickly into the coffeehouses, though it was much more expensive, in the late seventeenth century more than double the price of tea and coffee, eight sous a cup in the Left Bank.

Chocolate was a delight that could also terrify. A Jesuit insisted that in Mexico, chocolate caused "a number of homicides by the Spanish ladies taught by Indian women, who, by the use of chocolate had corresponded with the devil."[75] In France, Madame de Sévigné warned her pregnant daughter that "the Marquise de Coëtlogon drank so much chocolate when she was expecting last year that she was brought to bed of a little boy as black as the devil, who died." (Others suspected that the child's dark skin color had more to do with the attractive young African slave who served the marquise her chocolate as she lay abed.) Scaremongers failed to frighten people away from chocolate, which steadily increased in popularity. As it did, sugar consumption rose proportionately.

"THE TEA" COMES HOME

After coffeehouses, home was becoming the second home of tea and, to a lesser extent, coffee and chocolate, all three being vehicles for sugar. Some commentators worried that the bitter beverages were an excuse to indulge in sugar, while others worried about the excessive amounts of the sweet stuff consumed. England was the worst offender, importing 10,000 tons in 1700 and, one century later, 150,000 tons, a staggering increase.

Sugar figured prominently in "the tea" taken now at home, as Catherine of Braganza's tea rituals were replicated first by the upper classes, then by middle-class families. By the eighteenth century, tea—which might offer coffee, chocolate or both as well—was becoming well established. The tea gardens truly popularized it. London's Ranelagh Rotunda and Gardens, opened in 1742, charged half a crown admittance and provided tea, coffee and bread and butter, period. (The notion of tipping allegedly originated in the Tea Gardens, where a locked wooden TIPS—To Insure Prompt Service—box on each table encouraged or perhaps bullied guests into donating a few coins.) Women gathered at these gardens and chatted over cups of tea. Before long, they began to do the same thing at home.

Before it evolved into "afternoon tea" and "low tea" in the nineteenth century, "the tea" was first likely served to women after an early dinner, when men and women separated into different rooms, freeing the men to partake of wine or brandy. P. Morton Shand, a British food historian, writes that "this purely feminine development of a dish of tea into a 'light refection' may be considered as an imitation of the old French 'goûter,' at which sweet wines ... biscuits and petits-fours were served to both sexes."[76] Over time, the sexes remained together in the drawing room (actually the withdrawing room, because women withdrew to it) and took their post-prandial tea and wine there.

In the first three decades of the seventeenth century, "the tea," replete with sugar, often milk or cream, and accompanied by anything from buttered bread to dainty pastries, had become a ritual in English and Dutch upper- and middle-class homes. The increase in the amount of tea and sugar imported was correspondingly immense. In 1660, Britain consumed one-third of the 3,000 hogsheads (1 hogshead = 63 gallons) it imported from its sugar island. In 1730, consumption was up to 104,000 of 110,000 hogsheads imported.[77]

The tea developed its own trappings, with the very wealthy acquiring elaborate sterling silver tea services including a teapot, hot water pot and often a matching coffee pot, along with a sugar pot and a small milk jug. Until the late eighteenth century, before which the guests of even very rich hosts were expected to bring their own cutlery and traveled with *necessaires*, elegant boxes designed to hold a knife and fork, such tea services were considered a great luxury. Tea services were produced in less fancy and expensive versions as well, in earthenware and, after French king Louis XVI's mistresses, Antoinette Poisson, Marquise de Pompadour, began to design them for the royal factory at Sèvres, in ornate rococo porcelain. Before long, Sèvres tea services were prized all over Europe, and French ambassadors routinely offered them as state gifts.

Tea sipped in Sèvres, or as a cuppa slurped in a coffeehouse bowl, had taken hold of England, Holland and, later, other European nations. (Germany's Meissen Royal Manufactory, opened in 1710, also produced highly desirable porcelain tea services.) As a status symbol, tea conveyed respectability, legitimizing the family circle and guests who partook of it. The tea-and-sugar ritual—knowing how to make and serve it, and having the proper accoutrements to do so—showed good taste and refinement. Manners mattered; the ritual became "to some extent a training process of adolescents and ... a reminder to adults about how to behave in the world at large," explains historian Woodruff D. Smith.[78] Significantly, women were as central to the tea ritual as they were to its preparation.

The tea was also evidence of restraint, providing sugar in healthy (as opposed to gluttonous) amounts, and of temperance, replacing alcohol or wine. And it was a patriotic act, for sugar and tea (but not coffee and chocolate) now came, in monopoly form, from British colonies. "Sugared tea and coffee ... constituted one of the most important dynamic ensembles of consumer goods in eighteenth-century Europe," concludes Smith, and "thus became the preferred 'soft drugs' of Western Europe because they afforded access to respectability and bourgeois standing."[79]

The institution of afternoon tea, as opposed to post-supper tea, evolved only in the early nineteenth century. The story is that Anna, the seventh Duchess of Bedford, confessed to a "sinking feeling" as, surely, millions of others did in the long hours between their heavy noon-time dinner and their late, light supper. To assuage it, the duchess ordered a repast brought to her Woburn Abbey boudoir: tea and a few sweets. She felt so restored that she began to invite a few friends to join her. They came at about five o'clock, and enjoyed the little meal in the parlor. The duchess served them tea in the European tea service mode, accompanied by bread-and-butter sandwiches, dainty little cakes and other sweets. The duchess's tea party was such a happy event that she often repeated it. Soon other hostesses held teas of their own, and—so the story goes—the afternoon, or low, tea was born.

Low tea was so called because it was served from a low table in the parlor, at the height of the modern coffee table. Low tea took on the character of a quasi-meal, with "little cakes ... the real lure, the *pièce d'abandon....* Tea is an excuse for eating something ... a break, a challenge to the crawling hours, it 'makes a hole in the day.'... Another advantage is the extreme elasticity of its hour, so that one can order it at any time from 4 P.M., till half-past six."[80] The hostess would serve from one pot of tea, which she replenished from an accompanying pot of boiling water. (Far away in Russia, the tea ritual revolved around the samovar, a spigoted metal tea urn, often large enough to dispense scores of cups of hot tea sweetened with sugar or honey. Some Russians developed the habit of clamping a sugar lump between their

Seven little girls in party finery waiting to enjoy their tea and birthday cake glare in mock annoyance at their photographer. Third from the left is Eleanor (Dudy) Ball (Mansur), sister of Lady Henrietta Banting, whose husband, Frederick, discovered penicillin with Charles Best.

With Lillie Ballantyne, Babs and Joe O'Gara enjoy an outdoor tea party near Ottawa, October 10, 1892. Sadly, Lillie died of tuberculosis a few years later.

teeth and sipping tea through the dissolving granules.) Until 1870, when tea merchants began to offer standardized varieties, tea blends were carefully guarded secrets, as ambitious hostesses blended their own. Along with the repast, card games and gossip, hostesses often entertained with short harpsichord or pianoforte concerts.

Most crucially, tea drinking was relatively cheap compared with coffee, and so flexible in how it could be prepared and served that throughout the seventeenth century it was adopted by more and more members of the lower-middle classes, then by the working classes and finally by even the lowest, most miserable classes, indeed by anyone able to scrabble together something approximating its ingredients. In an era of revolutions, this apparently innocuous domestic activity proved to be unwittingly revolutionary.

*Everyone loves afternoon tea. Fourteen Tsimshian women, four children and one
man enjoy theirs under a lean-to at Metlakatla near Fort Simpson, B.C., on
July 1, 1889, perhaps celebrating Dominion Day.*

High Tea and the Industrial Revolution

The second half of the eighteenth century spawned two fundamental
social and economic transformations: the Industrial Revolution and the
Sugared Tea Revolution that sloshed into being within it. Led by
England, the Industrial Revolution recast primarily agricultural Europe
into ever-urbanizing industrial societies fueled by capitalism, overseas
trade, growing consumption and changing mores. Technological innovations, most notably the cotton gin, the spinning jenny and the steam
engine, transformed how English cotton was produced. Historian
David Landes provides this eloquent summary: "The abundance and
variety of these innovations almost defy compilation, but they may be
subsumed under three principles: the substitution of machines—rapid,
regular, precise, tireless—for human skill and effort; the substitution of
inanimate for animate sources of power, in particular, the introduction
of engines for converting heat into work, thereby opening to man a new
and almost unlimited supply of energy; the use of new and far more

abundant raw materials, in particular, the substitution of mineral for vegetable or animal substances. These improvements constitute the Industrial Revolution."[81]

The nature of work changed. Cottage industry, in which family members produced goods at home, declined. Factories, where workers toiled for wages beside strangers, sprang up. Standardization became the norm: hours of labor, productivity, wages and working conditions were all controlled. Social life changed drastically. Rural workers forced off the land by the Enclosure Acts of 1760 to 1830 crammed into cities scarcely able to accommodate them, and poverty forced women and children into the factories. Family life disintegrated and re-formed in the pulsating, filthy and merciless but exciting cities where miracles sometimes happened.

The English population nearly doubled. Millions of men, women and children toiled from 6 A.M. to 7 P.M. or later, with few breaks. Dust and filth polluted work spaces. Machines without safety features mutilated workers who were then fired without compensation; many also died of their injuries. Workers performed repetitive and onerous procedures, risking their health and suffering exhaustion and physical deformities. Supervisors were often brutal men who beat underlings and fined and punished them for infractions such as unpunctuality, talking or making mistakes. Most factories were fearful and violent places.

Domestic life was seldom a refuge for exhausted parents and their sickly, rickety and malnourished children. Child mortality skyrocketed, to nearly 50 percent before the age of five. Survivors often entered factories at five or six years old, and some employers sought them out. "The fingers of children at an early age are very supple, and they are more easily led into habits of performing the duties of their station," a nineteenth-century reformer explained.[82] Laws reforming the lot of child laborers were enacted in 1833, but decades passed before they covered all workplaces and were effectively enforced.

Darkest London, the greatest and also the worst of England's cities, was populated by what one historian styles "vast, miserable, unmanageable masses of sunken people."[83] In all industrial cities, rented hovels were expensive, crowded and unsanitary, icy in winter and broiling in summer. Water and toilet facilities were deficient, with a single tap serving several streets. Disease and depression ran rampant. Streets were dangerous and thick with pickpockets. Prostitutes, often seamstresses or shop girls supplementing their meager wages, stalked most corners.

In their former agrarian life, most laborers had had access to gardens where they could grow vegetables and fruit and perhaps raise poultry or even a cow. In the cities, and even in rural areas affected by the enclosure laws, workers had to purchase their food and they often changed their diets in response to cost and availability. For the first time, they had access to non-European foodstuffs previously restricted to the privileged, and soon potatoes, rice, maize, tea, coffee, chocolate, sugar and tobacco were staples of the English diet. The combination of these developments suggests "a time of great change in consumption levels and eating habits," writes economic historian Carole Shammas.[84]

Sugar, cheaper and more plentiful than it had been, had the greatest impact on the working-class diet. By 1680, sugar cost only half what it had in 1630. By 1700, the percentage of imported foodstuffs, notably tea, coffee and sugar, had more than doubled from 16.9 percent to 34.9 percent, with brown sugar and molasses the most popular. These imports translated into sugar consumption that likely quadrupled between 1700 and 1740, and more than doubled again in the period 1741 to 1775. In roughly the same period, from 1663 to 1775, England and Wales consumed sixty times more sugar though their populations did not even quite double, so that over the years, people consumed vastly more sugar and related products (molasses, syrup and rum) than before, and in a ratio that greatly outstripped those of bread, meat and dairy products.[85] Sugar historian Noel Deerr estimates that per capita sugar consumption was four pounds in 1700, eight pounds by 1729, twelve by 1789, the year of the French Revolution, and eighteen pounds by 1809.[86]

Let's take a look at sugar in the context of the working-class diet that would commonly include bread, peas, beans and perhaps turnips and cabbages, beer and (inferior) tea, supplemented by small portions of much-loved but expensive meat (bacon and salted or pickled fish), butter and cheese. Fruit, considered dangerous for children and generally unhealthy, was widely avoided. Thanks to lower prices and easier access to water, beer and tea were beverages of choice, and by the eighteenth century, tea outstripped beer. Sugar was used to sweeten everything, especially tea. "The unprecedented heavy use of sugar was by far the most important of the developments," Shammas writes, "because it made puddings of wheat, oats, or rice much more palatable…. Tea was another byproduct of the sugar revolution, and together the two changed the composition of breakfasts and suppers. Brown bread, cheese, and beer gave way to the new drink, its sweetener, and white wheat bread with butter."[87]

When wages were low, or a worker was unemployed, bread and tea became the staple meal. Indeed, "bread makes the principal part of the food of all poor families and almost the whole of the food of … large families," reported Rev. David Davies in 1795.[88] Bread was dry and dense and, when yeast was unavailable, unleavened. Unsurprisingly, workers gladly abandoned it for lighter, moister white bread made from heavily refined flour. The rising cost of fuel often made it cheaper to buy white bread from a baker rather than bake brown bread at home, and saved precious time. Workers saw white bread as a status symbol, and associated its whiteness with the privileged upper classes. Similarly, they preferred refined white sugar to brown sugar or molasses, and bought it whenever they could afford to.

Dr. James Phillips Kay, a concerned contemporary physician, described a typical cotton worker's day: he rose at five, gobbled a breakfast of tea and oatmeal porridge or bread, then rushed off to the factory. Lunch was potatoes flavored with lard or butter and perhaps bacon fat. Back home late in the evening, supper was more potatoes, bread or oatmeal, washed down with weak, sugared tea.[89] Sometimes the tea leaves had been used once already, purchased from enterprising domestic servants who sold the dregs of an employer's teapot. "Tea leaves" might also be bits of charred toast brewed in hot water, a sad approximation. But the sugar was real, and it made the tea potable and even delicious.

TOM & BOB, *taking a Stroll down Drury Lane at five'in the Morning*

Gentlemen Tom and Bob, strolling at dawn in Drury Lane, London's notorious slum, see a Genuine Tea stall serving its "wholesome beverage" to both "industrious" and ragged passersby. They learn that poor people's tea was often adulterated and that "moist sugar was made from the best red sand."

By the eighteenth century, the medieval habit of two meals a day had been replaced by three, even in boarding schools, hospitals and work-houses for the indigent. At the same time, fewer of those meals were now cooked at home. Women worked and had less time; they lacked ingredients and fuel, and eventually they lost the knowledge of how to make the broths and stews that had simmered on medieval hearths. It became unusual for a woman to cook every day. Instead, she made do with baker's bread served, if she could afford it, with cold meat or cheese, and washed down with beer or sweetened tea, sometimes with milk added.

During the Industrial Revolution, urban water supplies were erratic and often tainted, so boiling water for tea purified as well as heated it. (Milk, however, was notoriously impure and often adulterated with unclean water.) Beer was safe to drink and nutritious, but a growing temperance movement attacked its ubiquitousness in the working-class diet. Tea, on the other hand, stimulated, refreshed and, heavily sugared, delivered much-needed calories to the undernourished working class. In the second quarter of the nineteenth century, improved water supplies and falling prices made tea Britain's most popular beverage. Sugar had much to do with propelling it there. As British historian D. J. Oddy notes, "The principal change from the late eighteenth century was the growing use of sugar. By the mid-nineteenth century sugar consumption had reached half a pound (0.2 kg) per head per week."[90] That's a fair amount of sugar, and over the decades it would increase until, by the end of the century, weekly per capita consumption exceeded one pound.[91]

But those figures are misleading, because they imply equal consumption among family members. What actually happened, because there was not enough nourishing food for everyone, was that women and children ate more of the family's sugar, while men ate far more meat, milk and potatoes. Nineteenth-century medical officer Dr. Edward Smith was continually told "'that the husband wins the bread and must have the best food.' The labourer eats meat and bacon almost daily, whilst his wife and children may eat it but once a week, and ... both himself and his household believe that course to be necessary, to enable him to perform his labour."[92]

Even this does not tell the whole tale, because Dr. Smith's sources implied that only men worked. Yet other surveys found that even factory women survived on bread, sugar and fat supplemented by portions of meat (anything from chops to cow-heel, sheep's trotters, pig's ear or red herring) and potatoes equal to one-quarter the amount served their husbands.[93] In 1895, "The Diet of Toil," published in the medical journal *The Lancet*, confirmed that factory women ate mostly bread with jam or treacle, and tea with sugar; every week the women surveyed consumed 21 ounces of sugar (68¼ pounds annually) to their men's 15 (48¾ pounds annually).[94] This meager but tasty diet was typical of lower-income families. "We *see*," wrote B. Seebohm Rowntree in his 1901 *Poverty: A Study of Town Life*, "that many a labourer, who has a wife and three or four children is healthy and a good worker, although he earns only a pound a week. What we *do not* see is that in order to give him enough food, mother and children habitually go short, for the mother knows that all depends upon the wages of her husband."[95]

Astonishingly, these skimpy, badly balanced and sugar-saturated meals fueled not only the working classes but also the Industrial Revolution that their labor made possible. As the decades passed and England grew less hungry, its standard of living rose, its caloric intake grew and its choices increased. As workers consumed more, they also "bettered" themselves, addressing and sometimes satisfying other hungers such as self-esteem and respectability.

Sugar scholar Sidney Mintz has shown how sugar was integral to these developments. Sugar was much more than a mere sweetener. Like tobacco, for centuries a luxury of the rich, sugar became "the general solace of all classes," especially "the emerging proletarian classes, who found sugar and kindred drug foods profound consolations in the mines and in the factories."[96] A case in point is an eighteenth-century washerwoman, "a queasy and ragged creature who came into a shop with two children … asked for a pennyworth of tea and a half-pennyworth of sugar, and said she could not live without drinking it every day."[97] By 1750, "Sugar, the inseparable Companion of Tea, came to be in the Possession of the very poorest Housewife"[98]—remember Gladys? Sugar as consolation—the ultimate comfort food—gave it a psychological dimension that transcended taste and caloric force. The wage-earning worker's ability to buy this previously unattainable luxury connected the "will to work and the will to consume." The working poor could now aspire to pamper themselves as the rich had long done.

One way working-class families did this was through the ritual of high tea, a modest new meal that was rather different from low tea. High tea was served on the high table in the dining room, *not* on low tables next to sofas and chairs in the drawing room. And high tea became the family supper, prepared after working parents arrived home.

High tea was easy for an overtired and overworked woman to assemble. It saved money and fuel, and avoided the need for refrigeration. In the short run, it was satisfying enough to substitute for real food. High tea required tea with sugar, and bread heaped with butter, jam, preserves, cold meat, cheese or an egg. Whatever was served tasted better and more substantial when washed down by even the wateriest cups of sugared tea. "Tea, coffee and sugar were essential to the display, and even more to the self-perception, of respectability, which was in turn a very important, possibly definitive, element of bourgeois consciousness," writes Woodruff D. Smith, which is why sugared tea and to a lesser extent coffee became "the preferred 'soft drugs' of Western Europe ... they afforded access to respectability and bourgeois standing."[99]

Sugar also sustained these high tea workers during their dull and difficult days, during brief breaks when they snatched time to gulp down a sugary cuppa. Mintz stresses the significance of sugared tea being "the first substance to become part of a work break."[100] Sugared tea breaks proved to be a key element in how factories managed and motivated their workforces. These tea breaks served many functions, Mintz explains. They came about because new industrialized production methods changed proletarian work schedules, incorporating tea breaks into them that gave the working classes "new tasting opportunities and new occasions for eating and drinking."[101]

In this context, sugared tea promoted self-respect and the illusion of upward mobility. It also provided a welcome jolt of energy as it delivered calories to workers who, after their break, resumed work with renewed vigor. The sugared tea break inspired workers to work harder so they could earn more and thereby afford more sugared tea and other delights, a dynamic that transformed them into consumers intent on consuming more and more. Mintz sees this as doubly significant in that it represented a "crucial feature of the evolution of modern patterns of eating"—*what* was eaten, and *how* it was eaten. Tea and sugar were initially new, exotic and previously unobtainable foods that quickly became essential, as did the work break they represented. Tea and sugar were also the main components of breakfast and, for workers' wives and children, the principal ingredients of lunch and supper.

The acceptance of, and soon the reliance on, these foods extended to the occasions on which they were consumed, so that workers easily integrated the new habit of eating at work rather than at home. This helped them adapt to other major changes: new work schedules, new kinds of labor and, inevitably, the new way of life shaped by all these other transformations.

Sugar played the nefarious role of opiate of the people. It was a psychologically addictive substance that energized and delighted; it deadened appetite and satisfied hunger pangs; and it opened up new possibilities of consumption and social respectability previously unattainable to all but the privileged classes.

Candy was one of these possibilities, boiled hard, distinctively flavored and shaped, and delicious. By the 1840s, new technology allowed mass production of hard candies that were, confectionery historian Tim Richardson writes, "good-quality, uniform, dependable and affordable ... packaged and branded with the name of the manufacturer rather than sold loose on the street or from the market barrow."[102] The working classes, no longer excluded from the delights of confectionery, happily satisfied their growing sweet tooth from among hundreds of different kinds of candies.

These possibilities extended to sailors in Her Majesty's navy, who by the mid-nineteenth century were allotted two ounces of sugar daily, or forty-five pounds annually. Even paupers confined in forbidding poorhouses were each allotted twenty-three pounds annually. The inmates of the Nacton poorhouse were so fond of sugar that they petitioned to forgo their usual dinners of peas porridge and instead to use their food money to buy the flimsier bread and butter washed down by tea and sugar. Thanks to the sugared tea, noted a concerned observer, this meager fare had become "their favourite dinner."[103] In the latter half of the nineteenth century, England's poorest people, paupers as well as workers, ate even more sugar than the rich, and made England the world's largest sugar consumer.

Across Europe, as other nations also urbanized and industrialized, the same pattern of transformations ensued. Factories swallowed up workers, changing their meals and mealtimes to suit the new working schedules. Workers who had once eaten at home grew accustomed to eating at work, or at commercial establishments close to work. Their menus changed to include more prepared food—bread, cold cuts, jams, preserves—and they consumed more sugar.

Reflecting on the deeper meanings of sugar as it was transformed by capitalism and the Industrial Revolution from an unobtainable luxury into a daily necessity, Mintz summarizes what made it such an ideal substance: "Sugar ... served to make a busy life seem less so; in the pause that refreshes, it eased, or seemed to ease, the changes back and forth from work to rest; it provided swifter sensations of fullness or satisfaction than complex carbohydrates did; it combined easily with many other foods, in some of which it was also used (tea and biscuit, coffee and bun, chocolate and jam-smeared bread).... No wonder the rich and powerful liked it so much, and no wonder the poor learned to love it."[104]

A RUM STORY

There was another dimension to sugar's enormous power, collectively known as the Sugar Interest and, in these pages, as "the Interest." It included the West Indian planters; the slavers who traded in its sugar slaves; the shipowners who transported sugarcane; the bankers who underwrote its production; the insurers who insured it; the importers, wholesalers and grocers who sold it; even the factors, longshoremen, bakers and confectioners who dealt in it. The Interest was so influential that its reach extended into policy-making, which is how rum, made from molasses, a by-product of sugar, came to be included in English naval rations.

Until the mid-seventeenth century, the English navy's beverage rations consisted of beer that was sometimes supplemented by brandy. After the 1655 British conquest of Jamaica, many ships replaced the brandy with Jamaican rum distilled from Jamaican molasses. (The word *rum* was coined in Barbados in the seventeenth century. Also known as Kill-Devil, it was "a hott, hellish and terrible liquor," a visitor reported.)[105] In 1731, this hellish drink became part of the "Regulations and Instructions Relating to His Majesty's Service at Sea."

Sailors who requested it were served daily rations of rum ranging from one-half pint in the seventeenth century to one-eighth of a pint in the nineteenth. Officers took measures to avoid drunkenness and the binge drinking that undermined discipline and caused sailors to fall out of masts. They had the rum barrel hauled out twice a day, at noon and again at four-thirty, and the rum doled out in the metal cups that were part of each man's kit. Because "Spirituous Liquors" had to be diluted with water, the rum was doled out with water and, often, lime juice. Officers, however, got theirs neat. To ensure the perception of fairness, three officers supervised the grog mixing and distribution, to the peppy tune of "Nancy Dawson," aka "Here We Go Round the Mulberry Bush" or "I Saw Three Ships Go Sailing By." Thrifty, temperate men could sign up on the T (Temperance) List and, in return for forgoing their rum ration, earn three pence more per day. In the cause of sobriety, the rum ration was reduced over time, and served only once a day.[106] It was eliminated in 1970, on Black Tot Day, after temperance supporters won Parliament's Great Rum Debate.

Ever since 1805, when naval captain Horatio Nelson was pickled in (rather than by) the amber liquid, naval rum rations have had a curious nickname. The story is that after Nelson was fatally shot during the Battle of Trafalgar in which he crushed Napoleon's fleet and saved England from a French invasion, quick-thinking officers preserved his body in his ship *Victory*'s rum barrel. Quicker-thinking sailors prised open the barrel and drank the embalming rum; since then, naval rum has been known as Nelson's Blood.

Naval rum served several useful purposes. It killed bacteria in the water, which usually turned rancid after a few weeks in the ship's storage barrels. It compensated for inadequate food supplies by providing calories. It was believed to have nutritional value. Although it addicted, maddened and enraged many sailors, it calmed and, at least temporarily, cheered others. (Of course, any alcohol would have done these things.) In the final analysis, the main beneficiaries of the naval rum ration were the West Indian sugar planters. The rum ration guaranteed steady sales of their difficult-to-sell molasses; it represented an important commercial opportunity; and it was a victory over brandy, which grape-growing France promoted as assiduously as the West Indians did their sugar-based rum.

The imperializing sugar interests encouraged the spread of their addictive product. They also made sure that across the Atlantic, millions of enslaved Africans toiled in the cane fields, chained for life to the English zest for sugar. Food historian Maguelonne Toussaint-Samat celebrates the culinary genius brought to bear on sweetness but laments its costs: "So many tears were shed for sugar that by rights it ought to have lost its sweetness."[107]

Part 2

Black Sugar

Chapter 3

The Africanization
of the Cane Fields

The Middle Passage

Let's meet Prince Apongo, one of the Africans who cut the cane and
process the sugar that sweetens Europe's teacups. It's mid-eighteenth
century in Jamaica, and the cane fields are now heavily Africanized.[108]
Like so many other Africans, Apongo has learned the hard way that
fraternizing with European slave traders is dangerous. He had been
a guest of John Cope, governor of Cape Coast Castle, where fifteen
hundred slaves were crammed into dark, dank dungeons ventilated only
by ten-inch-square openings, gasping for air until they were forced
through the ominously named Door of No Return into slave ships.
Sitting upstairs with Cope, Prince Apongo must have heard the frantic
shrieks and moans from below—even the townsfolk complained about
the noise. Neither he nor his host could have missed the stench of
human effluvia that wafted upward.

The castle's reputation was so grim that Apongo showed up there
with a hundred well-armed guards. He was captured later, hunting in
the forest, and held either in the castle's dungeons or farther west, at
Whydah. At Whydah, the slave barracoons were simpler but equally
stark and, unlike the castle, a good distance from the slave ships. When
it was time to board, coffled slaves shuffled in a heartbreaking march
through the verdant countryside down to the port.

Cape Coast Castle was an important slave-trade post and a seat of British colonial government. Here John Cope, later a Jamaican sugar planter, conferred with Prince Apongo, later a Jamaican sugar slave, atop the dungeons that confined Africans destined for slavery on New World plantations.

In Jamaica, Apongo never forgot his royal status or acquiesced in his enslavement. Yet he seems to have absolved John Cope, by then retired from the civil service to plant sugar in Jamaica, from complicity in his capture. He even managed a visit to the plantation and, as in the old days, Cope reportedly "had a table set out, a cloth, etc., laid for him." In later years Cope's son, also a sugar planter, claimed that his father had planned to buy Apongo and return him to Africa. Had this happened before 1760, Apongo would not have become a ringleader in Tacky's Rebellion, which killed sixty whites and four hundred blacks, Apongo among them.

The prince was one of millions of Africans sold along the 3,400-mile coastline from Senegal to Angola. Over four centuries, the international slave trade wrenched at least thirteen million Africans from their homes and killed upward of two million. Of the eleven million transported to foreign slavery, sugar consumed by far the most: six million.[109]

Those Africans entered the cane fields profoundly scarred by the Middle Passage, their ocean journey from Africa to New World slavery. Slaving was a competitive business with enormous financial stakes. Fortunes could be made but also lost, given the amount of capital necessary to acquire and transport Africans from one continent to another. Guidelines were developed about ship design and management, about the human cargo and about relations with African traders. The Africans' experience of the Middle Passage reflected all these factors.

Africans were selected in response to buyers' demands regarding age, condition, sex, even ethnicity. Sugar planters preferred strong and healthy males fifteen to thirty years old, but had conflicting views about which tribe made the best slaves: many considered Coromantees rebellious but capable, while Ibos were docile but suicidal. Occupation seldom mattered, and slavers captured whomever they could, whether farmer, fisherman, hunter, artisan, tradesman, domestic, slave, shaman, scribe, chieftain or noble. Two queens were sold into slavery, one by a jealous stepson, the other by a jealous husband. Occasionally slavers had "special orders," for instance for Jamaican sugar planter John Cope's wife, Molly, who specified "an Ebo girl, about 12 years of age, with small feet, not bow-legged, nor teeth filed, small hands long, small taper fingers, &c, for a sempstress [*sic*]."[110]

A pre-boarding triage sealed the Africans' fate. A ship's surgeon or another officer examined the captives, checking for such flaws as broken teeth, skin eruptions or other symptoms of disease. (Lucky) captives with crooked limbs or missing fingers might be rejected and released.

The examination was designed to degrade as much as to select. The naked slaves were made to jump and perform other exercises. The surgeon peered into their open mouths and "is forc'd to examine the privities of both men and women with the nicest scrutiny." One examiner twisted, poked and prodded, "pinching breasts and groins without mercy,"[111] supposedly in the interests of weeding out pendulous genitalia. Traders often doctored their goods, disguising older people's graying hair or flaky skin, so shaved and greased testicles were suspect. The Africans who passed muster during this triage were branded with a hot iron, then herded onto waiting slave ships.

On board, the males, who constituted two-thirds of the human cargo, were shackled and pushed below deck into suffocating holds former slave Olaudah Equiano recalled as "absolutely pestilential."[112] Whether "tight packed" or "loose packed," slaves were intolerably crowded. The official "Dimensions" for slave ships were "five foot in length, Eleven Inches in Breadth, and twenty three Inches in height" per slave. On most ships, slaves were forced to sleep nestled spoonlike against their fellows in quarters contaminated by vomit, urine and feces. Women and children, unshackled, were held separately. Sailors, mistreated and underfed, abused and raped the women.

In this morass of misery, captains aimed for maximum profit, which meant keeping their cargo alive and in salable condition: a dead slave was a dead loss. To avoid this, they attempted to implement so-called sanitation and health measures, both supervised by a slave driver armed with a cat-o'-nine-tails. Sanitation consisted of forcing the slaves to

Slaves endured the Middle Passage crammed into filthy holds in ships like the Brookes. *Survivors afterward treated their "shipmates" as blood relatives.*

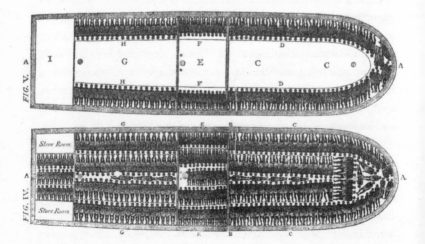

scrape down and sluice the filthy holds, preserving health by bringing them up on deck and forcing them to exercise and dance, often grotesquely.

There was nothing sanitary or healthy about the Middle Passage. Food and water were always in short supply, especially when ships had to wait for months for a full cargo of Africans. Embittered and despairing, or horribly ill, the Africans often refused to eat. Then sailors force-fed them, even if the process broke teeth or choked them. Disease, suicide and brutality killed at least two million. On some ships, a handful died; others arrived full of the dying, having already flung the dead overboard.[113] One captain lost 320 of his cargo of 700 Africans to death, then cursed them as "a parcel of creatures nastier than swine."[114]

Along with the challenges of feeding, watering, exercising and otherwise keeping their charges alive, captains confronted slave mutinies. More than a million rebelled, inciting insurrections on one in ten slave ships. "Keep [the slaves] shackled & hand bolte[d] fearing their rising or Leaping Overboard," one captain instructed.[115] Slave ships became "floating prisons" manned by warrior sailors who treated their human cargo as hostile and dangerous.

African women figured prominently in shipboard revolts. Unshackled and sometimes privy to information gleaned from sailors who raped them, these women encouraged, warned and provided vital information to the male rebel leaders. Revolts began off the African coast and continued throughout the Middle Passage. Historian David Richardson is aware of 485 insurrections, 93 by Africans attacking ships from the shore, 392 revolts by slaves aboard ship. The unarmed rebels rarely triumphed, but every insurrection was a declaration of defiance and hatred and set the tone for the slaves' new lives.

Those new lives began anywhere from five weeks to two or three months later. Then slave traders cleaned and prepped their wares, feeding the too-thin, shaving and oiling the graying, disguising as best they could the ravages of scurvy, scabies and syphilis, even plugging the anuses of those afflicted with dysentery. Some traders clothed their merchandise in cheap garments, others left them naked.

Potential buyers jabbed, squeezed limbs, handled genitals, inspected orifices. They peered inside mouths to check for unhealthily pale gums or lips and for teeth filed into sharp edges or points, an African fashion that whites universally disliked and considered barbaric. Barbadian planters were notorious for grappling large-breasted females.

Slave sales, on board or in onshore barracoons, were the terrifying climax to the Middle Passage. They were usually auctions conducted as "scrambles" or by "inch of candle." Equiano described the slaves' terror as buyers rushed or "scrambled" at their slaves of choice, shrieking and grabbing at them. In auctions by "inch of candle," bids were taken until a candle burned down one inch. Black and white witnesses never forgot the heartrending wails as slaves were sold apart from their family and friends.

The Cane Fields

The next phase of their ordeal was "seasoning." The new slaves were by now disoriented, grief-stricken and displaying "all the symptoms of a broken trauma-ridden personality."[116] To erase their sense of identity and to crush what remained of their spirits, their master renamed them: Prince Apongo became Wager, and Olaudah Equiano became Gustavus Vassa. Next he issued them identical shapeless garments of cheap, coarse Osnaburg linen, then branded them again, searing his personal-property logo into their cheeks or shoulders. Jamaican overseer and slave owner Thomas Thistlewood's was "TT" inside an inverted triangle. The Society for the Propagation of the Bible's was "Society."

Next came a sad shackled march to the plantation. There the newcomers were lodged with Creole slaves who could orient them and teach them the rudiments of plantation life, and perhaps moderate the recalcitrance so common in Africans. White overseers welcomed them with the whip, jeers and humiliation and, in the case of women, with sexual assault.

The Africans did not "season" easily. An estimated two out of seven died of disease and despair. The survivors refused orders, lashed back at drivers and overseers and ran away. They ceaselessly mourned their lost lives and loved ones and their African homeland. Shocking numbers chose suicide over slavery. Frustrated and angry planters resorted to the whip and other punishments to force them to work and to obey the plantation's rules. Slaves, their greatest capital investment, simply had to be productive.

SUGARCANE PLANTATIONS VARIED in size and structure over time and place but, whether in Brazil, Mexico, Jamaica, Antigua, Barbados, Cuba, Martinique or St. Domingue (later Haiti), they shared common features dictated by the nature of the crop, the demands of sugar consumers and the goals of the planters.

Plantations were self-contained villages with dozens of buildings. These included a mill, boiling and curing houses, often a rum distillery, sheds in which to repair and maintain equipment, and storage sheds and barns for the cane and its leavings—*bagasse*—and for livestock and plantation supplies. There was a Great House for the planter or his agent, and more modest dwellings for the overseer, the chemist and other white employees. The slave quarters were set at a distance from the white homes and built as barracks or as rows of shacks with thatched roofs. In Brazil but rarely elsewhere, planters provided a small chapel and house for the resident chaplain. Most plantations had a slave "hospital" and a "jail" or dungeon.

The plantation was surrounded by hundreds or thousands of acres of cane fields known as cane pieces, as well as pastureland, woodland for fuel, and usually slave provision grounds. Cane fields were located close to the mills and cut into rectangles bounded by lanes that accommodated oxen-pulled wagons and served as fire breaks. Farsighted planters rotated their planting schedules so that maturing cane did not overwhelm the slaves and the mills.

The most characteristic feature of sugarcane plantations was that they operated with factory-like scheduling and job specialization; Sidney Mintz proposes that they were the first to institute assembly-line production. Most of the slaves, "the Main Sinews of a Sugar Plantation,"[117] were divided into cane-field gangs—the Great Gang, the Second Gang and sometimes a Third Gang, each with its own drivers.

Other slaves worked as boilermen, coopers, mechanics, wheelwrights, carpenters, blacksmiths, masons, carters, loaders, mule handlers, stock-keepers, cooks, grass cutters, rat catchers, nurses, babysitters, fishermen and watchmen. The Hogmeat Gang, composed of children, seniors and the disabled, scavenged food for the animals, weeded gardens and did odd chores. Housekeepers, cooks, laundresses, babysitters and other domestics ran the Great House.

Gang members were selected carefully, their strength and ability matched to the work assigned.[118] The Great Gang was the largest and hardest worked. The Second Gang was a smaller reflection of the first. Today's exhausted Great Gang slave might work tomorrow in the Second Gang; a less weary Second Gang slave might find herself toiling in the Great Gang. The Third Gang, if there was one, would include adolescents and slaves too old or debilitated to keep up with the demands of the Great and Second gangs. On most estates these workers were assigned to the Hogmeat Gang, which also included all slave children between four or five and ten to twelve years of age.[119]

Age was of overriding importance. "The masters valued their slaves, as property and human capital, largely on the basis of age," notes historian B. W. Higman, with fourteen- to forty-year-olds considered prime workers.[120] Except in the earliest years of slavery, when male slaves outnumbered females two to one, women predominated in the field gangs. Male slaves had many more options. They could train to become coopers, masons, boilers or mechanics or learn any number of trades closed to women. Women could become distillers or slave drivers, the only job promotions open to them. The Hogmeat Gang driver was often a "careful old woman."[121]

Color played a starring role in work assignments. Mixed-race or colored slaves were usually exempted from such laborious work and were sent into the fields only as punishment. In 1790, for instance, mulatto Ned, a misbehaving stable boy, was "stripped of his livery, degraded to a field negro, and for six months, dug cane-holes, weeded and cut down the crop with a fifty pound weight fastened to his body."[122] A white plantation manager's "Mulatto sweetheart" caught cheating on him with a black slave lover had "chains put on her neck &

sent into the field."[123] Only after the 1807 abolition of the slave trade, and the resulting labor shortage, did planters send more lighter-skinned slaves into the cane fields.

The Great Gang's work was onerous, dangerous and, under hot-tempered drivers and the even hotter sun, debilitating. In July or August, they prepared the land for planting, slashing and burning grass, shrubs and old cane. This was skilled work best done in windless weather. Even then slaves could be gouged by a swinging machete, inhale smoke or be scorched or bitten by fleeing snakes and rats. At the best of times, cane fields hosted armies of rats so destructive to the uncut cane that planters called them "the most expensive of the planter's enemies." On Matthew Lewis's Jamaican plantation, slave rat catchers caught three thousand in a six-month period, and rat-hunting cats caught untold numbers more.

The next step, readying the soil for planting cane tops, was the hardest. Few planters were willing to rest and improve their fields with fallow periods, which, in the short run, cost them sugar production. Instead, the effects of aridity and galloping erosion taught them to plant cane in holes rather than trenches. Cane holing was tedious and back-breaking work. White supervisors marked off the land into precise five-foot squares, then strung knotted strings between them in taut lines along the cane rows. At each knot, slaves dug a shallow hole, six to nine inches deep and two to three feet long, and used the scooped-out soil to form a ridge around each hole.

The slaves, each equipped with a hoe, worked in two-person teams, sometimes "sorted so as to match each other in size and strength,"[124] at other times with a strong worker paired with a weaker one. They inserted three cane tops into each hole and, on many plantations, packed it with manure, seaweed or sludge before covering it with earth.[125] (A Martinique planter estimated that fertilized cane produced 31 percent more sugar, and fertilized ratoon cane 36 percent more.)[126] Forty slaves planted one acre or approximately 3,500 cane holes per day.[127] By the mid-eighteenth century, the average plantation in Jamaica, the premier English sugar colony, was more than one thousand acres. Each slave's daily quota was one hundred cane holes. In the less compacted soil of the French Antilles, the standard was twenty-eight holes per hour. Failure to achieve this guaranteed a whipping, the sugar planter's standard motivational tool. In Antigua, a young army officer observed "a huge slave-driver flogging most unmercifully an old decrepit female negro, who appeared bowed down with misery and hard labour … one of a gang … working with spades under a midday tropical sun."[128]

Slaves had their own motivational tools. Despite perpetual white surveillance, they chanted and sang out their rage and pain. "Hard work kill de neger, O dear, he must die." A Hogmeat Gang chanted, "One Monday morning they lay me down / And give me thirty-nine on my bare rump." Some slaves sang seditiously, "One, Two, Three, / All de same, / Black, White, Brown, / All de same, / All de same, / One, two three."[129] Cuban slaves already in the fields before sunrise startled Great House visitors awake with the "prolonged wailing cadences of their barbaric chants,"[130] "A-a-b'la!" "E-e-cha! E-e-cha!" as the boilers cried out to the stokers, and the gangs loading the wagons or filling the troughs chanted "a barbaric, tuneless intonation."[131]

Slaves were sometimes silenced. In St. Domingue, Swiss traveler Justin Girod-Chantrans observed sweating, sun-baked slaves, naked or in rags, cane holing in "dead silence … The merciless eye of the plantation steward [overseer] watched over the workers while several foremen [drivers], dispersed among the workers and armed with long whips, delivered harsh blows to those who seemed too weary to sustain the pace … none escaped the crack of the whip if they could not keep up the pace."[132]

Cane holing exacted such a toll that many overseers hired jobbing gangs to assist. Jobbing gangs were owned or co-owned by white settlers engaged in slave rental, or by small farmers looking to make money between harvests. In a brutal system, they were the hardest-worked and the most abused. The planter's own slaves were his greatest capital investment and, if only for that reason, worth keeping alive. Cane holing, "although equally hard on the hired negroes … at least relieves my own," Jamaican planter Matthew Lewis admitted.[133]

Sugar slaves so dreaded cane holing that jobbers got higher rates for cane-holing gangs than for prostitutes or pastry chefs. In alien cane

William Clark, from Ten Views in the Island of Antigua, in which are Represented the Process of Sugar Making, and the Employment of the Negroes, in the Field, Boiling-House, and Distillery. *1823.*
Holeing a Cane-Piece, on Weatherell's Estate *shows a gang of mostly male slaves supervised by a black-hatted driver performing the precise and arduous work of cane holing. A female slave and two children stand next to a crowded pen of cattle.*

Planting the Sugar-Cane, on Bodkin's Estate *shows two gangs overseen by two drivers. Cattle graze in the distance and the Monks Hill Military Station, also known as Fort George, looms large. The fort was built to protect Antigua from Arawak and French attacks.*

Cutting the Sugar-Cane, on Delaps' Estate *portrays a gang cutting cane under the watchful eye of a brown-hatted driver. Another gang, including women and children, bundles the cut cane, which is carried to waiting horse-drawn carts. A horse-mounted white overseer speaks to a slave.*

Interior of a Distillery, on Delaps' Estate *shows slaves ladling cane syrup into copper vats. Opposite them, in formal suits and top hats despite the intense heat, white men examine the sugar.*

fields, supervised by drivers who had no stake in their welfare, the jobbing gangs, almost always African males, were overworked, whipped, starved and, at night, left to sleep out in the fields. Once in a gang they had a life expectancy estimated at seven years and, lamented a nine-teenth-century observer, died like "overwrought or over-driven horses."[134]

For the next twelve months (fifteen for ratoon cane), the slaves rein-forced the growing cane with banked soil, weeded the thousands of rows between the cane holes and removed dry stalks. When the soil was parched, as it commonly was in the West Indies, they had to irrigate it. As the cane grew, they pruned it. Many plantations staggered their planting schedules so that the mills could be fed continuously. This also meant that slaves finished one onerous job only to have to repeat it on a neighboring field.

In addition to their work, deprivations and punishments, female field slaves had to cope with pregnancy, childbirth and, hardest of all, childrea-ring. Sugar planters regarded slave children (and old slaves) as a drain on the plantation's coffers and made no concessions even to women in advanced pregnancy. From the age of two weeks to two months, infants who survived were slung onto their mothers' backs, African style, and carried out to the fields. Some women worked like that all day, stooped under the little burden. Others had to set their babies down "in trays beneath an arbour made of boughs" or cushioned on soft cloth or goat or sheepskin where they lay "like so many tadpoles," naked and exposed to the weather and the mosquitoes, sucking at a morsel of sugarcane and watched over by an old slave "grandee" (a midwife or babysitter).[135] On some plantations, nursing mothers took shifts, minding babies for two hours and then returning to work. On others, "drivers curse both them and their squalling brats, when they were suckling them."[136]

When they were weaned or their mothers were not permitted to nurse them in the cane fields, slave babies survived on "parrada," bread, flour and sugar mashed into pap. Caring for these toddlers in the cane fields was difficult and dangerous. Most mothers left them back in the quar-ters, in the "nursery" that was really a euphemism for a dusty patch where older children and decrepit old slave women watched them. On a few plantations, determined mothers "suffer the pickaninny to sit astride upon their backs, like St. George a horseback … as she continues her painful stooping posture" weeding and cane holing.[137]

Large Cuban plantations kept slave infants in "nursery rooms" in the grim slave quarters or barracoons, but permitted their mothers to come in from the fields twice or three times a day to breast-feed them. An American woman found these little ones "preternaturally quiet and docile,"[138] while a white male visitor described them as "little black, naked sinners, running and tumbling over each other in great glee."[139]

In the Service of Cane

As the cane grew, slaves tended the fields full of corn and other crops that would feed the human and animal livestock, repaired roads, walls, buildings and equipment, and finished shipping last season's cane. When the cane was mature, the gangs harvested it, expertly hacking it with machetes, cutlasses or the fascine knives known as bills. For the five months of crop time, the slaves worked day and night. The cane, cut about four feet long and immediately bundled, had to be milled within two days; any delays and it would dry out, reducing the sugar content.

After loading the heavy cane stalks onto waiting wagons, the slaves in turn made slaves of the groaning, heaving oxen struggling to haul the laden carts to the mill. From the time the carts drew up at the mills and slaves unloaded their cargo of raw cane, the slaves worked without respite. Cart after cart lumbered back and forth from the fields, and slaves loaded and unloaded them. Meanwhile, wheelwrights and black-smiths made emergency repairs to the carts, and carpenters mended wooden equipment.

The cane passed through a series of slave-operated assembly lines. It was crushed in the mill to release its sweet sap, immensely dangerous work. Slaves, many of them women, were then working eighteen to twenty hours a day, and often fell asleep or faltered as they fed cane through the huge rollers. The rollers easily caught a careless hand and pulled its owner along through the roller, crushing her to death. This was such a frequent occurrence that many overseers kept a hatchet or saber at the ready so they could chop off the trapped limb to save the slave's life. In Brazil and St. Domingue, slave women with missing arms, hands or fingers were common. Theresa, an African queen sold into Brazilian slavery, had both arms amputated after she caught first one then the other in the roller. In Barbados, where two female mill feeders were chained together as a punishment, one caught her arm in the roller and "every effort was used, to stop the mill, yet that was impossible to be done, before the other female negroe, was dragged so close to those cylinders, that her head was severed from her body."[140] Haiti's Maroon rebel, the African-born Makandal, fled his plantation after his hand was severed in an accident in the sugar mill. In Voltaire's *Candide*, a maimed Surinamese slave explains why he is missing one arm and one leg: "When we work in the sugar mills and we catch our finger in the mill-stone, they cut off our hand; when we try to run away, they cut off a leg; both things have happened to me. It is at this price that you eat sugar in Europe."

One remarkable Cuban plantation, the three-thousand-acre Ingenio Hormiguero, had a sitting room right inside the mill. The owners' wives, in rocking chairs with sewing in hand, watched "every piece of cane that goes between the rollers ... [and] the entire interior of the mill.... The ladies ... can tell to a nicety just what proportion of juice the cane is yielding, whether the engine is running steadily, and whether the last new team of mules is likely to turn out well."[141]

After the cane was milled, the sap was piped along a long wooden gutter system into the boiling house, into the first and largest of a train of copper receptacles known as the Jamaica Train. In mule-driven mills, mule drivers lashed the animals round and round. In the intolerable heat, slaves shoveled firewood or dried *bagasse* to stoke the boilers. They heated sap with lime to clarify it. They repeatedly skimmed impurities from the juice and, with long-handled dippers, ladled it into the ever-smaller boiling pans. The sap in the last and smallest boiler, the teache, was a sticky, taffy-like syrup. This clarifying process was also dangerous, and exhausted slaves were often scalded by the boiling fluid.

C'est à ce prix que vous mangez du sucre en Europe.

Candide Chapitre 19

J. M. Moreau le J.^{un}   1787   Baquoy filius sculp.

A slave explains his mutilations to two Europeans, adding, "It is at this price that you eat sugar in Europe." Illustration from Voltaire's Candide.

The boiler-house slaves had to be highly skilled; if they made mistakes, they could ruin the sugar. A plantation's head boiler was arguably its greatest asset. He had to discern the nature of the incoming cane: its species, whether it was grown or ratooned, and in what kind of soil, how often it had been watered and fertilized, whether it had been attacked by pests or rats, how long it had been grown and how ripe it was when cut. On the basis of this information he would decide how much lime to use—a hundred pounds of cane needed anywhere from two ounces to three pounds of lime—and how long to boil the sap. The head boiler effectively determined the quality of sugar the planter would export to Europe: would it be suitable for the Duchess of Bedford's low tea, or would it be the crude sort of sugar that Gladys could afford? When Jamaican overseer Thomas Thistlewood hired the "famous boiler" Witte from a neighboring plantation, he was so pleased with Witte's work that he rewarded him with 4 bitts—half a Spanish-American dollar—and two bottles of rum, double what he gave slave women he had sex with and the same as he gave those he was infatuated with.[142]

The next stage was to cool the syrup and cure it in the procedure described in chapter 1. Some of the molasses that dripped out of the barrels known as hogsheads was collected and reboiled. Many plantations also distilled rum, fermenting equal amounts of molasses with sap skimmed from the first boiling, and twice distilled to produce proof rum (half alcohol by volume). Female slaves worked in distilleries and could even aspire to be distillers because planters thought women were less inclined to tipple the finished product.

On large plantations, the cutting-milling-boiling-distilling cycle went on night and day for five months. Each segment of that agricultural-industrial assembly line depended on the one preceding it, and each slave had to accommodate its exigencies. Specifically, they had to work inhuman hours. In Puerto Rico, "one sees the blacks going to the mill by three o'clock in the morning and continuing until eight or nine o'clock in the evening, having as their only compensation, the pleasure of eating cane. They never even get twenty-four hours of respite during the year," French abolitionist Victor Schoelcher observed.[143] In Cuba, a visitor asked an overseer if allowing slaves only three hours for sleep would not shorten their lives. "Sin duda," the overseer replied. Without doubt.

If it had not been for biological limitations, planters would have forced their slaves to work even longer. As it was, they relaxed their rules and motivated their exhausted slaves by allowing them to sample the hot, sweet cane juice and sometimes gave them tots of rum laced with sugar. Energized and comforted, the slaves redoubled their efforts to finish the sugar.

"THE MUSIC OF THE NEGRO IS THE WHIP": THE WORKING LIVES OF SUGAR SLAVES

Martinique's Pierre Dessalles spoke for thousands of other sugar planters when he declared that reason "is a language the negro does not understand. The music of the negro is the whip."[144] In slave quarters everywhere, it was the music that began their day and gave rise to the expression "the crack of dawn," when the head driver cracked his whip as a collective wake-up call. (Some overseers blew on conch shells or rang bells instead.) In Cuba, where planters and colonial officials believed that "in order for a man to be loved by his slaves, he must be feared,"[145] an American visitor described "horrible places in the interior of the Island, where the crack of the whip pauses only during four hours in the twenty-four, where, so to speak, the sugar smells of the blood of the slaves."[146]

Before trudging off to the cane fields, slaves had chores to complete around the plantation. These "before-day jobs" included cleaning animal dung and the onerous task of finding fodder for the livestock. After completing these tasks, they carried their hoes and food up to the fields, where they assembled for roll call. The tardy, even mothers who had been tending their infants, were whipped. Nonetheless, some slaves were late every morning.[147] After roll call, the unfed slaves worked in the field for about two hours, until 10 A.M., when they stopped to eat whatever provision they had scrounged together and brought with them. Hunger was ubiquitous, and in the season of ripening cane, they risked the whip to alleviate it. A few quick machete slashes transformed a slice of cane into fast food that fueled the next torturous burst of labor. If the driver noticed, he would let loose a hail of blows. Thomas Thistlewood subjected the slaves Phillis, Egypt, Hector, Joe and Pomona to "Derby's dose," his own bizarre punishment for eating cane, forcing the slave Derby to defecate in the other slaves' mouths.

After breakfast came another sustained spurt of labor. It was interrupted by two hours for lunch when the sun was highest, the fields shimmering with reflected heat and the slaves weary after six to eight hours of labor. Lunchtime was often a euphemism for gardening, as many slaves preferred to tend the provision grounds that were often their sole source of food and income. They also fed their chickens and pigs with the grass and plants their children had gathered. A cracking whip or melancholy conch shell summoned them back to the fields.

The afternoon session lasted until sunset. Here the Great, Second and sometimes even Third gangs toiled along the taut rows of cane. White overseers roamed the fields, checking crops, monitoring slaves. Drivers—"commonly called dog-drivers, who are mostly black or mulatto fellows of the worst dispositions"—strode alongside the slaves, threatening and whipping them to exact every last ounce of their energy. Janet Schaw, a Scottish visitor unsympathetic to slaves, described a cane field in St. Kitts: "Every ten Negroes have a driver, who walks behind them, holding a short whip and a long one.... They are naked, male and female, down to the girdle, and you constantly observe where the application [of the whip] has been made."[148]

Cane-field drivers, almost always males, were among the most important workers on the plantation. They were "official tyrants" who commanded the respect or at least the fear of the slaves they literally drove, and planters or overseers made sure they had a stake in the process. Some overseers and planters tolerated their drivers' sexual predations on the slave women if they were efficient. Some planters went so far as to ask their drivers' advice about new slaves, even bringing them along to slave auctions. Drivers were often the husbands, brothers and fathers of field slaves, which greatly complicated their family relationships.

Former Antiguan slave Mary Prince heard Henry, a black driver, confess in church "that he had treated the slaves very cruelly; but said that he was compelled to obey the orders of his master.... He said it was a horrid thing ... to have sometimes to beat his own wife or sister; but he must do so if ordered by his master." Worse, Mary added, he had to strip them, even "women that have had children exposed in the open field to shame!"[149] A Wesleyan missionary watched as "a female, apparently about forty years of age, was laid, her stomach upon the ground, her clothes were most indecorously turned up and whilst two persons held her hands and one her feet ... the driver inflicted stroke after stroke."[150]

That driver's overseer would have approved. Overseers and planters tolerated no leniency in drivers. At harvest time, a furious Pierre Dessalles punished a driver who told him that "he was not in the habit of killing people"; Dessalles "had three stakes driven into the ground and had him tied to them; he was given fifty lashes.... Yet he persisted in saying that he would continue to act as before. So I had him put into an iron collar."[151] Most drivers were compliant, and when slaves underperformed—intentionally or because of illness, disability or lack of skill—they were subjected to their driver's ire.

At harvest's end, after they had prepared the sugar for shipping and before the new season began, the exhausted slaves enjoyed a brief celebratory respite. Planters and overseers rewarded them with rum, sugar and sometimes food. "Served the Negroes 15 quarts of rum out of the butt a filling in the curing house, and 2 large bottoms of sugar to make them merry, now crop over," Thistlewood noted.[152] Slaves came to expect these tokens of appreciation, and mutinied if they were deprived of them.

HUMAN AND ANIMAL LIVESTOCK

The cane fields were the heartland of every sugar plantation, but sugar production required more than just cane. Livestock was essential to the operation, especially on plantations with animal-powered mills. On average, large estates in the French Antilles needed thirty-five to fifty of both oxen and mules, smaller ones perhaps twenty-five or fewer of each.

Both oxen and mules were worked hard, transporting cane and powering mills. As well, their droppings made excellent fertilizer for cane.

Despite their value to the sugar operation, planters treated animal livestock just as they did the slaves they recorded in their estate account books as human livestock, and provided minimal sustenance, inadequate shelter, cruel treatment, indifferent care. Pens were established on land unsuitable for planting cane whether or not it was good pastureland or had sufficient water sources. Pens were usually ill conceived, roofless enclosures that left the malnourished, overworked animals unprotected even during the rainy season. Sugar regions had few or no veterinarians, and medical care was makeshift or nonexistent. Planters showed the same callousness to animals as to slaves, and relied on the pain of the whip to force them to perform Herculean feats of strength and endurance. The result was that the average sugar-plantation mule survived only six to eight years, and oxen four to six, less than half their potential life spans.

Quite apart from overwork, inadequate nutrition and brutal treatment, the bizarre, counterintuitive dynamics of the plantation system pitted field slaves against livestock they were expected to nurture. Predictably, the slaves targeted the animals, laming, mutilating, starving or poisoning them, pilfering their fodder for their own animals, surreptitiously selling or even butchering and feasting on them. Overseers and planters waged constant war against slave sabotage of their animals.

The problem was exacerbated because the overseers required desperately overworked cane-field gangs to provide fodder for the animals. After an exhausting day in the fields, the slaves had to tramp out into the pasture or other fields and, in the darkness of nightfall, pick their allotment of grass. Even on Sundays, when the slaves were freed to tend their own gardens and some lucky ones could sell extra yams or plantains at the local market, cattle fodder took priority. "On Sunday morning," Mary Prince recalled about an Antiguan sugar plantation, "each slave has to go out and gather a large bundle of grass; and, when they bring it home, they have to sit at the manager's door and wait till he come out: often have they to wait there till past eleven o'clock, without any breakfast."[153] Only when the manager approved her offering could a slave eat, garden and engage in commerce.

Slaves detested gathering grass. Memoir after memoir emphasizes how they begrudged the time it consumed, and the backbreaking effort of picking through inhospitable, stony fields for vegetation, grass and weeds to hand feed to the cattle. "At the best of times the labour of searching 'about the fences, in the mountains, and fallow or waste grounds' was exhausting," writes Caribbean historian Elsa Goveia. "In dry weather it became an almost intolerable burden."[154]

Rev. James Ramsay and Rev. Clement Caines, contemporary observers of sugarcane cultivation, singled out grass gathering as a hardship so extreme it warranted legislative intervention. Caines decried it as "an unnecessary and abominable custom; but which, like all other customs, no reasoning will be of enough force to eradicate."[155] Both he and Ramsay claimed that droves of slaves ran away to avoid being punished for failing to gather enough grass.

Meanwhile, despite the slaves' prodigious efforts, cattle were often underfed and too weak to do work that then fell to slaves. When cattle could not manage it, slaves had to fertilize fields, staggering up hillsides with basketfuls of manure on their heads; such treks were, Caines believed, "the source of more racking and incurable pains in the stomach, than every other species of plantation labour united."[156] Furthermore, owners often opted to spare cattle by transferring their heavy loads onto slaves when moving up steep hillsides. Slave laws, such as St. Kitts's "It is a Rule never to do by Slaves what Cattle can accomplish," were obeyed mostly in the breach. The most striking example was the notoriously grueling cane holing, which could have been accomplished, Jamaican planter Bryan Edwards asserted, "with greater facility and dispatch by the [oxen-drawn] plough than by the hoe."[157] Instead, wretched slaves hand hoed acre after acre.

Slaves were so busy tending the plantation's fields and livestock that they struggled to scavenge enough guinea grass, weeds, cane tops and other vegetative *bagasse* for their own animals. They worried that hunger would drive their cows or pigs to break into the estate's pastureland to graze. When this happened, the overseer would punish the straying creature's owner or even kill the animal.

CANE GANGS

Pen slaves worked full time on livestock maintenance, and the Hogmeat Gang helped them. In marked contrast to the cane-field slaves, as regimented as a military operation, pen slaves worked relatively independently, and their work was steady and regular. They had quotidian chores—gathering and distributing fodder, planting guinea grass and corn, sweeping, cleaning, repairing fences, branding. Contemporaries agreed that pen work was much easier, and sometimes assigned young women to work in the pen rather than the cane fields where the backbreaking work contributed to the low fertility rate. "A Penn is certainly better calculated for Negroes to breed at than Estates for there is no light work on them for negro women," planter Simon Taylor believed.[158]

The pen slaves also sabotaged their owners by victimizing the livestock entrusted to their care. To avert attacks, some overseers bribed pen slaves with little gifts of money. When animals died, even of undiagnosed disease, or an oxen or mule was lamed or went missing, the pen slaves were punished.

Slave children were known as pickaninnies, a corruption of the Spanish *pequeños niños*—small children. At the age of four or five, their childhood ended. Then, as an absentee Jamaican planter reported after a fact-finding visit to investigate why his estate was no longer profitable, they were "put to clean the Paths, bring Fire-wood to the Kitchen, etc. when a Boy Overseer with his Wand or White Rod, is set over them as task Master."[159] When they were about nine, girls and boys joined the Hogmeat Gang, collecting grass, tending livestock and doing other chores. As they matured and grew, planters or overseers assigned them to adult work gangs. It was not unheard of to send twelve-year-old girls into the cane fields.

An English visitor to Cuba ached for the gang of fifty or sixty children he saw outside a cane-crushing house, piling cane onto an elevator that carried it to the crushing wheel: "Toiling away for their very lives in the broiling sunshine, the poor little wretches kept a constant eye on a formidable cow-hide whip, wielded by a negro who stood by, ready to crack it across their bare backs if they attempted to idle or eat the sugar-cane."[160]

The Hogmeat Gang accomplished more than chores. It also social-ized its little members into slavery. The women promoted to drive the Hogmeat Gang took pride in being supervisors, but their owners saw them as instructors in slavery. A "benevolent" French planter expected the driver to "teach them how to perform all their duties well…. She must also instruct them to obey orders without question and to resist bickering among themselves…. At a young age, children are very recep-tive. Thus, much depends on authority figures who mold them into either good or bad subjects."[161]

Longevity was rare among sugar slaves, but some defied the enormous odds and survived into their fifties and sixties and sometimes even longer. Old age brought them little respite. Planters assigned old women to child care, to assist in the kitchen or the slave hospital or to gather grass for fodder. They sent old men into the cane fields to work as cane "tiers," a job still performed by the oldest cane cutters. Tiers waited beside the carts where other slaves deposited the cut cane. Then they bundled and tied the heavy, wet stalks and heaved them into the cart. This was onerous and unremitting work and very difficult for old men to perform.

Other old men became one of the many watchmen employed on the theft-plagued plantations. Each watchman had his specific guard duty: the Great House, the pen, the mill, the boiling house, the vast barns and storerooms, the fields, the gardens. He had to endure the mosquito-ridden nights and fight sleep. If stealthy intruders—a slave of his acquaintance, renegade slaves from other plantations or Maroons seeking supplies—succeeded in raiding the plantation, he faced severe punishment. Thistlewood, "finding many corn cut up by the roots, and the corn stole, flogged Pompey [the watchman] well."[162]

Some aged slaves were unable to work. A few planters gave them plantains, but most were fed by other slaves or not at all. Many planters expelled old slaves from their plantation to fend for themselves, often after cynically manumitting them. In Barbados, these old field slaves "crawled" to Bridgetown to beg and were "often to be seen in the street, in the very last stage of human misery, naked, famished, diseased and forlorn."[163] Abuse-by-manumission of old or disabled slaves was so prevalent that colonial laws outlawed it, but these laws were not enforced. One vicious eighteenth-century planter simply threw his oldest slaves over a cliff.

DOMESTIC SLAVES

Domestic slaves worked in the Great House, on the periphery of the quarters. Most lighter-skinned women, some their master's own progeny, were domestics. So were favored or talented blacks, an adept cook or a nimble-fingered seamstress. Although domestic labor was less physically onerous than field and pen work, the constant presence of whites made it more stressful. Even nighttime brought no escape. Domestics were always on call, and were often forbidden to visit the quarters. These men and women slept in the Great House, in the cupboard, or the cookhouse, or under the stairwell; many were forced to take what rest they could on their snoring masters' bedroom floor so they could jump at the snap of a finger to pour a glass of water, drag the chamber pot from under the bed or bat pesky mosquitoes away.

Female domestics were sexual targets, "compelled under pain of corporal punishment to yield implicit obedience to the will of the master."[164] Thistlewood "took" scores of women, both domestic and field slaves, and watched his drunken employer do the same. "Mr. C[ope] in his tantrums last night," he noted, "forced Egypt Susanah in the cook-room; was like a madman most part of the night, &c." Most female slaves who dared resist their white assaulters were punished for their "impudence."[165] Cope had Egypt Susanah and another woman whipped for refusing sex with him and a lustful visitor.

Alone of sugar plantation slaves, domestics had no role in sugar production except their contribution to the well-being and comfort of the planter or his representative. Great Houses boasted astonishingly large staffs. To do the work of five or six, "from twenty to forty servants is nothing unusual," one observer noted.[166] St. Kitt's resident Clement Caines, a critic of the slave system, asked rhetorically, "Was it necessary that [slaves] should wait in our houses and on our persons?" and answered, "No, it was not necessary. Yet it has been done,"[167] a perfect example of the twisted logic at the heart of sugar slavery.

This superabundant domestic flock filled myriad positions: butlers, coachmen, footmen, assistants, storekeepers, servers, housemaids, laundresses and, the most privileged, cooks, nannies, seamstresses and housekeepers. The cooks had to be trusted not to poison their masters, the nannies not to harm the little white heirs, and the seamstresses not to spoil imported fabric with crooked seams. The housekeeper, often her master's mistress, was the most important of all, as long as she maintained the authority of her sex appeal and loyalty, and navigated the pitfalls of cohabiting with his wife, who supervised her.

Compared to the field slaves, domestics had more and better clothes, including the white family's cast-offs, wore jewelry and ate much better; whites did not want ragged and dirty men and women under their roof. Many domestics received small gifts of money and used it to buy trinkets or saved it. Despite these benefits, most toiled at thankless jobs, dreading demotion to the cane fields. Insecurity was rife, and they were continually shifted to other jobs. They were, one observer opined, "the most miserable creatures that we own, the most corrupt and the most dangerous."[168]

OVERSEERS

Outside of the Great House, the most pervasive white presence in the sugar slave's life was the overseer. Unlike planters, even those who were not absentees, overseers spent considerable time in the fields and, during cane season, in the mill and boiling house. They were full-time plantation residents and, in the planter's absence, often served as de facto master. Only attorneys superseded overseers in authority, but because attorneys often supervised several plantations, they were more likely to visit than to live on any one plantation.

Overseers were both Creoles and expatriates, either younger sons hoping to improve their fortunes in the colonies or ambitious young men with poor prospects in Scotland or Ireland. Overseers often began their jobs knowing little about sugar cultivation, that most complex, rigorous, risky and capital-intensive operation. They traveled the length and breadth of sugar islands, making contacts, exchanging information, gaining experience and seeking work. When hired, they negotiated annual salaries ranging from £50 to £300 plus accommodations and other perks.

Overseers were usually bachelors, because many planters objected to "employing married Men, on the Supposition that their Families use more Sugar, and keep more Attendants about the House than Bachelors."[169] Nevis absentee planter John Frederick Pinney suspected married overseers would "neglect my estate by laziness and lying in bed mornings and afternoons (too much the Creole practice) or by visiting and being visited."[170] But though unmarried, overseers were seldom celibate and were notorious for raping slave women, keeping slave mistresses and fathering mulattoes. Thistlewood, who helpfully recorded the details of his every sexual encounter, confirmed the accuracy of the stereotype. So did the overseers whom Pierre Dessalles constantly complained about.

Overseers were the plantation's chief disciplinarians, and were commonly linked with brutality toward slaves. They had little fear; planters rarely chastised them if they were efficient. Planters lived in fear of slave uprisings and considered it important to show solidarity with other whites. And, living as they did in splendid isolation, surrounded by blacks they oppressed, exploited and degraded, many whites espoused severe repression as the best policy to keep safe. As a result, most planters intervened only when an overseer's cruelty was jeopardizing the slaves' cooperation and, therefore, sugar production and overall security.

Such intervention happened in 1824, when Dessalles sacked his overseer after prolonged lobbying by enraged slaves. What tipped the balance was the suicide of a just-whipped slave. "Say hello to M. Chignac, and tell him that he won't find Césaire to beat him again," Césaire cried out, then threw himself from the top of the sugar mill's wheel. "Your negroes are giving in to despair," other slaves warned Dessalles, "nothing amuses them, they no longer get dressed, and when they think of M. Chignac, the hospital fills up, and they let themselves die." Although Dessalles believed that "the race of men we must command is diabolical and treacherous," he justified firing Chignac because "All our misfortunes were caused by the slaves' hatred for him."[171]

Thistlewood was a harsh overseer, yet he denounced another overseer for acting "like a madman amongst the Negroes, flogging Dago, Primus, &c. without much occasion." When another overseer "came home sometime in the night in liquor, quarrelled with [African slave] Nanny, whom he kept, and shot her with small shot, one of which struck her head near the top, and the other her ankle, [and] both these shots seem to be lodged," Thistlewood fired him.[172]

Overseers were the instigators or the purveyors of slave punishments, and their policies and personalities directly affected slave life. Thistlewood's journals, written over a thirty-six-year period, are a litany of the violent punishments he inflicted on both house and field slaves, and are fair representations of life on sugar plantations elsewhere.

Like most overseers, Thistlewood was especially brutal with runaways. He confined the runaway Hazat "in the bilboes"—a long, iron bolt with locked shackles—"both feet; gagged him; locked his hands together; rubbed him with molasses & exposed him naked to the flies all day, and to the mosquitoes all night, without fire." He severely flogged another runaway, "then washed and rubbed in salt pickle, lime juice & bird pepper." After authorities executed Robin, a runaway, and sent back his head, Thistlewood stuck it on a pole so the other slaves could reflect on Robin's fate. He also had an elderly slave whipped for having shared a meal with Robin when he was AWOL. When the runaway Port Royal was recaptured, Thistlewood "gave him a moderate whipping, [and] pickled him well."[173]

Thistlewood flogged slaves for innumerable other infractions: eating sugarcane, eating mud (now known to be symptomatic of hookworm), failing to catch enough fish, "for scolding & disturbing Mr. Wilson," "for letting the cattle break into the Trumpet Tree Bottom and for getting drunk in the night & making the most infernal noise I ever heard," "for villainy & neglect," "for drumming last night." He had the ear, cheek and jaw of a slave who had stolen corn sawed away with a machete.[174] In nineteenth-century Martinique, Pierre Dessalles also used the whip, chain and iron collar, the bilboes, and also a *cachot*, a coffin-like dungeon, for similar offenses. He considered food theft a serious crime and punished it harshly: "I punished my negroes by taking their half-Saturday because they stole three bunches of bananas from me," he noted.[175]

In all the centuries of sugar slavery, slaves endured and died from a plethora of brutal and often grotesque punishments: they were roasted to death, flayed, hanged, dismembered, buried alive. Jamaican planter Tom Williams killed a slave girl suffering from diarrhea by "stopping her A— with a corn-stick."[176] Other punishments included castration, mutilating genitalia, amputating limbs or parts of limbs—half a foot for running away, for instance—riveting iron rings around the neck or stopping up the mouth with a metal spur. The abuse of slaves shook even hardened observers. In 1790, Royal Navy Captain Hall, no stranger to the harsh handling of sailors, testified tersely that the treatment of plantation slaves was "rather inhuman."[177]

THE QUARTERS: LIFE AFTER HOURS

Sugarcane dominated the lives of slaves even in their own quarters, where they made their own world. These men, women and children were the principal force in a unique project, "one of the rare cases of a human society being artificially created for the satisfaction of one clearly defined goal: that of making money through the production of sugar," sociologist Orlando Patterson observes.[178]

Over the centuries, that human society was rocked by wars and rebellions, politics and abolitionism, hurricanes and droughts. The most powerful blows were the stamping out of the slave trade and, at staggered intervals over five decades, of slavery itself. Yet through it all, the core of the sugar world remained so little altered that a cane cutter in seventeenth-century Brazil would have readily grasped how her nineteenth-century Jamaican counterpart lived, and the eighteenth-century Jamaican overseer would have been at home in St. Domingue. Because of the common denominators in the lives of sugar slaves, the following sketch of life in the quarters, reflecting a multiplicity of experiences, conveys a fair approximation of the world the sugar slaves made.

Slave quarters were set far enough away (a half mile was usual) to separate their sounds, smells and activities from the Great House, but close enough for the overseer to monitor all activities. Typical cabins were simple mud-and-wattle dwellings, detached or barracks-style, with thatched roofs and packed-earth floors. Many had only one door and one uncovered window or, as in St. Domingue, no window at all, leaving them without ventilation in the tropical heat. If the plantation owner provided whitewash, the walls were whitened; if not, they were the pale yellow, red or gray of the loam used in the plaster. Most shanties were so low that taller slaves could not stand upright in them. They were very small, and the one or two rooms of each cabin housed several slaves.

These dwellings were furnished with sleeping mats, cooking utensils and perhaps a little table, low stools and a cherished article of clothing reserved for special occasions such as a dance or a funeral. Many slaves slept on the ground, prompting whites to quip that slaves didn't go to *bed*, they went to *sleep*. In the Danish West Indies they lay on the floor "jumbled together like cattle."[179] During the rainy season, roofs leaked and floors turned into oozing mud. The shanties were hot, infested with mosquitoes, and devoid of privacy. The ground outside served as the kitchen, nearby woods as the toilet and remoter knolls and fields the sites of lovemaking.

Privileged slaves—wheelwrights, carpenters, coopers, blacksmiths, masons and mechanics, and some domestics released from the Great House at night—had larger and more solidly constructed houses that reflected their status and accommodated their possessions, including several changes of clothing. Some of these slaves had boarded their floors and, with their own money, had acquired furniture that white observers considered very comfortable. A few had mosquito nets to stave off the nightly assaults that tormented everyone else in the quarters.

Large Cuban sugar plantations housed their slaves in barracoons, grim, dirt-floored, unventilated barracks built of wood or cement. Runaway slave Esteban Montejo described the barracoon he fled: "The place swarmed with fleas and ticks that gave the entire workforce infections and sickness…. There was always some fool dog sniffing around looking for food. People had to stay in the rooms.… Rooms! In reality they were furnaces…. The barracoon was bare dirty, empty, and lonely.

A black man couldn't get used to that.... The slaves did their business in a latrine ... in a corner of the barracoon.... Afterward, you had to use plants like feverfew and corncobs."[180]

As if Cuban sugar slaves weren't wretched enough, they were locked in at night, imprisoned in their cells, overseen by two watchmen who were to report any suspicious activity. American visitor Julia Woodruff described her deeply troubling visit to a barracoon: "We look into some of the rooms, and wonder if life is worth living at such a scanty measure of comfort or attainment. There is a bed of rude plank with a blanket on it, a stool or two, a few pots and pans, two or three coarse garments hanging on the wall, occasionally a little crucifix or an image of the Virgin,—that is all! ... merely a place for eating and sleeping, where the slaves ... are driven nightly, like sheep to a pen, and locked in, until the morning's call to labor."[181]

THE SLAVES' FOOD

On most days, exhausted slaves rushed home from the fields to prepare whatever food they could before falling into desperately needed sleep. Slaves were perpetually hungry. "Evidence is consistent from the beginning of the sugar economy to the end of the colonial era that slaves did not receive an adequate ration," Latin American historian Stuart Schwartz writes about Brazilian slaves,[182] and this was true of sugar slaves everywhere.

Individual planters had widely different policies about feeding their slaves. Many provided meager rations they expected slaves to supplement by growing vegetables and raising animals on "provision grounds," small plots of land allocated for that purpose. Some provided only provision grounds and expected their slaves to feed themselves. Others refused to allow their slaves any free time and provided food. Still others neither fed their slaves nor provided provision grounds. In 1702, one of Haiti's wealthiest planters remarked that "Negroes steal at night because they are not fed by their masters." Eighty years later, an observer estimated that "three-quarters of the masters do not feed their slaves."[183] Many Barbados planters followed this same policy, providing no food and assuming that their slaves would "subsist, as they could, by committing nightly depredations on the neighbouring sugar plantations."[184]

Planters shortchanged their slaves by failing to provide them with the amount and quality of rations prescribed by colonial slave laws. In Cuba, slave law stipulated a daily diet of six or eight plantains or the same amount of starchy tubers, eight ounces of meat or fish and four ounces of rice or flour. In reality, food allowances ranged from two or three miserly meals, a breakfast of tassajo—dried, salted beef—and a dinner of plantains and Indian corn, or a potage of sweet potatoes. In Cuba as else-where the provision grounds were the slaves' salvation. "They were little strips of dirt for gardening ... real close to the barracoons, almost right in back," former slave Montejo recalled. "They grew everything there; sweet potato, squash, okra, corn, peas, horse beans, beans like limas, limes, yucca, and peanuts. They also raised piglets."[185] Those piglets ate potatoes and, when they were grown, slaves ate or sold them.

In Barbados, Antigua, St. Kitts and Nevis, where most of the land was planted to cane, and also in the colonies later known as British Guiana, slaves had to rely on rations and were permitted only small gardens, known as *polinks*, around their huts. Their rations were meager, starchy and, if cooked into mush for them, sometimes so coarse that it sickened them. They were also monotonous: "Massa gib me Guinea-corn too much," a slave complained:. "Guinea-corn today, Guinea-corn to-morrow—Guinea-corn eb'ry day."[186] On top of this, the salted cod that became a staple of the slave diet was rancid and substandard, "fit for no other [than slave] consumption,"[187] and the herrings had "as little nutrition as the brine in which they lie."[188] In 1788, slaves in St. Kitts reportedly received *weekly* allowances of four to nine pints of flour, corn, peas or beans, and four to eight salted fish; they got the lesser amount when cane liquor was given out as a food supplement. Skilled slaves got double rations, children a half ration.

Stealing food, with accessible, comforting sugarcane heading the list, was a fact of life on most plantations. In Antigua as in Brazil and other sugar colonies, "slaves ate whatever they could lay their hands on. Besides their issue of rations, slaves cajoled, begged, and stole additional food."[189] Incredibly, some masters doled out quantities of cheap rum instead of food, with predictable consequences: some slaves sold theirs and bought food, but many drank it, went hungry, then stole to survive.

Slaves without provision grounds were the hungriest and the worst off. Their masters usually planted almost all their land to profitable cane and relied on importing food, usually from the American colonies. During times of war and other economic dislocations, these slaves actually starved; the outbreak of the American Revolution cut off supplies of imported food, and in Antigua as in other sugar islands, hundreds of slaves died of hunger.

Provision grounds provided better and more foodstuffs, but at a high cost to overburdened slaves; instead of rest or relaxation, they had to devote their scarce free time to tending their crops. When, as in Martinique, the provision grounds were on marginal land and in lieu of rations, slaves struggled for sustenance. The usual practice was to give them time off to garden, often half-Saturdays and Sundays. On many estates, they rushed off during their lunch break to garden rather than relax and eat. If they had chickens and small livestock, they tended them as well.

Despite its obvious hardships, slaves preferred this system, and so did their masters. In one respect it "directly benefited the master, because the expense of maintaining the slave population placed a heavy economic burden on him," economic historian Dale Tomlich writes. "The burden of responsibility was shifted directly to the slaves themselves ... just to secure the basic necessities of life."[190] Even when hurricanes, poor soil, marauding animals or slaves, drought, negligence or myriad conditions caused crop failures, planters seldom offered to supplement their slaves' rations, even if they were starving.

Provision grounds represented much more than food. More than any other facet of slavery, they gave slaves hope, especially women who gardened assiduously. If a slave worked hard and the soil cooperated, she could cook tasty meals that were a mélange of improvised, Creole and remembered African dishes. She could sell some of her yams, plantains, coconuts, pumpkins, bananas, ackee, okra, spinach, fruits and other foodstuffs, or the chickens she raised in their midst, and spend her profit as she wished, on better-quality fish or meat, eggs, goods for her children, tobacco, a piece of cloth, cooking pots and utensils, or a trinket or jewelry.

Often her best and surest customer was her master if he, like so many planters, planted most of his land in sugar rather than food crops. One disadvantage was that he or his wife used their power to underweigh and underpay. Another was that in times of crop failure, neither master nor slave had any food unless it was imported. By the nineteenth century and the advent of the Amelioration Laws, slaves owned cows as well and also became the main source of livestock and poultry.

Over time, slaves expanded their customer base. Instead of just their masters and neighboring whites, they "higgled" or hawked their provisions at nearby town markets. That market was the slave's lifeline to hope, "the day of mirth and recreation, when the whole negro population seems to be in motion."[191] From daybreak until mid-afternoon, when the rum shops opened, the marketplace swarmed with black, brown and white higglers and their customers. Then slaves departed, their profits or purchases tucked securely away, though some gave in to temptation and drowned their sorrows in rum or gambled away their profits. But however slaves disposed of their earnings, market day altered their perceptions of life and inspired dreams of freedom: some saved enough money to purchase and manumit themselves.

Provision grounds spawned traditions as well as vegetables and fruit. On many plantations in English colonies, slaves assumed a proprietary right to their portion and willed it to their heirs, a practice many masters honored. Jamaican sugar planter William Beckford noted that "negroes absolutely respect primogeniture and the eldest son takes possession of his father's property immediately after his decease."[192] Slave masters also punished their slaves through these provision grounds, taking away their free time so they could not garden, or denying them "tickets," the day passes granting them the right to travel off the plantation to specified market locations.

Slave higglers did not always confine their wares to produce. Ironically, one of the most profitable goods was sugar, difficult for the townsfolk of any color to obtain. Enterprising slave higglers quickly met that demand, stealing from their plantation's storerooms the sugar they

The marketplace, St. John's, Antigua, shows black people buying and selling provisions. A dignified older woman adorned with bean neck-laces carries what look like a dried fish and a pipe. This image suggests the bustle and excitement of slave-era markets.

devoted their lives to but did not own, and carting it to town in calabashes. They also stole and sold anything else their eager customers demanded, and sold items they scorned to use, such as the despised coarse cloth doled out to them once or twice yearly to make clothes.

SLAVE FAMILY LIFE

The world the sugar slaves created had all of the tensions of any immigrant society. In the earliest days, all slaves were Africans, and tribal differences had separated them. Creoles gradually gained the ascendant until the slave trade ended, when Africans counted for about 40 percent of the slave contingent. From then on, as Africans died off, most slaves were Creoles. There were the usual conflicts. Some Creoles mocked the newcomers as "salt-water Negroes" and Guineybirds" and jeered at their tribal scars, filed teeth and halting efforts to communicate in a new language. At the same time, they respected and envied the Africans' knowledge and their refusal to accept their bondage or acknowledge the social structure of the estate. Although they wore the uniform of slavery, the Africans were aliens in their hostile new world.

In the quarters there were other tensions. There was a hierarchy, with field slaves at the bottom and skilled slaves, who had superior lodgings, finer and more extensive wardrobes and access to more of the niceties of life, higher up. They even cost more in the market, roughly double the price of a field slave. Privileged slaves expected a certain deference from their fellows. For instance, "the daughter of a skilled slave would never entertain the idea of marrying or forming a couple with a field slave," writes Haiti scholar Carolyn Fick.[193]

Domestics who visited the quarters added another dimension to the social brew; they were the best fed and dressed, the best spoken, the most assimilated but also the most chained to the Great House and its ways. Most were also the lightest-skinned, and their color betrayed their special connection with whites as well as to the black women who had given birth to them.

Slaves navigated the tensions in their society, and analyses of their housing arrangements reveal how they formed families and partnerships.

The most common social units were simple nuclear families, and large ones lived alone. Smaller families shared their lodgings with single men and women or with seasoning Africans assigned to them. Older single women, often widows, lived with younger single men they likely cooked and cleaned for. Some rooms housed the solitaries, usually African men and older women.[194]

Extended families were also in evidence, though given the tiny size of slave houses, not under the same roof. Sons often lived near their mothers while daughters moved away, usually to be close to their mothers-in-law. Extended slave families could include adopted rather than blood sisters, brothers, aunts and uncles. Shipmates from the Middle Passage always treated each other as kin.

The complexities of slavery prompted some slaves to enter polygamous unions. Most commonly, a man sold away to another plantation would pair up with a woman on his new plantation. However, if he was granted permission for a "ticket" or temporary pass to visit his former home, he resumed marital relations with the wife he had had there.

As circumstances changed, so did the nature of marriage. When, in the early years of sugar production, a majority of slaves were male—the ratio was often two males to one female—many men could not find a mate, while women were in great demand. Visitors to Cuba often described estates with few or even no female field hands, "where the wretched laborers have not the privileges of beasts, but are only human machines, worked and watched. There, not even the mutilated semblance of family ties and domestic surroundings alleviates the sore strain upon life and limb."[195]

Even when creolization corrected the gender imbalance, slaves could not marry whomever and whenever they wished. Their masters interfered in and regulated this most intimate dimension of their lives as they did all others. Planters in all the sugar colonies deplored their slaves' sexual mores but could not decide if marriage was the solution. There was much at stake. Recognizing slave marriage, especially with Christian rites, could easily give slaves unwelcome notions, for instance that all souls are equal before God. Slave marriage also raised thorny property issues. Intermarriage between slaves of different owners, or between a slave and a free black or person of color, could be complicated. Spouses would want to visit each other. They would demand not to be sold away from each other, and the Catholic and other Christian churches that condemned separating a wife from her husband, and parents from their children, would support them. Unmarried slaves, on the other hand, could be sold or rented out without any problems.

Given these concerns, the planters' anti-marriage contingent was as vociferous as its pro-marriage opponents. Leeward Island legislators attempted a compromise. They opposed religious marriage rites for slaves but urged masters to encourage the monogamous relations that would produce badly needed slave children.

Slaves had their own perspective on marriage, and their own customs. Even if they had Catholic masters who encouraged them to unite in Christian nuptials, few did so. They had no financial stake to consider, being property themselves. And given their custom of ending unhappy relationships to live alone or try again, they were sceptical about pledging to remain united until death. They also rejected arguments about the morality of marriage. "Sensible negroes have been known to object to it as a solemn contract; saying that they understood that many of the white people, both here and in England, were as bad afterwards as before marriage," one contemporary noted.[196] As well, slaves feared committing themselves to unions so easily shattered if one spouse were sold away.

At the same time, slaves fell in love and formed unions that ranged from lifelong to brief interludes cut short by a new passion or the sale of one spouse to a distant owner. Many masters required their slaves to seek approval for these relationships. They were particularly loath to allow domestics to marry, not wanting to lose their services such as nighttime babysitting. Thistlewood permitted Cudjoe, a slave from a neighboring estate, "to have" Abba, whom he often sought out for sex, but afterward continued his sexual relations with her. Pierre Dessalles, on the other hand, as a devout Catholic who believed that marriage fostered slave morality, stability and fertility, was inclined to marry off those slaves who asked his permission. "I am giving them advantages that will turn to our benefit and re-establish morality. To my mind, this is the only way to ward off evil and bad intentions," he explained.[197]

Dessalles also described the anguish of the wife of one of his slaves whom he had ordered to return to her owner's estate. She "cried and entreated me so much that I decided to buy her," enabling the couple to remain together.[198]

Slave holders arranged many slave unions, not without resistance. A Guadeloupean "bride" whose master paired her with a slave groom informed the priest at the beginning of the service that she was *not* willing to marry him. "I do not wish to marry this or any other man," she said. "I am miserable enough as it is without having to bring children into this world to be more miserable."[199]

Like many slave masters, Thistlewood and Dessalles recorded slave unions and afterward identified slaves with references to their partners. They also noted the dissolution of marriages, frequently after blatant infidelities. In the days of gender imbalance, women were often the offenders. As a cuckolded Brazilian slave demanded of his master, "If there are so many men and so few women upon the estate, how is it to be expected that the latter are to be faithful? Why does Master have so many men and so few women?"[200] Thistlewood mentioned many such instances. "Cobenna catched London and Rosanna [Cobenna's wife] at work upon London's bed. London got a good thumping as I hear." Thistlewood often intervened, flogging the unfaithful partner, for instance "Maria for cuckolding Solon ... and stirring up quarrels, &c.," and both Lincoln and Violet for cuckolding Violet's partner, Job.[201]

In all societies, bearing and raising children is integral to the concept of marriage and family. Sugar slaves, however, had a universally low rate of reproduction. Until the slave trade ended and childbirth became the only source of new slaves, few sugar planters cared about this, and many actively discouraged their female field workers from becoming pregnant. Even in the early days of sugar, planters had severely penalized white indentured field hands who had babies on the grounds that motherhood "disabled" them and their "bastards" cost money to feed.[202] When Africans replaced whites in the cane fields, this attitude persisted. Mid-eighteenth-century Bahian planters, for instance, calculated that, in three and a half years, a slave's labor would equal his purchase price and annual upkeep, making it cheaper to buy Africans than to raise slave babies, whom a Jesuit slave owner noted cost "a great deal to raise,"[203] or even to keep adult slaves alive.

During the eighteenth century, with the abolition of the slave trade looming and the slave population decreasing by about 3 to 4 percent each year, planters had to adopt new strategies. They had attributed their slaves' low birthrate to promiscuity, abortion and infanticide. Now, in a tacit admission that lethal working and living conditions had contributed, they began to encourage childbirth by providing slightly better living conditions and medical care and by giving pregnant and nursing mothers preferential treatment.

Death at any age was the sugar slave's constant companion, the consequence of the same hardships that kept their fertility so low. Sugar culture killed males off in even greater numbers than females, as children and again after the age of forty. As a general rule, the larger the sugar estate, the higher the mortality rate among its slaves, particularly males. Compared to other forms of slavery, sugar slavery was the deadliest. Dessalles' complaint about the "crescendo of illness on the plantation," which in eight months killed ten of his slaves, was a familiar one.[204]

The relentless overwork and poor nutrition slaves endured in the living hell of the cane fields caused delayed menarche, weight loss, amenorrhea and their notably low fertility rates. In addition, a high proportion of babies did not survive childhood. As late as 1813, for example, fewer than half of Trinidadian slave children survived their fifth birthday. In French colonies, planters often punished both midwives and mothers when a newborn died, accusing them of murdering the child.

Plantation journals are filled with notes about deceased children. In January 1771, Johnie, the six-year-old son of Abba, the most prolific slave on her plantation, died of lockjaw. "His mother almost out of her senses," overseer Thistlewood wrote, "quite frantic & will hear no reason." The following October, Abba delivered a daughter, perhaps Thistlewood's progeny, who died a week later. In 1774, her son Neptune died after complaining "of pains all over him. &c., a most violent cold, got I suppose by the water running thro' her house & making the floor wet." In June 1775, Abba delivered a son who died a week later. Another slave, Nanny, lost child after child including five-year-old Phibbah, worm-ridden and afflicted with yaws.[205]

The same diseases that killed their parents killed these children. A study of Jamaican parishes from 1807 to 1834 identifies lockjaw, caused by tetanus, as the leading culprit, especially for infants, followed by a plethora of conditions—general debility, yaws, whooping cough, fever, worms, malaria, yellow fever, convulsions, dropsy or edema of the lungs, dysentery, apoplexy, convulsions, bloat, pleurisy, tuberculosis, hookworm, cocoa-bay or leprosy, and the vaguely defined complaints of "visitation of God" or "bowel complaint." Grown slaves died as well from venereal disease, the complications of pregnancy and post-natal infections. During the harvest, slaves succumbed to exhaustion. In Brazil in 1816, for example, the slave Francisco was so tired he stumbled into a vat of boiling sugar syrup and died.[206]

Planters were responsible for their chronically unwell slave population's medical care and dispensed it in slave "hospitals" where slave nurses, midwives and doctors cared for the patients. Some planters' wives also visited the quarters and the hospital to assist ailing slaves. In Cuba, the barracoon hospital was a bare room with thick planks for beds. "On these lay the patients, in their usual working garments, with a blanket over them if they liked," American visitor Julia Woodruff reported. "The blank, stolid, utterly unilluminated faces on those beds were pitiful to behold!"[207] The quality of care was usually inferior. Exceptions were found on estates where planters took pains to provide better facilities and directed slave women to clean the premises, wash and feed the patients and ban unauthorized visitors.

Some planters hired white "doctors" to care for their slaves, but these were very often unqualified quacks whose incompetence cost many lives.[208] Those with medical training subjected patients to treatments that included bleeding with leeches and purging. Thistlewood, who suffered chronic gonorrhea, detailed his own forty-four-day treatment, which combined blood-letting, twenty-four mercurial purging pills, salts, cooling powders, balsam drops and a mixture of herbs and other less benign ingredients. It also required him to bathe his penis twice daily in new milk, and catheterize it—agonizingly—with thin, specially designed candles. In accordance with contemporary medical practices, slaves were often bled, purged with mercury, dosed with medication, steamed and massaged. Nonetheless, they died in such numbers that planters accused them of complicity with the Grim Reaper.

SLAVE LIFE IN THE SHADOW OF THE GREAT HOUSE

Except when they slept, the slaves' cramped, dank and dark lodgings drove them outside. There they gossiped, quarreled, flirted, dressed their hair, preserved folktales and invented new ones. There they stretched out, lounged and fanned themselves cool. There they congregated to play games remembered from Africa: *kai* in Haiti, *warri* in Jamaica. There they worshipped their ancient gods, and mocked and lamented their cheerless lives in song and dance. They chatted about their days in the broiling and deceptively tranquil cane fields, where thousands of rats feasted off uncut cane, and in the boiling house with its cannibalizing machinery and intolerable heat. They shared stories about the mighty feats of well-fed rats. They discussed their masters, overseers, drivers and each other, and plotted against those who enslaved and exploited them. They shared news and gossip passed on by domestics who transmitted everything that happened in the Great House back to the quarters.

One of the curiosities of the quarters was the stream of whites who came and went, men prowling for sex, women offering health care, visitors of both sexes seated ringside at the slave dances and celebrations they witnessed as entertainments and later laughed about, although among foreign observers, the white fascination with slave life was not always derisory. France's Baron Maximilien de Wimpffen wrote, "One has to hear with what enthusiasm, with what precision of ideas and accuracy of judgment, these creatures, gloomy and taciturn during the day, now squatting before their fire, tell stories, talk, gesticulate, reason, express opinions, approve or condemn both the master and all those around them."[209] Sitting around the campfire as they roasted corn on the cob, vegetables and sometimes meat, and made corn or cassava bread wrapped in leaves in the ashes, slaves shucked off their personae as sullen drudges and revealed themselves as thinking, feeling—and judging—beings.

The slaves also had holidays, including Christmas—in some colonies a three-day legal holiday—Easter and Whitsuntide, and to celebrate such events as their master's birthday and his children's weddings, when masters customarily gave their slaves gifts of money, clothing, special food or rum. On one such occasion Pierre Dessalles offered his field hands a slaughtered cow and, after his twenty-two white guests had eaten, a "copious and good" meal.[210] Then, in his courtyard lit with torches, the slaves danced till midnight. Thomas Thistlewood, a man of more modest means, doled out rum and large slabs of meat for his slaves' Christmas celebration. Over the years the slaves redefined these customary gifts as their right. Whenever a planter failed to provide them, his slaves would grow surly and rebellious.

Slaves of all ages, decked out in their finest garb, were welcome at slave parties and dances that whites referred to derisively as "Balls, Assemblies, and Coffee Treats."[211] White onlookers were astounded at how these ragged drudges metamorphosed into high-spirited, flirtatious beings, their garb spotless and dramatic. The women especially went to great lengths and expense to beautify themselves. Their limited resources and imagination spawned ingenious fashions. Some wore Great House cast-offs; others paid slave seamstresses to design glamorous dresses from fabric, often imported, purchased with money earned from higgling. "One finds the extent of the spending done by a female slave woman hard to fathom," remarked Creole observer Moreau de Saint-Méry.[212] It should be easy to fathom. When a bathed and perfumed sugar field worker donned a stunning dress, she shed her degradation along with her filthy, sweat-corroded rags, and reaffirmed her humanity and her femininity. When she accessorized with earrings, headscarves tied in innovative or remembered African styles, or when she improvised with Great House bonnets, ribbons or beads, she was expressing her individuality and rejecting the uniform of slavery.

Slave dances were joyous and informal, with mostly barefoot revelers spinning and whirling to the beat of the drums and of rattles or percussion instruments carved from hollowed-out cedar trunks or sticks. In Cuba, some dances were so complicated that men alone performed them; the *mani* was too violent for women, who watched and cheered

Agostino Brunias spent decades in the West Indies and his much-copied paintings convey false images of carefree slave life. Here slaves dance while a white man importunes a finely dressed mulatto woman. A drummer and tambourine player provide the music.

as men whipped each other to win the right to dance, a grotesque perversion or perhaps an exorcism of the brutality of the cane fields and sugar mills.

Holidays and entertainments helped slaves make sense of their lives. In male-heavy Cuba, former slave Montejo recalled, slaves gravitated to wood and palm frond "taverns" where army veterans extended them credit to buy overpriced rum and rice, beef jerky and beans, biscuits and cookies. They also played games; "the cracker" and "the jug game" were two of the most popular. The cracker was a contest of genital power in which slaves attacked salt crackers with their penises; to smash the crackers, which were laid on a board, was to win the game. The jug game measured penis length; each contestant inserted his penis into a jug with soft ash at the bottom, then withdrew it. The winner could prove his penis had touched the bottom by the ash that coated it. In a society that emasculated male slaves socially, legally and psychologically, and killed most of them off at a relatively young age, the men fought back by asserting their masculinity in whatever ways they could.

Slaves sustained hope through dreams and schemes of escaping slavery. Some succeeded, through self-purchase, manumission, resistance, running away, marronage or suicide (these are the subject of chapter 6). Most also found spiritual sustenance and meaning in religion, remembered African beliefs and rituals often enriched with Catholic saints and ceremonies. These religions were animistic and incorporated the natural and the supernatural worlds, the rocks and the trees with the spirits. Vodun (in French colonies), obeah (in English), Santería (in Spanish) and Candomblé (in Brazil) were non-hierarchical healing religions whose shamans or priests and priestesses summoned the gods through prayer and incantation, gifts and sacrifices.

Unlike the slave dances whites found so amusing, these shamanistic ceremonies troubled and terrified them. This was because the special men and women who could invoke the supernatural had other skills: they could inspire their fellow slaves to rise up against their oppressors. Whites were so terrified of their power that they sought through colonial laws to suppress them. The 1792 Consolidated Slave Act of Jamaica is a case in point: "Any slave who shall pretend to any supernatural power, in order to promote the purposes of rebellion, shall, upon conviction thereof suffer death, transportation, or such other punishment." The overarching reality of the sugar world was that white prosperity, security and even survival depended on the relentless domination of the bodies, if not the souls, of the denizens of the slave quarters.

Chapter 4

The World
the Whites Made

The Great House

The slave quarters stood at a strategic and symbolic distance from the
Great House where the planter, his family and his associates were building a different world. The Great House was as much a metaphor for the
values, meanings and dichotomies of white Creole society as it was a
lodging for its privileged residents. It was also a structural challenge to
the hurricanes and earthquakes that haunted the sugar colonies, and, an
eighteenth-century writer warned, "We must not look for Beauties of
Architecture here."[213]

A typical Great House was spacious, raised off the ground and
usually a single story because anything higher seldom withstood "the
Shock of an Earthquake, or the Fury of a Storm," and solidly built of
stone or brick.[214] Wide stone steps led up into the long, airy gallery used
as the main sitting room, and bedrooms ran off to each side. Great
Houses were designed to foil the debilitating heat. Venetian blinds or
louvered windows blocked the glaring sun while admitting welcome
breezes. The only windows that closed completely were in the back
rooms that were more exposed to the pounding rain. Great Houses were
floored with planks of mahogany or other hardwood, uncarpeted and
highly polished. The furniture was fashioned from hardwood. A few
storerooms underneath the house completed the structure.

Europeans expecting manor houses were shocked and disappointed. Lady Maria Nugent, the governor of Jamaica's patrician American wife, found them downright hideous. Absentee Jamaican planter Matthew Lewis considered his inherited Cornwall House "frightful to look at," though in the stifling Jamaican heat he appreciated its cool interior.[215]

Great Houses were also designed for security against the ever-troubling black presence, far enough removed from the quarters and high enough to protect against a sudden slave attack. In Cuba, planter Edwin Atkins built impenetrable walls several feet thick. In St. Croix, the Whim Plantation Great House had three-foot-thick walls made of stone, coral and molasses. In other Great Houses, basement shelters were common.

That distance, those walls and those basements underscored the essential dichotomy at the core of Great House life. Whites relied on blacks to produce their sugar, counted them as their biggest capital investment, enslaved and mistreated them, vilified their race, sexually assaulted and fell in love with them, and lived dependent on and surrounded by them. No Great House was without an overstaffed contingent of domestics, "negroes, men, women, and children, running and lying about, in all parts of it, perfectly in the Creole style,"[216] Lady Nugent commented. Most also kept a cute slave child or two as pampered pets who, in uncute adolescence, were banished to the quarters and the cane fields. Like their quarters, Great Houses were permeated by fear and tensions.

Slavery was the great issue. Resident planters and their families had to reconcile slavery, specifically their brutal version, with Christian morality. They presented themselves as the sugar world's landed gentry, and yearned—or so they claimed—for genteel refinement. Yet they indulged in conspicuous consumption so extreme that (often envious) Europeans condemned them for their crassness and their obscene, slave-ridden riches, and coined the contemptuous expression "rich as a Creole." Maria Nugent echoed countless others when she described white Creoles as "indolent and inactive, regardless of every thing but eating, drinking, and indulging themselves."[217]

This Great House gluttony contrasted grotesquely with the hunger in the quarters. As the sugar slaves subsisted on their meager "provisions," their white owners gobbled gargantuan meals: breakfasts of oily fish, cold veal, tarts, cakes, fruit, wine, tea and coffee, and wine-sodden dinners with upwards of twenty dishes, including sugar-rich desserts and fruit preserves. The Creole men "ate like cormorants and drink like porpoises," Nugent wrote.[218]

Janet Schaw, a well-connected and wealthy Scot who in 1774 paid a lengthy visit to Antigua and surrounding islands, initially shared Nugent's reactions to Creole extravagance, but within a short time succumbed to its seductions. "Why should we blame these people for their luxury?" Schaw wondered.[219]

Schaw framed her question rhetorically because she had already answered it: we should not blame these people. Her defense of their sumptuous lifestyle reflected the seductive powers of the sugar world, seemingly irresistible to those it embraced. Schaw's first reports about her sugar-island sojourn expressed her incredulity at what she was seeing. Before long, however, she began to rationalize her experiences until she came to see excess as generosity, ostentation as the grand manner and the kindnesses extended to her as evidence of admirable hospitality. She was one of legions who scoffed at the immoderation and the sheer vulgarity yet described Creole society as fundamentally gracious and welcoming.

The planters were the first to point to these values as part of their social psyche. They also invoked racialist arguments to justify the chasm between their opulent lives and their slaves' destitution. Blacks, they explained, were childlike inferiors with savage and lascivious inclinations who benefited from the civilizing morality of Christianity; their relation to planters was of children to benevolent masters. Planters also argued that slave life compared favorably with that of Europe's working classes, which they complimented as more diligent, efficient and honest. They pointed to their heavy managerial and marketing responsibilities and the enormous outlays of capital they made to underwrite the infrastructure of the sugarcane plantation; these were problems slaves didn't have to worry about, and were reason enough that planters deserved the grand life.

Although Schaw disagreed with Nugent's view that Creole life failed standards of taste, the women's judgment about the morality of slavery coincided: nothing Schaw saw in Antigua and nothing Nugent saw in Jamaica persuaded either that slavery was wrong. To the contrary: they both reiterated the planters' own justifications for the institution that was at the core of the sugar economy.

WATCHING EYES, LISTENING EARS

Tens of thousands of other witnesses interpreted white Creole culture rather differently. These were the domestics who were as integral to that way of life as the slaves in the cane fields. Unlike visitors, domestics were expert witnesses with intimate knowledge of their subjects. Domestics were such ubiquitous and familiar presences that whites scarcely noticed them and seldom bothered to hold their tongues in their hearing.

This lack of restraint astonished visitors. "They introduce their favourite topic, the conduct of negroes, and their particular management of them," a missionary noted disapprovingly. "Every thing relative to them is freely discussed: the colonial laws, the observations made upon them at home, and in the public prints in this island, together with those instances that have occurred of trials before Magistrates, etc., respecting any violation of the laws. Don't we know that servants have got *eyes* and *ears* as well as ourselves?"[220]

This observation was entirely correct. Domestics stored away this table talk and other conversations overheard during their long days of service. Later, they mulled it all over with other slaves, embellishing and interpreting it and shaping their version of the sugar planters' world.

They had an impressive range of information to process. They heard that sugar production mattered more than anything else. They heard a botanist's much-repeated witticism that "were beef stakes [*sic*], and apple pies ready dressed, to grow on the trees, they wd. be cut down to make room for cane plants."[221] They heard that slavery was justified because blacks were difficult, dishonest, treacherous and lazy, good-for-nothings, childlike beings who reveled in "short-lived and baby-like"

*Typical of planters who lived in the constant presence of black slaves,
this Brazilian woman sews and her daughter reads while three adult slaves work
and two infants play at their feet. A clothed monkey seems to oversee a baby's basket.*

pleasures."[222] They heard that some of them were "ungrateful scoundrels" and "so obstinate and so wilful in their general character." They even heard that "unless a negro has an interest in telling the truth, he always lies—in order to keep his tongue in practice."[223]

They heard that field slaves roused themselves to work only on their provision grounds, and earned substantial (not to say fabulous) sums selling the produce and—the horror!—their *master's* sugar, then, being "so thoughtless and improvident," wasted their earnings on trinkets and rum and, "at the end of the week … come to beg a supply from the master's storehouse."[224] They heard that "the poor blackies" were poor housekeepers.

They heard whites debate the relative merit of punishments, which were essential to manage blacks. They heard that "when one comes to be better acquainted with the nature of the Negroes, the horrour [*sic*] of it must wear off. It is the suffering of the human mind that constitutes the greatest misery of punishment, but with them it is merely corporeal.... [Their] sufferings are not attended with shame or pain beyond the present moment."[225] They heard that "slow punishments make a greater impression than quick or violent ones. Twenty-five lashes of the whip administered in a quarter of an hour, interrupted at intervals ... are far more likely to make an impression than fifty lashes administered in five minutes and less a danger to their health."[226]

Domestics heard their whites confide to other whites that the plantation was teetering on bankruptcy and that other mortgaged

Whippings were often public spectacles as warnings to other slaves. Black drivers had to whip their victims under white supervision.

estates were being sold to the highest bidder. They heard about a fellow planter's ploy to outwit his creditors by selling off his slaves "so they will not be included in the assessment of his property,"[227] and that the price of sugar had plunged catastrophically. The domestics of one of Martinique's wealthiest planters heard him complain that "we are more poverty-stricken than ever, and our sugar is without value."[228] They heard that the overseer was sulking because his wages were (again) in arrears, and that their master would try to squeeze more revenue from his estate by driving his slaves to produce yet more (worthless) sugar. As they served roast pig and duck and ham and fish and turtle and veal and chicken with all the fixings, the domestics heard that feeding slaves was an expense planters begrudged and tried to minimize.

They heard how apprehensive and angry whites were about slave uprisings and attacks, and how greatly they feared their own treacherous domestics. They heard that Minette, a fifteen-year-old domestic enslaved on a Jamaican sugar plantation, poisoned her master's nightcap of brandy and water, then, at his bedside, "witnessed his agonies without one expression of surprise or pity."[229] They heard about the respected planter who escaped death in a coffee cup only because he generously served it to his bookkeepers instead and then watched in horror as they dropped down dead.

They heard about the crudeness of supposedly superior whites: how when old Jamaican planter Tom Williams saw a slave cleaning an already clean room "he shit in it and told her there was something for her to clean,"[230] and how Mr. Woodham "got tipsy, and beat his wife the other day."[231] They heard how the young planter John Cope "took all Mrs. Cope's china, glasses, &c.... and smashed them with all his force against the floor, and broke them in pieces," because he suspected that the china was a gift from her former sweetheart.[232]

They heard about the fate of domestics who were also their master's mistresses, the mistress of the planter Irvine, whom he murdered in a jealous fit, and the mulatto mistress of overseer Francis Ruecastle, whom he beat to death. They heard that overseer Harry Weech, who worked for Thomas Thistlewood, "cut off the lips, upper lip almost close to her

Nose, off his Mulatto sweetheart, in Jealousy, because he said no Negroe should ever kiss those lips he had."[233]

They heard the more encouraging news that a popular mayor in Martinique permitted "the little mulattoes, his bastards," to run free in the house, that an army captain had willed his entire estate to his black "chère amie" and their bastard, and that Barbadian planter Jacob Hinds had left large properties to his children with three of his black slaves, couched in the cryptic words, "I would call them my children but that would not be legal as I never was married."[234] They heard that, despite the ignominy, some white women cast their lot with black men. They heard that "more than one or two *white* Ladies … had, tho' married, borne Children of Negroes."[235]

Domestics who took their social cues from whites, who emulated their expressions and mannerisms and could be as snobbish as Maria Nugent or Pierre Dessalles, heard that a wealthy planter's little pet black pig snorted throughout dinner, and that another white fellow propped his feet on the dining table so that his slave could gouge out chiggers, the parasitic mites that tormented black and white alike. They heard that Brazilian Creoles raised on sugar plantations were indifferently educated and could converse only about dogs, horses and oxen while their women, nearly illiterate, lazed about on hammocks while slave women picked lice out of their hair with their fingernails.

Domestics serving at males-only Creole dinners heard tawdry conversations about business and sexual exploits, including unpleasant details about the venereal disease that ravaged both black and white. They heard an elderly planter joke that he pleased "his mistress yet twice a night: first by putting his thigh over her, which pleases her by putting her in expectation—next, he pleases her by taking it off, when she is weary of the weight."[236] They heard Martinique planter Pierre Dessalles rail against the younger generation's heresies: that "Jesus Christ is a prodigious *man*; to kill oneself when one is unhappy is a perfectly simple and natural thing. Seducing two sisters in the same family, running away with another man's wife—all of this is considered very nice."[237]

Domestics heard incessant complaints about centipedes, bats and rats, and about the ants and cockroaches that invaded chairs, sofas, fruit baskets, books and clothes. They heard that before reading a book, Henry Koster first closed it "violently so as to crush any things that might have crept in between the leaves."[238] They heard about "the innumerable mosquitoes, that have almost eaten us up, and certainly spoilt our beauty.... [and] tormented us all night ... innumerable insects, that put out our candles, in spite of the large glass shades."[239] They heard about the merciless climate, autumn's "sickly season" and the seasons of extreme heat, buffeting winds and, in the rainy season, torrential downpours and cold dampness. They heard about the "swampy soil" and its noxious vapors, the "noisome frogs" and the "swarms of flies and gnats."[240] They heard and were reminded of their own sleepless nights devoted to killing the creatures that interrupted the sleeping whites and the nighttime torments of those confined to the quarter's cramped, airless and unprotected shanties.

Domestics were reminded constantly of how hurricanes terrified whites above all else, and how these savage acts of nature often ruined even the wealthiest. They heard that Barbadian planter William Senhourse was "sickened at the sight" of the damage done to his Grove plantation by the hurricane of 1780 that also killed six of his slaves and thousands more on the island. They heard heirs to sugar estates bemoan their futures as Barbadian Walter Pollard did when he despaired, "Lo! The fatal hurricane! It lays our properties in the dust, the hard earnings of the past, the hopes of the rising generation."[241] Any of these conversations might be interrupted by a crying white baby's urgent need for his slave nanny's breast milk; she would stand or sink into a chair and suckle her little charge. The ladies present might help to get the milk flowing, "slapping, pressing, shaking about and playing with the long black breast of the slave, with very indelicate familiarity," as a visitor recalled.[242] At this point domestics might hear white males titter about distended breasts, perhaps repeating the witticism that, as field slave women, naked to the waist, stooped down to cane hole, "You would think they had six legs!"[243]

Occasionally, if the meal was unsatisfactory, domestics heard and saw one of their own being punished, for instance a St. Domingue cook grilled to death in a fiery furnace or, in Martinique, after the cook "Philippe got drunk, and our dinner showed it," a brief whipping.[244] Afterward, the interrupted discussion would resume, perhaps laced with reflections on the efficacy of slave punishment.

ABSENTEEISM, THE ROOT OF EVIL

From any perspective, the sugar world was riddled with contradictions, but absenteeism is usually identified as the most egregious. At any one time, large numbers of the planters, perhaps 20 percent, fled to Europe, and many stayed there. In Cuba and Brazil, absentees retreated to gracious colonial cities, or to Fifth Avenue in New York, leaving their estates in the hands of attorneys and, from time to time, returning to visit.

Only the wealthiest planters with the most acreage, the greatest number of slaves and the largest capital investment could afford to leave. Absentees said they were fleeing the heat and humidity that made them feel "fricased,"[245] diseases that struck suddenly and fatally, the devastation of tropical storms and hurricanes, the embarrassment of the Creole world's reputation as a cultural wasteland, and the constant fear of attack from the blacks who outnumbered them. Above all, they hoped to save themselves from an early grave. The mortality rate for whites was "horrific," even worse than that of their slaves, and few managed to live out a normal life span.[246]

Orlando Patterson identifies absenteeism as "the basic and dominating element in Jamaican slave society ... central to the whole social order ... and so much was it the root of all the evils of the system, that we may describe the white Jamaican community as an absentee society."[247] This widespread defection from the sugar estates was just as true in the rest of the sugar world. Those who remained were rarely the most solid citizens. In Antigua, for instance, Governor Hugh Elliot described the "few white inhabitants who remain, [as] Managers, Overseers, Self-created lawyers, Self-educated Physicians, and adventurous Merchants, with little real capital and scanty credit."[248]

A Grand Jamaica Ball! Or the Creolean Hop a la Mustee as exhibited in Spanish Town (*London, 1802*) *ridicules the decadence of Creole society as Creole women dance lewdly to attract red-coated local militiamen and slaves serve drinks or watch from the wings. A biting inscription reads,* "Farewell ye girls! and still alas! As Mama bids sad Red Coats shun! / But soon will each forsaken Lass, / Most keenly rue the Dance she's run! Charmless you'll grow in person, face and eye, / Joyless in youth, old maids you'll useless die!"

Absenteeism had serious consequences. It reduced the pool of potential officeholders, adversely affecting colonial administration. Some well-connected absentees held office anyway, to the detriment of the colony. The plantations and their mostly black residents suffered the most, because employees hired to replace absent owners had little stake in the success of the enterprises other than keeping their jobs. As Henry Drax, a wealthy Barbados planter, noted, absenteeism was "very pernicious to all Proceedings there, every Person being more diligent in his Employ, when the Master is at home, although he stirs not out of his Chamber ... therefore it must be observed for a Rule, that you never be absent from the Plantation, but in Case of Necessity."[249]

Few wealthy planters followed Drax's advice. Instead, they left and made incessant demands for remittances to support them in European luxury. To comply, the attorneys, agents or overseers hired to run their plantations had to overwork the depleted soil and the exhausted slaves. On the Cuban Olanda plantation, heavily mortgaged because its absentee owner lived beyond his means, the attorney ran Olanda into the ground and worked the slaves almost to death. A visitor reported that they looked "jaded to death, listless, stupefied, haggard, and emaciated," wore rags made of burlap sacks and lived in huts "unfit for the habitation of wild beasts."[250]

With their bosses safely transatlantic, white employees adopted the Great House lifestyle. Bachelor overseers moved into vacated Great Houses or furnished their modest lodgings as lavishly as possible. Most installed slave mistresses or even harems in their houses. They aped the planter's standard of eating, consuming extraordinary amounts of meat, wine, liquor and other delicacies, and offering the same to visitors. Thistlewood, for instance, hosted one dinner that included goose in papaya sauce, roast pork and broccoli, roast duck, stewed pork, shaddock (or pomelo), watermelon, oranges, Madeira wine, porter, punch, grog and brandy.

These were the often reckless and poorly qualified employees to whom the management of large estates was entrusted. Many overseers and attorneys gave priority to their own social and monetary goals. They diverted slaves, land and resources to their personal use and supervised their own crops and livestock to the detriment of the plantation's. By milking it, they accumulated enough money to buy slaves and, eventually, a plantation of their own, often purchased from a bankrupt planter.

Absentees bled dry by their employees found few sympathizers. Had they stayed, critics charged, their fortunes would have been different. Yet resident planters were noted more for their deficiencies than for possessing good judgment, efficient management skills, agricultural expertise and general ability, including a willingness to invest in improvements ranging from manure to equipment. Instead, they were notorious for sacrificing the needs of their plantations to their own desire for an extravagant lifestyle.

Whether bankrupt or ostentatiously resplendent in European cities, absentees demoralized and undermined the sugar world's fledgling societies. They shirked their civic duties and relegated leadership to those they despised as inferiors. Instead of contributing their support, taste and patronage to the new world under construction, they voted with their feet for the cultural, social and physical superiority of European metropolises. They capitulated to the hardships of the sugar colonies rather than attempting to alleviate or cope with them. And, even more than resident planters, they encouraged the environmental and human degradation of their plantations with their relentless demands for money. By default, it fell to those few wealthy planters who stayed, and to the thousands unable to leave, to operate the plantations and related enterprises, and to shape the racial meanings at the heart of the sugar world.

Sexual Liaisons in the Great House

The byzantine structure of the new sugar world was rooted in emotional confusion about slaves whom the whites trusted, confided in and loved yet at the same time hated, mistrusted, bullied, beat and betrayed. This was especially true of domestics who surrounded them and were often their blood relatives, the offspring of white men and black women or, as the mulatto class grew, mulatto women.

These sexual liaisons were landmines in Great House relationships. If a slave mistress was a domestic and the white wife was aware of or even suspicious about the relationship, she might punish the mistress because she could not punish her husband. In a philandering, patriarchal society, a white wife had little leverage to restrain a philandering husband.

Consider Molly Cope, sugar planter John Cope's teenaged wife. Molly's slaves confided in her that John and his guests had gang raped Eve, a domestic. Molly investigated and found the bedsheets "amiss," but what could she do? She could only pretend not to notice that John drank himself into a frenzy, then raped domestic and field slaves, and also "kept" Little Mimber as a mistress.[251] Molly was herself the apparently white daughter of her father's not-quite-white mistress, Elizabeth Anderson. Like all Creoles, Molly knew, as Maria Nugent discovered early on in her Jamaican sojourn, that "white men of all descriptions, married or single, live in a state of licentiousness with their female slaves," and that "no man here is without one."[252] Barbados governor George Poyntz Ricketts even installed his mulatto mistress in the Governor's Mansion.

Sympathetic visitors described the emotional devastation provoked by the birth of mulatto or quadroon (someone with one black grandparent, often the offspring of a white and a mulatto) infants bearing their master's features and perhaps even his name. The presence of these special little ones saddened and infuriated the white wife, her family and her white children. In Martinique, the unmarried Adrien Dessalles shamed his father by acknowledging his quadroon daughter Palmire, referring to her as Mlle Dessalles and dining with her.[253] In Barbados, a guest was shocked when she realized that a handsome fourteen-year-old Barbadian mulatto who served two young women at meals could be none other than "their own brother, from the likeness he bears to their father."[254]

Her husband's affair with a slave humiliated and often hurt his wife and undermined her authority with the domestics she was supposed to manage. Sometimes it was easiest to ignore the situation, as Molly Cope apparently did. Other women remonstrated, sulked, despaired. A few managed by allying with other domestics or by focusing entirely on childrearing, a task made lighter by slave nannies. Many cuckolded

Rachel Pringle was the free daughter of a black Barbadian woman and her Scottish schoolteacher master. In this 1796 portrait by Thomas Rowlandson, Pringle, aged thirty-six, sits in front of her business, the Royal Naval Hotel cum bordello, popular with the white elite. One repeat client was the visiting Prince William Henry, later William IV.

wives took out their fury and frustration on the offending mistress. Brazilians repeated the story of a woman who gouged out a pretty mulatto slave's eyes and presented them to her husband in a jelly-dish, dripping in blood. Less innovative women had their rivals disfigured and maimed. The motive for these brutalities, "almost always, was jealousy of the husband. Sexual rancor. The rivalry of woman with woman," Brazilian historian Gilberto Freyre writes.[255]

Even where sexual jealousy was absent, the women of the sugar elite could be as sadistic as their menfolk and many made the lives of the domestics under their authority a daily torment. Thistlewood reported that "Mrs. Allwood, dr. Allwoods wife, has flogged another wench to death and buried her in the buttery, this is said to be the 3rd she has killed."[256] Edward Long described a white woman burning just-flogged slaves with scalding sealing wax, and another who forced slave women to embroider with bloodied thumbscrews tightly screwed onto their left thumbs. In the world of white sugar planters, there was scant evidence of sisterhood overcoming the racism at the heart of society.

The effects of sexual aggression extended to black men, who were infuriated by the assaults on their women. Sometimes, despite their legal and social impotence, they acted aggressively. Enraged because Harry McCormick, Thistlewood's white distiller, relentlessly pursued slave women, male slaves retaliated by cutting down a tree so that it fell onto him and crushed him to death. Matthew Lewis was so conscious of the violence that sexual abuse could engender that he threatened to dismiss any white employee who made advances to any slave "woman known publicly to be living as the wife of one of my negroes."[257]

But when the white man was a powerful plantation owner or a slave woman welcomed his advances, her black partner had little recourse. Many women chose the benefits of an intimate relationship with a white master. To prove their love and loyalty, and to retain his, they were "exceedingly faithful and useful in overlooking the others in their master's absence."[258] They had much to gain, including relaxed working conditions and gifts of clothing, jewelry, perfume, rum or money. If any children resulted from the union, their white father might offer them vocational training or even manumission. The mistress, too, might be manumitted.

The clever and ambitious mistress of a single man could become his housekeeper, a prestigious and responsible position. But she had to make sacrifices, notably getting married. Lewis described this from the white male perspective: "the *brown* females ... seldom marry men of their own colour, but lay themselves out to captivate some white person, who takes them as mistresses, under the appellation of housekeepers."[259]

"Nutmegging," as these relationships were called, and the growing number of mixed-race children challenged the ideological foundations of sugar slavery. Nothing could entirely disguise the love and the bonds that transcended racial boundaries and undermined racial justifications for slavery.

Another difficult dimension to the situation was that in adulthood, the lighter-skinned children formed a separate caste; sometimes it was a bridge between white and black but more often it was a chasm. In that race-obsessed society, there was too much at stake. "No freed or unfreed Mulatto ever wished to relapse into the Negro," Jamaican planter Edward Long observed.[260]

To define and control the new "race" they had created, whites devised bizarre and complex classifications. The offspring of a black and a white was a mulatto. The offspring of a mulatto and a black was a sambo; the offspring of a sambo and a black was a black. The offspring of a mulatto and a white was a quadroon; the offspring of a quadroon and a white was a mustee; the offspring of a mustee and a white was a musteephino; the offspring of a musteephino and a white was a quintroon; and the offspring of a quintroon and a white was an octoroon. Most quintroons and octoroons successfully passed for white and therefore *were* white. Brazilian, French and Spanish sugar colonies had racial distinctions with as many as 128 permutations of mixes between native and white, native and black, and mestizos (people of mixed European and native ancestry) and mulattoes. In Brazil, for example, a black-native was a *cabra*. A mulatto with light skin was a *pardo*.

Increasingly, this caste structure determined an individual's place in society. Given the vagaries of genetics, only proof of genealogy could really distinguish a very dark mulatto from a very light sambo. Because society recognized these refinements, the caste system solidified into a

social and personnel tool. Matthew Lewis's black slave Cubina was
shocked by the suggestion that he might marry Mary Wiggins, a very
pretty slave woman. "Oh, massa, me black, Mary Wiggins sambo; that
not allowed," Cubina exclaimed. "The separation of castes in India
[cannot] be more rigidly observed, than that of complexional shades
among the Creoles," Lewis wrote.[261] Similarly, mulattoes and lighter-
skinned slaves were assumed to be unfit for the cane fields and were
assigned to less onerous work, often in the Great House. The darker-
skinned were consigned to backbreaking work in the cane fields or the
sugar mills.

This reverence for whiteness crammed overflowing Great Houses
with domestics and kept likely workers out of the fields. It greatly
increased the likelihood that the lighter-skinned would be manumitted
and that blacks would not be. Most freed blacks had to buy themselves
or had to wait until they were old, like the nannies of Pierre Dessalles
and his children. "The social order of the whole community hung upon
the distinctions established between its constituent races," writes
Leeward Island historian Elsa Goveia. "This ... has been extremely
influential and persistent in the historical development of the West
Indies"[262]

After the abolition of the slave trade in 1807, the sugar slaves' chronically low fertility and infant-survival rates meant that, without African
reinforcements, the cane-field workforce shrank. At the same time, the
manumission of lighter-skinned slaves continued, with almost two-
thirds being women under forty-five. This trend further skewed the
already complicated social order and injected further racialism into the
society. Many observers commented that free women of color, "being
brought up from their infancy among the whites, ... acquire all the
habits and vices of the Europeans, they look down with contempt upon
their ignorant and uncivilised brethren."[263]

Despite the racially tinged tensions in Creole households, some white
women raised on secluded plantations in the midst of large contingents
of domestics acquired "the habits and vices" of their slaves. Maria
Nugent was vitriolic in describing how "many of the ladies, who have
not been educated in England, speak a sort of broken English, with an

indolent drawling out of their words, that is very tiresome if not disgusting." One Creole woman, referring to the cool air, told Nugent, "Yes, ma-am, *him rail-ly too fra-ish*."[264] When attended by slave midwives as they gave birth, Creoles incorporated African fetishes into the procedure. They surreptitiously turned to slave remedies for illness and affairs of the heart. Creole women wrapped their heads in African-style scarves and, scarcely realizing what they were doing, imitated their domestics' carriage and mannerisms.

These cultural borrowings did not soften many white hearts. The assertion of racial superiority began in childhood. An observer deplored "the inbred arrogance of a white child brought up among black children.... At even two years of age the black child cowers and shrinks before the white child, who at all times slaps and beats it at pleasure and takes away its toys without the smallest manifestation of opposition on the part of the piccaninni."[265] Braz Cubas recalled how, as a child in Brazil, he bashed a slave girl's head for refusing him a piece of coconut candy. He used to make the slave Prudencio play horsey, mounting and riding him, whipping him hard again and again. If Prudencio moaned, Braz Cubas would shout, "Shut your mouth, beast!"[266] Nugent, a young mother, was struck by how spoiled white Jamaican Creole children were, "screaming the whole day ... allowed to eat every thing improper, to the injury of their health, and are made truly unamiable, by being most absurdly indulged."[267]

In adulthood, they bullied their domestics, spoke to them imperiously and criticized them for laziness. The irony of this was not lost on European visitors who documented their Rabelaisian appetites, sexual profligacy and cruel treatment of slaves. The continual interplay of the forces of race, slavery and gender stamped the face of the Creole sugar world's white society with their indelible marks.

Repressing slaves was also a collective endeavor, and sugar society was heavily militarized. Colonial militias were organized and controlled by white planters. The militia's primary function was to police slaves and subdue slave rebellions. Eventually, as part of the white society's divide-and-rule strategy, trusted blacks were enlisted as well. Throughout the sugar colonies, the militia system formed what Barbados historian

Hilary Beckles describes as "the most developed military and hegemonic structure for the control of slaves in the New World."[268]

Racial Meanings and Sexual Desire in the Sugar World

How did people negotiate the intricacies of their society's rules? How, in the face of myriad restrictions, regulations and Slave Codes, did they manage their daily lives and relate to each other? The following stories offer some answers.

We have already met Jamaican overseer Thomas Thistlewood, the expatriate Englishman who managed John Cope's sugar plantation, bought, seasoned and punished slaves, had sex with them and documented their existences as he did those of his white companions, peers, employers and underlings. Despite Thistlewood's gonorrhea-ridden, nymphomaniacal sex life, which he detailed in Latin abbreviations, he shared thirty-three years of his life with Phibbah, a black Creole slave he loved and treated as his wife.

It was not love at first sight. Months after arriving at the Egypt sugar estate, Thistlewood flogged Phibbah severely for hiding a slave who had plotted to murder him. Eighteen months later, he had sex with her. Soon after, he made her his mistress.

Back then, in 1754, Phibbah was well into her twenties, the Copes' head housekeeper and cookhouse manager, and the devoted mother of a daughter, Coobah. She was clever, articulate and ambitious, and understood the complexities of sugar plantations. She maintained cordial relations with white acquaintances and slept only with white men, including the overseer who had preceded Thistlewood. In the cookhouse, Phibbah ruled supreme. Field slaves, too, respected her, and she sometimes tried to intervene on their behalf with Thistlewood. He was not responsive. "Reprimanded Phibbah for intermeddling with the field Negroes business with me," he noted.[269]

Phibbah had clear goals. She wanted property, including livestock, land and slaves, as well as the finery to which her status as a privileged domestic and Thistlewood's mistress entitled her. She wanted money and the power to help her sister, Nancy, enslaved on another plantation, her daughter and her friends. She wanted mulatto children who might be manumitted. She wanted security, to be Thistlewood's only lover except during the later phase of pregnancy, when she chose another slave for him "to keep as Sweetheart the Time she lies in."[270] Phibbah was completely loyal and usually faithful, though Thistlewood noted jealously that she sometimes slept with John Cope and, in later life, seemed far too interested in a handsome mulatto worker.

Phibbah did not rely on erotic appeal to bind Thistlewood to her, though they had a hearty sex life: 234 times in their first year. Afterward, she was his partner in 65 percent of his sexual encounters.[271] When she was angry with him, she withheld sex, flounced out of his bed and maintained a stony silence: "Phibbah did not speak to me all day."[272]

Early on, Phibbah became this prickly, cruel, hardworking and lonely man's helpmeet. She was his liaison with the slaves. She listened to his concerns and advised him. When slaves were difficult, she suggested punishments, such as smearing a runaway with molasses and tying her outside all night, naked, to be devoured by mosquitoes. She kept Thistlewood abreast of everything that happened on the plantation. When he was short of cash, she lent him money that he scrupulously repaid.

Phibbah's most serious challenge came when Thistlewood accepted a better position managing another sugar plantation. "Phibbah grieves very much, and last night I could not sleep, but vastly uneasy, &c.," Thistlewood wrote. He "begged hard" for the Copes to rent Phibbah to him, but Molly Cope refused. "Poor girl, I pity her, she is in miserable slavery," he lamented.[273] This quasi-epiphany gave Thistlewood new insight into the nature of slavery. Phibbah wept and suffered. So did Thistlewood, though he soon fulfilled her worst fears and found sexual comfort with slaves on the new plantation.

Phibbah refused to let the relationship die. She sent gifts of turtles, crabs, eggs, biscuits, pineapples and cashews. She gave him a gold ring. She managed to visit, and Thistlewood escorted her around his new home and introduced her to the slaves. She brought him news and gossip from Egypt, and he missed her sorely when her visit ended. This unsatisfactory arrangement lasted for six months, during which Phibbah negotiated for Thistlewood's return to Egypt, acting as the indefatigable intermediary between him and the Copes. On Christmas Eve, the lovers were reunited and spent the night together.

In 1760, Phibbah and Thistlewood had a child, Mulatto John, whom the Copes manumitted. Thistlewood acknowledged his son and helped Phibbah raise him. He bought John books, scolded him about undone homework and reproached Phibbah for spoiling him. John was educated, apprenticed to a carpenter and inducted into a free colored militia unit. Sadly, Phibbah's high hopes for her son were shattered when, at twenty years old, he died delirious with fever, perhaps poisoned at the hands of the jealous lover of a slave woman he had impregnated. Thistlewood grieved. "I am exceedingly dejected and low spirited etc a parched mouth and great inward heat," he wrote.[274]

By then, Thistlewood had again left the Copes and bought his own small livestock pen. This time the Copes allowed him to hire Phibbah, his "wife." Thistlewood farmed, raised livestock and rented out slaves as jobbing gangs at sugar-plantation harvest time. Phibbah traded in livestock, sewed, baked and higgled, and steadily accumulated money. Unofficially, she also owned slaves, although as a slave herself she was not allowed to. She cultivated land that Thistlewood considered hers and fenced in for her. Through the opportunities open to her as Thistlewood's mistress, combined with unremitting hard work, Phibbah became the matriarch of what historian Trevor Burnard calls "'protopeasants'—subsistence farmers engaged in independent production on their own." She also "demonstrated her concern that her family prosper."[275]

Phibbah and Thistlewood shared an emotional attachment that must define love. They were involved in the smallest details of the other's life, including chronic illnesses. Thistlewood "got up and tended her ... no rest in the evening,"[276] and Phibbah was equally solicitous of him. Thistlewood was respectful of Phibbah and of her accomplishments. He accepted Coobah and the rest of Phibbah's family as his own, and never returned to England. He became less cruel to his slaves, though he was never a lenient master. He showed concern for their health, provided decent health care for them and did not, like so many other planters, always assume they were malingering.

Thistlewood provided for Phibbah in his will, leaving the Copes enough money to manumit her. Six years later, they did so. He also left her money to buy land and to build a house and, once she was freed, legal ownership of her slave woman and her son. After Thistlewood's death, Phibbah became a propertied, slaveholding freedwoman.

Phibbah understood how slavery operated and, in that context, set her goals and achieved them. Knowing that whites were all-powerful, she wanted some of that whiteness for her children, and preferred lighter-skinned friends. Knowing that neither her work nor Thistlewood's could advance without the cooperation of slaves, she punished slaves who defied her authority, and helped Thistlewood do the same. Phibbah's values centered on family solidarity, friendship, prosperity and hard work. She must have experienced her life as a personal triumph. It was also a triumph over slavery, and an indictment of the premises of racial inferiority that underpinned it.

The story of Guadeloupe sugar planter Guillaume-Pierre Tavernier de Boulogne, his Senegalese slave mistress, Nanon, and their son, Joseph de Boulogne, le Chevalier de Saint-Georges, began on Christmas Day 1739, when fifteen-year-old Nanon gave birth.[277] The child grew into a tall, strong and graceful boy with strikingly good looks. His father introduced him to all aspects of sugar production and his mother showed him the Rue Case-Nègre, the slave quarter, with its misery and its music. In time they moved to St. Domingue, where sugar was cheaper to produce. But after an overseer struck Joseph as he tried to intervene in a slave's whipping, Guillaume-Pierre moved mother and son to France. There, realizing that Nanon was an obstacle to his social success, Guillaume-Pierre dismissed her with a large pension and married a white woman.

The story now shifts to Joseph, whom Guillaume-Pierre continued to raise as an aristocrat, and whom Nanon cared for. The boy excelled at everything. He was ranked France's best fencer. He swam the Seine using only one arm. He was a brilliant equestrian and an elegant dancer.

Joseph de Boulogne, Le Chevalier Saint-George.

He was also a musical virtuoso and delighted guests with his Amati violin (Amati was Stradivarius's teacher), a gift from his proud father. Only marriage proved elusive. White women adored him, but because of his color, could not marry him; gossips said that his pillow was stuffed with his lovers' hair.

Saint-George, the anglicized name he affected, soared in the French musical world. He became a leading orchestra's first violinist and later a conductor. He performed for Queen Marie-Antoinette and taught her music. He composed concerti written for the full range of instruments, string, wind and brass. He became the focus of a racial scandal after Louis XVI named him director of the Opéra, then, under pressure from three operatic divas, revoked the appointment but refused to name any director at all.

As Saint-George matured as a composer, orchestras and soloists performed his works as they did those of Mozart and Haydn, whom critics considered his peers. He commissioned Haydn, a struggling musician like Mozart, to compose six major pieces; Haydn produced his "Paris" symphonies, which Saint-George presented to the Parisian public in the revolutionary 1780s.

Saint-George's extraordinary talents did not protect him from racial hatred. Voltaire, who considered it a witticism to wonder whether

Africans descended from monkeys or monkeys from Africans, disliked him because he was a mulatto. Racial prejudice and personal uncertainty about his own identity haunted Saint-George. He became a Jacobin, dropped the aristocratic "de" from his name and assumed command of a black and mulatto revolutionary regiment. After someone denounced him, he languished in prison for a year until he was pardoned, and died a few years later.

Ferocious racial prejudice buried Saint-George's music, which the musical community joyfully rediscovered only in the late twentieth century. That same racism warped his mother's life and tainted his. In France, where only a few thousand other blacks lived and where artists portrayed them as monkeylike demons, they could not escape the racism exported with sugarcane.

In Martinique, planter Pierre Dieudonné Dessalles held typical attitudes about slaves and the racial basis of slavery.[278] He was a practicing Roman Catholic with spiritual and moral concerns about slaves, but he never doubted that they were inferior beings. He encouraged them to marry as a means of curing their "licentious" ways and putting an end to the turmoil caused by sexual conflicts. He also believed married slaves would produce the additional slaves he needed for his cane fields.

Dessalles and his wife, Anna, had two sons and two daughters, usually resident in France. Occasionally Dessalles visited them there and was singularly unhappy: "Why did we come to Paris, for God's sake? To eat badly and suffer privations of every kind? … [In Martinique] I had fresh fruit all year long, fresh compotes every day, and cream custard at every meal."[279]

What Dessalles really missed in Martinique was the companionship of Nicaise, the mulatto slave he loved more than his white children and certainly more than his wife, whom he systematically schemed to keep away from Martinique. Understandably, Anna was vitriolic about her husband's passion for Nicaise, who was either his lover or, what is more likely, his son.

As a political conservative who believed fervently that racial "impurity" was incompatible with legitimacy, Dessalles never acknowledged

Nicaise, but he loved and favored him and, self-pityingly, forgave him interminable transgressions. He admitted that he cared for Nicaise "as if he were my child, to whom I give unlimited marks of confidence … I decided to treat this young slave as a part of myself."

Dessalles wanted Nicaise to stop cheating, lying and stealing and to "deposit in my breast even his most secret thoughts." In return, he showered the young man with "pretty things," trusted him with his storehouse keys and his money, and confided in him "about the particular heartaches my affairs and my family might cause me." Clearly, Dessalles had extraordinary expectations of this relationship.

Nicaise was Dessalles' manservant, his constant companion and, in the turmoil of revolution and abolition, his trusted lieutenant. They often dined together, and Nicaise slept in Dessalles' room at night. But Dessalles fretted about what Nicaise did when he was out of his sight. "I wish he had a better understanding of his status. Since I treat him kindly, he should sense that he no longer ought to be so familiar with the negroes. I do not mean that he should be haughty with them, but I wish he were more careful about his body and his cleanliness. After all, he sleeps in my room and should not rub himself against everything. I would be very happy if I could instill delicate tastes in him and make him lose those that come with the sad state of slavery."

Dessalles acted as Nicaise's marital matchmaker and took "what can only be called prurient interest" in the young man's sex life. (Dessalles noted that male domestics were "endowed by nature with enormous instruments!") Nicaise, he wrote, "is a bit of a spendthrift and loves dissolute parties, so I always tremble that he will catch a nasty disease. He assures me that he is not after women, but can I count on that?"

Dessalles took Nicaise with him on extended trips to Paris, gave him free rein in the city and, as best he could, shielded him from French racist bigotry, and from Anna Dessalles. On one visit to Martinique, Anna demanded that her husband get rid of Nicaise. "She claims that he is harmful to the interests of the plantation, that he treats the other negroes as if he were the master, and that, of course, everyone is jealous of him," Dessalles wrote. But Nicaise was there to stay.

The impulsive and elegant young man got married, had children and christened them, and served Dessalles throughout his life, even after Dessalles freed him. Nicaise whipped recalcitrant slaves for him, lent him money and helped him through the difficult period before and after slavery was abolished. He identified with Dessalles' interests, alienating other mulattoes. Nicaise died in 1850, with Dessalles at his deathbed. Until his own death seven years later, Dessalles grieved for the younger man.

Dessalles' profound love for Nicaise, whether sexual or paternal, was steadfast and reciprocated. It should have undermined Dessalles' racial assumptions about slavery and challenged his worldview about white people ruling and non-white people serving them. Yet for most of his life, Dessalles held these ideological conflicts at bay by prevaricating, rearranging his marital life, estranging his family and never allowing himself to look clearly into his own heart for fear of what he would see there.

The passionate and conflicted relations between white and black men and women were testaments to the illogic at the heart of sugar slavery. But what ultimately mattered in the sugar world was the business of selling sugar and of expanding the fortunes of the related industries that linked four continents and were essential to the imperial economy.

Chapter 5

Sugar Stirs the Universe

Across the Atlantic, at the other end of the bridge that carried the Old World to the New, the metropolises were bound up in their colonies' fortunes. Britain in particular had its sugar colonies and its people's voracious sweet tooth to thank for its expanding empire. Together with the tea and coffee it sweetened, sugar was one of the most important founding blocks of the British Empire. The eighteenth-century Abbé Raynal went further, exclaiming that the "scorned [sugar] islands … double perhaps triple the activity of the whole of Europe. They can be regarded as the principal cause of the rapid movement which stirs the Universe."[280]

The slave-sugar complex was all-pervasive. It linked field slaves and slave boilers to colonial carters and dock workers; seamen, captains and ship's bursars to freight forwarders, insurance agents and customs agents; harbour officials, longshoremen and carters to refiners, grocers, confectioners; people who took sugar in their tea and spread jam on their bread to refiners, packagers and bakers; and shipbuilders and shipyard workers to brokers and commercial agents known as factors.

Sugar and slaving were intertwined, and slaving was big business. It supported important industries: building and provisioning slave ships and manufacturing the items to be traded for Africans. The slave ships and their sailors generated enormous orders for coils of lashing to caulk ships, rope, fabric for uniforms, canvas for sails, silk for flags, locks, tallow and hundreds of other items.

The African trade spawned yet more production. In 1787, one typical cargo included the following items, all made by British workers or imported by British companies: coarse blue and red woolens, wool caps, cottons and linens, ruffled shirts, coarse and fine hats, beads and glass trinkets, guns, ammunition, iron bars, sabers, pewter, copper and iron pots and pans, hardware, glassware, earthenware, leather trunks, silver and gold jewelry, rum and tobacco.[281]

Slaving and the African trade also generated employment, albeit notoriously underpaid and coerced, for seamen. In 1787, for instance, 689 ships manned by 13,976 seamen, about one-eighth of the national total, plied the Atlantic between England and the West Indies. Seamen who survived the rigors of the journey, rampant tropical disease and mistreatment were sought out as "seasoned" veterans. When European nations waged war against each other's colonies, which represented enormous capital investment and economic production, these veterans were enlisted into their nation's navy.

Sugar slavery provided jobs manufacturing the items every plantation needed in its arsenal, including the iron collars, handcuffs and shackles, tongue depressors and ball-and-chains originally designed for medieval torture chambers. Sugar works needed brass fittings for the boiling house, iron sugar stoves and cane-crushing rollers, iron hoes and agricultural implements, knives and machetes, barrels, casks and staves, account books, pens and ink and reams of paper for the overseer and other managers, and bolts of Osnaburg linen and cheap cotton, shoes, gaudy jewelry, ribbons, buttons, thread and other notions for slaves.

Great Houses with their insatiable demand for furniture, rugs, pianos, books, magazines and newspapers, fashionable clothes, hats and shoes, jewelry and medicine provided employment for metropolitan manufacturers and artisans. Creole whites also ordered large quantities of refined sugar for which they paid double to quadruple what consumers paid in Europe, where it was refined. They were inveterate buyers of the livestock that, like slaves, were too brutalized to reproduce themselves and had to be replenished from foreign sources.

The slave-sugar complex operated on triangular routes between the metropolis, the African Slave Coast and the sugar colonies, then back to the metropolis. Specifically, Europe traded its finished goods for African slaves who were transported and sold to its West Indian colonies, which supplied sugar and other tropical commodities to the metropolis, which supplied these colonies with refined sugar, cloth, tools and other manufactured goods. This triangle satisfied the requirements of mercantilism, the post-medieval economic system premised on the need for bullion accumulation achieved through balances of trade that favored the metropolis and its industries at the expense of subservient colonies and their raw produce.

An important consequence of mercantilist policy was that England forbade its colonies to refine the sugar they produced. Shipping interests furiously defended this illogical practice because they earned more by transporting the much bulkier unrefined sugar. In Europe, refineries and associated trades also gained. The sugar colonies, on the other hand, remained economically infantilized and dependent. To ensure that they would not rebel and establish refineries, the metropolis imposed onerous duties on refined sugar.

In the case of England, the mercantilist triangle was supplemented by an additional, unmercantilist zigzag back and forth between its North American colonies and its sugar colonies. North Americans supplied foodstuffs and livestock in return for sugar, molasses and slaves and earned sufficient profit from this commerce to purchase manufactured goods from England's growing industrial heartland, which muted metropolitan grumbling about deviance from the economic model. Vocal sugar planters defended this trade, letting it be known that without North American wheat, maize and salted beef, their slaves would likely starve, and without mules and oxen to power their boilers and their mills, their sugar operations stood idle.

Sometimes a second and rival triangle developed, with North Americans refining their imported molasses into rum they sold to slavers who traded it for slaves they sold to the West Indian planters for more molasses. France's sugar colonies, which needed similar supplies, also traded with British North America, paying for their goods with large quantities of the molasses that France, protecting its brandy industry from competition, did not want distilled into rum. Spain, effectively excluded from the African slave trade since the end of the sixteenth century, made do with asientos, licenses that granted foreign slavers, usually British, the right to supply slaves to Spanish territories.

Reinforced by these commercial improvisations, the Europe-Africa-colonies triangular trade was remarkably efficient. Its mercantilist bans on colonial manufactures eliminated the need for much ballast because ships from Europe, especially Britain, could generally be filled with salable goods on every leg of their journey. Metropolitan coffers swelled and underwrote an expanding merchant and military marine. Empires grew and Europe urbanized and industrialized. All over Europe but especially in England, sugar sweetened even the poor man's palate.

In his passionate and groundbreaking *Capitalism and Slavery*, Trinidadian historian Eric Williams argued that the triangular trade contributed so heavily to British industrial development that its profits "fertilized the entire productive system of the country" and "made an enormous contribution to Britain's industrial development."[282] By the eighteenth century, the West Indies had become the hub of the British Empire. Sugar slaves had a direct connection to English workers; Williams cites one claim that calculates the combined needs of one planter or manager and ten of his black workers, including their foodstuffs, clothing and tools, as providing jobs for four Englishmen. Other sources provide more extravagant ratios: that one white West Indian created £10 net profit for England, 2,000 percent more than an Englishman; that every sugar worker outproduced every English worker in a ratio of 130 to 1; and that the combined worth of the sugar plantations was anywhere from £50 million to £70 million.[283]

To support his hypothesis, Williams noted Pitt the Younger's 1798 estimate that the annual income from the West Indian plantations was £4 million, and that all other sources together totaled only £1 million. He argued that little Barbados, a mere 166 square miles, was more valuable to British capitalism than the vastly larger colonies of New

England, New York and Pennsylvania combined; that British imports from tiny Nevis were double those from New York; and that those from Antigua three times those from New England. Satisfying Britain's sweet tooth had created colossal capital, fueled its factories, encouraged its imperial ventures, helped finance its wars and enriched both its nation's coffers and its people, Williams concluded.

Since its publication four decades ago, scholars have debated and tested *Capitalism and Slavery*'s fundamental premises. They have reached no consensus, but many conclude that, despite a certain wobbling in his macroeconomic calculations, Williams was essentially correct. Although capital from the slave-sugar commerce did underwrite some factories, the evidence now suggests that it was not a primary source of investment for the Industrial Revolution. But its influence on Britain's economic growth, which "was chiefly from without inwards," was enormous because it generated so many subsidiary businesses. And planters and other investors spent so lavishly on home furnishings, clothing, jewelry and entertainment that they had an economic influence on these businesses. After emancipation, most of the planters' compensation money remained in England.[284]

Shipbuilding, Slaving and Sugar Refining

The dynamics of the slave-sugar industry spring to life when they exit the realm of mercantilist theory and enter real life. Starting from the British tip of the triangle, let's focus on three economic activities—the major ones of shipbuilding, slaving and sugar refining—in the context of how they generated employment and capital, transformed sleepy towns into thriving commercial cities, and were urbanizing magnets that drew droves of country folk into them. Bristol, which the sugar and slave trades catapulted economically into second place only to London, "could not feel the iniquity of the merchandise, but they could feel it lucrative."[285] Late in the eighteenth century, Liverpool overtook Bristol and London in the slave and the sugar trades.

Until then, Liverpool was an obscure borough, home to fishermen and farmers, and a port for the Irish trade. By 1740, its brilliantly conceived commercial dock, England's first, with its entourage of ware-houses, offices, commercial buildings and dock-related structures, provided the infrastructure for Liverpool's commercial and industrial expansion. This included shipbuilding. Liverpudlian shipyards built pirate ships, naval vessels and slavers. Slavers were designed to accommodate hundreds of slaves and had different specifications from other vessels.

Slave trading and shipbuilding were integrally linked. Half of Liverpool's sailors worked in the slave trade, and many shipwrights engaged in it with their own ships. The shipbuilders Baker and Dawson, for instance, had eighteen slaving vessels, worth £509,000, and a contract to supply at least three thousand slaves to Spanish colonies. They were also one of the largest suppliers of slaves to the British sugar islands.

A growing number of Liverpudlians were economically dependent on shipbuilding and slaving. An abbreviated list hints at the range of trades-men involved: carpenters, painters, mechanics, ironsmiths, rope makers, sail makers, repairmen and general handymen. Clerks and supervisors processed purchases, deliveries, payments, hiring and payroll. Insurance agents calculated and levied insurance premiums and assessed damages and losses. Customs clerks collected duties. Men and women operated food stalls for dockyard workers. Longshoremen loaded ships bound for Africa and unloaded sugar and molasses from the West Indies. By 1760, Liverpool could sell slaves to the West Indies more cheaply than London and Bristol, the other major slave-trading port cities.

From the sailor who had forced wretched Africans to "dance" on deck, to the foundry worker who turned out brass collars and silver padlocks designed "for Blacks or Dogs,"[286] Liverpudlians knew all about the slave trade and the Middle Passage. Citizens eager for profit—"attor-neys, drapers, grocers, barbers and tailors"—invested in the slave trade, with a common share being one thirty-second.[287]

A few Liverpudlians refused to participate in the slave trade. John Kill, a major shipbuilder, declined orders for slavers, and William Rathbone refused to supply timber to build them. An actor jeered by his Liverpudlian audience shouted from the stage, "I have not come here to be insulted by a set of wretches, every brick in whose infernal town is cemented with an African's blood."[288]

Liverpool's artisans and semiskilled workers produced the goods used to trade for slaves. A very good slave cost one trader thirteen coral beads, half a string of amber, twenty-eight silver bells and three bracelets. Traders placed orders for vast amounts of these sorts of goods, and factories obliged them. Mills rolled out bolts of gaudy cloth made from American cotton, and lengths of wool from British, Spanish, Portuguese and German sheep and, after 1815, Australian sheep as well. Glassworks manufactured beads and trinkets of glass. Gunsmith shops mass-produced specially designed inferior guns for African slave traders to use to capture new victims. Processing plants used vast amounts of salt, Liverpool's "Nursing Mother," to preserve substandard codfish that, salted into stiff boards, was exported to the West Indies in ships that returned with sugar.

The slave-sugar complex darkened Liverpool's complexion. Slaves were sold there as domestics, advertised in the *Liverpool Chronicle* and sold by auction at such venues as the Merchants' Coffee-house, George's Coffee-House, the Exchange Coffee-House and other establishments on Negro Row. Sugar planters fleeing their plantations returned home to England (and France and Spain and Portugal) with slaves they could not function without, and who were the ultimate status symbol.

Liverpool also hosted dozens of young African aristocrats whose princely fathers were encouraged to send them abroad to strengthen the ties between Britain and their respective homelands to which they would return and, it was hoped, promote British values. Most went home, thoroughly Europeanized; other remained in Liverpool, marrying there, sometimes to white women, and later sent for relatives to join them.

The mixed-race children of wealthy white fathers who brought or sent them "home" for an education or to escape the intolerable atmosphere of West Indian racism and slavery settled in Liverpool as well. One was Jamaican William Davidson, the son of a white official and a black slave woman. By curious coincidence, he joined Thomas Thistlewood's nephew, Arthur Thistlewood, in the revolutionary "Cato

Street Conspiracy" to assassinate the British cabinet. Davidson and Thistlewood were betrayed, arrested, hanged and beheaded, in Britain's last public decapitation.

Most blacks lived in the poorest areas and suffered discrimination. As waves of impoverished whites immigrated into the city, they competed with blacks for jobs. Only black sailors were relatively untouched by prejudice, working alongside whites who usually treated them as colleagues. The plight of black Liverpudlians sparked few abolitionist sentiments. Too many of their white fellow citizens depended for economic survival on slaving and shipbuilding or on the growing sugar and tobacco businesses. Between 1704 and 1850, more sugar refineries opened, and imports of raw sugar increased from 760 tons to 52,000 tons. In 1850, Liverpool also imported 726,000 gallons of rum.

Those who grew, imported, sold, refined, insured and speculated in sugar transformed the industrial face of Europe by creating an administrative infrastructure to facilitate their commerce, and political alliances and lobbies to promote it. That commerce employed or otherwise affected millions of Europeans. A much smaller group, the sugar planters, had the closest and most primary connections to sugar.

Capital Sugar

Sugar plantations were complex and expensive operations. In the *Historical Account of the Rise of the West-India Colonies*, Sir Dalby Thomas estimated that, at the end of the seventeenth century, a one-hundred-acre sugar plantation would cost £5,625. This would include fifty slaves and land, houses, mills, vessels and all tools and implements.[289] In *The Sugar Cane Industry*, historical geographer Jock Galloway examines seventeenth- and eighteenth-century literature for evidence about what it took to establish them. First of all, a planter needed suitable land, at least a few hundred acres. If he lacked the connections to arrange a land grant, he had to buy his property. He needed workers, and once sugar became a slave-produced commodity, that meant purchasing slaves, his largest expense. He needed a mill, boiling and curing houses, a distillery, a pen, slave quarters, housing for his white employees and a Great House for himself. He had to equip and furnish these edifices and stock his pen with expensive livestock. He had to buy wagons and agricultural tools. He had to pay legal fees. He needed capital to operate his plantation, yet it would be about two years before he made any money from his sugar.

In the mid-seventeenth century, Galloway calculates, a five-hundred-acre Barbadian plantation might cost £14,000, an enormous sum. In the mid-eighteenth century, an average Antiguan plantation of two hundred acres and a hundred slaves had a value of £10,000. A decade or two later, a much larger Jamaican plantation of six hundred acres and two hundred slaves represented an investment of £19,027. Other Jamaican estates were worth more than £20,000, excluding the value of land. Slaves were usually any sugar plantation's largest investment. The slaves on a modest Cuban plantation in Santiago de Cuba accounted for 33 percent of its value, the land only 17.6 percent and the mill and boiling house 6 percent and 8.8 percent respectively. In mid-eighteenth-century Brazil's sugar-rich Bahia, planters agreed that the breakdown of their investment would be 20 percent for land, 30 percent for slaves and the remaining 50 percent divided between equipment, livestock, furnishings and other essentials.[290]

In the context of sugar's power to transform, these figures translate into capital investment, methods of banking and borrowing, and rates of return that influenced unrelated but less profitable areas of investment. Such a powerful but complicated and risky commerce had serious political implications, for planters were in perpetual need of legislative support. Specifically, they needed the protection of mercantilism. Although it outlawed colonial enterprise and commercial expansion, mercantilism embraced individual planters and investors as beneficiaries of its heavy-handed economic management.

The nature of plantation-style sugar production forced planters into the world of high finance and commerce. They needed capital, credit, exporting and importing expertise, insurance, and customs and commercial contacts to finance and operate their sugar estates. This applied as well to those who inherited plantations or had access to large sums of money, and to absentees. If they neglected any one of these essential matters, they jeopardized their opulent lifestyle or, as frequently happened, risked losing the plantation.

Sugar was an investment that frequently produced better than average returns: in the second half of the eighteenth century, close to 10 percent annually compared with 5.5 percent on government bonds and 6.5 percent on land mortgages. But like other speculative investments, sugar's high interest rates alternated with disastrously low ones. Sugar and hence its profits were exposed to a plethora of risks, hurricanes chief among them. Hurricanes laid waste plantations, killing slaves and whites. They smashed fortunes, bankrupting once-powerful families. Hurricanes were, writes historian Matthew Mulcahy, "central forces helping shape the economic experience of colonists in the Greater Caribbean.... The risk from hurricanes was distinct because the destruction was so complete, so sudden, and so frequent."[291]

Other threats to the successful sugar operation included drought, rats, pest infections, disease, soil erosion and aridity, wars and invasions, and its sullen and uncooperative labor force. Potential catastrophes were dramatic drops in the price of sugar, sharp increases in sugar duties, competition from such foreign sources as the French sugar colonies, the advent of cheaper imperial sources such as the East Indies, bad publicity about the brutality of sugar slavery and, from early on in the nineteenth century, the advent of sugar processed from European sugar beets.

ABSENTEES IN ATTENDANCE

We've seen how the white planters lived. Let's now consider how the absentees managed their sugar interests far from the colonies they abandoned. In England they were so conspicuous for their lavish spending that "rich as a Creole" became a common expression. Grasping Englishmen and their sisters chased after marriageable West Indian heirs and heiresses. The wildly popular *The West Indian*, Richard Cumberland's 1771 dramatic comedy, perpetuated the stereotypical view of Creoles as fabulously wealthy and socially inept. Protagonist Belcour, a young sugar-plantation heir "accustomed to a land of slaves" and accompanied by a few of his own, has just landed in England with mountains of luggage and a menagerie of two green monkeys, a pair of gray parrots, a Jamaican sow and pigs, and a Mangrove dog. Audiences roared as impecunious English schemers, having discovered that "he was a West Indian fresh landed, and full of cash; a gull to our hearts' content; a hot-brained headlong spark," target him for a major sting operation involving a beautiful young woman. At one point, the impulsive and passionate Belcour laments, "I had better have stayed in the torrid zone: I shall be wasted to the size of a sugar-cane."[292]

One talented expatriate contributed a poetic elegy to the growing literature about the phenomenon of West Indian sugarcane. "The Sugar-Cane," by James Grainger, neither romanticized nor humanized cane but considered it as a commodity central to Britain's commerce and empire. The poem described its agricultural cycles and the African slaves who

Tom Sugar Cane, a West Indian, is nineteenth-century British illustrator George Spratt's caricature of a sugar planter. Tom is composed of the tools and produce of his trade, including a cane stalk, a barrel and glass of rum, and metallic cutters. Behind him, slaves work the cane fields.

produced it. It acknowledged that slavery was regrettable but qualified this with the standard rationale that slaves endured less punishing conditions than Scottish miners.

"The Sugar-Cane" attracted a good deal of attention among literati. Dr. Samuel Johnson, who hated slavery and once toasted "the next insurrection of the negroes in the West Indies," praised it in public. His private reaction was less positive. "One might as well write the 'Parsley-bed, a Poem'; or 'The Cabbage-garden, a Poem,'" he confided to James Boswell. At one public reading, the stanza "Muse, let's sing of rats," a lament about how rats devastated cane fields, provoked derisive laughter.[293] It was one thing to eat sugar and deplore the slavery of unknown Africans, it was another to contemplate sugarcane as a difficult food crop, and no amount of poetic talent could overcome this.

Jane Austen, on the other hand, approached sugarcane in its human dimensions, weaving the declining fortunes of absentee Sir Thomas Bertram's Antiguan plantation into those of *Mansfield Park*, published in 1814 and set in 1810 to 1812, and considered by some to be her finest novel. In those days of mostly arranged or, at the very least, parentally condoned marriages, the machinations of parents and their unmarried children dominated the plot. The background to the plot was Sir Thomas's urgent and lengthy trip to Antigua to reverse his plantation's "poor returns," which left "a large part of his income … unsettled." An important subtext was the African slave trade, very recently abolished; mention of it elicited pained silences among the novel's characters. Specifically, the posh life of Mansfield Park, including the "near-fatal fatigue" Lady Bertram incurred by "embroidering something of little use and no beauty … not to mention a healthy dose of opium every day," depended absolutely on the continued profits from the Antiguan sugar plantation.

Austen opposed slavery and favored abolition, and she understood the link between slave-operated sugar plantations and much of England's high society. *Mansfield Park* was, in the words of Antiguan-born classical scholar Gregson Davis, "a subtle moral critique of the British landed gentry in terms of their presumed allegiance to the institution of slavery. Such a conclusion is congruent with her ongoing denigration—expressed with exquisite irony and incomparable elegance of style—of the landed gentry's obsession with financial status and the concomitant social climbing endemic to the marriage market."[294]

Mansfield Park's West Indians modeled their behavior on the English patricians who scorned them as nouveaux riches yet pursued and married them until the two groups were so interconnected that it was difficult to disentangle them. Sir Thomas Bertram, a long-term absentee with serious revenue problems, an engaged member of Parliament and the respected head of an established English family, was the personification of this confused identity.

In the real life that art reflected, the Beckford family was at the apex of the sugar plantocracy. In 1670, absentee planter Sir Thomas Beckford netted £2,000 annually from Jamaican sugar, while his relative, Peter Beckford, a resident planter, held high offices in Jamaica and died "in possession of the largest property real and personal of any subject in Europe."[295] Peter's handsome and imposing grandson William, who preferred England to Jamaica, became the most powerful of all the absentee planters.

William understood the importance of political connections and through his financial and commercial resources made himself useful to William Pitt the Elder. William also held several elected positions, the last as chief magistrate of London. Fonthill Splendens, his English estate, was a vast stone edifice with two wings connected by corridors, and a vaulted ceiling. It was lushly furnished and boasted fine artwork and splendid decor. Beckford entertained there on a scale beyond the reach of almost anyone else; at one of his dinners he served six hundred dishes at a cost of £10,000. He also arranged for his son, heir and namesake to have the best educational experience available, even hiring Mozart to give the boy piano lessons.

In 1770, William Jr. inherited his father's estate, which brought him an annual income estimated at about £100,000 and earned him the nickname "England's wealthiest son." William Jr. was indifferent to the Jamaican source of his fortune that he so enthusiastically dissipated, most spectacularly when he built Fonthill Abbey, a Gothic curiosity with a 275-foot tower that kept collapsing. William was a more talented writer than architect, and his gothic novel, *Vathek*, influenced Mary

Shelley's *Frankenstein*. Unwisely in those homophobic times, William also wrote about his erotic desire for young men. His homosexual liaison with a young patrician caused such a scandal that he fled to Switzerland, where his wife, Lady Margaret Gordon, died.

Beckford later returned to England and took refuge in Fonthill Abbey, where he lived in seclusion with a contingent of servants including a physician, a musician and Pietro, a dwarf. Beckford earned a reputation as a bibliophile, art collector and genealogist, and as "the most isolated man of his day." He delegated control of his Jamaican estates to agents and managers who neglected them and likely cheated him. Beckford lost one plantation, worth £12,000 annually, for failing to produce a title deed. By 1823, when he was sixty-four, his fortune was gone and he was forced to sell Fonthill Abbey and his vast art collection.

Absentee Robert Hibbert supplemented the revenues from his sugar plantation by trading in cheap cotton and linens destined for both the African slave trade and the sugar plantation slaves. His relative, George Hibbert, combined his business interests as a London merchant by serving as Jamaica's agent in England as well. He was also a prime mover in the establishment of the privately capitalized West India Docks, and its board of directors elected him their first president.

The West India Docks were a massive undertaking and, when they were built, the largest in the world. In July 1799, Hibbert and the West Indian merchants secured passage of legislation granting them a twenty-one-year monopoly to unload and load all West Indian produce there. The thirty-acre unloading dock could accommodate three hundred ships, the twenty-four-acre loading dock two hundred ships. Adjacent warehouses, five stories high, held the sugar, rum and other goods until duties were paid. Before this, the London port, where Canary Wharf is now located, was hopelessly overcrowded, and ships queued for weeks until they could be unloaded. Their perishable merchandise, namely sugar, was exposed to foul weather and deterioration, and to gangs of thieves such as the River Pirates, Night Plunderers, Heavy Horsemen, Scuffle-Hunters and Mud Larks, who stole £150,000 worth of sugar every year. When the West India Docks opened, they employed two hundred armed men as a private security force.

The Long family lived in English splendor on income drawn from their fourteen-thousand-acre Jamaican holdings. After his father Samuel's death, Edward Long, an English-born lawyer, visited his inherited estates. His sister, Catherine Maria, had married there, to Sir Henry Moore, the island's governor. Long, too, married in Jamaica, to Thomas Beckford's daughter Mary. Long spent twelve years in Jamaica, then in 1769 returned to England to devote himself to literary pursuits. His most famous were his three-volume *History of Jamaica*, along with *Letters on the Colonies* and *The Sugar Trade*.

Bryan Edwards was raised primarily in Jamaica but returned to England as an adult and remained there. His knowledge of sugar production and his personal contacts helped him prosper as a West India merchant. Edwards stoutly defended his fellow absentees against critics, denying that they were vulgarly ostentatious social climbers who fawned on patrician Englishmen and yearned to marry their daughters. He also wrote the four-volume *The History, Civil and Commercial, of the British Colonies in the West Indies*, an excellent source for West Indian history.

Edwards failed in his attempts to polish the West Indian absentee planters' reputation. They were their own worst enemies. They traveled in showy carriages driven by liveried drivers and frequented spas and holiday resorts like Epsom and Cheltenham. They attended posh social events resplendent in extravagant clothing and jewelry. They sent their coddled and imperious sons off to Eton, Westminster, Harrow and Winchester and provided them with enormous allowances the boys used to lord it over other boys. It was rumored that at least one of these scions of West Indian planters paid another student to do his math homework.

The sugar-planting Pinney family had its share of wealthy and influential absentees whose lives and fortunes are re-created in historian Richard Pares's *A West-India Fortune*. The Pinneys owned large sugar plantations in Nevis and substantial property in Bristol, their metropolitan home base. Their story begins with Azariah Pinney, who in his youth joined the Protestant Duke of Monmouth's rebellion against the Catholic James II. Captured and condemned to hang, Azariah was instead transported to the West Indies for a term of ten years. He arrived in Nevis in 1685, with a Bible, ten gallons of sack and brandy and £15.

Azariah flourished. He acquired several sugar plantations, acted on behalf of absentee planters, served as a colonial officer and established businesses. One was the sale of lace and other dry goods such as sugar bags and scissors, which he ordered from his family in Bristol. As was common in the chronically coin-short West Indies, he remitted his payments to them in sugar and other local produce. Azariah occasionally visited England and, in 1720, died there.

Azariah's more or less estranged wife raised their son, John, in England. John, whom Azariah considered a wasteful dilettante, married Mary Helme, an heiress to Antiguan sugar plantations, and moved to Nevis, where he served as a councilor and then chief justice. John died a few months after his father and left his estate to John Frederick, his only surviving child.

John Frederick was raised in England while attorneys managed his Nevis and Antiguan properties. In 1739 he visited Nevis, intending to implement improvements that would permit him to return to England an even wealthier man. This was a wise plan. All sensible absentees visited their estates at least once a decade to prevent feckless agents from running them into the ground. John Frederick's experience in Nevis left him extremely critical of Creoles, particularly how they hated to pay their debts, but as he grappled with the complexities of operating sugar plantations, he gained an understanding of the problems Creoles faced. He stayed longer than he had intended and even served in the Assembly. A few years later, John Frederick returned to England and luxurious comfort as a sugar-financed West Country squire and an unexceptional member of Parliament. Cannily, he increased his Nevis holdings by calling in an unpaid loan from another planter.

In 1762, John Frederick died unmarried and childless, and left the bulk of his estate to John "Jackey" Pretor, a poor and distant cousin he had taken in and educated. John Frederick had been a stern and unaffectionate benefactor to Jackey, whose legacy depended on his adopting the surname Pinney. Suddenly, meek and fawning Jackey Pretor became John Pinney, a rich absentee sugar planter. His new life transformed him. He gained confidence and drove himself—and all around him—

A glimpse of the high life that expatriate West Indians flocked to join. The wealthy Englishmen Bob and Tom attend a dance in Vauxhall Gardens, where thousands of lamps illuminate the night, cold food and drinks are served, and the genteel classess—and ambitions courtesans—mingle.

This 1822 engraving is based on William Hogarth's satirical "Taste in High Life." A fashionable woman pets her black page boy, who holds a doll. An old woman takes tea from a foppish man. A liveried, monocled monkey reads a menu featuring "Ducks Tongues" and "Rabbits Ears." Dominating the scene is a large painting of a woman missing the back of her dress.

mercilessly. "Idleness and dissipation will never suit my disposition," he declared. The reborn John Pinney rejected the corrupt life of the West Indian absentee and he loathed debt, the albatross that burdened so many absentees. He shuddered at the thought of debt and interest, which he likened to "a moth in a man's garment, never asleep."[296]

Like his mentor John Frederick, John decided to sacrifice a few years in Nevis to "get mastery of plantation industry."[297] He arrived in 1764 and, also like John Frederick, disdained most of his fellow planters as lazy and indolent, interested only in making and keeping money and in the price of sugar. In the heartland of sugar, with its vagaries of weather, crop and personnel, he fought a duel over a debt and saw another planter murdered over one, and learned that creditors who assiduously called in debts from desperate planters could pay a high price. Yet he risked the dangers of exacting repayment and lent large sums to planters, prudently arranging for repayment in English sterling.

John Pinney shed his distrust of Creoles sufficiently to marry one. Jane Weekes was plain, dumpy and unassuming and, he complained, continually "[took] it into her head to breed," producing a stream of little Pinneys: John Frederick, Elizabeth, Azariah, Alicia, Pretor, Mary and Charles. He sent some of his sons to England to be educated and longed to follow them there, if only he could find loyal employees to churn out sugar and send him the profits. But the timing never seemed right, and Pares likens John and other planters to Sisyphus: "Just when he was near the top of the mountain a hurricane, or the American revolution, the French war, bore the stone down again."[298]

In 1783, after nineteen years in Nevis, John and Mary Pinney finally returned to England. Pares describes their reunion with their sons as "one of those scenes which made West-Indian life so absurd and touching." Neither parents nor sons recognized each other, and greeted each other as strangers. "Don't you know them, they're your children?" their English guardian exclaimed. John was stupefied. Mary, so shaken that she was half senseless, set her nightcap on fire with a candle. "Such a scene of distress and joy I never before experienced," John Pinney recalled.[299]

Pinney knew firsthand the high financial cost of absenteeism, and that a good resident planter could squeeze more from his sugar estates than a delegate. But he was also a lovelessly raised orphan who had heard too many horror stories about planters' children alone in England. His bittersweet reunion with his sons persuaded him to stay with them in England and to sacrifice revenues from the plantations. His subsequent troubles with attorneys or managers—they drank, lay abed, ignored instructions, squandered money, mired the plantation in debt—prompted him to sell his sugar holdings rather than leave his children and return to Nevis. He sold three plantations to Edward Huggins, whose cruelty to formerly compliant Pinney slaves would be the subject of a notorious law case.

The Pinney dynasty was the exception to the rule that by the third generation, incompetence and high-living dissolved West Indian sugar fortunes into nothingness. After John's death, his sons' squabbles over their legacy of his share in the House of Pinney and Tobin—Pinney's friend James Tobin was an anti-abolitionist pamphleteer—seemed ominous. Then Azariah, whom John had identified as his most competent successor, died. Of the unprepossessing survivors—John Frederick, excitable and ineffective; Pretor, so mad he was locked up for life; and fragile Charles, "a cold-hearted, evangelical Pecksniff"—it was Charles who became the family's commercial helmsman.

Like other absentees, Charles understood the importance of local political power and footed the cost of his election as mayor of Bristol in 1831. His tenure, however, was brief and disastrous after a civic riot escalated into violence and five hundred people died. The military commander, facing court-martial, shot himself. Mayor Pinney was luckier, and a court acquitted him of charges of neglecting his duty. Charles was markedly more effective as a merchant than he had been as a mayor. He visited Nevis to learn at first hand how sugar and related West Indian businesses operated, then returned to England and headed his family's business as sugar factors.

SUGAR BUSINESSES

Like the Pinneys, who were a microcosm of the sugar commerce that fueled the engine of the British Empire, other absentee planters, factors, merchants and bankers, refiners, distillers, shippers and insurers, often one and the same, followed tried-and-true strategies to protect and strengthen their commercial interests. Like John Pinney's daughter Elizabeth, who married Peter Baillie, a member of a major West Indian commercial firm whom her father brought into the family business, the West India Interest arranged matrimonial alliances and socialized together at their exclusive societies and clubs. In London, they met monthly at the Planters' Club, which by 1780 merged with other sugar interests into the Society of West Indian Planters and Merchants. Bristol and Liverpool, too, had West Indian societies with officers, elected members, archives and working capital. There they dined, established contacts, shared information and concerns, plotted strategies and consolidated alliances.

Provided a merchant had a good reputation, these contacts made the always-difficult sugar business a bit easier. They could, for example, facilitate the sale of warehoused sugar. Sugar had no one price and, like other commodities, could fluctuate wildly in response to myriad factors, including its quality, supply and demand, and competition from beet sugar or East Indian cane sugar.

A planter's sugar arrived at different times, on different ships, and the quality, too, was different. A trusted sugar broker would try to negotiate the sale of a planter's entire stock, making sure that the best quality rather than the worst set the standard for the selling price. If he showcased the very best sugar and sold it separately for a high price, he would lose overall because he would then be forced to accept a low price for the sugar of lesser quality.

Buying and selling sugar involved considerable expertise. Different islands produced different grades. Barbados's clayed sugar was very fine, while Nevis's and Jamaica's brown sugars were at the low end of the scale. (The claying process cleansed sugar of molasses and produced a loaf of sugar white on top and darker at the bottom.) The price differential was significant. The grocers, refiners, re-exporters (to the Continent) and speculators who bought raw sugar all had diverse needs. Grocers liked brightly colored sugar. Refiners wanted it strong, to withstand the refining process. Distillers could use molasses. Speculators had standards too slippery to define. Supply was more seasonal than demand, which increased only when grocers wanted more sugar at Christmastime. The crucial thing was to beat the hurricane season, officially from August to October, and the hurricane-related insurance rates that doubled just before the first of August.

Planters were always frantic for higher prices, and when prices were low, many pressured their brokers to warehouse their sugar for sale later, hopefully for a higher price. But molasses continued to drain from the hogsheads, decreasing the weight of sugar, and warehousing cost money. Even if prices rose, new shipments would sell better than "old" sugar. It was challenging enough to extract payment from the planters without adding the additional cost of warehousing unsold sugar. When planter clients demanded that the Pinneys sell their sugar for higher prices, the Pinneys invoked their excellent reputation to justify the prices they had negotiated. But not all factors were as financially sound as the Pinneys. Those with less capital to front freight, duties, warehousing and other costs were often forced by their urgent need for cash to accept lower prices.

Sharing information helped members of the West Indian societies make important decisions. News of a hurricane, a slave uprising, a measles epidemic or a war usually raised prices, whereas increased supplies of sugar beet or East Indian sugarcane, or the addition of such sugar sources as Trinidad and Mauritius, lowered them. "We sadly want the report of a war, a hurricane, or a something to give it a lift!" the Pinneys once lamented in a time of low sugar prices.[300]

Factors and everyone else connected to the sugar business had to keep abreast of current events and interpret them to calculate the effects of war and peace on sugar prices. In 1832, for instance, during the Anglo-French dispute over Belgium, Charles Pinney predicted that a European war "should bring back the good old times when sugars sold at £30 and £40 [per hogshead]."[301] In Eastern Europe, Pares writes, "Tsar Paul was a 'bear' point for sugar, Tsar Alexander I a 'bull' point, until he made peace with the French at Tilsit."[302] When Napoleon occupied Hamburg, an important consumer of English sugar, the Pinneys worried that unless the English government devised some way of increasing consumption, "God only knows the consequence to ... those connected with the West-India colonies may be fatal ... we must be completely done up."[303] Fortunately for them, the war took another turn and the price of sugar skyrocketed.

Many sugar merchants were also shippers. In the eighteenth century, so were some planters; the Pinneys, for instance, owned two ships. Regular ships had scheduled runs to specific islands, and their captains developed relations with the planters who entrusted them with their valuable and perishable cargo. Ships often had other routes in addition to their regular runs; the Pinney vessels also visited the Baltics, Bombay and Singapore.

Shipping was an intrinsically precarious business. Shippers faced competition from each other, from "seekers"—unscheduled ships hoping to attract business—and from foreign ships that illegally serviced the islands. Shipping was vulnerable to war, piracy and, until the West India Docks were built, forced idling at anchor in ports with insufficient warehouse space to take their sugar. To all these uncertainties and vagaries was added the danger of rumor. Planters shunned ships reputed to be shoddily maintained, and captains dreaded how rumors galloped through the sugar colonies. True or false, these rumors could ruin their business. The best way to counter them was to maintain close social ties with their planter-clients.

The regular ships carried much more than sugar. They brought planters' supplies, agricultural implements including hundreds of cheap hoes for the slaves, riding gear, brass and copper fittings for the mills and boilers, iron shackles to confine runaways, and draft animals. Captains found these mules, horses and oxen difficult passengers. Their fodder took up space, they soiled the holds and they suffered and died, which caused quarrels about financial accountability.

Another important part of sugar factoring was filling planters' orders for personal items, then packaging and shipping them, all without compensation for labor. These items included fashionable hats and clothing, pianos and music scores, magazines and books, pipes and Madeira wine, toiletries and medicines, salted and cured meat, even sugar refined in England and re-exported. Factors even had to arrange tutoring and schooling for Creole schoolchildren. At holiday time, if the children had no relatives in England, many factors took them home as nonpaying guests.

Factors agreed to these time-consuming and unremunerative services to retain their clients. They made money on commission sales of sugar and on shipping, but their big profits came in the form of interest on loans to their planter-clients. These loans were an inescapable feature of the sugar business. Most planters lived wastefully, extravagantly and primarily on credit, and were overwhelmingly indebted to their factors. When, as so often happened, a planter defaulted, the factor became de facto the absentee planter and then faced the exact same problems that had bankrupted the planter.

The West Indian sugar business was riskier than other monocultures, and its profits depended on intelligent maneuvering, cooperation between the interested parties and good luck. The West India societies were indispensable in conceiving and coordinating the strategies that kept sugar lucrative. They orchestrated protective shipping convoys during wartime, and faster mail service for the sugar islands. They took on technological issues; in 1796, for instance, they sent Dr. Bryan Higgins, a chemist, to Jamaica to conduct experiments to improve sugar-refining methods.

THE WEST INDIA LOBBY

The West Indians also threw themselves into politics and established England's most formidable lobby. In the days of rotten boroughs, they invested some of their sugar capital in buying parliamentary seats. In the mid-eighteenth century, four of the Jamaican Beckford brothers sat in Parliament. Of the fifteen members of one of the Society of Planters and Merchants key committees, ten held parliamentary seats. In 1764, fifty or sixty West Indian MPs held the balance of power in the House of Commons. The West Indians constituted a voting bloc large enough to save governments from nonconfidence votes, a service for which governments later repaid them. The West Indians also allied with the landed aristocracy and with the seaport merchant class, likewise dependent on monopolies for their financial lifeblood.

The West Indians infiltrated the House of Lords, parlaying their political support into peerages. One of many sugar-connected nobles was Lord Hawkesbury, later Earl of Liverpool, a West Indian plantation owner, president of the Privy Council for Trade, and a fervent advocate for the West Indian Interest, including the slave trade and slave owners. Like Charles Pinney, West Indians held municipal offices; William Beckford was twice Lord Mayor of London. "Contemporaries laughed at his faulty Latin and loud voice; they were forced to respect his wealth, position and political influence," Eric Williams notes.[304]

The West Indians set new standards for political pressure tactics and may well have created modern-day lobbying. They were organized, focused, capitalized, intermarried and allied to influential landed and mercantile interests. They had well-defined agendas for their propagandists to promote. Even after their defeat on such major issues as slavery and, even more crushingly, free trade, they were enduring. More than a century and a half later, the sugar lobbies in the United Kingdom and the United States are equally notorious for their bulldog tenacity, ingenuity, disproportionate influence and problematic ethics as they confront the issues of health, obesity, fair trade and environmental degradation.

One of the West Indian lobby's legislative victories was the naval rum ration. That half a pint per seaman translated into rivers of rum and established the tradition of naval grog. When critics challenged the relative merits of rum versus brandy, the Society of West Indian Planters and Merchants hired a pamphleteer who produced "An Essay on Spirituous Liquors, With Regard to their Effects on Health, in which the comparative Wholesomeness of rum and Brandy Are particularly considered," which—in three thousand subsidized copies—came down strongly on the side of rum.

SNOW FOR SUGAR AND OTHER VICTORIES

After the Seven Years' War, the West Indians geared up for their most important campaign ever: to persuade the English government to return the prolific sugar island of Guadeloupe to France and to retain instead the giant fur-trading colony of Canada. Guadeloupe would have competed mercilessly with their own eroding sugar operations, though it would have meant cheaper sugar for English consumers. The West Indians did not care about British consumers. They had, in the Earl of Hardwicke's words, "but one point in view, which is how it may affect their particular interest; and they wish all colonies destroyed but that wherein they are particularly interested, in order to raise the market for their own commodities."[305] The West Indian lobbyists fought with all their might to ensure their own interests, and they won. The result was Snow for Sugar, shorthand for the provisions in the 1763 Treaty of Paris that restored Guadeloupe to France while England kept Canada.

The West Indians could not, of course, vanquish all problems or control all governments. Most notably, they could not stop the American Revolution. Although most were inextricably linked to Britain and British interests, they had close commercial relations with the Thirteen Colonies, which supplied much of their slaves' foodstuffs and the lumber they needed to build and repair their houses and sugar mills. West Indians were deeply alarmed at the prospect of war, and many defended the colonists' complaints.

After the American Revolution erupted, the British government had to send emergency food supplies to famished Barbados. The governor of Montserrat reported that "many Negroes have Starved, the same has happn'd in Nevis.... Antigua has lost above a thousand Negroes, Montserrat near twelve Hundred & some Whites—Nevis three or four Hundred, & [St. Kitts] as many from the Want of Provisions."[306] In Jamaica, Barbados and the Leeward Islands, prices of common staples such as rice, Indian corn, flour, lumber, shingles and white oak staves doubled, tripled and quadrupled.

The West Indians, struggling with this crisis of supplies and the debilitated slave labor force, watched as France, the Americans' ally against England, attacked and captured St. Kitts, Montserrat, Nevis, St. Vincent, Grenada, Tobago and Demerara, with Antigua, Barbados and Jamaica next in line for conquest. In England, George III warned that "if we lose our Sugar Islands it will be impossible to raise money to continue the war."[307] A miracle happened in the person of Admiral

George Rodney. In 1782, under his command, the British defeated the French fleet, saving both the sugar islands and the British Empire.

Having failed to prevent the American Revolution, the West Indians scrambled to recoup their losses. Many planters among them were ruined. As production plummeted, the price of sugar skyrocketed. Consumers responded by buying less, though many grocers began to sell it at little more than cost in an effort to keep up their sales of tea; many of their customers preferred to forgo tea rather than drink it unsweetened. Metropolitan refineries began to fail, and by 1781, one-third had closed their doors. Associated businesses were hit just as hard. Half of the potteries that supplied refineries were bankrupted. Coopers, coppersmiths, ironworkers and other artisans and tradesmen were ruined.

The Society of Planters and Merchants retreated to lick their wounds. Then they turned their attention to the possibilities of the loyalist British colonies as markets for their sugar and suppliers for their plantations. But these colonies imported far less than the more densely populated Thirteen Colonies with their voracious appetite for sugar and rum. And though they willingly supplied the West Indians, the British colonies charged double to quadruple more than the American prices thanks to their greater transportation costs and their higher wages.

The American Revolution left the sugar colonies in dire straits. Antigua's plantations were mostly mortgaged to members of the West Indian interest in England. In Jamaica, 324 out of 775 sugar estates that had been operating in 1772 had been sold for debt, or repossessed. Under such financial pressure, smuggling from foreign Caribbean colonies resumed. The West India interest lobbied for legislation to ease the planters' crushing financial problems. In 1787, their efforts resulted in legislation that established much-needed West Indian free ports while preventing competing goods, in particular cheaper East Indian cane sugar and European beet sugar, from entering Britain.

The terrifying news of whites murdered in the Haitian Revolution put a great pall on the abolition movement, which pleased the West Indians. The economic consequences of the revolution had an equally welcome though temporary effect on their sugar interests. Nothing could change the impending decline because, as historian Lowell Ragatz explains, "that grand edifice, the old plantation system in the British West Indies, was tottering from structural weakness." The revolution propped it up and delayed its total collapse for a quarter of a century.[308] Haiti's 792 sugar plantations had been munificent suppliers to France and had supplied 43.3 percent of the European continent's needs. When the revolution abruptly terminated Haiti's huge shipments of sugar, Europeans urgently sought other sources, namely re-exported sugar from England, which had previously supplied only 36.7 percent. Suddenly sugar was in great demand and at high prices.[309]

The planters alone applauded sugar's new high prices. English grocers and refiners complained bitterly, and argued strongly that the privileged position of West Indian sugar should be ended, and East Indian sugar allowed into England on the same terms. The West Indians fiercely defended their right to their monopoly. Increasingly, however, they were battling other interest groups, namely British consumers, the men and women who shaped the market. Many of these were low-wage earners who loved and needed sugar and deeply resented paying artificially high prices they knew could be easily lowered by importing East Indian sugar on equitable terms.

East Indian sugar was easy to champion. Bengali labor was free rather than slave; East Indian plantations required less capitalization than West Indian; East Indian sugar plantations had great potential for expansion whereas the West Indian, eroding and overplanted, did not. The East Indian market for British manufactured goods seemed infinite, the West Indian modest and shrinking. And, the East Indian interests claimed, the great distance between Bengal and Britain would provide a training ground for sailors who, in times of war, could be co-opted into the navy. The West Indian lobby, unable to refute these arguments, struck back hard by invoking law, history and patriotism. Through an unwritten but inviolable compact, the mother country had guaranteed them a monopoly in English markets in return for a monopoly over colonial produce. Favoring (as the West Indians put it) East Indian sugar would ruin the West Indies, the West Indian planters and all their commercial and financial associates in England. It would be like murdering a family member to benefit a foreign newcomer.

The issues raised in the escalating contest between the two competing sugar interests were rooted in Britain's mercantilist system and its imperialist aspirations. They could not be resolved by strictly economic reasoning. The West Indies, having been colonized and governed on mercantilist principles, were creatures of Britain's imperial goals. The nature of their economy, notably their reliance on monocrop sugar, and the prohibition against colonial refining and manufacturing had shaped them as economic dependencies operating in an infrastructural wasteland. Their land was overworked and eroding. Their labor force was wretched and hostile. They (usually) bought British manufactures rather than lower-priced American ones. During the American Revolution, they were inclined to sympathize with the rebels but remained loyal to Britain, sacrificing slaves' lives, their profits and their population's safety to do so. Then, in times of war, Britain's enemies attacked and invaded them.

When they took on the issue of East Indian sugar, the West Indians did not bother to deny that it could be produced and delivered more cheaply. Instead, they asked rhetorically why the interests of a vast consuming public should take precedence over the commercial well-being of their historically entrenched sugar commerce. Had the West Indians not acted as agents of civilization and Christianization to native and African heathens? Britain had treated the sugar colonies as pawns in its empire, the West Indians concluded, and it should be clear to everyone that Britain was in their debt.

The West Indians once again bested their economic rivals through legislation that confirmed an unequal system of duties on sugar. But their victory was incomplete because the immensely complicated sugar duties were fixed rather than calculated on a sliding scale or, as the West Indians wished, ad valorem. The consequence was that when prices were high, the duties were reasonable, but when they fell, the duties could be ruinous. This was what happened in 1803 and 1806, when duties represented 55.7 and 61.7 percent of the wholesale price, and planters suffered terribly.

DEBT, DISEASE AND DEATH

As the Napoleonic war continued, the situation worsened. The West Indians could no longer re-export sugar to the Continent and lost lucrative markets. But American ships, protected by their neutral flag, delivered colonial sugar to those same European markets. West Indian sugar was also burdened by war duties—Pitt raised millions of pounds for the war effort through a rising scale of sugar duties (which doubled in 1805 alone)—and sky-high wartime shipping and insurance charges. By 1806, with the Americans undercutting them at every turn, the West Indians' sympathy for them evaporated in anger. That anger resonated in England, and British ships began to seize American vessels. War between the former colony and mother country threatened and was narrowly averted.

The sugar planters were in crisis. "Bankruptcy is universal," Antigua's governor reported in 1805, "and is not confin'd to the Public Treasury, but extends to the Generality of Individuals resident in the Colony."[310] It got worse: by 1807, Jamaican sugar was sold in England at less than its cost of production. St. Lucia's governor echoed the same sad refrain. "This colony is in a most deplorable situation.... The planters have no Money to purchase nor can they get credit from the Merchants who cannot afford to give any for the Sugars made here as the Duties, Freights & Insurance would absorb the whole at the British market."[311] Planters abandoned their plantations or sold them at whatever price they could get. Slaves wore rags and went hungry. Thousands died.

The sugar colonies now had only three topics of conversation: debt, disease and death. English parliamentary committees investigated and agreed that the situation was dire but disagreed about how to remedy it. Even the West Indians and their lobby offered conflicting advice. British consumers were unsympathetic. "We see West India Merchants still living like princes; but when they come before Parliament they have ... the whining cant of beggars," scoffed abolitionist Macall Medford, author of the pamphlet "Oil without Vinegar, and Dignity without Pride: or, British, American, and West Indian Interests Considered."[312]

In 1808, those whiners won a small and unconscionable victory on behalf of their rum interests. They convinced a parliamentary committee that corn was in short supply and should be reserved for food and not used in distilleries. English corn farmers angrily pointed out that there was no such shortage, and that forbidding distillers to use grain would drastically decrease the demand for corn. The West Indian interest, however, was still strong enough to drown out these legitimate arguments. The prohibition against grain was instituted, forcing distillers to use sugar instead. In 1809, after Martinique fell to the British, the West Indians successfully lobbied for foreign duties to be levied on Martinican sugar. However, their victories over corn and Martinican sugar were minor at a time when only truly drastic changes could have halted the West Indian decline. The War of 1812 made things worse.

A brief recovery followed the collapse of the continental system, Napoleon's attempts to block Britain from trading with the European continent. English sugar exports to European markets soared and demand forced up the price in the home market. But the recovery was short-lived because Europeans, wanting cheaper sugar, turned to new sources: Cuba and Brazil. Cuba and Brazil had deep, fertile soil and were not constrained by mercantilist policies. Per hundredweight, Cuban sugar could be sold at 30 shillings compared to Jamaican at 53 shillings. The West Indies plunged into another period of crisis, exacerbated by English legislation that restricted their trade with the Americans. They had few buyers for their rum and molasses. Rum shipments plunged from nearly two million gallons in 1818 to less than 54,000 in 1820; shipments of molasses plummeted from more than a million gallons to 12,000. Plantations lost so much of their value that lenders no longer accepted them as collateral for desperately needed loans, and the West Indians described their plight as calamitous.

Their lobbyists tried again to pressure the English government to lower duties on sugar. But the times and the politics were changing. The constraints of mercantilism and its concomitant of protectionism were now under serious challenge from economic theories that favored liberalization and free trade. In addition, the relaxation of previous restrictions had removed one of the West Indian sugar lobby's most important arguments, that they deserved preferential treatment to compensate for those restrictions.

West and East Indian sugar interests were now in open conflict. It was futile to deny that East Indian sugar was cheaper and produced by free laborers and that, unlike the West Indies, East Indian sugar plantations cost Britain nothing to protect. Nor could it be denied that, if West Indian shipping provided maritime training to future navy men, the East Indies provided even more. Lastly, the conquest and retention of French and Spanish sugar islands had given just-conquered foreigners the same privileges enjoyed by the once-favored English sugar islands.

The West Indians were now fighting for a dying way of life, and their arguments reflected their desperation and bitterness: that they were British subjects entitled to the rights of British farmers and manufacturers while East Indians were conquered foreigners; and that they had invested nearly a billion pounds sterling in the sugar colonies on the promise of preferential treatment, yet in 1807, the slave trade they depended on had been abolished. Would England not intervene to salvage what remained of their former glory? England would not. The West Indian lobby and the West Indians were fast fading into political oblivion.

On sugar plantations, despair reigned. "The pressure of the times is severe," wrote one colonial official, "the future prospects are gloomy, the days of West Indian prosperity are probably terminated."[313] The final blow, emancipation of the slaves beginning in 1834, would strike "the final, mortal blow at the old plantation system" and, in the form of a slow slide with short-lived reprieves, complete "in spectacular fashion the downfall of the planter class," Ragatz writes.[314]

French Sugar

The French also liked their sugar, though without English passion. Until the Haitian Revolution, her prolific colonies produced enough sugar to sate her sweet tooth. The wealthy liked it refined, the working class were content with clayed and, until the nineteenth century, the rural folk did without. Parisians, however, gobbled it up, anywhere from thirty to fifty pounds per capita every year.[315]

As in England, France's sugar business was a huge employer. In 1791, the Duc de la Rochefoucauld-Liancourt estimated that the livelihoods of 713,333 French families, from which he extrapolated more than three and a half million people, were directly linked to or dependent on the West Indian trade.[316] That trade, much like England's, was governed by strict metropolitan decrees against trading with foreigners. The operation of the sugar colonies also resembled that of the English, including their cruel treatment of sugar slaves and their planters' heavy indebtedness to metropolitan merchants, with slaves the costliest expenditure.

In other ways, French law, policy and practice differed from England's. French civil law prevented foreclosure on plantations, and metropolitan creditors complained that their planter-debtors had no incentive to change their inefficient management habits or to reduce their personal extravagances. Like their English counterparts, French planters and merchants often intermarried and socialized together. But they did not ally to create a powerful lobby and instead treated each other as rivals. For these reasons and because of a weaker marine presence, France's sugar business was differently organized. It also inspired widespread and ingenious schemes designed to bypass government control.

One elaborate colonial scheme involved Martinican sugar. Martinican planters would borrow groups of their neighbors' slaves and declare them, at the Bureau des Domaines, as merchandise bound for St. Domingue. Afterward, the slaves returned to their plantations. Meanwhile, in dead of night, ships loaded with sugar would sail to the Dutch colony of St. Eustatius, where it would be exchanged for the same number of slaves, who were then sold away to St. Domingue. This subterfuge was so successful that it sustained a robust and secret trade in both sugar and slaves with a foreign colony.

Another strategy was to mislabel barrels filled with clayed sugar as "syrup" or "tafia" (a cheap rum), which were then exported to the Thirteen Colonies. This "illegal commerce is conducted openly,"

France's consul in Boston reported.[317] Simpler scams to avoid paying intermediaries and commissions involved selling sugar directly to the captains of foreign "seekers" or, more problematically, to foreign smugglers. The failure of French plantations to make large profits encouraged smuggling and other illegal schemes. Based on pre-revolutionary sugar sales, plantation expenses and losses with capital investment and annual profit, historian Robert Stein calculates at best a 5 to 6 percent return on investment. A 1787 committee studying Martinican planters' finances found that all plantations returned a net profit of about 2 percent. Although French sugar was much cheaper to produce, its rates of return were much lower than in England, where the price of sugar was kept artificially high.

The French government and importers operated on the principle that local interests were paramount and must be protected. This precluded the establishment of a national French sugar business, but it stimulated small local industries, especially in the three major sugar ports: Nantes, Bordeaux and Marseille. In the eighteenth century, three-quarters of France's sugar imports entered through them.

In Nantes, the sugar and slave trades were closely linked; the city's merchants sold slaves in return for tropical produce. This trade in slaves was the only way Nantes could compete with Bordeaux, which exported a vast array of European goods to the sugar colonies. By the advent of the French Revolution, more than one-third of the city's sugar imports represented payment for slaves. In Nantes, "sugar merely followed the paths charted by the slavers."[318]

Sixty to 70 percent of Nantes' sugar imports were muscovado, ideal for refiners and for re-export to Spain, Portugal, Holland and Germany. Bordeaux imported more clayed sugar and Marseille imported almost nothing else; both re-exported large quantities, because clayed sugar needed no refining and was therefore in great demand. These three ports and others involved in the sugar trade operated as bitter rivals. The notion of a national sugar business did not exist.

Although little sugar was refined in France, refining was "at the gastronomic heart of the French sugar business."[319] Refining was complicated and dangerous. The sugar was prone to bursting into flames in the intense heat of the boiling and drying operations. The refining process polluted the air, and nobody wanted to live near a refinery. Early in the eighteenth century, when refiners substituted ox blood for eggs as a cleansing agent, refineries also polluted the ground and emitted an intolerable stench.

A few refineries produced small quantities of *sucre royal*, considered the most exquisite sugar and correspondingly expensive. Its refiners enthused that it was "very pure and marvellously transparent … even, fine, dry, brilliant, and easy to break."[320] Eggs rather than ox blood cleansed these heavenly granules, which were usually made from top-quality clayed sugar. A slightly less perfect but still expensive version was sold as *demi-royal*. Various other qualities of sugar were produced for the wider poorer market.

In the national spirit of internecine commercial rivalry, French refineries competed with each other rather than trying to expand their businesses by finding new export markets. They all sold only to the Paris market and tried to sabotage each other. The consequence was that, despite having the world's greatest sugarcane colonies, the French refining business was disappointingly limited.

NAPOLEONIC BEET

The early years of the French Revolution seemed to have little effect on sugar production. But between the eruption of the Haitian Revolution and Napoleon's defeat at Waterloo, the sugar business changed fundamentally. France was particularly hard hit. After France's humiliating naval defeat at the Battle of Trafalgar in 1805, Napoleon declared economic war on British commerce (and hence British power) by blocking ships from Britain and her colonies from trading through European ports.

Britain retaliated with a counterblockade, and continental Europe suffered a punishing shortage of colonial produce. Cane sugar began to disappear from grocery stores. Napoleon, justifiably worried about the popular fury that sugar rationing or, worse, no sugar at all would provoke, gambled on replacing cane with French-grown sugar beet, even though the process of extracting sugar from beets was still in the experimental stages.

Early-seventeenth-century French agronomist Olivier de Serres had observed that "the beet root when boiled yields a juice similar to syrup of sugar,"[321] and a century later, German chemist Andreas Sigismund Marggraf produced sugar crystals indistinguishable from cane sugar crystals by slicing, drying and pulverizing eight ounces of beets, drenching them in alcohol, heating them to boiling point, filtering them into a container then waiting weeks for sugar crystals to form. But it was Marggraf's French expatriate student, Franz Carl Achard, who refined his mentor's techniques so that large amounts of beets could be processed into sugar.

Achard's work was advanced enough to frighten English cane-sugar interests, who allegedly offered him enormous sums to abandon it, while Frederick the Great and his successor, Frederick William III, encouraged Achard with valuable land grants and highly paid positions. Napoleon offered bounties and urged Frenchmen to rise to the challenge.

Industrialist Benjamin Delessert responded and opened a small processing factory in Passy. Napoleon was so impressed with the quality of the beet sugar the factory produced that he presented Delessert with his own Legion of Honor sash. The next day Napoleon declared that England would have to throw its sugarcane into the Thames because sugar beet would now sweeten Europe.

To make good his word, Napoleon established six experimental sugar-beet stations and scholarships to send one hundred science and medical students to study there. Through the Ministry of the Interior, he set aside nearly eighty thousand acres to plant sugar beets, required farmers to grow them and financed sugar-beet factories, allocating one million francs to his sugar-beet projects. His strategy worked. By 1812, forty factories refined 3.3 million pounds of sugar from 98,813 tons of beets grown on 16,758 acres.[322] Germany, Russia and other European countries also developed significant sugar-beet industries.

The peace that followed Napoleon's downfall in 1815 led to an influx of cane sugar onto European markets and ruined the fledgling industry. Its low-quality beet and imperfect processing techniques could not compete with cane and, for a time, only one European factory, in Arras, France, survived. But the prewar status quo of the cane-sugar industry was not reestablished. At the Congress of Vienna, Britain, which had abolished its slave trade in 1807, pressured France and its allies to agree to do so as well, though illegal slaving would continue for decades. Another major change was that sugar production in the newly independent nation of Haiti plunged from 200 million pounds a year to almost nothing, and there were no new French sugar colonies to replace it. Millions of pounds of sugar now came from Martinique, Guadeloupe and Réunion, in Africa, and over time, from European sugar-beet sources. Cane remained dominant, although beet still had its believers and would later resurge in popularity.

EMBITTERING AFRICA

Nowhere in the world did the sugar business have a more destructive effect than in Africa, the third leg of the triangular trade. European traders dealt mostly with African merchants or nobles to obtain slaves. The consequences were horrific and, in an era when tribes organized the continent's people and pan-Africanism did not yet exist, set off tribal wars. Dahomeyan kings captured their northern neighbors with European weapons and sold them. African traders invented reasons to destroy villages and enslave their inhabitants. To fill their quotas for slaves, raiders attacked other tribes and took captives. Other Africans were sold for debt, or were already enslaved.

The slave coffles of shackled men and women shuffling from interior villages to coastal barracoons marked the consciousness of everyone who witnessed them. These coffles often traveled five hundred miles, passing through village after village, their misery on public display. Until they were transported, the prisoners were held in centrally located barracoons in sight or at least hearing of the local townspeople. Whydah had six barracoons near the center of town, and in Cape Coast, the wailing, shrieking drone from the Castle's dungeon was audible from a distance. Africans did not know exactly what lay in store for the slaves, but everything suggested that it must be terrible.

Captive Africans chained and force-marched in coffles was a dreaded but common sight. The illustrator, Verney Lovett Cameron, served in the British navy, suppressing the East African slave trade.

Six million Africans went to the sugar colonies, the majority males in their prime, and in such numbers that the West African population remained static, unable to grow. Agricultural communities were shattered and terrified by raids and kidnapping. Leaders, husbands and sometimes wives and children were snatched away, leaving social confusion or chaos in their stead.

As in Europe and the sugar colonies, the slave trade affected Africa economically. It stimulated the need for a common currency, with cowries and iron bars becoming standard. Slave ports developed services to facilitate the slave trade, which employed many people as porters, guards and canoemen. Farmers were encouraged to grow the foodstuffs needed to provision the barracoons and slave ships: rice, yams, manioc and maize.

At the same time, the slave trade's stranglehold monopoly over sub-Saharan external commerce stifled Africa's economic development. Slaves were more profitable than any other commodity. Even palm oil at its highest price could not compete with slaves. For centuries, farming lost out to raiding, and the European goods traded for slaves dampened interest in African goods, stymieing any infrastructural or institutional developments that might otherwise have occurred. "All the slave trade did was to create social and political structures hostile to peaceful economic development," writes historian Joseph E. Inikori.[323] The consequence was that manufacturing and agriculture failed to develop as they surely would have.

Some of the most popular European goods—brandy, rum, tobacco and guns—were intrinsically harmful. The perils of spirits and tobacco are self-evident. Guns, the backbone of English trade to West Africa in the eighteenth century, were in such demand—in January 1772, the firm of Farmer and Galton received orders for more than 15,900—that Birmingham gun manufacturers struggled to fill orders. This led to shoddy workmanship, and contemporaries worried that weapons would explode the first time they were fired. Their most dangerous feature was that they were used primarily in slave raids.

Sugar stirred the universe and fueled the engines of empire. The profits were huge but the costs were greater. The African continent lost its way along the shackled path toward the future. African expatriates, enslaved or free, confronted a lopsided new world poisoned by the racism at the core of sugar slavery. Their resistance to that world and to that racism was a relentless battle that would culminate, at the dawn of the nineteenth century, with the armed revolution that established the world's first black republic.

Part 3

Abolition Through Resistance and Parliament

Chapter 6

Racism, Resistance, Rebellion and Revolution

Sugar Spawns Racism

Sugar slavery's most insidious creation was the racialism that justified enslaving Africans and forcing them into the cane fields. (As Eric Williams writes: "Slavery was not born of racism; rather, racism was the consequence of slavery. Its origin can be expressed in [the] words: in the Caribbean, Sugar; on the Mainland, Tobacco and Cotton.")[324] After it became evident that slaves would replace and not merely supplement European indentured labor, race became an essential reference point for slaveholders and everyone else involved in sugar production, from Creole overseers to European sugar refiners. It explained away the grotesque system that slavery clearly was and eased uneasy consciences.

Over time, whites elaborated racist ideology, borrowing elements of Christianity and reinforcing this mélange with anecdotal testimony. Slavery had been designed primarily for field labor, but the logic of racism expanded it into all spheres of work, including the domestic.[325] What had begun as a narrow economic system had evolved into Creole sugar society's guiding, organizing principle.

Whites had urgent practical reasons for inventing elaborate racial distinctions. They were surrounded and outnumbered by men and women they oppressed, and they needed social arrangements and power structures that would keep them safe from their victims. They needed mechanisms to divide and control the always-mutinous slaves for whom they felt a "corporal dread." And they needed to address the phenomenon of the growing number of mixed-race offspring.

In the sugar world, the existence of mixed-race people had to be redefined. Chapter 4 listed some of the names given to them. These pseudo-scientific attempts at rigorous classification, travesties of Linnaeus's careful work in the eighteenth century, lent an air of credibility to notions of race. Labeling them mulatto, a disdainful analogy to the sterile offspring of horse and donkey, implied that Mother Nature prohibited the "unnatural" offspring of white and black from reproducing. Matthew Lewis discovered from looking around him in Jamaica that they could, indeed, reproduce, but he still believed that mulattoes were "almost universally weak and effeminate persons, and thus their children are very difficult to rear."[326]

This carefully enunciated racism coexisted with its polarity of legal freedom. Manumission was possible. The children born to free women of any color, from black to musteephino, were born free. When the human heart beat harder than the whip, a white father could free his lighter-skinned child and perhaps her mother. He could also manumit his old nurse, a loyal slave or a decrepit one.

Freed or freemen naturally sought the same economic and social advantages they saw the whites enjoy. Seeing that slaveholding was the key, many of those prosperous enough became slave-owning planters. They bought their own relatives and freed them, but they also bought slaves to work their lands, and treated them as cruelly as whites did. Often the lighter-skinned internalized the colorism inherent in racial classifications and held themselves to be superior to the darker skinned. In Haiti, mulattoes recast this and decided that they were superior to everybody else, including whites. There, the caste system "played a major part in shaping the course of the revolutionary movement that eventually destroyed the colonial society, and also in determining post-revolutionary alignments," historian Elsa Goveia writes.[327]

Brazil's more porous caste system underscored the absurdity of racial classification. For example, mulattoes could obtain legal documents identifying them as whites and, thus armed, work in white-only professions. Sugar planter Henry Koster was told that a certain official was no longer a mulatto; "he was, but is not now." The man had had to cease being a mulatto because mulattoes were ineligible for the position he wanted and now held.[328] "In the sugar islands, it was possible to pass

Le Masurier, A Mulatto Woman with Her White Daughter Visited by Negro Women in Their House in Martinique, 1775.

The Barbadoes Mulatto Girl *and* The West India Washer Woman *by Agostino Brunias. Brunias, who sired a family with a free woman of color, perpetrated the image of mulattos as desirable, beautiful and seductive. The mulatto woman is stylishly dressed, bejewelled and self-confident as she bargains with black higglers. The mulatto washer woman is lovely, unself-conscious in her nakedness. In some of his images, Brunias painted himself peeking out at naked mulatto women.*

from black to white in three generations," historian Richard S. Dunn writes. In North America, by contrast, "black blood was like original sin and stained a man and his heirs for ever."[329]

BLACK CODES, SLAVE LAWS

As racial slavery evolved, colonial and metropolitan administrators wrestled the intricacies of its operation into legal texts known as Black Codes. They also appointed officials to oversee these laws. English colonies were the exception, having no code and usually no slave protector. Instead, each colony had its own slave code, often modeled on that promulgated in 1661 in Barbados. Jamaica's 1664 law was almost verbatim, Antigua's in 1702 was very similar. The British Amelioration Laws of the late eighteenth and early nineteenth centuries, however, were intended to reverse the low birth and high child mortality rates by improving slaves' conditions in light of impending abolition.

Black Codes and slave laws varied little from colony to colony. Their underlying premise was that "Negroes were Property, and a species of Property that needed a rigorous and vigilant Regulation."[330] Black Codes "legitimised a state of war between blacks and whites, sanctioned rigid segregation, and institutionalised an early warning system against slave revolt."[331] They prescribed such punishments as branding; whipping while tied up by the hands in the mill house, with pepper and salt afterward rubbed into the raw wounds; nose slitting; amputation of an arm or a leg; and "gelding," or amputating genitals. Punishment for striking a white or rebelling was savage and lethal, for example "burning them by nailing them down on the ground with crooked sticks on every limb and then applying the Fire by degrees from the feet and hands, burning them gradually up to the head, whereby their pains are extravagant." Slave codes specified how the punished-to-death slave's owner could claim compensation for loss of his property.

Black Codes criminalized almost every slave misdeed. Murdering and assaulting whites headed the many capital offenses, which included killing another slave. Running away, a much more common crime, was considered a theft, because the slave stole himself from his owner. Black Codes also criminalized harboring or aiding runaways and specified rewards for capturing them or, after a certain time elapsed, killing them. As towns developed, the laws specified that townsfolk must not employ runaways, as so many did.

Black Codes dealt harshly with marronage, running away to live in settlements inhabited by fugitive slaves who afterward raided plantations and, by their very presence, inspired other slaves to emulate them. Because they had no choice, most colonies acknowledged and accepted a few Maroon settlements. But laws preventing marronage were draconian. Punishments included branding with a fleur-de-lys, hacking off ears, hamstringing or, if the runaway were armed, execution. Freedmen helping such runaways could be sold back into slavery. France's Black Code of 1685 also banned slave assemblies; even celebrants at weddings or funerals might use the occasion to plot.

The Black Codes sketched out slave working conditions, specifying hours of work, food allowances and the nature and extent of punishments. Their object was twofold: to keep slaves alive, and to rein in the cruelest masters. The reality was that most laws were practiced in the breach, and few of the whites who starved, abused, tortured and overworked their slaves were charged. When they were, only a handful were convicted.

By the late eighteenth century, with revolutionary sentiments inflaming public opinion, France's Black Codes were modified to reflect the growing metropolitan concern over slave abuse. Against planters' protests, whippings were limited to twenty-nine lashes. The 1789 Black Code of Trinidad, then under Spanish control, was praised for its leniency: lashes were restricted to twenty-five and could not draw blood; slaveholders could not unburden themselves of old or sick slaves by manumitting them; they were to assign to female slaves jobs suitable for females; and any slaveholder who violated these provisions could be heavily fined. Soon after, however, Trinidad came under the control of the British, who imposed severe new slave laws that even forbade slaves to free themselves by self-purchase.

Cuba's Black Codes, on the other hand, provided for self-purchase—*coartació*—either outright or in installments. A slave valued at $600 who could afford to pay his master only $25 would own one-twenty-fourth of himself. A slave thus manumitted, even partially, was called a *coartado*. Many slaves bought all but a small percentage of themselves even when they had the money to complete the transaction. Naturalist and observer Alexander von Humboldt believed they did this so that in times of trouble, they could rely on their (fractional) owner for counsel, influence and protection.[332]

Many sugar colonies enacted Deficiency Laws intended to rectify the always terrifying imbalance between the black and white populations. Deficiency Laws required employers to hire one white employee for every twenty to thirty slaves.[333] In white-deficient colonies like Jamaica, most planters and pen owners paid fines instead of complying, and the laws became cynical sources of government revenue. "Deficiency men" were easier to find in Barbados, with its larger white population descended from indentured laborers.

Black Codes set out minimum requirements for slave food, provision grounds and the free time to cultivate them, clothing and blankets, the establishment of slave "hospitals," and record keeping of slave births, deaths, marriages and punishments. In Barbados as elsewhere, raping a slave was not a crime, and murdering one carried only a £15 fine. The Black Code of Catholic countries charged masters with their slaves' religious instruction, arranging for their baptisms and providing slave burial grounds in restricted areas of Catholic cemeteries. The laws standardized holidays, of paramount concern to slaves. An Antiguan law stated that slaves had committed "great Disorders ... and Murders ... because their Masters have not allowed them the same Number of Days for their Recreation at Xmas, as several of their Neighbours have done."[334] Catholic slave societies permitted more holidays; Henry Koster counted thirty-five in Brazil.

The Amelioration Laws applied to all British colonies and addressed the anticipated consequences of abolishing the slave trade. Goveia singles out the provision ordering a coroner's inquest to examine the corpses of slaves who had died suddenly as "probably ... the single greatest modification of enacted law that the new act introduced."[335] Another seldom-to-be-implemented provision decreed that anyone convicted of crimes against slaves should be punished as if their victims had been white.

Amelioration Laws tackled the issue of sugar slaves' failure to reproduce themselves in sufficient numbers, increasingly urgent in light of the impending abolition of the slave trade, whereupon the supply of Africans would dry up. Slave women, who dominated the cane fields, were to be better treated. Pregnant women had to be fed better and could no longer be whipped, though they could be imprisoned. They were also exempted from what abolitionists called "extreme and murderous agricultural labour,"[336] and were to be rewarded with small sums of money for each child born. Slave mothers of six children, the youngest seven years old, were excused from heavy (but not light) labor. The Amelioration Laws also freed slaves from the intolerable burden of gathering fodder after they had finished their field work.

In the last decades of slavery, the Amelioration Laws constituted the only official reforms in how slaves were treated. Their unenforceability, however, emasculated them. Until well into the nineteenth century, whites refused to act on complaints from non-whites, slave or free, and usually refused to testify against other whites. Instead of enforcing these "specious" new laws, they fought them. They acknowledged their duties toward slaves, but were ineffective, often hostile slave "guardians" who denied that slaves had any rights.

The case of Nevis planter Edward Huggins, charged with cruelty and murder, is an extreme example. When the slaves on the sugar plantation he had recently bought from John Pinney went on strike against his cruel treatment, Huggins marched them into town and had them publicly and savagely whipped. One slave died. In the subsequent trial, Huggins was acquitted by a jury of planters that included three of his sons. Neighboring planters applauded the acquittal as a victory against the slaves' intolerable insolence. Despite such travesties of justice, the West Indians bitterly resented their negative image in England and "the Charges of Cruelty and Oppression with which the West India Colonies have been so unjustly loaded."[337]

SLAVE RESISTANCE

Sugar slaves worked under threat of the lash and, at every turn in their daily lives, alternated between accommodation and resistance. Slave resistance was such a powerful dynamic that it is the never-resolved subtext of all contemporary literature, documents and Black Codes. A survey of the most common kinds of slave resistance is an ironic commentary on slavery as a labor system.

Among Africans, suicide was often the first line of defense and could be an act of self-affirmation as much as of self-destruction. Their misery would end and their spirits return home to Africa. The literature of slavery is replete with examples. The father of British abolitionist Ignatius Sancho drowned himself during the Middle Passage. In Martinique, two Africans hanged themselves, making a liar of Pierre Dessalles, who insisted that "nobody had done anything to them; they were having a perfectly gay and amiable time."[338] Slaves hanged, drowned and starved themselves, threw themselves into vats of boiling sugar, took poison or found other ways to kill themselves. "The blacks, an impossible race, prefer death to slavery," a slave trader concluded.[339]

Slaves were expensive, and suicides enraged their masters, who even accused sick slaves of willfully dying. Although illness, malnutrition, unsanitary conditions, poor medical care, overwork and depression caused most slave deaths, the absence of the will to live contributed as well. "Twelve have died since January, and several others are threatening to die," Dessalles complained. He called the slave Toussaint a "scoundrel" who, "in order to get out of work and to die, keeps up a stomach ailment that puts him into a horrible state.... These are things that the abolitionists would not understand. They would not fail to say that the despair at being a slave drove this negro to destroy himself. Laziness and dread of work, these are the motives that cause him to let himself die." When Toussaint died a month later, Dessalles exploded. "The criminal! He is the fourth member of his family to do this to his owner!"[340]

The deathly ill Toussaint was not a malingerer but droves of other slaves were. "The hospital has been crowded, since my arrival, with patients who have nothing the matter with them," Matthew Lewis wrote. Only four were genuinely ill. The others, with "a lilly pain here, Massa," or "a bad pain me know nowhere, Massa," passed the day chatting with their fellow fakers.[341] On a typical day, out of forty-five field slaves—one-fifth of the total—claiming to be ill, Lewis believed only seven or eight. On Santana plantation in Bahia, Brazil, a 1752 report noted that at any given time, fifty to sixty of 182 slaves claimed to be ailing. "The patience of Job is inadequate to suffer them in their sickness, which usually amounts to little more than nothing," the administrator complained.[342] Pierre Dessalles always had thirty to forty field hands in his slave hospital.

Faking insanity was a popular ploy because lunatics could not work. Self-mutilation was also common; a Barbadian cooper, for instance, protested an unreasonable order by chopping off his own hand. As Amelioration Laws modified the Black Codes, their pregnancy-relief provisions inspired many women to feign pregnancy. For fifteen consecutive, childless months, Pierre Dessalles' slave Zabeth insisted that her pregnancy prevented her from working.

Resistance continued into the fields. Slaves asked for frequent breaks to "go a bush," their toilet, complained of menstrual problems, limped and slacked off. They broke their hoes. They planted too many or too few cane tops in each hole. They "misunderstood" instructions. They included rat-gnawed cane in the loads destined for the mill, knowing that one "single damaged piece is sufficient to produce acidity enough to spoil the whole sugar."[343] They decided, all together, to stop working. This happened to Matthew Lewis, whose slave women "one and all, refused to carry away the trash (which is one of the easiest tasks that can be set) … in consequence, the mill was obliged to be stopped." Lewis reasoned, pleaded and finally threatened to sell off the most recalcitrant slaves; all in vain. The next morning, the mill remained closed, "no liquor in the boiling-house, and no work done."[344] Managers complained that such defiant women were a "great discouragement to the industrious." They were also nearly impossible to sell and so, until they submitted and returned to the fields, these "dreadful idlers" served time in the stocks or were punished in various other ways.[345]

Insolence was a favorite form of passive-aggression, and planters in all the sugar colonies reported that women excelled at it. They sang satirical songs rich with double-entendre, and they cursed and defied their masters. After a failed slave rebellion in Antigua, an observer noted that "by their Insolent behavior and Expressions," the women "had the utter Extirpation of the White as much at heart, as the Men, and would undoubtedly have done as much Mischief by Butchering all the Women and children."[346] Some slave women did kill their masters' children. In 1774, a young Barbadian slave admitted poisoning several white infants and, at her trial, explained that she detested babysitting. Antiguan slave Gemima was burned to death for attacking a white baby.

Domestic slaves also resisted. "They mislay, & break your furniture," reported an official in St. Vincent, "throw spoons and knives into the dust pan, —or out of the windows … if a lady's richest piece of dress were in the way, they wd. rub the table with it."[347] In 1796, in Barbados, plantation manager Sampson Wood described the two mulatto daughters of retired domestic Old Doll. Dolly and Jenny were "young, strong, healthy, and have never done anything." Never, Dolly declared, had she "swept out a chamber or carried a pail of water to wash … [and] would rather starve with hunger than grind herself a pint of corn."[348] Wood longed to force her into the cane fields to break her spirit. Instead, Dolly persuaded her employers to manumit her. Other domestics resisted more subtly. Seamstresses sewed crooked seams. Laundresses ripped a low-ranked white's precious clothing. Cooks poisoned. Maids stole.

Field slaves resisted in other ways. They laid down their tools and refused to work until a specific grievance had been addressed: when their masters' shortchanged them on their annual clothing allocations or their holidays or to protest a cruel new master or overseer. In 1744, on an absentee-owned plantation in St. Domingue, sixty-six slaves struck against a cruel overseer who retaliated by knifing a pregnant striker to death. Two months later, her companions killed him. Slaves on the Codrington estate in Barbados left the fields and lodged a complaint against their brutal overseer, Richard Downes, "a man of as hasty and passionate a temper as it is possible to conceive."[349] Soon after, their master fired Downes and the slaves returned to work. In Martinique, Dessalles also opted to fire a hated overseer rather than confront the fury of his slaves.

Slaves resisted by assuming a persona known as Quashee (for males) or Quasheba (for females), whose earnest, evasive, childlike, capricious and lazy bumbling concealed a crafty, confident, contemptuous and revengeful core. Cane fields full of Quashees and Quashebas confounded white slaveholders and their visitors. Maria Nugent thought she understood the fun-loving "blackies" until "a horrid looking black man" who had previously acted "very humble" cast aside his Quashee persona, grinned and gave her "a fierce look" that, she wrote, "struck me with a terror I could not shake off."[350] In Grenada, where they were as elsewhere "the most numerous and effective part of the field gangs of the estate," women or Quashebas were also "the most turbulent … of the slaves," impossible to control except by flogging.[351]

Slaves scratched their heads in mock bewilderment as whites repeated instructions. "The more you try to explain a matter that is disagreeable to him, the more incapable he appears of comprehension; or if he finds this plan ineffectual, he endeavours to render the matter ridiculous; and his talent at rendering ridicule sarcastic is really surprising," one witness recalled.[352] Henry Koster's slaves never answered directly, but only slowly released information in response to "four or five questions put in various ways."[353] These same slaves were astute students of character, identifying weaknesses they then used to outwit their white adversaries.

Lewis, who prided himself on his benevolence, discovered at 3 A.M., after his pen keeper allowed the livestock to escape into the cane fields and trample them, that:

Not a single watchman at his post; the watch-fires had all been suffered to expire; not a single domestic was to be found, nor a horse to be procured; even the little servant boys, whom the trustee had locked up in his own house, and had left fast asleep when he went to bed, had got up again, and made their escape to pass the night in play and rioting; and although they were perfectly aware of the detriment which the cattle were doing to my interests, not a negro could be

prevailed upon to rouse himself and drive them out … one of my best
cane-pieces was trampled to pieces, and the produce of this year's crop
considerably diminished!—And so much for negro gratitude.[354]

Slaves also stole as much and as often as they could, to the point
where thefts were a significant drain on a plantation's finances. They
stole as a form of not-so-passive aggression and because theft was often
their sole source of obtaining things. A slave caught with a lump of
sugar reproached his angry master: "Shall Buckra [white] man, who do
nothing, eat all; and poor Negro man, who do all dem tings, starve?"[355]

Many slave higglers stocked purloined goods, although colonial laws
forbade people to buy anything from slaves that was likely stolen from
their owners—"sugar, cotton, rum, syrup, molasses, wine, or other strong
liquor, and also plate, wearing apparel, household goods, horses, horned
and other cattle (excepting goats and hogs), building timber, cobbles and
other boats."[356] Antigua's 1794 Act for More Effectually Preventing the
Purchase of Stolen Iron, Copper, Lead and Brass in This Island" was an
expression of slaveholders' frustration but did not stop higglers from
selling "Iron Bolts from Mills and Carts … Pieces of Lead Copper and
Brass from Sugar Works and Plantation Utensils,"[357] even though these
items were essential to their owner's sugar operation. Higglers risked
being attacked in the woods or on the roads by other slaves, brigand
runaways or by poor white competitors on their trips into town to sell
their goods.

Thieving was not only an act of resistance. Some masters neglected
to feed their slaves, who then stole to survive. Those who lacked access
to the master's wares stole from each other or raided other slaves' provision grounds. Overseer Thomas Thistlewood continually requested his
neighbors to keep their slaves away from his slaves' provision grounds.

On some plantations, stealing undermined slave society. Slaves'
requests for their white masters to intervene confirmed white domi-
nance and vindicated whites' belief in their superior morality. Slaves'
hostility to losing their hard-earned property, especially food from their
provision grounds, often pushed them to turn away or even turn in
raiding Maroons they otherwise admired.

Livestock was a prime target for slave resistance. "My hogs get lamed and cut, almost every day, which is very surprising who does it, and where," Thistlewood noted. "Within this month past, have lost as follows: A young boar gone (never learnt how) ... A young barrow, his back broke and killed (can't tell how) ... A fine ewe, fit to lamb, found dead in a rock-hole ... [the cow] Rachael's young calf ... and young steer."[358] Thistlewood's horse, Mackey, died after his belly was slashed so deeply that his guts hung out. Countless animals suffered as slaves sought to damage their master's property. A Haitian slave justified his cruelty to a mule, saying, "When I do not work, I am beaten, when he does not work, I beat him—he is my Negro."[359]

Slaves resisted in so many ways that slaveholders saw resistance everywhere and accused the women of employing "gynecological resistance" in the form of abortion and infanticide. A few women did resort to infanticide to rescue an infant from slavery and to deprive their masters of a new slave. Barbadian slave Mary Thomas, assisted by her mother and sister, apparently killed her newborn baby out of spite because his father, the plantation's white bookkeeper, "did not consider her his favourite."[360]

The evidence suggests, however, that field slaves followed dangerous neonatal traditions that inadvertently contributed to the high mortality rate. The grandees (slave midwives or babysitters) gave babies "oils and other pernicious drugs," kept their navels wet, did not change their clothes and, for the first nine days, scarcely fed them. "Till nine days over, me no hope for them," a midwife told Matthew Lewis.[361] Survivors faced an uphill fight against malnutrition, tetanus, fever, worms and other debilitating conditions. So many died before the age of five years that there was a natural decrease in the slave population. In Trinidad, for instance, two out of three slave girls died before reaching sexual maturity.[362]

Until the advent of the movement to abolish the slave trade, many planters had welcomed child mortality. John Terry, a Grenadian overseer, testified that his employers felt that "suckling children should die for they lost a great deal of the mother's work during the infancy of the child."[363] When the discontinuation of the slave trade loomed, planters who had previously imported Africans suddenly focused on slave women's fecundity. Usually they attributed the lack of it to willful defiance.

Murder was an extreme form of slave resistance. Before he fell in love with Phibbah, Thistlewood whipped her as an accomplice in a plot to kill him. Ruth Armstrong, a white woman, and her three children were burned to death after three slaves set their house on fire. Barbadian slaves killed an overseer who failed to give the field gangs any food. In 1714, in Antigua, slaves Richard and Baptist killed a white man. Slave Mingo was executed for "almost strangling" his master. Slaves stabbed, poisoned, strangled and otherwise assaulted whites; their intent was murderous and sometimes they succeeded.

Arson was another fearsome weapon. The female slave Omer was executed for "Willingfully setting fire to a dwelling House." Slaves set cane fields afire when they were supposed to be burning *bagasse* and preparing for a new crop. Frequently, before running away, slaves would burn down the Great House, outbuildings and fields.

After theft, running away was the most common form of resistance. Sometimes slaves just wanted a break and later returned to the plantation. Many fled to be with spouses or family on other plantations. Amelia, who ran away in 1829, was "harboured by her father or his connections. This man has a sister or some family connection near Canewood-Moore estate, and no doubt his daughter meets with a welcome reception there," her owner wrote in an advertisement.[364] Polly Grace, who fled in 1831 with her three children, was likely with her sister or her husband. Because they could not stamp out running away, slaveholders devised a face-saving system whereby a repentant runaway could implore a neighboring planter or a kindly family member to intercede on her behalf with her owner; she could then return home with minimal or no punishment.

Many slaves were chronic runaways. The Barbadian Codrington estate's Quashebah, a field hand, ran away five times in nine years. In Jamaica, African slave Sally, whom overseer Thistlewood repeatedly had sex with, ran away two or three times every year for a few days. Sometimes she returned voluntarily, sometimes a slave catcher returned her.

Thistlewood barely survived his attempt to recapture an African runaway, Congo Sam, who slashed at him repeatedly with his knife. As Thistlewood defended himself Congo Sam exclaimed "in the Negro manner, 'I will kill you, I will kill you now,' &c." Terrified, Thistlewood shouted, "Murder, and help for God's sake." Slaves Bella and Abigail appeared, but after Congo Sam spoke to them in their native language they refused to help, and Thistlewood "was much afraid of them." He lunged, grabbed Congo Sam's knife and wrestled him into the river. Five black men and three black women crossing over the bridge would not stop, "one saying he was sick, the others that they were in a hurry." At last two white men happened by. With their assistance, Thistlewood captured Congo Sam and sent him home in irons.[365]

Incorrigible runaways were often sold away from the colony, a heart-breaking fate for those who had fled to be with their loved ones. Others, like Antigua's Judea, had one leg amputated. Many runaways were put in iron collars and chains. The runaways deprived their owner of their labor, disturbed the equilibrium of the slave workforce and became a living symbol of resistance. Other slaves fed and hid them under their master's nose, further undermining his authority. Some runaways survived by raiding plantations, including provision grounds. Others became highway robbers, preying on travelers, including market-bound higglers. Some whites flouted the law and hired them. Planters desperate to rid their cane fields of rats hired itinerant black rat catchers without asking awkward questions, and a runaway rat catcher who could trap sixty or a hundred rats each week was quite safe. In the towns, so was a good seamstress.

Even in hopeless slavery some slaves found hope, and set out to escape to freedom. To many seventeenth-century slaves, freedom was in Puerto Rico. In 1664, after four runaways arrived there, the governor decreed that "it does not seem proper that the King should reduce to slavery those who sought his protection" and the Council of the Indies agreed. Hearing about this, so many runaways from the Leeward Islands made it to Puerto Rico that by 1714 "they were organized as a separate settlement in the neighbourhood of San Juan." Jamaican slaves ran away to Cuba, sometimes paddling there in stolen canoes. Slaves from Dutch

Guiana fled to Spanish Guiana. Diplomatic tensions between Spain and the other slave metropolises intensified. The Spanish did not relent, and no fugitives were returned.

In 1772, slaves were overjoyed by the news of Lord Mansfield's judgment in favor of James Somerset, a Jamaican slave whose master, Charles Steuart, had taken him to England. Two years later, Somerset "departed and refused to serve." Steuart, egged on by England's pro-slavery interests, had him recaptured, held on a ship bound for the West Indies and brought before a court on a writ of habeas corpus. In the ensuing court case, Lord Mansfield ruled that "the state of slavery … is so odious, that nothing can be suffered to support it, but positive law. Whatever inconveniences, therefore, may follow from a decision, I cannot say this case is allowed or approved by the law of England and therefore the black must be discharged."[366] Somerset walked away a free man.

Other slaves, determined to get to England, discovered that if they could escape to a harbor they could enlist on a ship. During the American Revolutionary War, hundreds signed on to English ships in a bid for freedom. As well as young males, enslaved women, children and grandparents fled to the British side. Many died of disease, and those who reached England were appallingly treated there. But the very fact that they had run away gave enormous hope to the family and friends they were forced to leave behind and who would likely never hear from them again.

MARRONAGE

Marronage, running away and staying away permanently in Maroon communities, added another dimension to slave resistance. Maroons, whose name likely derived from the Spanish *cimarrón*—fugitive or runaway—devised ways to live defiantly parallel to the wider slave society, refusing to accept the legitimacy of its property relations and its notions of racial inferiority.[367] To slaves on plantations, Maroon communities represented the possibility of freedom; to slaveholders, they represented ever-present danger and humiliating failure.

Marronage existed in all sugar colonies but was most deeply entrenched in Jamaica and Surinam. Marronage grew out of an urgent need to flee slavery, a strong African presence and powerful religious inspiration. "More than any other single factor," writes historian Mavis C. Campbell, "African religious beliefs gave the unifying force, the conspiratorial locus, the rallying point to mobilize, to motivate, to inspire, and to design strategies: it gave the ideology, the mystique, and the [Maroon's] pertinacious courage and leadership."[368] Physical topography was also important, and Jamaica's landscape of mountains laced with hills, valleys, ravines, rivers and gorges was ideal for establishing and defending autonomous communities. Other variables included the slavocracy's policies and resources; the will of its leaders and the commitment of its militias; the state of the harvest and the effects of drought, hurricanes or infestations; the threat or presence of warmongering enemies and external attacks; and just plain luck.

A runaway sugar slave became a Maroon when he founded or joined a community dedicated to freedom, defended militarily and governed on an African model. Maroons built impregnable villages, often atop steep mountainsides accessible only by single footpaths and guarded by sentries. As best as they could, they replicated remembered African ways of life. They communicated over wide areas by blowing the *abeng*, a cow horn. Maroon women were agriculturists, their men hunters and warriors. Because Maroons usually lived in a state of perpetual warfare, wartime measures were routine and offensive rather than extraordinary and defensive.

White militias reinforced by black slaves trained and entrusted with guns, one of the many anomalies of sugar slavery, fought back. The Maroons were usually victorious. They terrorized the countryside, attacking plantations and roads, burning buildings and cane fields, maiming or slaughtering livestock or carrying it away for their own use, stealing food, tools, weapons and ammunition, and selectively recruiting other slaves. They refused to accept slaves who lacked drive and discretion, and even killed those they suspected might return to their master and betray Maroon secrets. Those they accepted into their communities were bound by a sacred oath.

Because Maroon communities had gender imbalances of about 60 percent male to 40 percent female, all women were prized additions to the community, and whenever they could, Maroons seized them from the plantations they raided. Women did the domestic chores and tended the gardens and livestock; when necessary, they also fought off the militia. They were "the morale sustainers, the hope-givers, the organisers of meetings and feasts."[369]

To earn money, Maroons marketed their goods, disguising themselves as free blacks or as slaves with passes. The market was a primary source of their supplies, especially ammunition. In 1730, Jamaican Maroons captured two literate white boys and forced them to forge passes identifying two Maroons as slaves authorized to buy gunpowder for their master.

At their most audacious, Maroons took over entire plantations, inspiring slaves elsewhere to refuse to work. "Nor dare their master punish them for the least Disgust will probably cause them to make their Escape and join the Rebels as many from several plantations frequently do," an observer reported.[370] Some of the slave soldiers employed against the Maroons deserted to join them. Slave military porters were particularly keen on "transferring" white supplies to the Maroons they had been fighting. On the other hand, slave soldiers who did not switch sides were instrumental in the militia's occasional triumphs. Sometimes their grateful owners even manumitted them.

Campbell shows how marronage in Jamaica paralleled white planter absenteeism, as the planters fled the predations of the Maroons, until "cause and effect became entangled."[371] Other planters attempted to save their estates by paying the Maroons protection money. Many tried to sell their holdings, but potential buyers were equally frightened. The Maroons had effectively paralyzed the society they had renounced.

Early on, in 1662 to 1663, the British had brought temporary peace by signing agreements with the Maroon leader Juan Lubolo, trading land grants and manumission (until then only de facto) for his cooperation. They accepted his leaders as magistrates and named him Colonel of the Black Militia. In return, the Maroons had to make a few compromises: they had to teach their children English rather than African languages, and Lubolo could no longer call himself Governor of the Negroes.

A century later, it was time to negotiate a new peace. This time the leader was Cudjoe, born into a Maroon community and "rather a short man, uncommonly stout, with very strong African features" and "a prodigious hump on his shoulders or back."[372] Thomas Thistlewood, who frequently crossed his path and referred to him as Colonel Cudjoe, described Cudjoe wearing "a feathered hat, sword by his side, gun upon his shoulders, &c. Barefoot and barelegged, somewhat a majestic look. He brought to my memory the picture of Robinson Crusoe."[373]

Despite his military victories, Cudjoe agreed to the "Treaty of Peace and Friendship." The perpetual warfare had debilitated the Maroon communities just as it had the whites, who, "wearied out from the tedious conflict [were desiring] relief from the horrors of continual alarms, the hardships of military duty, and the intolerable burthen of maintaining an army on foot."[374] Before negotiations could begin, Col. John Guthrie, whom Gov. William Trelawney had ordered to deal with Colonel Cudjoe, had to swear, in an Ashanti ritual, that he would not fight the Maroons. (The Dutch had to do the same when they sued for peace with their Maroons in Surinam.) Blood drawn from black and white signatories was mixed with rum and quaffed as a "blood treaty." The treaty of 1738/9 declared that the Maroons would be forever free, and recent conscripts could either return to their plantations without punishment or remain free with the Maroons. The Maroons were granted Trelawny Town and many other guarantees, and would henceforth act as slave catchers, using "their best Endeavours to take, kill, suppress or destroy" slave rebels. Peace restored equilibrium to Jamaica's beleaguered planters. Slaves understood that the Maroons, now allied with the whites, had become their adversaries. Indeed, until Tacky's Rebellion of 1760, there would be uneasy peace.

In 1795–96, when the specter of the Haitian Revolution haunted all the sugar colonies, Maroon wars again erupted in Jamaica. Slaves, resentful at what they saw as Maroon indifference to or even complicity in their bondage, did not join in large numbers. Lord Balcarres, the lieutenant-governor, whose brother, General Lindsay, had just suppressed Fedon's rebellion in Grenada, in which seven thousand slaves died, sent to Cuba for nearly a hundred vicious mastiff-type dogs that had been trained on African-looking effigies stuffed with animal blood and guts to hunt runaway slaves. The canines arrived with forty-three handlers. "The Negroe all over this Island has been struck with Horror at hearing of this measure," Balcarres gloated.[375] The dogs, led by a small black one with an especially discerning nose, discovered and savaged the concealed Maroons. Others, helpless against the beasts, surrendered. Balcarres transported the Maroons of Trelawny Town to cold and forbidding Nova Scotia. Later, they were sent on to Sierra Leone and further misery.

Cuba, too, had its Maroons, many of them Africans who had escaped toward the east, where they expected to find a route back to Africa. Despite the concerted efforts of poor whites hoping to earn the reward money for their return, many of these runaways remained free. When more than seven settled together, their hamlet was called a palenque. Between 1802 and 1864, there were seventy-nine palenques. The largest, Gran Palenque del Frijol, had a population of four hundred. A military expedition inadvertently discovered another palenque in the middle of a dense forest. "The settlement is so-well hidden that one could pass by many times without suspecting the presence of a living soul," an admiring officer reported.[376] A mysterious, impenetrable palenque on the Sierra del Cristal's wild mountainside was legendary as the home of a large number of runaways.

Armed Uprisings

In sugar-packed Barbados and other colonies lacking mountainous, forested or swampy refuges, marronage was doomed to failure. Instead, slaves had to channel their hatred and rage and their need for freedom elsewhere. The odds were always heavily weighted against winning a wide-scale uprising. They had to enlist only trustworthy colleagues and somehow keep their plans secret from slave informants. Slave leaders had to coordinate with supporters on plantations they could visit only with special passes, forcing them to rely instead on trusted emissaries. They had to draft plans of action and coordinate them over large territories. They had to acquire weapons and ammunition, often stolen from their masters.

Much could go wrong. There were slave catchers aprowl. The militia could be quickly dispatched. Some slaves might be too frightened of post-rebellion punishment to join in. Slaves who had accumulated property might not want to jeopardize it. The free coloreds had mixed loyalties and could be valuable allies or dangerous opponents. There was little to sustain hope; slave rebellions were always stamped out, and spectacular punishments followed: being roasted to death over a slow fire, gibbeted, broken on the wheel, beaten to death or, if one were particularly lucky, dying quickly on the gallows. Still slaves rose up, time and time again, and planters discovered too late that "those who are our chiefest favorites, and such that we put most confidence in are generally the first and greatest conspirators."[377]

In 1760, Tacky's Rebellion vindicated decades of white anxiety that "the Island [of Jamaica] must be overrun, and ruined by its own Slaves,"[378] and sent shock waves through the official chain of colonial command. Tacky and the other rebel leaders were Gold Coast Africans from different plantations who planned "the entire expiration of the white inhabitants; the enslaving of all such Negroes as might refuse to join them; and the partition of the island into small principalities in the African mode; to be distributed among their leaders and head men."[379] The rebels planned to set fire to entire towns and kill the whites who ran out to extinguish the flames. Back on the plantations, the slaves would overpower their overseers and assume control.

The rebellion began at 1 A.M. on Easter Monday. Led by Tacky, the rebels fought from estate to estate, gathering reinforcements, burning plantations, killing whites and beating back the militia. They attacked Fort Haldane and obtained forty firearms and gunpowder. Militiamen and Maroons set out to stop them. Tacky fought until Davy, a Maroon sharpshooter, killed him. Tacky's head was stuck onto a post in Spanish Town as a dire warning. Some of his rebels committed mass suicide rather than surrender.

Despite Tacky's death, the rebellion simmered across Jamaica for months. Thistlewood learned of it from four terrified and nearly naked whites who described the carnage they had escaped and warned that he "should probably be murdered in a short time, &c &c."[380] On July 3, the African Apongo, renamed Wager and now known as King of the Rebels, was captured and hung up in chains. Before he could be cut down and burned, he died. Another rebel leader was condemned to be burned. "The wretch," Thistlewood wrote, "was made to sit on the ground, and his body being chained to an iron stake, the fire was applied to his feet. He uttered not a groan, and saw his legs reduced to ashes with the utmost firmness and composure; after which, one of his arms by some means getting loose, he snatched a brand from the fire that was consuming him, and flung it in the face of the executioner."[381]

When Jamaica finally quieted, nearly sixty whites and four hundred blacks were dead, and the terror and tension among whites were palpable. Hundreds left the island, and those who stayed were wary and vigilant. The legislature mandated the death penalty or transportation out of Jamaica for anyone practicing obeah. When the obeah priestess Sarah was caught "having in her possession, cats teeth, cats claws, jaws, hair, beads, knotted clothes, and other materials relative the practice of obeah to delude and impose on the minds of the negroes," she was transported.[382]

Ironically, the abolition of the slave trade inspired Barbadian slaves to rebel because they believed the island now belonged to them and not to the whites they intended to kill. Their rebellion began on the evening of Sunday, April 14, 1816, in the southeastern parish of St. Philip, and spread through half the island. The rebels burned a quarter of the sugar crop and a good deal of property in an attempt to ruin the planters and to signal other rebel groups with the smoke rising from the smoldering fields. They also looted as much as they could, taking jewelry, silver, furniture, dishes, even floor tiles; in the frenzy, some whites joined in the pillaging. Many old whites died of stress provoked by the rebellion.

The militia, assisted by imperial troops that included black slave soldiers in the West India Regiment, crushed the rebels. By the end, one militia man, two soldiers and about a thousand slaves were killed in battle or executed. The rebel leader, African-born Bussa, had been killed as he led his followers into battle.

The uprising had been well planned and, like Tacky's, scheduled to coincide with Easter festivities. The leadership was strong and included slaves respected on their plantations. One was Nanny Grigg, a domestic who read English and Barbadian newspapers and informed the other slaves about the Haitian revolution and the abolitionist campaign. The rebels were aided by free colored men who visited slaves on different plantations and converted them to the rebel cause.

But several things went wrong. A drunken conspirator set events in motion days early, taking fellow conspirators by surprise. The slaves failed to get sufficient ammunition and had to fight with machetes, pitchforks and other farming tools. The majority of the colored slaves and freemen declined to join the uprising. After a few days, the rebellion was stamped out, and Barbados went back to making sugar.

THE HAITIAN REVOLUTION

In 1791, the French colony of St. Domingue was known as the Jewel of the Caribbean. It produced more sugar more cheaply than anywhere else and supplied half of Europe's consumption of tropical produce, including coffee, cotton and indigo. St. Domingue accounted for two-thirds of France's overseas trade, employing one thousand ships and five thousand sailors. It was so linked to the metropolis that before their own revolution, foppish Parisians, extolling the superiority of its laundering, shipped their dirty clothes there to be pounded clean and dried in the burning sun.

In the terrifying, exhilarating years between 1791 and 1804, slaves transformed St. Domingue into Haiti, the world's first self-liberated black republic, whose military and moral triumphs against slavery the white world never forgave and the black world never forgot. The story of those thirteen years is a convoluted and magnificent chronicle of fierce fighting with brief interruptions as the militants realigned their forces then struck out again with renewed fury. When it finally ended,

Abolitionists portrayed slaves as supplicants or grateful recipients of white bounty. But images portraying the brutalities of the Haitian Revolution, including the slaughter of white families, preyed on white fears of unchecked black vengeance.

at least a hundred thousand Haitians and fifty thousand foreign soldiers lay dead, and the French commander, Donatien-Marie-Joseph de Rochambeau, had capitulated.

Like the other West Indian colonies, St. Domingue had all the ingredients for conflict. It was rigidly divided by color and caste. Its aristocracy was arrogant and cruel. Its less advantaged whites—overseers, clerks, attorneys—envied and aped them, while poor whites struggled and had to compete with blacks. The slaves, 500,000 strong, were half African-born. There were Maroons and free blacks, and enslaved and free mulattoes, some of the latter slaveholding planters. This unhappy society had had experience with two major revolutions. During the American Revolution, the future Haitian rebel leaders Henri Christophe, Jean-Baptiste Chavannes and André Rigaud had fought for the colonists against England. More recently, the goals and deeds of the French Revolution inspired the suffering slaves.

The revolution developed in stages as allegiances changed, participants regrouped and European nations fought against the rebels and also against each other. It began when mulatto Vincent Ogé, aided by British and French abolitionists, attempted a military assault designed to force the government to extend equal rights to all free people, mulatto or black. Defeated and captured, Ogé, his brother Jacques, and his colleague Jean-Baptiste Chavannes had their limbs broken and were tied face up on a wheel, to expire in a slow agony of thirst, starvation and pain. Afterward, their heads were chopped off and stuck onto poles to warn off would-be rebels.

Ogé's revolutionary frisson caused shivers, but it was only when the slaves of Cap François in the north rose up that the true dimensions of what was now truly a revolution were revealed. The slaves planned meticulously, their object to kill all the whites, burn down all the plantations and take over the colony. Their coordination was superlative. Thousands kept the uprising secret. Their leaders, two hundred strong, were mainly trusted slave drivers or skilled workers. Toussaint Louverture, who later emerged as their principal leader, was a freed coachman who used his pass to carry messages between the isolated plantations.

The slaves had been told—incorrectly—that the king and French National Assembly had granted them three free days per week and abolished the whip, and that they were preparing to enforce this against the wishes of the planters and colonial authorities. The uprising was led by the massive Boukman, a driver, coachman and vodun priest who presided over a rousing vodun ceremony at Bois Caiman that galvanized those present and has descended into legend.

Afterward, the slaves rose up. They killed their plantation managers and other whites, and torched the *bagasse* storage sheds and other structures. The Northern Plain became "a flaming ruin," writes C. L. R. James, "the whole horizon was a wall of fire. From this wall continually rose thick black volumes of smoke, through which came tongues of flame ... a rain of burning cane straw, driven before the wind like flakes of snow, flew over the city and the shipping in the harbour, threatening both with destruction."[383]

As the revolution rolled on, the rebels took refuge in mountainous hideouts and organized themselves into bands that, a French general recalled, were "mutually able to come to each other's aid whenever we partially attacked them."[384] They had surveillance posts and prearranged rendezvous points. They improvised what they lacked. "They camou-flaged traps, fabricated poisoned arrows, feigned cease-fires to lure the enemy into ambush, disguised tree trunks as cannons, and threw obstructions of one kind or another into the roads to hamper advancing troops, in short, any means they could invent to psychologically disori-ent, frighten, demoralize, or otherwise generally confuse the European units in order to defend their own positions," Fick writes.[385] Their motto was Death to All Whites, their martial music African. They devised bullet-resistant vests. But they were not impervious to bullets, and Boukman was shot dead and his head displayed in a city square.

Three months had passed. Toussaint Louverture, who had taken the name Louverture—Opening—to signify that nothing remained closed to him, began to assume a leadership role. The revolution continued, confusingly. France's revolutionary government abolished slavery in August 1793, but from 1796 to 1801 in Haiti, the newly freed blacks, headed by Louverture, and the mainly mulatto already-freemen, headed by André Rigaud, fought each other over political and economic inter-ests, personal rivalry and the ever-present, toxic question of color. As the revolution continued, it widened into civil war.

Toussaint soared as a leader, a model of determination and pride, the black liberator, the First West Indian. He was born on a northern plan-tation, the enslaved son of an African-born prince. He tended livestock and served as a coachman until his owner manumitted him. He was literate and had some knowledge of geometry, French and Latin, but preferred Creole to French and needed secretaries for his correspon-dence. Like Jamaica's Cudjoe, Toussaint was small, ugly and majestic. He took inspiration from the Jamaican Maroons: "I am black like them, I know how to fight," he said.

Toussaint consolidated his power, and also France's, after a brief alliance with Spain. He overpowered the Spanish, who conceded French control over the eastern part of the island, and in 1797 defeated English invaders. One of his strategies was to wait until the yellow fever, which flourished in the rainy season, sickened and killed off legions of whites.

Since 1793, England and France had been at war. English politicians saw in the Haitian Revolution an ideal opportunity to punish France for her military assistance to the now independent Thirteen Colonies, and they coveted St. Domingue as a prize that would partially compensate them for the loss of those colonies. To this end, they plotted with anti-revolutionary planters to restore slavery to St. Domingue, which they invaded in 1794. By 1798, however, England had to concede military defeat to Toussaint Louverture.

The situation was volatile and byzantine. "From the vantage point of international politics," writes Fick, "Saint Domingue was being manipulated as a piece on a chessboard, and the outcome of its internal struggles would be a key to the particular political and economic advantage that each of the three contending foreign powers [France, England and the United States] intended to reap."[386] Napoleon Bonaparte's ascension as First Consul further obfuscated the situation. While Toussaint proclaimed a new constitution in 1801 and concentrated on clarifying Haiti's future commercial relations, guaranteeing the ex-slaves' freedom but envisioning a return to the plantation system as the only profitable way to raise sugarcane and other commodities, Napoleon was naysaying St. Domingue's independence and contemplating the wisdom of re-establishing slavery.

In 1802, Napoleon sent his brother-in-law, Gen. Charles Leclerc, to retake St. Domingue and crush its "gilded Negroes," a scheme slave-holding England approved. In nearby Jamaica, Governor and Lady Nugent were preoccupied by Haiti's unfolding drama and shuddered at stories of "the horrible bloodshed and misery that must take place, before any thing can be at all settled on that wretched island." Nugent deplored Toussaint's successes, dismissed most visiting French officials as "a set of cruel heartless wretches," and sympathized with French planters who plotted to turn Haiti over to the slaveholding English, "a most embarrassing situation" for her poor husband, she lamented. She was consoled, however, by Pauline Bonaparte Leclerc's gift of the latest

Parisian fashions, especially a "crape dress, embroidered in silver spangles ... scarcely any sleeves ... but a broad silver spangled border for the shoulder straps. The body made very like a child's frock, tying behind, and the skirt round, with not much train. A turban of spangled crape, like the dress, looped with pearls, and a paradise feather; altogether looking like a *Sultana*."[387]

Two of the Nugents' special friends were Gen. Philibert Fressinet, "a true Frenchman," and Marie-Adelaide, his petite and very pretty new bride, a St. Domingue property owner who spoke with "astonishing *sang froid*" about her "disastrous" experiences there. Months before, General Leclerc had arranged for the "gentleman-like" Fressinet to trick Toussaint Louverture into attending a meeting at which he was overpowered, arrested and taunted: "Now you are nothing in Saint-Domingue, give me your sword," one of them, perhaps Fressinet, told him.[388] Now both Leclerc and Louverture were dead, Leclerc a victim of the yellow fever that had wiped out so many of his troops.

Toussaint's death, on April 7, 1803, was closer to murder. He died of pneumonia and apoplexy in an icy prison cell in the Fort-de-Joux, three thousand feet high in the Jura mountains. On Napoleon's instructions, his mocking jailers deprived him of sufficient food, firewood and clothing. "I am to-day wretched, ruined, dishonoured," Toussaint wrote, appealing to Napoleon's mercy.[389] But Napoleon, merciless, wanted Toussaint to die.

Toussaint's successor, Jean-Jacques Dessalines, had been a black man's slave. He was short, stocky and middle-aged, a courageous and vigorous man who inspired both terror and admiration. *Coupé tet, boulé kay*—cut off heads, burn houses—Dessalines advised his men. He was illiterate and unpredictable, sometimes appearing in embroidered splendor, sometimes in slave-like rags. During the revolution, he married the beautiful and accomplished former mistress of a rich planter; Madame Dessalines tried but mostly failed to soften her husband's ferocious disposition. As a military strategist, Dessalines was as brilliant as Toussaint and as devious in his dealings with whites.

The revolution continued under Dessalines, whom General Rochambeau had once promised, "When I take you, I will not shoot you like a soldier, or hang you like a white man; I will whip you to death like a slave." But the French mission was hopeless. Even the dreaded Cuban attack dogs failed to distinguish between black and white and attacked both. In November, Rochambeau capitulated to Dessalines. On January 1, 1804, Gen. Jean-Jacques Dessalines, who had torn the symbolic white strip from the tricolor flag, issued a Proclamation of Independence against France, against racism and in honor of the new nation he called Haiti, Land of Mountains, its Arawak name.

The French "are not our brothers ... they will never be.... Anathema to the French name! Eternal hatred of France!" his proclamation declared.[390] Stunningly, it eliminated the racial classifications that, everywhere, fed the corrosive racism at the core of sugar slavery. Henceforth, all Haitians would be considered black, even whites who embraced the new nation's vision.[391]

The Haitian Revolution was the ultimate resistance to slavery and had profound consequences. It hastened the abolition of the slave trade. It laid bare the nature and effects of racism. It inspired black pride. It articulated the notion of universal freedom and it challenged colonialism, directly influencing future revolutionaries. It embraced the biblical idea of diaspora, as Dessalines invited blacks and coloreds who had relocated or whose fleeing French masters had taken them to the United States, often Louisiana, to return home. He also offered ship captains forty dollars for each male they transported back to Haiti.

Within Haiti, the revolution's promises of hope and prosperity were swiftly dashed as the rest of the slaveholding world united to punish the ex-slaves for their victory. Commercial embargos, diplomatic ostracism and moral indifference stifled the new nation's first breaths. Internecine quarrels between blacks and their lighter-skinned compatriots undermined reconstruction of the shattered economy, the burnt-out countryside and the devastated sugar, coffee and indigo plantations. In the final years of the war, black and colored had fought together under Dessalines. But because many of the colored owned property, and most of the blacks did not, postwar conflicts over property flared up and seemed irreconcilable. After Dessalines's assassination in 1806, Haiti split into two entities, a northern kingdom and a southern republic, its cultural and political renaissance paralleled by economic and ecological decline.

The Haitian Revolution was a morality play that pitted racism against resistance and recapitulated the conflicts and the inconsistencies at the heart of sugar slavery. In the end, Dessalines eviscerated racism, elevating blackness and offering it to anyone, of any color, who accepted the new Haiti. But when the curtain went down on Dessalines's dream, racism resurged in Haiti. Resistance became internecine. Sugar, once the heart of the matter, sweetened less and less. Cuba, Louisiana and other producers rushed to replace Haitian sugar in the world markets.

Chapter 7

Blood in the Sugar:
Abolishing the Slave Trade

WHITE ABOLITIONISTS

Until the late eighteenth century, most abolitionists were blacks, usually slaves fighting to free themselves, or at least extricate themselves, from slavery. Sugar defined and dominated their existence. They produced it, stole it, ate it and sold it. They trod on mounds of still-warm sugar with their bare feet, pounding out lumps with iron picks, and droplets of sweat and blood from their wounds dropped into vats of sugar destined for export. The sight shocked and repulsed visitors. "Your blood will be drunk in England," one of them scolded a slave who had just washed his injured hand in a puncheon of rum. "You no think, Massa, when you eat our sugar, you drink our blood?" the slave retorted.[392]

That bitter query encapsulated the horror of slave-grown sugar, which came to symbolize injustice and the defects of colonialism. By its very nature, sugar connected the West Indian colonies to the millions of European homes and eateries that consumed it. By the late eighteenth century, growing numbers of religious and reform-minded citizens focused on its centrality in ordinary people's homes and private lives. The contents of the family sugar bowl became a personal embarrassment. For women, overseers of their family's nutrition and their moral character, sugar began to lose its power to sweeten.

A serendipitous chain of events transformed abolitionism from an impulse into a movement. First, Granville Sharp, an ordnance clerk at the Tower of London, intervened on behalf of Jonathan Strong, a runaway black man whose master had retrieved and beaten him, thrown him into prison and sold him to a Jamaican sugar planter. From then on, Sharp devoted himself to saving blacks from West Indian slavery. An autodidact, he pored over law books to gain expertise. His studies deepened his loathing of slavery and oppression in all forms, including animal abuse, which he considered "that *unsuspected test of moral character*, by which he might safely ascertain the worth of every man's heart."[393]

Sharp's most memorable case involved James Somerset, whose successful bid for freedom in 1772 was discussed in chapter 6. Before he could be sent into Jamaican slavery, Somerset contacted Sharp to protect him. Lord Mansfield's judgment in the Somerset case was a stunning victory for both Somerset and Sharp: "*Fiat justitia, ruat coelum*"—Let justice be done, though the heavens may fall—Mansfield declared in his tension-filled courtroom as he freed Somerset.

Abolitionists were ecstatic, and widespread misinterpretation of Mansfield's judgment—that he had abolished slavery in England—lent his words even more power. Blacks and abolitionists exulted, and at least fifteen English slaves were freed by judges who cited Somerset as their precedent. "Slaves cannot breathe in England; if their lungs / Receive our air, that moment they are free: / They touch our country, and their shackles fall," the poet William Cowper rejoiced in "The Task." Mansfield himself issued no clarification, except to mention privately that his ruling was merely that "there was no right in the master forcibly to take the slave and carry him abroad."[394]

West Indian whites and their allies lamented the Mansfield judgment, and Jamaican planter Edward Long predicted that hordes of slaves would escape to England where, with "the lower class of women ... [who] are remarkably fond of blacks, for reasons too brutal to mention," they would mongrelize the English, who would soon resemble the darker-skinned and degraded Portuguese.[395] Slaves in the revolutionizing American colonies yearned en masse for Somerset's England, and at least one, nineteen-year-old Bacchus from Virginia, attempted to get there. In later years, Mansfield's judgment remained deeply influential in shaping American judicial decisions.

In 1783, Granville Sharp confronted Lord Mansfield over an insurance claim involving 132 slaves thrown overboard the *Zong*, a slaver, after its captain, Luke Collingwood, decided to cull the sickest of his cargo of Africans. Using the legal excuse that the ship was nearly out of water, Collingwood claimed reimbursement from the insurance company for the drowned slaves.

The insurers disputed the legitimacy of the claim, accusing Collingwood of acting negligently and improperly. Although court spectators shuddered as they heard the story, the jurors quickly decided against the insurers, who were ordered to pay £30 per slave. Sharp might never have heard of the *Zong* had a letter to *The Morning Chronicle and London Advertiser* not called the court case a villainous act that would provoke divine wrath.[396] The African Olaudah Equiano read this letter and hurried to Granville Sharp's office to implore him to avenge the Africans. Sharp lobbied unsuccessfully to bring murder charges against those who threw the Africans overboard. Despite his failure, the breathtaking brutality of the *Zong* murders and their reduction to a disputed insurance claim clarified for many people the urgency of abolishing the slave trade.

Enlightened Thought and Spiritual Conviction

Sharp and his abolitionist colleagues interpreted such current events as the Somerset and the *Zong* cases in the context of Enlightenment ideas that condemned slavery as an abomination and an affront to human civilization. Montesquieu, for instance, denounced slavery as intrinsically evil, degrading the slave and corrupting the master whose "unlimited authority over his slaves" made him "fierce, hasty, severe, choleric, voluptuous, and cruel."[397] Many of Sharp's contemporaries believed that Montesquieu's measured insights, his analyses of law systems and his moral philosophy amounted to a call for reform and for abolition of slavery. Prominent political philosopher Edmund Burke translated Montesquieu's *Spirit of the Laws* into

English and denounced the slave trade. The great jurist Sir William Blackstone's magisterial four-volume *Commentaries on the Laws of England* was influenced by Montesquieu and argued that slavery was "repugnant to reason, and the principles of natural law."[398] The Abbé Raynal's *Philosophic and Political History*, which vociferously opposed the slave trade, attracted so many readers that it was published in fifteen English editions between 1776 and 1806, and abolitionists frequently cited it to justify their views.

Abolitionists like Granville Sharp were driven by intellectual conviction reinforced by intense spiritual conviction. They rejected centuries of Christian sanction of and involvement in slavery and reinterpreted the fundamental meaning of Christianity and scriptural texts. The simplest and most important was the New Testament's decree "Thou shalt love thy neighbor as thyself," "the sum and essence of the whole Law of God," in Granville Sharp's words.[399] Christianity's central story, the sacrificial death of Christ to save mankind, reinforced theological arguments against slavery, and the late-eighteenth-century intellectual climate made it easier to conclude that mankind included blacks.

Except for Bartolomé de Las Casas, who focused international attention on the plight of Indian and, belatedly, black slaves, little Christian-derived concern for slaves had penetrated sugar culture. From the earliest days, Catholic religious orders, including the Jesuits, Dominicans and Franciscans, owned slave-operated sugar plantations; later, so did the Moravians. In 1710, the Anglican Society for Propagation of the Gospel in Foreign Parts accepted sugar planter Christopher Codrington's bequest of two Barbadian sugar plantations complete with slaves, whom the society duly branded.[400] Even plain-living Quakers were slave traders and owners, including the Barclay and Baring banking families; one slaver was named *The Willing Quaker*. Christian churches justified slavery as divinely ordained, and described Africans as savage pagans whose exposure to civilizing Christianity and European mores was a blessing.

That exposure, such as it was, was minimal. In French, Spanish and Portuguese sugar colonies, it usually consisted of a slave chapel with a chaplain or, in his place, planters who felt godlike and personally conducted religious services. English planters seldom did even this much. Absentees and many others were indifferent financial supporters of churches and did not respect colonial clerics, all too often undereducated, irreligious "men that have dissipated their patrimony ... [and fled] to the church as their last refuge from poverty," as one contemporary noted.[401] Unsurprisingly, these undermotivated clergymen had no interest in ministering to slaves as well as to indolent whites.

However, missionaries were different, and after 1754, Moravian, Methodist, Presbyterian, Baptist and Anglican missionaries competed for the souls of black folks. Most respected their home churches' warnings against causing slave discontent and taught that slavery was ordained by God, that monogamous relationships were essential and that one must render unto Caesar that which was Caesar's. The London Missionary Society's 1816 caution to Rev. John Smith was typical: "Not a word must escape you in public or private which might render the slaves displeased with their masters or dissatisfied with their station. You are not sent to relieve them from their servile condition, but to afford them the consolations of religion."[402] Many missionaries bought slaves, explaining that by treating them humanely, they were leading by example.

Nevertheless, many planters banned missionaries from their plantations. They feared the spiritual strength slaves might draw from a religion whose central deity washed poor people's feet. As missionary wife Jane Smith explained, "Many of the planters ... apprehended that the religious instruction of the slaves was incompatible with their condition in life, and that as soon as they became a little enlightened, they would revolt."[403] They were also leery of the social and legal consequences of baptizing slaves.

A few planters saw in Christianity an antidote to what they suspected was obeah's revolutionary bent and welcomed missionaries onto their plantations. But slaves, always straining against slavery, interpreted Christ's suffering as proof of his willingness to defy authorities even unto death. As Christianity spread among slaves, it produced leaders, a forum for self-expression, scriptural ammunition and new ways of organizing. As always, slaves were the staunchest abolitionists.

As abolitionism gathered steam, a new breed of missionary infiltrated the field. These men were horror-struck at what they witnessed on

the plantations. Some rejected their customary complicity and minis-
tered to slaves in ways planters considered subversive. Missionaries
also documented, most often in journals and letters to friends and
congregations at home, the realities of sugar slavery and sugar production, and their narratives were important contributions to abolitionist
literature.

THE ABOLITION MOVEMENT

After centuries of the slave trade and slavery, an English coalition of men
and women merged into an anti-slavery movement that resembled a
hybrid spider propelled by unmatched legs. Each leg was formed by
members of the following groups: men and women of the working class;
blacks resident in England; West Indian slaves, free blacks and coloreds;
renegade West Indian missionaries; Quaker and religiously motivated
non-Quaker men; Quaker and religiously motivated non-Quaker
women; politically minded reformers; and anti-protectionist free traders
and East Indian sugar interests. From time to time over the more than
half century of anti-slavery efforts, a leg would shrivel away or be cut
down and then regenerate.

Moving from metaphor to the year 1783, these disjointed limbs
joined together to create a Quaker society committed to ending the slave
trade. Four years later, this society became the Society for the Abolition
of the Slave Trade, nondenominational though Quaker-dominated
and attractive to Christian evangelicals.

Quaker and evangelical women believed fervently in the humanity
of blacks and in their own Christian duty to help them. Despite their
exclusion from Parliament and ineligibility to vote or even to sign petitions, these women clasped hands and joined the abolition movement.
Most were middle class and upheld their society's values about the
sanctity of family and motherhood. They were deeply moved by images
of cruelty to slaves and by stories of slave auctions that tore families
apart, snatched children from their mothers' arms, denied slave women
"all aspects of maternal leadership, direction and discipline,"[404] and left
them vulnerable to sexual exploitation by degraded whites. Trading

places with such sinned-against women in their imaginations transformed these British women into fervent crusaders against slavery, which, they declared, "practically insults the feelings of every female on earth."[405]

They also came to understand the role that sugar played in the misery of the slaves, and acknowledged that as homemakers who purchased, prepared and served slave-produced sugar to their families, they had been shoring up the very institution they now abhorred. They identified sugarcane as slavery's primary raison d'être, and as a vital symbol of the evil they were dedicated to destroying.

Large numbers of working-class men and women, motivated by religious fervor, especially Methodism, and by the reformism that was suffusing the political landscape, supported abolition. When Olaudah Equiano visited London, for instance, he stayed with Lydia and Thomas Hardy, white working-class sympathizers. Many others, however, complained that slaves' needs were prioritized over theirs. But those who believed that the rights of slaves and workers had a common denominator understood the need for solidarity. Historian James Walvin describes how its universality empowered the anti-slavery movement. It also sensitized abolitionists to the condition of the working class, and some began to employ the rhetoric of abolitionism to argue for the rights of England's "white slaves."

The most visible abolitionists came from urban England's black community. Free blacks, usually poor and downtrodden, eagerly joined in the fight to liberate their fellows. They organized their communities, raised money for those in direst need and showed up en masse at courtroom hearings for such slave-related legal proceedings as the *Zong* case.

In the eighteenth century, their most influential leaders were Olaudah Equiano and his African-born friends Ottobah Cugoano and Ignatius Sancho. The trio was intelligent and erudite, and their published narratives were invaluable weapons against slavery. They provided channels of communication between white abolitionists and the black community. Equiano in particular, exemplary in his personal life and known for his sincerity, was a towering abolitionist figure.

West Indian slaves, free blacks and coloreds formed the most committed and autonomous of abolition's legs. Their every instance of defiance, sabotage or rebellion weakened the institution of slavery. Ironically, every account of these events carried in newspapers, magazines and published journals converted more whites to the necessity of achieving abolition through Parliament and the legal system as the only way to avoid abolition by revolution or by mass destruction of whites.

Renegade missionaries who spoke out against plantation slavery and preached sedition were few in number but, as respectable white men, contributed a disproportionately influential sixth leg. A seventh consisted of abolitionists driven by reform idealism. They strove for social rights and justice, freedom for workers and freedom of conscience and worship, and included slaves in their mission.

The eighth leg was provided by economically inclined reformers who challenged the old colonial mercantilist system that protected slave-grown West Indian sugar and called for laissez-faire or free trade. They condemned the slave trade and slavery as obsolete institutions that shored up an artificial trade in sugar and hurt Britons who had to pay artificially high prices for this essential item.

These reformers found allies of a sort among members of the East Indian sugar interest, who had an obvious interest in free trade and promoted it through self-serving declarations against slave-grown sugar, though they failed to create an East Indian abolitionist bloc. Other reformers pointed out that free-grown beet sugar, already invading the continental market, was in any case a death knell for slave-grown cane sugar.

As its various members joined together in common purpose—to avert revolution and to work through legally sanctioned means—England's anti-slavery movement commenced its long, slow march. Its members recoiled from the news of French and later Haitian bloodletting, even in the cause of abolition. The primary locus of the English struggle was Parliament, where the weapons of choice were ideas, religion and law, propagandizing and lobbying, and where men were the only players. The growing numbers of women joining the movement focused their struggle on British sugar bowls and fought their battle with boycotts, deprivation and substitution.

In the earliest days, abolitionists had to agree on common goals, no easy task given the diverse options, which ranged from improving slave conditions to sending slaves (or even all blacks) back to Africa, specifically Sierra Leone, where rebellious Jamaican Maroons had been transported. Abolition's first wave settled on abolishing the slave trade as a way to stamp out the worst abuses of slavery as well as the brutality of the Middle Passage. The rationale for this was simple: if slaveholders could not replace dead slaves with African imports, they would be forced to treat their slaves humanely. Slavery would die a natural death, and waged labor would replace it. Abolitionists often cited the example of sugar planter Joshua Steele as proof that such a transition would work. Steele had moved to Barbados in 1780 and paid his slaves instead of terrorizing them. They worked much harder and required less supervision, and Steele's profits tripled.

The gradualist approach won out over the more radical goal of abolishing slavery, and so the Society for the Abolition of the Slave Trade was formed. Leaders emerged and coordinated their efforts, among them Granville Sharp, Thomas Clarkson, William Wilberforce, James Stephen, Josiah Wedgwood and the Reverends James Ramsay, John Wesley and John Newton.

Sharp had already devoted decades to pursuing legal justice for individual blacks. Clarkson was a devout and brilliant Cambridge classics student whose research for his essay "Is It Lawful to Make Slaves of Others Against Their Will?" converted him to abolition. (The professor who set the topic was outraged by the *Zong* case.) Clarkson cofounded the abolition society and became its chief fact finder. Wilberforce was only twenty-one when he won the first of many parliamentary elections for Hull, the sole British port that did no trade with Africa or the West Indies. Clarkson plied Wilberforce with abolitionist literature and contacts, including his friend William Pitt, the prime minister. Clarkson experienced "the happiest day I had then spent in my whole life" when, at Pitt's urging, Wilberforce finally agreed to take up the abolitionist cause in Parliament.[406]

Stephen was an angry young lawyer in practice in St. Kitts who contacted Wilberforce and became a de facto witness and fact finder for the abolitionists after he saw such travesties of justice as two slaves burned alive for an unproved rape. He returned to England, where his keen legal mind, powerful writing (*The Slavery of the British West India Colonies Delineated, as it exists both in law and practice*), belated conversion to evangelical Christianity and political success made him a most valued colleague and the architect of the abolitionists' parliamentary strategies.

Wedgwood, the great Quaker potter whose magnificent porcelain vases, busts and other objets d'art were beloved of royalty, was another of the society's cofounders and created its official seal, a kneeling slave in chains, arms raised toward heaven, pleading, "Am I Not a Man and a Brother?"

Wedgwood traveled to the West Indies to see for himself the conditions on the sugar plantations, including John Pinney's on Nevis. Pinney had warned his manager about Wedgwood's visit: "Do not suffer a negro to be corrected in his presence, or so near for him to hear the whip." He advised giving the slaves less work and said, "Point out the comforts the negroes enjoy beyond our poor in this country … the property they possess in goats, hogs, and poultry, and their negro-ground [provision grounds]. By this means he will leave the island possessed with favourable sentiments." Despite Pinney's precautions, Wedgwood returned to England a committed abolitionist.

Ramsay joined the abolitionists after a bitter career as an Anglican priest and doctor to sugar slaves in St. Kitts. He had welcomed both black and white to his services, befriended his slave parishioners and sought to convert them to Christianity. This so incensed those whites who believed that Christianizing slaves was dangerous that they stopped attending church. Ramsay, like Stephen, kept detailed notes about how sugar slavery worked. He married Rebecca Akers, a wealthy planter's daughter, but alienated the plantocracy by speaking out publicly against their abuse of slaves and trying to improve slave conditions. The planters made his life so intolerable that, in 1781, he returned to England, where he wrote his influential *Essay on the Treatment and Conversion of African Slaves in the British Sugar Colonies* and *An Enquiry into the Effects of the Abolition of the Slave Trade*, both still valuable sources for research on sugar slavery.

John Wesley, the founder of Methodism, was so profoundly moved by abolitionist Anthony Benezet's *Some Historical Account of Guinea* and the Somerset case that he published his own *Thoughts Upon Slavery*, which caused slave-trading interests to hate him. In it he asked the slave trader rhetorically, "What is your heart made of? ... Do you never *feel* another's pain? ... When you saw the flowing eyes, the heaving breasts, or the bleeding sides and tortured limbs of your fellow-creatures, was you a stone, or a brute?" and warned, "The Great GOD [will] deal with *You*, as you have dealt with *them*, and require all their blood at your hands."[407] On his deathbed Wesley was reading Olaudah Equiano's narrative, and one of his last letters was to Wilberforce.

John Newton was a slave ship's captain who had a religious epiphany and committed himself to Christianity. Years later, when he had stopped sailing and had been ordained as an Anglican priest, he renounced slavery, repented his participation in it and preached abolition. (He also composed the stirring hymn "Amazing Grace.") Wilberforce read Newton's 1764 *Authentic Narrative* about his life in the African slave trade and enlisted him as a supporter.

The abolition society began as an all-male organization, and for some time women figured more as behind-the-scenes influences and financial contributors. Lady Margaret Middleton, wife of Capt. Charles Middleton, later Lord Barham and First Lord of the Admiralty, hosted and attended political dinner parties and spoke persuasively about the horrors of the slave trade; her like-minded husband did the same in Parliament. Lady Middleton was a close friend of Hannah More, a popular playwright and conservative evangelical tract writer, and the women colluded at social events to promote abolition. More reached a wide audience with her pamphlets and such sentimental poems as *The Negro Woman's Lamentation*, helping to convert homemakers who in turn converted their husbands, brothers and sons who, as males, could petition and vote to keep or make new laws.

Women also contributed to the society's coffers or persuaded their husbands and fathers to do so. Most were well-to-do Quakers, evangelical Anglicans or Protestants. Few working-class women could afford the high price for membership subscriptions to the society. Aristocratic women were largely absent from abolitionist ranks. Except in cities, where commercial interests were unrelated to either slavery or the slave trade, they would not or could not compromise their families' social and commercial connections by supporting this alien cause.

Like the West India Interest, the abolitionists, too, were interconnected. Bristol-based Nevis sugar plantation owner Charles Pinney, whose father had tried to hide the true condition of his slaves from Josiah Wedgwood, was brusquely reminded of this in 1827. Charles, an absentee slaveholder, wished to marry abolitionist Wilberforce's daughter. Their marriage, Pinney argued, was "most likely to produce beneficial results to the improvement of the slave population." After Wilberforce learned how deeply his potential son-in-law was involved in the West Indian trade, his disapproval ended the relationship.

On the other hand, when dedicated abolitionist and widower James Stephen fell in love with Wilberforce's sister Sally, Wilberforce showed great flexibility. Stephen had repented his wild ways, but his sorry past had included fathering a child with his best friend's fiancée while he, too, was engaged to be married. Wilberforce was forgiving. "Stephen is an improved and improving character," he wrote, "one of those whom religion has transformed and in whom it has triumphed by conquering some natural infirmities."[408]

Their interconnectedness encouraged abolitionists to resolve their different visions about abolition and other issues and find a workable common denominator. Some were gradualists, others immediatists. Wilberforce was a politically astute compromiser who believed that women belonged in the home, while Clarkson was an inflexibly principled "moral steam-engine"[409] who strongly supported female independence. Sharp was passionate about the rights of men and animals but fiercely rejected equal rights for Catholics and denounced cross-gender theatrical presentations as unscriptural. Most blacks and a great number of women thought slavery rather than the slave trade should be the primary focus of attention but, for the sake of solidarity and moving forward together, acquiesced in their leaders' more gradualist decisions.

Merging their differing ideals raised difficult issues: was it respectable for women to canvass door-to-door to drum up support or was it, as

Wilberforce insisted, unseemly? Was sending blacks to Sierra Leone an honorable solution or did it pander to anti-black prejudices? Was abolition morally incumbent on whites or should blacks first have to demonstrate their fitness for freedom? Should slaves be civilized and Christianized as preparation for freedom or would and should that follow? Should the emancipation of mulattoes be expedited in tacit recognition of their white bloodlines, or should all slaves be treated equally?

Another serious issue was how slaves were portrayed. For abolitionists such as Ramsay and Stephen, who had lived in the West Indies, the brutality and injustice of slavery was indictment enough. But others felt that a stronger or more legitimate case could be made if slaves were described as demoralized and broken beings thirsty for freedom and the right to work (hard) for (low) wages. Even degraded slaves should seem virtuous, their faults either concealed or blamed on slavery. They should never be ferocious or willing to resort to violence to free themselves but rather depicted as long-suffering victims who yearned for righteous whites to grant them freedom. Female slaves should seem especially meek, longing only to stay at home raising their adorable, born-in-wedlock children.

This implicit impulse to present blacks as deserving of freedom meant that black abolitionist leaders in England were held to high standards about every aspect of their lives, including the strictly personal. One of their irksome habits was to marry white women; even the otherwise irreproachable Equiano committed this fault. Sancho, a Westminster shopkeeper, married Anne Osbourne, a West Indian, but his amorous adventures were notorious and, it was rumored, racially unrestricted. The lack of black women caused marriageable black men to take white wives, triggering sexual jealousy or insecurity, or both, in whites. This sexual tension was one of many the abolitionists had to deal with as they planned their campaigns.

The abolitionist campaigns had distinctive peaks: 1788, 1792 and 1814 against the slave trade; 1823, 1830 and 1833 against slavery; 1838 against the "apprenticeship" of former slaves. The campaigns focused on sugar as the central reason for West Indian slavery and the symbol of its evils and looked to legislation to achieve their goals. This required them to participate in the official inquiries and studies that always preceded new laws, and to be involved in the political stratagems and alliances that move the parliamentary process along. The founding society spawned a network of local abolitionist associations: more than two hundred in 1814 and, by the mid-1820s, more than eight hundred, including forty-three women's anti-slavery societies. Just before emancipation in 1833, there were thirteen hundred of these associations. This abolitionist network cooperated in petitioning Parliament, teaching and preaching the tenets of abolitionism, raising money to publish and distribute tracts and other literature, writing pro-abolition letters and articles for newspapers and generally raising awareness about anti-slavery issues in every forum they could.

Fact finding was a crucial tactic. Parliamentary committees needed data, and so did abolitionists confronted by naysaying opponents. Clarkson, indefatigable, developed a list of 145 questions and visited the major slaving ports chasing after reluctant witnesses from among seamen involved in the slave and West Indian trades. To locate Isaac Parker, a sailor who had seen English slavers capture Africans in armed raids on villages, Clarkson got permission from Sir Charles Middleton to board every ship in the harbor. He located Parker on the 317th vessel, and triumphantly introduced him to a parliamentary committee. Former ship captain and surgeon Harry Gandy was one of Clarkson's few cooperative witnesses. "I had rather live on bread and water, and tell what I know of the Slave Trade, than live in the greatest affluence and withhold it," Gandy declared. Other ships' officers fled from him like "a wolf, or tiger, or some dangerous beast of prey," Clarkson wrote.[410] So he could describe slave ships, Clarkson went inside two and measured: each adult African had three square feet of space.

Clarkson also disputed the widely believed notion that the slave trade was a nursery for the navy; his statistics proved it was a grave that swallowed more sailors than slaves. Of 5,000 sailors plying the triangular trade in 1786, only 2,320 came home; 1,130 died and 1,550 were unaccounted for in either Africa or the West Indies, and Clarkson knew the names of each one. Clarkson's official evidence on the "monstrous inequity" of the slave trade ran to 850 folio pages for the Privy Council report, and 1,300 pages for the House of Commons.

The abolitionists also used images to make their case. One that struck a collective nerve was the unforgettable image of a Liverpool slave ship, the *Brookes*, with 482 recumbent Africans jammed into its hold and an accompanying note adding that the *Brookes* sometimes carried as many as 609. Wilberforce had first displayed a wooden model of the slaver in the House of Commons as he urged members to vote against the slave trade. Prints of the *Brookes* became wildly popular decorations. The abolitionists printed 8,700 copies to display in homes and pubs, making it the first mass-distributed political poster. To this day, the *Brookes* illustrates books and articles on the slave trade and abolition.

The abolitionists' strategies were to cover every issue, defend every pronouncement, counter every criticism and suggest palatable alternatives to what would be abolished. They cited material from all credible sources, especially missionaries, former slaves and repentant slave captains and slave owners. Ramsay's *Essay on the Treatment and Conversion of African Slaves in the British Sugar Colonies* took readers into the cane fields and hovels of the sugar slaves, and was one of the most influential pieces of abolitionist literature. Congregations throughout England listened in fascination as other missionaries' reports were read out.

In his *Authentic Narrative* told in the first person, former slaver John Newton described how, despite his affection for his wife, Polly, he had had lustful thoughts about enslaved African women and had curbed them by drinking only water and abstaining from meat. Other narratives revealed that many seamen had had no such compunctions and had sexually assaulted the Africans. Brutalities were detailed. *Felix Farley's Bristol Journal*, published in 1792, described how John Kimber, a Bristol slave-ship captain, punished a sick fifteen-year-old African for not eating by having her suspended upside down by one ankle and whipped so savagely that, five days later, she died of her injuries. A satirical cartoon by Isaak Cruikshank depicts a gloating Captain Kimber and a sobbing trio of slave women watching as the flailing, upside-down, naked woman holds her head in despair as angry sailors prepare to whip her. The cartoon, shown below, is titled "The Abolition of the Slave Trade."

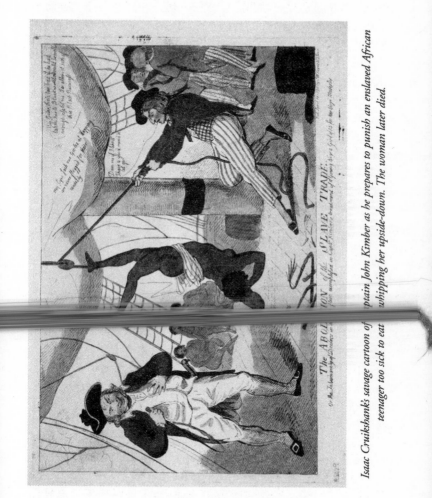

Isaac Cruikshank's savage cartoon of Captain John Kimber as he prepares to punish an enslaved African teenager too sick to eat by whipping her upside-down. The woman later died.

The published testimonials of African victims of the slave trade were especially powerful, and Equiano's *The Interesting Narrative of the Life of Olaudah Equiano, or Gustavus Vassa, the African* (1789) and Cugoano's *Thoughts and Sentiments on the Evils and Wicked Traffic of Human Species* (1787) generated intense interest. Sancho's *Letters of the Late Ignatius Sancho, an African*, published posthumously in 1782, were said to prove that "an untutored African may possess abilities equal to an European."[411]

Equiano promoted his seven-shilling pamphlet so ably that, for five years, he traveled throughout Britain on what historian Adam Hochschild styles "the first great political book tour."[412] His narrative, in some respects modeled on *The Life and Most Surprizing Adventures of Robinson Crusoe* (1719), appealed to intellect as well as sentiment. His fears that his white captors intended to stew and eat him reversed cultural notions about cannibalism. Equiano also accused planters, greedy for cheaply produced sugar, of destroying Africa's rich and peaceful societies.

Cugoano's account, edited by Equiano, described how the "browfow, that is, the white-faced people," took him from Africa to Grenada and how, during the Middle Passage, "it was common for the dirty filthy sailors to take the African women and lie upon their bodies." On a Grenadian sugar plantation, Cugoano saw "most dreadful scenes of misery and cruelty ... for eating a piece of sugar-cane, some were cruelly lashed, or struck over the face, to knock their teeth out.... Some told me they had their teeth pulled out, to deter others, and to prevent them from eating any cane in future." Cugoano was the first African to propose "a total abolition of slavery ... an universal emancipation of slaves" and an immediate end to the slave trade.[413]

Abolitionism—and the West India Interest—spewed out advertisements, newspaper articles, letters to editors and pamphlets. Abolitionists lobbied editors and worried that the West Indians and their allies were resorting to bribery or intimidation to have editors exclude abolitionist articles or letters from their newspapers. To persuade editors to support abolition, Clarkson traveled with a grim show-and-tell, a set of implements sold in Liverpool shops for use in the slave trade: handcuffs, shackles, thumbscrews and a tool to pry open the mouths of slaves attempting suicide by starvation.

ABOLITION OF THE SLAVE TRADE, OR THE MAN THE MASTER.

This British cartoon illustrates whites' terror that if the slave trade ended, slaves would retaliate and treat whites as they have been treated, forced to labor, beaten and deprived while they—the new masters—cavort and enjoy their prosperity.

Both abolitionist and pro-slavery groups distributed cheap or free pamphlets, many simple and satiric. "Valuable Articles for the Slave Trade," one spoof abolitionist handbill announced: "To be SOLD at and under Prime Cost, in Consequence of the EXPECTED ABOLITION ... About Three Tons Weight Hand and Feet Shackles and Thumb Screws ... Enquire of the Slave Mongers. Specimens of the Whole (except the Thumb Screws, the Sight of which it is thought would too deeply wound the Feelings of those not inclined to purchase) are NOW exhibiting on the Exchange."[414] Cartoons could be biting and unforgettable. As a commentary on the treatment of sick slaves, James Gillray's 1792 "Barbarities in the West Indies" depicts a grim-faced white man using a long baton to hold a struggling slave down in a vat of boiling sugar.[415]

Most propaganda was more serious. Bristol Quaker James Cropper's "Another Bonus to Planters: or the Advantage Shown of an Equitable Purchase of the Monopoly and Bounty on West India Sugar" argued that free-grown East Indian sugar should be substituted for slave-grown West Indian. To catch the attention of members of Parliament, Cropper sent them packets of free-grown sugar and coffee.

The West India Committee, formed in about 1775 as a London-based association of absentee sugar planters and merchants connected with the West Indian trade, developed as a powerful lobby for the sugar and related industries. The committee also strongly opposed abolition-ism and, after Cropper's gesture, volleyed back. Five thousand copies of *An Abstract of the Evidence favourable to the Africa trade* were printed, *A Defence of the Planters in the West Indies* was sent to members of Parliament, and eight thousand copies of a pamphlet describing the sugar slaves' darling little cottages and gardens were distributed. Theatergoers were treated to Thomas Bellamy's short play *The Benevolent Planters*, which dramatized the compassion of planters who offered to replace sold-off lovers with new ones then, in a crashingly happy ending, reunited them instead.

For more critical thinkers, the West Indians sponsored the weightily titled pamphlet "No abolition, or, An attempt to prove to the convic-tion of every rational British subject that the abolition of the British trade with Africa for Negroes would be a measure of unjustice as impolitic, fatal to the interests of this nation, ruinous to its sugar colonies, and more or less pernicious in its consequences to every description of the people." The tone of this pamphlet, as well as of most other West Indian propaganda, was economic reasonableness. As Stephen Fuller, an influential planter and the agent for Jamaica, reported, "The stream of popularity runs against us; but I trust never-theless that common sense is with us, and that wicked as we are when compared with the abolishers, the wisdom and policy of this country will protect us."[416] Another anti-abolitionist believed that nomencla-ture was the problem: "Instead of SLAVES, let the Negroes be called ASSISTANT-PLANTERS; and we shall not then hear such violent outcries against the slave-trade."[417]

The guilt-inducing theme of "blood as sugar," an abolitionist favorite, was used to counter West Indian economic fearmongering. *No rum!— No sugar! Or, the voice of blood; being half an hour's conversation between a Negro and an English Gentleman, Shewing the Horrible Nature of the Slave Trade,* one pamphlet was titled. Another identified anyone who ate sugar as "the prime mover, *the grand cause of all the horrible injustice."*[418] Other abolitionists shocked readers into acknowledging the direct link between sugar and living and breathing (and sweating and bleeding) slaves. In *An Address to the People of Great Britain, on the Propriety of Abstaining from West India Sugar and Rum,* Quaker William Fox calculated that for every pound of West Indian sugar "we may be considered as consuming two ounces of human flesh."[419]

Thus, "blood as sugar" inverted African cannibalism by attributing it to whites who ate sugar. It also echoed Christian transubstantiation, wine as Christ's blood, as poet Samuel Coleridge thundered in a 1795 lecture: "Gracious Heaven! at your meals you rise up and ... say O Lord bless the Food which thou hast given us! A part of that Food among most of you is sweetened with the Blood of the Murdered. Bless the Food which thou hast given us! O Blasphemy! Did God give Food mingled with Brothers blood! Will the Father of all men bless the Food of Cannibals—the food which is polluted with the blood of his own innocent Children?"

BOYCOTTING SUGAR

If sugar was literally polluted with slaves' blood and sweat, clearly no reasonable person could eat it. The abolitionists decided to boycott sugar, and William Fox calculated that if every family accustomed to using five pounds of sugar and rum per week abstained from slave-grown sugar, every twenty-one months they would save one African from enslavement and death. Every nineteen and a half years, eight families would save one hundred Africans. London debating societies borrowed the topic, resolving in January 1792, "Is it not the duty of the people of Great Britain, from a principle of moral obligation and regard to their national character, to abstain from the consumption of West

India produce till the Slave Trade is abolished and measures are taken for the abolition of Slavery?" and in February 1792, "Which might be considered the most Criminal, the Merchants and Planters who carry on the Slave Trade; the British House of Commons, who have refused to abolish it, or the People who encourage it by the Consumption of Sugar and Rum?" To this was added "An Appeal from the suffering Negroes" addressed to "the Judgment, as well as the compassionate Feeling of the Fair Sex ... to dissuade them from any longer consuming an Article of Luxury that is polluted with the Blood of innocent Fathers, Mothers and Children."[420] In the early stages of the boycott, abolitionist conviction coincided with the rise of the price of sugar during the Haitian Revolution and drove 300,000 English people to abstain from West Indian sugar. Wilberforce had clearly erred on the side of caution.

James Gillray lampoons the abolitionist campaign to abstain from sugar. The daughters sulk as their parents laud the deliciousness of their sugarless tea.

Abstention was usually a family matter directed by the female head. Both well-to-do and working class abstained. "There is more people I think hear [*sic*] that drinks tea without sugar than there is drinks with," Lydia Hardy wrote to Equiano about her village of Chesham.[421] Abstainers came from all denominations as abolitionists urged all Christians to shun the sugar and rum that orphaned slave children by murdering their parents through "excessive labour and cruel treatment." In response to their customers' concerns and demands, grocers and refiners quickly located East Indian sources and announced that their sugar was "produced by the labour of FREEMEN." Sugar planters protested that the abolitionist movement was frightening away capital investment in the West Indies.

In fact, the boycott harmed the sugar business less than the fact that sugar was in short supply and therefore increasingly expensive. Then, as the French Revolution generated a backlash against anything smacking of Jacobinism, the abolition society quietly decided to stop promoting the boycott. Although the boycott failed to end slavery, it was a propaganda victory. It linked sugar to slavery and spelled out the individual sugar consumer's complicity in perpetrating slavery. And, by acknowledging women's power in buying and using and serving sugar, it enlisted women as participants in a campaign that had until then largely excluded them. A few decades later, women would revive the sugar boycott. Since that first boycott, and as a direct result of it, boycotting as an economic weapon has become a standard feature in major justice campaigns.

Abolition also evoked a steady literary outpouring, as poets, writers, essayists and dramatists expressed their sentiments through art.[422] Poet William Cowper, a dedicated abolitionist, tackled a range of themes. "The Task" condemns racism: "There is no flesh in man's obdurate heart, / It does not feel for man. The natural bond / Of brotherhood is severed as the flax / That falls asunder at the touch of fire. / He finds his fellow guilty of a skin / Not coloured like his own, and having power / To enforce the wrong, for such a worthy cause / Dooms and devotes him as his lawful prey." And again in "The Negro's Complaint," "Fleecy locks and black complexion / Cannot forfeit nature's claim; / Skins may differ, but affection / Dwells in white and black the same."

Cowper also indicted sugarcane: 'Why did all-creating nature / Make the plant for which we toil? / Sighs must fan it, tears must water, / Sweat of ours must dress the soil. / Think, ye masters iron-hearted, / Lolling at your jovial boards, / Think how many backs have smarted. / For the sweets your cane affords." The narrator of "Pity for Poor Africans" rationalizes his moral confusion about sugar slaves: "I pity them greatly but I must be mum / For how could we do without sugar and rum?"

Some poetry was shamelessly hagiographic. Anna Letitia Barbauld's 1791 "Epistle to William Wilberforce, Esq., On the Rejection of the Bill for Abolishing the Slave Trade" elevated Wilberforce to the apex of a movement millions strong. In his 1807 poem "To Thomas Clarkson. On the Final Passing of the Bill for the Abolition of the Slave Trade," William Wordsworth genuflected to "Duty's intrepid liegeman": "Clarkson! It was an obstinate hill to climb: / How toilsome—nay, how dire—it was, by thee / Is known; by none, perhaps, so feelingly: ...The blood-stained Writing is for ever torn; / And thou henceforth wilt have a good man's calm, / A great man's happiness."

As the poetry suggests, Clarkson's and Wilberforce's elevation to secular sainthood reinforced the abolitionist focus on parliamentary solutions. The pair was an effective team. Clarkson investigated and amassed information. Wilberforce incorporated Clarkson's data into forceful and moving parliamentary speeches, and used his friendships with politicians to hammer out political deals.

The West India Interest

On its road to success, abolition suffered many defeats and faced formidable opposition from the West India Interest, their political and commercial allies and their influential family connections. The West Indians worked diligently within Parliament to respond to every abolitionist remark, offering counterevidence, denials or justification. A preferred tactic was to favorably compare the lives of wretched slaves with those of England's wretched workers. Their strongest arguments were economic: sugar had made fortunes and was a mainstay of the empire.

The West Indians resorted as well to smear tactics to destroy their opponents' credibility. The most egregious example was their vilification of abolitionist James Ramsay. They attributed his limp to his falling onto a stone floor as he kicked a slave as punishment for a minor misdeed. The planter Molyneux testified in the House of Commons that Ramsay had abused slaves. Although other West Indians refuted these charges, Ramsay's enemies attacked relentlessly. When the abolitionist finally succumbed to his grief and died, Molyneux gloated to his illegitimate son, "Ramsay is dead—I have killed him."[423]

Another West Indian tactic was to justify slavery by portraying Africans as savages. When Haiti erupted in revolution and insurrections spread in the West Indies, they declared that interfering with slavery would lead inevitably to such horrors. White Jamaicans reviled Haitians as "black barbarians," and in England, Wilberforce worried because "people ... are all panic-struck with the transactions in St. Domingo."[424]

That did not stop the hero-hungry British public from admiring Haiti's martyrs. Wordsworth assured Toussaint Louverture, betrayed and mistreated by France, that "thou hast great allies; / Thy friends are exultations, agonies, / And love, and man's unconquerable mind." Wilberforce enthusiastically fulfilled the self-appointed Emperor Henri Christophe's request for qualified English school and college teachers, and tutors for the now-imperial children, and confessed, "How I wish I was not too old ... to go."[425]

Abolitionists sympathized with the Haitians' longing for freedom but deplored their violent tactics. Many people noted with displeasure that the freed blacks did not appear interested in the hard work needed to run sugar plantations. In the face of revolution and public dismay, the abolitionists lay low until they resurged in the new century, revitalized. In 1805, the eleventh abolition bill in fifteen years was defeated. In 1806, the London Abolition Committee demanded that political candidates pledge themselves to abolition in the November elections. Even politicians with poor records on the issue hastily embraced it. *Felix Farley's Bristol Journal* exulted that "the friends of the oppressed African race will be pleased to learn that during the course of the election in

Philanthropic Consolations, after the loss of the Slave-Bill *is James Gillray's savage depiction of abolitionists William Wilberforce and Bishop Samuel Horsley as debauched libertines whose real love for enslaved blacks is erotic in nature.*

various parts of the kingdom the popular sentiment has been very strongly expressed against the continuance of that traffick in human flesh."[426]

The embittered West India and slaving interests battled on, but Lord Grenville's new Whig government, which included abolitionist foreign secretary Charles Fox, were in tune with the popular will. In January 1807 the Abolition Bill made its sixteenth appearance. The House of Commons debate elicited such passionate tributes to Wilberforce, including "three distinct and universal cheers," that he wept uncontrollably, "so completely overpowered by my feelings ... that I was insensible to all that was passing around me."[427] The bill passed 115 to 15 in the Commons and 41 to 20 in the House of Lords. It became law on March 25, 1807.

After decades of struggle, and at the beginning of a new century, the slave trade—but not slavery—was now illegal.

Chapter 8

Slaying Monsters: Slavery and Apprenticeship

SLAVERY LIVES ON

The slave trade may have been abolished, but in the sugar colonies slaves were bitter that they had not been freed. Some plotted insurrection, and Creole whites reported that their slaves wished to exterminate them. In England, however, abolitionists were as exhausted as they were exhilarated, and many were convinced that ending the slave trade would improve the condition of existing slaves and ultimately destroy slavery. In any case, the political climate made another abolition campaign a losing proposition, and there was too much else to do. The African coast and the West Indies needed monitoring for slave smuggling. The United States had abolished its slave trade, but what about France, Spain, Portugal and other European nations with slave-run sugar colonies that might compete against English colonies now forced to rely on natural slave reproduction? The new abolitionist priorities were to enforce the 1807 law, and to pressure other nations to end their slave trades.

In 1814, after the Treaty of Paris granted France five more years to end its slave trade, 806 abolitionist petitions denouncing this article gathered a record 750,000 signatures. Privately, Thomas Clarkson warned the government that if the "obnoxious article" remained, "both houses of Parliament, as well as the newspapers will be let loose against you."[428] In response, the government authorized loans and overseas territories as incentives for foreign nations to end their slave trades.

Much besides the slave trade was involved. In 1814, Portugal and Spain, although major slave-trading nations, were staunch British allies against France. Only the unequivocal popular will as expressed in the giant petition campaign persuaded British officials to push for an end to the French, Dutch, Portuguese and Spanish slave trades at the 1815 Congress of Vienna. In 1817, Spain agreed to immediately end its slave trade north of the equator and, after three years, to end it south of the equator.

In that same year, Wilberforce's Slave Registration Bill passed, requiring slaveholders to register each slave. This measure was an effective clerical tool to detect new African imports and to determine the slaves' mortality rate, and it passed against ferocious West Indian opposition.

The next wave of abolitionism targeted slavery. In 1823, the Anti-Slavery Society was founded, followed by the first of many ladies' anti-slavery associations. In 1824, the movement was revitalized by the news that John Smith, a frail young Methodist missionary accused of complicity in a slave rebellion, had died in a wretched jail in Demerara, a Dutch colony Britain had taken over in 1814. Smith had run afoul of the governor on their first meeting, when he explained his plan to teach slaves how to read. The governor, Maj.-Gen. John Murray, who was also a planter, was horrified. "If ever you teach a negro to read and I hear of it, I will banish you from the colony immediately," he warned.[429]

Smith was not frightened off. He called the slaves "brethren." He spoke out publicly against slavery, lamenting, "O Slavery! Thou offspring of the devil … when will thou cease to exist?"[430] He documented the evils of sugar plantations: the "charnel houses" that passed for hospitals, "the grossest licentiousness," the merciless floggings, the pitiful huts, the inadequate clothing and food allowances, the "abundance of rum, to make them drunk." He and his wife also counted the daily whippings: on April 30, 1821—105 on the slave Philis, for running away; May 1—86 lashes; May 2—81 lashes; May 3—34 and then 72 more. On Sundays, as slaves defied their masters to attend

Smith's services, fifty lashes for going to church instead of working in the cane fields. "I have influence over the negro minds, which influence is great," Smith unwisely informed one planter, "and I will ... preach to them in defiance of all the authority you possess."[431]

In July 1823, a delegation of slaves demanded that the governor free them, because "their good King had sent orders that they should be free." The governor, enraged, blamed Smith for the slaves' insubordination and jailed both him and his wife, Jane. As Smith gasped for breath in a hot, airless ground-floor cell permeated by the stench of stagnant water underneath, the slaves rose up in rebellion. On the Batchelors Adventure plantation, they slapped their owner, dosed him with medicinal salts and confined all the whites to the stocks. Elsewhere, slaves locked up and jeered at their whites. The insurrection was not violent, but its suppression killed more than 250 slaves.

Smith's trial was a travesty of justice. The prosecution argued that he had incriminated himself by reading biblical references to the Israelites whom Moses had delivered from Israel because they were slaves under Pharaoh. This convinced the court, and Smith was convicted of promoting discontent among the slaves and failing to report their planned insurrection. He was sentenced to death.

John Smith beat the hangman. Wasted by disease and racked by pain, he died in prison. Vindictive officials barred Jane from attending his burial, and uprooted railings that mourning slaves erected at his grave. A week later, before this news crossed the Atlantic, King George commuted Smith's death sentence to banishment from Demerara. "The day of reckoning will come," Wilberforce predicted when he heard the news.[432]

A grieving Jane Smith returned to England. Abolitionists raised money for her and were galvanized by her sorrowful story, Smith's anti-slavery writings and the London Missionary Society's published accounts of his ludicrous trial and piteous death. In April and May of that year, Parliament received two anti-slavery petitions. Many abolitionists saw proof in Smith's life and death that amelioration, even if recalcitrant planters were to implement it, was not enough. Emancipation was the only possible solution.

ABOLITIONIST GOALS:
GRADUAL VERSUS IMMEDIATE EMANCIPATION

"Missionary Smith" was the clarion call to abolitionist women to renew their efforts for the cause. In this conflicted era in which Mary Wollstonecraft urged the vindication of the rights of women who could neither vote nor even petition Parliament, middle-class abolitionist women drew on their moral authority as keepers of the domestic hearth, as mothers and wives, and as sisters and daughters. At the urging of their male counterparts, they formed their own associations and prepared, printed and distributed abolitionist literature. They raised money, petitioned the government and once again boycotted slave-grown sugar.

The women's associations reflected their own goals and management styles. The influential Birmingham Ladies' Society for the Relief of British Negro Slaves, later renamed the Female Society for Birmingham, decided on "the diffusion of knowledge on the wrongs inflicted by the people of Britain on the African slaves, to contribute donations to the Anti Slavery Society, to relieve deserted and neglected slaves and to promote the education of British slaves."[433] Like the other societies, they kept detailed reports, minute books and an accounting ledger, transferring their skills as chatelaines to their volunteer work. The Birmingham women also compiled an Album of the Female Society containing poems, articles, letters and other documents.

In 1824, Elizabeth Heyrick's bestselling *Immediate, Not Gradual, Abolition: or, An Inquiry into the Shortest, Safest, and Most Effectual Means of Getting Rid of West Indian Slavery* caused a sensation and changed the tone of anti-slavery. Wilberforce's first reaction was to suppress it. Heyrick dismissed gradualism, the hallmark of male abolitionism, as "puerile cant" and "the very master-piece of satanic policy," and women tended to agree with her.[434]

Tensions grew between male and female abolitionists. At one point, Wilberforce forbade his colleagues to speak at women's meetings. In 1830, at Heyrick's urging, the Female Society for Birmingham threatened to withhold its funding from the male Anti-Slavery Society unless gradualism was dropped. As Heyrick knew, the female societies donated more than 20 percent of the society's funds, and so the threat, and changing perceptions, had their effect. In May 1830, the Anti-Slavery Society opted for immediate abolition of slavery.

Unlike the men, abolitionist women were not sanctified, though Elizabeth Heyrick, Anne Knight, Lucy Townsend, Sarah Wedgwood, Mary Lloyd, Sophia Sturge and others were equally outstanding abolitionists. Their goals often differed from their male counterparts', their insistence on immediate abolition being the most striking example. The women understood the power of unity and vowed that "no cruel institutions, or ferocious practices could long withstand the avowed and persevering censure of the women of England."[435] As they carved out their territory and merged their resources, they also forged alliances that extended across the Atlantic to American abolitionists.

The women believed strongly in proselytizing for abolition through education, books, pamphlets, lectures and symbols. In 1828, they added a female version of the Wedgwood cameo to their arsenal, a kneeling, chained and piteous woman who pleads, "Am I not a Woman and a Sister?" They incorporated this image in bracelets and hairpins and had it printed on all manner of objects. A good abolitionist sugar pot, for instance, had the image on one side, and on the other a reminder that

> East India Sugar not made
> By Slaves.
> By Six families using
> East India, instead of
> West India Sugar, one
> Slave less is required.

The women also sewed and distributed thousands of workbags decorated with embroidered replicas of the Wedgwood cameo or mottos and containing abolitionist tracts. Even young girls and housebound women who could not publicly declare their views indicated their support for abolition by weaving the Wedgwood symbol into needlework samplers.

In the second phase of their campaign, the women initiated a national boycott of slave-grown sugar and promoted it by arguing that individuals who consumed sugar were complicit in the brutality of slavery. By buying sugar, "we participate in the crime," one of their pamphlets explained. "The West Indian planter and the people of this country, stand in the same moral relation to each other as the thief and the receiver of stolen goods," Heyrick elaborated.[436] "The laws of our country may hold the sugar-cane to our lips, steeped in the blood of our fellow-creatures; but they cannot compel us to accept the loathsome potion.... The slave-dealer, the slave-holder, and the slave-driver are the agents of the consumer ... he is the original cause, the first mover in the horrid process."[437] "As he sweetens his tea, let him reflect on the bitterness at the bottom of his cup," another writer urged. "Let him ... say as he truly may, this lump cost the poor slave a groan, and this a bloody stroke with the cartwhip; and this, perhaps worn down by fatigue and wretchedness and despair, he sunk under his misery and died! And then let him swallow his beverage with what appetite he may."[438]

As the women conceived it, the sugar boycott had moral, ideological and strategic appeal. It personalized the relationship between an unknown sugar slave and the English homemaker. By boycotting slave-grown sugar, that homemaker could make a moral statement and wield her economic purchasing power as a weapon to bring down the enemy. As her family's chief food buyer, she and millions of other women could lead the war against sugar slavery.

Heyrick argued that boycotting sugar would also end slavery much faster than the "panic-struck" abolitionist men's slow march, strewn with long petitions, to legislative abolition. "Abstinence from West Indian sugar alone, would sign the death warrant of West Indian slavery."[439]

Abstention, however, had to be taught, and the ladies' associations knew just how. They were experienced in benevolent visiting and so began to go door to door lending or selling tracts such as "Consumers of West Indian Sugar, the Supporters of West Indian Slavery." These described slavery and its evils, and urged substituting East Indian for West Indian sugar. The straight-talking "What Does Your Sugar Cost— A Cottage Conversation re British Negro Slavery" went to working-class women. "Reasons for Substituting East India Sugar for West" was for the "higher classes." To stop children from complaining at any reduction in their family's sugar rations, they distributed fourteen thousand copies of "Pity the Negro; or an Address to Children on the Subject of Slavery." (Abolitionists of both sexes were prolific pamphleteers. The Anti-Slavery Society alone distributed 2,802,773 tracts in the years 1823 through 1831.)

In the early 1830s, women also began to petition, an activity previously denied them. In 1833, four men lugged into Parliament a "huge featherbed of a petition" signed by 187,157 abolitionist women.[440] All the signatures had been gathered in just ten days, a reflection of how expertly the women organized the signature collecting. Men drafted their petition, printed it in several copies to be posted around town and advertised it. Supporters then signed, and organizers collected and collated all the copies. Women, however, orchestrated door-to-door blitzes, assigning volunteers to circulate the petitions in specific neighborhoods. This safeguarded the petitions from being ripped up or stolen, and it produced petitions inscribed by so many signatories that they represented one-quarter to one-third of the total number of all abolitionist signatures.

Abolitionist women took a special interest in the unique problems facing female slaves deprived of occupying their "proper Station as a Daughter, a Wife and a Mother." They reminded Victoria, their queen, that women were flogged, chained together by the neck with iron collars and placed on treadmills for trivial offenses. Through their petitions, well crafted and massively supported, abolitionist women forged a peculiarly female public stance on issues relating to sugar slavery and especially to slave women.

In an unusual lapse of common sense, abolitionist women assumed that slave women shared their English ideals about marriage, marital fidelity, modest behavior, childrearing and religious practice. They portrayed slave women as gentle, kneeling victims grateful for the intervention of their white sisters. They were never like Sally, who retaliated against Thomas Thistlewood by defecating in a kitchen strainer, or like the slave women who went on strike at Matthew Lewis's Jamaican plantation.

The exception to idealized images of enslaved womanhood was Mary Prince, the Antiguan slave whose 1831 *History* was the only slave narrative of a British West Indian woman. Mary's back was so "chequered" with the "vestiges of severe floggings [and] ... lacerated with *gashes*, by some instrument wielded by most unmerciful hands," and her *History* was such a scorching indictment of slavery that her abolitionist amanuensis did not suppress Mary's account of her complicated relationships with white and black lovers.[441]

EMANCIPATION

In the seething West Indies, sugar slaves unable to endure the wait for abolition rebelled and sometimes killed their whites. This happened in Jamaica during the Christmas season of 1831. The initial plan was for the sugar slaves to go on strike. But the strike escalated into an insurrection as twenty thousand slaves razed and burned plantations and cane fields, caused more than £1,000,000 in property damage and killed several whites.

The rebellion was crushed at the huge cost of £161,570 and the deaths of two hundred slaves. The remainder laid down their arms after a duplicitous promise of freedom, and 540 were hanged. Planters and officials allied with them turned viciously on the missionaries they blamed for inspiring the rebellion. Two Baptist missionaries fled to England and campaigned against slavery. Thomas Burchell described a "furious" white mob "hissing, groaning and gnashing at me with their teeth.... Had it not been for the protection afforded me by the coloured part of the population—natives of Jamaica—I should have been barbarously murdered—yea, torn limb from limb, by my countrymen—by so-called enlightened, RESPECTABLE! CHRISTIAN BRITONS!"[442] William Knibb recalled "the cries of the infant slave who I saw flogged on Macclesfield Estate, in Westmoreland ... the blood streaming down the back of Catherine Williams ... who preferred a dungeon to the surrender of her honour.... the lacerated back of William Black of King's Valley, whose back, a month after flogging, was not healed."[443]

In England, the Christmas Rebellion heightened the sense that anything short of emancipating the slaves was futile. As the rebellion leader, Samuel Sharpe, had said, "I would rather die on yonder gallows than live … in slavery." An investigation revealed that the rebellion leaders were trusted and privileged slaves motivated by their desire for freedom and for their masters' property. Slavery was in its death throes, and interminable parliamentary debates about abolition were contributing to rebellion. As a Jamaican put it, "The slave … knows his strength, and will assert his claim to freedom. Even at this moment, unawed by the late failure, he discusses the question with a fixed determination."[444]

On July 28, 1833, the Emancipation Act was passed in England, to take effect on August 1, 1834, but it emancipated only children under

Sam Sharpe, a slave-born Baptist preacher, urged, in 1831, slaves to refuse to return to the cane fields after Christmas. His peaceful protest turned into Jamaica's largest slave rebellion, killing hundreds, including fourteen whites. In 1832, just before he was hung for his role in the rebellion. Sharpe said, "I would rather die in yonder gallows, than live for a minute more in slavery." Sharpe officially became a Jamaican national hero in 1975, and fifty-dollar bills carry his image.

six, and "apprenticed" domestic and non-field workers to their former masters for a period of four years and plantation workers for six years. To its authors, "apprenticeship" meant learning how to live free, understanding that freedom meant working hard for wages, obeying the laws and embracing Christian ideals such as stable, Church-blessed marriages.

The concept of apprenticeship was designed to satisfy both panicked planters and gradualist abolitionists. Planters worried that freed slaves, given any choice, would refuse to work on the plantations; abolitionists believed that equitable conditions, strong legislation and moral suasion about the intrinsic value of labor would prevent this. The legislation mandated a forty-one-and-a-half-hour work week, with slave-era remuneration: food, clothing, housing and medical care. Field apprentices had twenty-six free days per year to either tend their crops or offer to work for their master for wages. Other days were designated for their gardens. Additional work, essential during sugarcane crop time, would be paid. To ensure compliance by both apprentices and planters, Britain paid and trained special magistrates who went out to supervise the new system. (In the absence of enough expatriate special magistrates, locals were enlisted as well.)

The Emancipation Act resolved the thorny question of compensation, setting aside a fund of £20 million to pay out claims from planters after apprenticeship ended. Compensation was seen as a moral duty and a political necessity, but British taxpayers were infuriated that planters were once again to feed from the public trough, this time through compensation rather than the preferential sugar duties that kept sugar prices artificially high. Working people complained bitterly that distant slaves were being coddled while English tots were apprenticed as chimney sweeps, beaten and starved. Many abolitionists vehemently opposed compensation for slaveholders rather than ex-slaves.

Compensation was one of the most important, albeit obscured, aspects of abolition. The West Indian Interest accepted that no government could withstand the abolitionist pressure for emancipation, though they fought it long and hard until the end. In *The Economics of Emancipation: Jamaica and Barbados, 1823–1843*, historian Kathleen

Butler documents the details of the compensation settlement. Sugar planters were heavily indebted to their metropolitan creditors—the West Indian Interest—and both feared that emancipation would devastate the sugar business and the financial system integral to it. The Interest warned that if slavery were abolished without compensation, they would stop issuing credit, honoring bills of exchange and shipping out essential supplies. In other words, "the Interest threatened to destroy the colonial economies and to bring down the government."[445]

The Whigs, cornered, negotiated a settlement that included compensation for all slaves, even runaways, and forced most slaves into an unemancipated labor arrangement with their former owners. Apprenticeship was a transitional arrangement devised to help planters develop a waged labor system. With the Interest driving the negotiations, there was no question of compensating slaves rather than—or as well as—their owners. Compensation per slave would be based on their average price for the preceding eight years in each colony. Claims had to be made in England, giving merchants and creditors the means to ensure that all outstanding debts were paid, and to influence how compensation money was invested.

EMANCIPATION'S WINNERS AND LOSERS

Emancipation had many winners, led by the abolitionists and the West Indian Interest. Abolitionists had created a movement that remains a model for reform movements today, most notably the animal rights movement, which has successfully adopted many of their strategies. Wilberforce, who died two days after the Emancipation Act passed, and Clarkson were hailed as heroes, Wilberforce for the cautious but steady abolitionism that became his life's story, Clarkson for his indefatigable research, powerful writings and perseverance in the cause. They also taught younger men politics, diplomacy and the art of compromise. One new leader they influenced was Joseph Sturge, the internationalist-minded Quaker who headed the movement from the mid-1830s.

Women abolitionists—perhaps ten thousand activists and the thousands more who signed petitions, sewed workbags and attended meetings and lectures, and the hundreds of thousands who abstained from West Indian sugar—also gained from emancipation. Their accomplishments were enormous. They personalized the concept of slavery so that English women saw the suffering of slaves in sugar lumps, and protested by boycott. They placed a moral duty on the woman shopping for her family's meals, playing "the ideology of consumerism in a heroic key."[446] The boycott had little effect on sugar imports, but it was immensely influential propaganda.

Emancipation also marked an important stage in the maturation of the women's abolitionist movement. Their success helped women challenge men's exclusive management of greater society, and it fostered a feminist consciousness. When women began to campaign for more rights, they drew on the experience of the abolition movement for inspiration and seasoned veterans. Abolitionist women, and men like Sturge, also extended their sights from sugar slavery to slavery everywhere, and their movement inspired like-minded men and women in America.

The sugar interest was a big winner of compensated emancipation. Members with sugar plantations as well as commercial connections did very well. Charles Pinney received £36,000, about $4 million in today's Canadian dollars. The Bishop of Exeter, the Right Reverend Henry Philpotts, and his partners received £12,729 for 665 slaves in Jamaica. Predictably, these nonresident sugar proprietors put little or none of their compensation money back into their West Indian holdings. Charles Pinney was typical; he invested his compensation fortune in English projects such as canals and railroads and in another slave-based business, the Great Western Cotton works. Local British industry and business benefited. So did the housing market, as claimants treated themselves to new homes. The Interest also did well by having first claim on the compensation money doled out to desperate and indebted West Indian planters. As *The Barbadian* newspaper angrily complained, "Very little of the 'monstrous sum' found its way to the West India colonies. It was paid for the most part, to mortgagees, in or about, the small circle of Threadneedle Street," home of the Bank of England. This was precisely what the English government predicted would happen when it "cynically submitted its emancipation plans to the [West India]

Interest before laying them before Parliament," observes Kathleen Butler.[447]

Nevertheless, emancipation crushed many planters who, despite compensation money, were forced to sell their estates. But this provided opportunities for new owners, which invigorated the plantocracy. Some small owners used their compensation to expand their holdings or to speculate. Knowledgeable estate managers scooped up likely plantations. Compensation had the unexpected effect of raising land values and encouraging land sales. It also led to a disproportionate number of white women, who usually owned mostly domestic slaves, taking advantage of their modest compensation money to enter the plantocracy, or to extend credit to planters. After decades of financial drought, the West Indies enjoyed a renewed surge of investment. For a decade or two after abolition, thanks to the generous compensation money and contrary to planters' doomsday predictions, emancipation did not annihilate the sugar business.

Emancipation was a bitter disappointment to slaves expecting freedom. In Trinidad, as the governor tried to explain the nature of apprenticeship, a crowd of former slaves shouted "old rogue!" and protested, "No six years, we do not want six years, we are free, the King has given us liberty!"[448] In Demerara, angry apprentices stopped working. In rare unity, plantation owners slaughtered the workers' pigs and cut down their fruit trees, hoping by removing their means of support to force them to stay on the plantations. Soon, seven hundred apprentices went on strike. The military intervened, the strike leader was hanged, and the strikers returned to the cane fields. Apprenticeship, in Eric Williams's words, was "Negro slavery ... perpetuated in a modified form."[449]

Antigua, crowded and heavily planted, skipped the apprenticeship years altogether. The planters did not act philanthropically. The cruel and prosperous planter Samuel Otto Beijer put it succinctly: "I have been making calculations with regard to the probable results of emancipation, and I have ascertained beyond a doubt that I can cultivate my estate at least one-third cheaper by free labour, than by slave labour."[450] Feeding old, infirm and infant slaves cost money; freedom would relieve the planters of this obligation. Instead, they would pay wages— 1 shilling daily for the Great Gang, 9 pence for other work—and provide housing, provision grounds and medical care. Binding labor contracts were required, with severe penalties if a worker violated them (for example, a week in jail at hard labor for two days' absenteeism), but a light fine (up to £5) if a planter did. In addition, strict vagrancy laws were drafted to force workers to stay on sugar estates.

Planters generally managed apprenticeship with a spiteful disregard for its spirit. Deviously, they registered domestics as field slaves, thereby extending their apprenticeship to six years and gaining new field hands. They responded mercilessly to demands for half-Friday to work the provision grounds, and sent apprentices who dared to demand them to the special magistrates, who routinely sentenced them to the treadmill. They purposefully prevented visits between spouses who lived on different plantations. They continued "the habitual indulgences of their passions" by sexually assaulting female apprentices, as did some black drivers. Just as before, male apprentices could not protect their women, who remained fair game for any man with authority or power. Apprenticeship became the new slavery—and the new focus of the abolitionists.

Jamaican apprentice James Williams's *A Narrative of Events* provided hard-hitting propaganda. His sufferings—floggings, confinement in tiny, damp, airless, rat- and vermin-infested dungeons and near-starvation—palled beside the torments of his fellow slaves. Williams had seen Henry James, an old African watchman, beaten so savagely for having allowed cattle to wander into an unfenced corn field that "he drop down dead—all the place cover with blood that he puke up."[451]

It was, however, Williams's testimony about the plight of female apprentices that shattered any remnants of abolitionist complacency about apprenticeship. For one thing, women were still corporally punished. The treadmill, originally used in English prisons, had been introduced into the West Indies for females specifically as a means of punishing them without exposing their naked bodies, as flogging did. Treadmills were giant wooden cylinders with attached steps; victims, strapped on by their wrists, swung in the air and had to "dance the steps" as the cylinder turned to avoid having their shins and legs scraped or smashed.

Williams's *Narrative* exposed the reality of this supposed improvement. Modesty was impossible; "the women was obliged to tie up their clothes, to keep them from treading upon them, while they dance the mill; them have to tie them up so as only to reach down to the knee, and half expose themself." A driver flogged two young women until he shredded their clothes, then boasted "that he see all their nakedness."

The floggings spared neither pregnant, nursing nor aged women. One woman "quite big with child" begged the overseer for relief but "him say, not him send her there, and he must do his duty." Another overseer responded to a woman who protested, "Massa, me no one flesh, me two flesh," by flogging her even harder. "He said he didn't care, it wasn't him give her belly." British visitors confirmed Williams's account of the floggings, testifying that the floors underneath the treadmill were bloodstained. Planters were indifferent when harshly punished women miscarried because, after August 1834, all children were born free and so they were not losing a little slave. Although apprenticeship transferred the power to punish from planters to special magistrates, apprentices, male and female, were punished as harshly as they had been as slaves. They were chained together, flogged, confined to the workhouse, house of correction or plantation dungeon, and sentenced to hard labor cane holing on sugar estates. They were fined, and their rations and allotted time for working provision grounds were reduced. Planters or their overseers also flouted the law and meted out "highly illegal punishments ... such as confinement in the estate's dungeon."[452] Abolitionist leader Joseph Sturge, who spent 1837 in the West Indies investigating working conditions and had brought Williams to England and sponsored his *Narrative*, confirmed in a voluminous report that apprenticeship was nothing more than another name for slavery "in its most ferocious, revolting, and loathsome aspect."[453]

The planters were not just indulging in vindictiveness. They were also aiming to make women's lives so wretched that they would surrender their youngsters as apprentices in Hogmeat Gangs and agree to put in extra hours in the cane fields. Planters were profoundly worried that

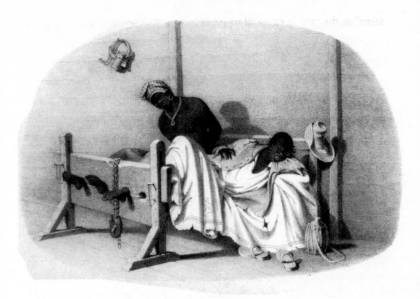

*Two exhausted slaves are forced into painful positions in the stocks,
a common punishment. One tries to sleep.*

when universal emancipation arrived in six years, women would
abandon the plantations, become homemakers and refuse to work in the
cane fields. It was a valid fear, especially as missionaries and abolitionists
were hard at work promoting just such a way of life as civilized and
Christian. Anticipating imminent ruin, planters tried to squeeze the last
ounce of work out of their apprentices, and to harass them in the process.

Williams described a typical case. Jamaican planter Mr. Senior
accused his hated field worker Amelia Lawrence, a mother of four, of
pushiness because she always worked in the first row, where her brother
was driver. Amelia's retort—"Massa ought to be glad to see apprentice
working at the first row, and doing good work"—earned her a week in
the workhouse and on the treadmill. That week was made yet more
distressing because Amelia had to leave her four children in the care of
others. Nancy Webb, summarily convicted of sassing a plantation
constable, was sentenced to seven days in the workhouse away from her
husband, Jarvis, and her seven children.[454] On plantations everywhere,

overseers tormented cane-field apprentice mothers. They forced those with more than six children, exempted from field work under the amelioration laws, back into the cane fields. Williams described the merciless treatment of nursing mothers: "Them women that have young sucking child, have to tie them on their back. When it rain ever so hard they have to work on with the children tied on their backs…. [The overseer] don't allow them to suckle the child at all, if it cry ever so much; him say the children free, and the law don't allow no time to take care of them; it is only the good will of the driver that ever let woman suckle the children."

In Jamaica, a group of nursing mothers arrived late at the cane fields because they had had to carry their babies and the ground underfoot was sodden with rain. When they lost six Saturdays as punishment, they protested that they could not survive without them. Their provision grounds were six miles away, they no longer had half-Fridays, their salted fish was finished and they no longer received sugar or flour for the children. For arguing, a special magistrate upheld the six Saturdays and added three days in the workhouse.[455]

The cane-field mothers protested even more fiercely when planters tried to bully them into letting their children tend livestock, collect grass and do other chores. The planters denied the children food and medical care, and some would not even feed apprentice mothers. When they were pregnant or nursing, the planters refused to allow them the time specified by the law for postnatal recuperation and breast-feeding, and forced them to make up any time lost in caring for sick or nursing children. At the same time, many planters shut down the "nurseries" and sent elderly nannies into the cane fields.

The mothers did not capitulate. They wanted their free children to remain free, to learn a good trade and to have a better life. Sometimes their fight to protect their children had tragic consequences. In St. Vincent, a measles epidemic killed many children whose apprentice mothers, fearing that the planter could claim the labor of any child treated by the estate's doctor, left them untreated. In other cases, mothers and a few fathers negotiated with the planter, agreeing to work extra days to pay for their children's medical care, six days if they had one child, nine days if they had more. "They … clung with tenacity to the right of expressing free will in respect of their unfettered offspring," reported Robert Pitman, special magistrate in St. Vincent, where planters succeeded in apprenticing only three, all the children of drunks.[456]

The cane fields and the quarters became the sites of guerrilla warfare between apprentices and planters. Women knew the new law and held their employers and supervisors to its provisions. They shouted "Six to six!" (6 A.M. to 6 P.M.) and resisted working longer hours. They were willing to strike against unfair treatment and to march to the nearest special magistrate to lodge complaints against their oppressors. Wisely, they emphasized their status as mothers, knowing how this resonated with British abolitionists. But unlike the meek Wedgwood slave woman who asked, on her knees, if she was a woman and a sister, these women angrily articulated their grievances and pursued them with legal authorities. Special magistrates listed case after case involving the rights of women who were pregnant, breast-feeding, caring for sick children, the mothers of six or more surviving children, and of women punished by now-forbidden flogging.

The fiction of apprenticeship as a training period for former slaves unused to freedom and working hard disintegrated quickly in the face of the blatant reality that it was simply a revised version of slavery that created a doomsday recklessness among planters. In England, abolitionists campaigned to end it immediately. In the West Indies, two years before it was due to end, the colonial legislatures voluntarily abolished it. On August 1, 1838, slavery, alias apprenticeship, really was abolished.

Throughout the West Indies and England, people rejoiced. In Jamaica, free and freed people surrounded a coffin inscribed "Colonial Slavery, died July 31st, 1838, aged 276 years." On the stroke of midnight, abolitionist missionary William Knibb cried, "The monster is dead! the negro is free! three cheers for the queen!"[457] Then the coffin, a chain, handcuffs and an iron collar were buried and, in the soil above them, a tree of liberty was planted.

Black deacons in Knibb's church used the occasion to express gratitude for the gospel—"The gospel bring we free," one said—and to focus on sugar slavery's legacy. Deacon Edward Barrett, a blood if not legal relative of the poet Elizabeth Barrett Browning, reminded the crowd how slavery

IMMEDIATE EMANCIPATION

In Alexander Rippingille's symbol-laden Immediate Emancipation in the West Indies, Aug. 1st, 1838, *a scantily clad former slave stands atop a whip, rejoicing under a palm tree to which the news of emancipation is tacked. Beside him two men bury shackles and a woman holds up her now-free child.*

had torn families apart through slave sales and by forcing men to whip their wives. William Kerr told the cheering crowd, "Let we remember that we been on sugar estate from sunrise a-morning till eight o'clock at night; the rain falling, the sun shining, we was in it all…. We get whip, our wives get beat like a dog, before we face, and if we speak we get the same; they put we in shackle; but thank our heavenly Father we not slave again."[458]

Freedom

Planters saw nothing to thank God for. Instead, they counted and cursed their enemies: missionaries who goaded slaves into rebellion; East Indian sugar producers and traders; beet sugar growers and their advocates; greedy London merchants; interfering colonial officials; self-interested manufacturers suddenly hostile to protective sugar duties; British consumers who boycotted West Indian sugar; self-righteous abolitionists; and competition from slaveholding sugar producers, notably Cuba and Brazil. Added to this was the planters' worst nightmare about emancipation: would the now-free Quasheba, insolent and intractable, and her partner Quashee, sly and supremely lazy, continue to toil in the cane fields as the abolitionists had promised?

If sugar were to remain king, or even pretender to the throne, the crop had to be tended. In Antigua and other heavily planted colonies with little spare land, freed blacks had few alternatives to the low wages that sugar planters offered them. In other colonies, where more land was available, few blacks accepted work with wages and conditions little better than they had endured in slavery. To coerce them into the fields, planters resorted to blackmail in the form of contracts that linked labor with housing. To remain in the home they already occupied and had often built, and to harvest the provision grounds they had cleared and planted, freedmen and women had to work on the plantation.

There was worse. They had to pay rent levied per inhabitant, not per house, and rental penalties for every day a tenant was absent from the field. Only children under ten were exempted. Rent was to be deducted from the weekly wages, making workers as dependent on the plantation owners as they had always been. The rent was a double blow for women.

Because they had been prevented from learning skilled trades, those who worked earned the lowest wages. Women who refused to return to the hated cane fields and earned their living gardening and higgling were even more vulnerable. Instead of the whip of slavery, planters wielded the bludgeon of housing and provision grounds.

In many places, missionaries intervened and advised workers against signing the proffered contracts, and black preachers organized labor strikes. Planters retaliated fiercely. They served eviction notices and ruthlessly executed them. They destroyed provision grounds bursting with crops and killed the freedmen's animals. In Jamaica, Shawfield plantation's owner demolished the house of Rasey Shaw, an old Baptist woman who was no longer able to work; Rasey "was driven into the road, without a shelter or a home," reported her pastor, William Knibb. A special magistrate wrote that the rent question hung, "like the sword of Damocles, suspended over the island."[459]

Other planters took a different approach and tried to create a landless workforce. They, too, linked labor with housing, and lodged their workers rent-free in the former slave quarters. Workers who remained in their homes did so at the planters' pleasure, and could be evicted for a wide range of causes: work disputes, illness or disability, affiliation with hated Christian churches such as the Baptists or, as very often happened, a woman's refusal to work, or a parent's keeping children at home or sending them to school instead of to work.

This planterly persecution crushed many dreams of life in freedom. At the same time, it drove other freedmen to buy or at least rent their own land with money they had earned during apprenticeship. The very poorest among them simply squatted. As sugar production plummeted, planters unable or unwilling to adapt to the new labor force declared bankruptcy or abandoned their plantations, and land-hungry blacks eagerly purchased plots carved from those larger holdings. "If a few sugar estates are abandoned so much the better, eventually it will be the making of Jamaica," Knibb declared. "Sugar is sweet but the liberty of man is much more sweet."[460]

Missionaries colluded against planters who refused to sell to blacks, presenting themselves as buyers then reselling to their parishioners.

14489—"Two Pretty Girls I Met in a Cane Field," St. Kitts, B. W. I.

Two old women, one clenching a corn pipe between her teeth, pose jauntily in their ragged dresses in the cane fields where they toil decades after emancipation.

Freedmen often continued to work for wages on the sugar plantations and harvested the crops already planted in the provision grounds. Freedwomen were much less likely to return to the cane fields. They lived and worked on their land, farming and higgling, raising children and homemaking. They also formed Afro–West Indian Christian religious sects that satisfied their desire to both worship and to lead. Most black women declined to reinvent themselves in the feminine domestic image abolitionists had confidently ascribed to them. They showed little enthusiasm for the pure domesticity that white women were already fighting to escape or for exchanging dependence on white men for dependence on black.

Missionaries encouraged the black rush to landownership, which they strongly believed was necessary to restore to black men the independence, security and sense of responsibility that slavery had stolen from them. The men could then reshape their relationships with the women they had been unable to defend and had been forced to flog.

Many missionaries established free "Negro Villages," and those unable to acquire their own land streamed into them. They were not, strictly speaking, really free: missionary societies or churches financed them at low or no interest, and most lots were designed to support a household but not to provide a living. The idea was that male villagers would work on the plantations, then return at night to their own Christian homes, dependent wives and obedient children. Knibb spoke for most missionaries when he described the Free Village population as "the germ of a noble free peasantry" and when he argued that freedom should be measured *not* by the tonnage of sugar produced "but by the cottager's comfortable home, by the wife's proper release from toil, by the instructed child, and by all that joy and peace which now gladdens the hearts of the beloved people of my choice."[461]

Within a decade, in Jamaica and other large colonies, two-thirds of sugar workers had moved away from their plantations; in more crowded islands, the numbers were smaller but still significant. The new communities drew on traditions from Africa, the Middle Passage and slavery, on dreams nurtured in oppression and fed by hope, and on the realities of lives in a broken society. Marriage became increasingly popular. So did churches whose missionaries had proved themselves in the fight for freedom. The family and the chapel replaced the sugar planter and his authority, and the emergent culture, though marked by the legacy of the sugar estates, was Afro-Creole.

With its labor force decimated, West Indian sugar was in trouble. Planters unable to corral sufficient workers looked elsewhere, for instance to the Leewards, where the scarcity of land available for blacks to escape to enabled local planters to offer risibly small wages—9 pence with housing, garden and medical care in Antigua, 4 pence with housing and garden in Montserrat and, in Nevis, only a share of the produce. In larger, richer islands, planters offered much more— 2 shillings—and sugar workers willing to trade familiar misery for foreign opportunities sailed away to new lives.

The influx of cane workers to Jamaica, Trinidad and British Guiana was too small to replace the flood of former cane workers who now lived as small farmers, higglers, tradesmen and small shopkeepers or, in a few cases, as landholders who hired their own employees. Desperate planters tried various measures to compensate for the lack of laborers, using the plow and harrow in place of the primitive hoe, and experimenting with different species of cane and better fertilizer. It was not enough. They advertised for immigrant cane workers, and shiploads arrived, a trickle from France, England and Germany and later a flood from China, Madeira, India and Africa. Within a few decades, sugar had a brand-new face, celebrated in now-independent, renamed Guyana's national anthem as "diverse though our strains ... one land of six peoples, united and free."

The travails of the sugar planters were additional proof that British sugar was no longer synonymous with slavery. But Cuban, Brazilian, French and Louisianan sugar and American commodities such as tobacco and the cotton that was fueling British industries were all produced by slaves. The abolitionists had new fields to conquer. In this new contest, men were more reluctant to participate, in part because their previous political and parliamentary strategies and expertise were of little use in dealing with foreign slavery. Women, however, willingly took up the cudgels and began to dominate the movement.

The abolition movement grew increasingly transatlantic, transcending political boundaries and focusing on the morality of the cause. The Quaker abolitionist tradition of corresponding with like-minded men and women across the ocean helped this process. Josiah Wedgwood had given anti-slavery cameos to Benjamin Franklin, who predicted that "they may have an effect equal to that of the best written pamphlet." The Liverpool Ladies' Anti-Slavery Society sent workbags and pamphlets to abolitionists in Philadelphia, Baltimore and New York. In America as in England, items decorated with the Wedgwood images were proudly displayed and treasured. In 1836, the Philadelphia Ladies' Society reissued Elizabeth Heyrick's *Immediate, Not Gradual, Emancipation*, which proved, as in England, immensely popular with female abolitionists. In 1837, when American women held their first national convention, they thanked British women for their help and support. Strategies that had been successful in England were adopted in America, with the same gender divisions. Although the bitterness, casualties and hardships of the American Revolution had ended less than three decades earlier, the common cause of anti-slavery erased former enmities as if they had never existed.

Chapter 9

Cuba and Louisiana: Sugar for North America

CUBAN CANE BECOMES BIG SUGAR

The triumph over slave-grown sugar was short-lived, and the English still ate slave-grown rice, wore slave-grown cotton and smoked slave-grown tobacco. They even imported sugar grown by foreign slaves, refined it and re-exported it to the Continent. In an 1845 parliamentary debate, Thomas Babington Macaulay, son of abolition-ist Zachary Macaulay, mocked the hypocrisy of this sugar policy: "We import the accursed thing; we bond it; we employ our skill and machinery to render it more alluring to the eye and the palate ... we send it to all the coffee houses of Italy and Germany; we pocket a profit on all this; and then we put on a Pharisaical air, and thank God that we are not like those sinful Italians and Germans who have no scruple about swallowing slave-grown sugar."[462] But banning its importation would cripple English refineries, and so slave-grown sugar continued to arrive.

A few years after emancipation, in an era of political and popular reform, the British government promoted free trade as the best way to offer consumers cheaper, fairer prices, especially on essential items such as sugar. Without the preferential duties that had protected West Indian sugar, competition among producers would lower the price. The West Indian lobby (predictably) predicted economic catastrophe, but the government, which no longer viewed the sugar colonies as essential elements of the metropolitan economy, was unmoved. In 1846, the sugar duties were repealed, and slave-grown sugar was no longer excluded from the domestic market.

Cuba's slave-holding planters, who by 1845 already exported 22 million pounds of sugar, half their production, to Britain, celebrated the news. Havana was "illuminated," a visitor reported, "in consequence of the news of high [sugar] prices from England." New plantations— *ingenios*—were opening up. Sugar planters took over coffee estates, "and the feeble gangs of old people and children were being formed into task-gangs, and being hired out by the month to the new *ingenios*."[463] Cuba, with more than three million slaves, had become the Caribbean's most spectacularly successful sugar producer.

Cuba also supplied the Americans' surging market, fueled by ambitious confectioners who used new technology to create alluring treats for the working classes and for children as well as for the wealthy. The cane fields of Louisiana could not supply the growing demand. Until the end of the nineteenth century, Cuba was America's principal supplier.

For 250 years, Cuban sugar had been a minor crop usually grown by cattle ranchers. During the Seven Years' War, Britain had briefly occupied Cuba and jump-started the island's sugar production. A giant market for Cuban sugar opened up during the American Revolution when Britain banned exports from her sugar colonies to rebellious American colonists. As Cuban planters stepped in, exporting sugar, molasses and rum in exchange for American food, naval supplies, manufactured goods, iron and slaves, "'sugar-fever' seized the island," historian Anton L. Allahar writes.[464]

The collapse of Haiti's sugar industry, the source of half of the world's sugar, propelled Cuba's rise to sugar greatness. Haiti even provided many fleeing French technicians who introduced improved technology into the Cuban sugar industry, just as seventeenth-century Jewish sugar financiers, merchants and planters fleeing Pernambuco after the defeat of their Dutch allies had disseminated new sugar technology throughout the Dutch Caribbean and Barbados. In 1792, 529 Cuban *ingenios* produced 19,000 tons; by 1846, nearly three times as many plantations—1,439—produced twenty-three times more sugar—446,000 tons. Increasingly wealthy and powerful sugar planters reshaped Cuban rural society for the benefit of the production and export of what had become Big Sugar.

Ironically, Haiti's exit from the sugar market transformed Cuba into a sugar slavocracy. Until the Haitian Revolution, most of Cuba's 85,000 slaves were domestics or city workers. By 1827, there were 286,942 slaves, and by 1841 there were 436,495, most of whom worked on sugar plantations. After Britain ended its slave trade, it pressured other nations to do the same. War-battered Spain agreed to do so by 1820. Before the deadline, Cuban planters imported as many Africans as they could, including 25,841 the year the treaty was signed, and 17,194 in 1820, when it was supposed to take effect. "Our existence is so tied into the maintenance of slavery that to want to destroy it all of a sudden will be suicidal," planter Ramóde Palma explained.[465]

Slave smuggling continued at least into the 1860s. Colonial officials accepted bribes for each African landed and, until the Civil War ended American slavery, American ships usually transported them even if they had to outrun British naval patrols. In the 1860s an American watched as more than a thousand Africans disembarked from a slaver in the dead of night. Within two hours, planters had purchased all of these "muzzled ones," as smuggled slaves were called, and they began their forced march to the sugar plantations. The slaver, "from stem to stern ... a mass of filth and noxious vapour," was towed out to sea and scuttled, leaving no trace of the illegal operation.[466] Cuban officials occasionally intercepted slavers. They freed the Africans, then put them to work on public projects such as the Canal de Vento.

A few planters believed that slavery was morally wrong, and many argued that waged workers would be more reliable and even cheaper. But slaves were readily available while free labor was not, and the Haitian Revolution had taught them that freed blacks would rise up against their white oppressors. Despite their terror of a Haitian-style uprising that would annihilate them, the planters defended slavery as an institution that both the state and the church had condoned, and continued to import slaves.

The planters' fears about slave uprisings were well founded. Their slaves, inspired by the Haitian Revolution and their own misery, rose up time and time again. Some revolts were spontaneous and slave-led, others were planned and directed by alliances of free mulattoes, blacks and slaves. The 1844 Ladder Conspiracy, which may have been a fictional plot invented by Cuban authorities to legitimize extreme repression, resulted in thousands of mulattoes, free blacks and slaves tied to ladders, tortured to extract confessions and sometimes executed.[467]

For frightened whites, the Ladder Conspiracy confirmed that even trusted slaves hated slavery and that "it was the kindest masters who were first massacred with their whole families."[468] Whites developed such an intense fear of blacks that Spanish officials used it as a club to keep the dissident Cubans in line, threatening to free the slaves if the Cubans defied the metropolis. "The fear which the Cubans have of the blacks, is the surest means which Spain has of guaranteeing her continued domination in that island," wrote Premier José María Calatrava.[469]

Sugar Modernizes

Cuban sugar planters had other pressing concerns. They needed new land to expand their cane operations, and new forests to fuel their boilers and their mills. They had to borrow money to import and install steam-driven mills and plows and other modern equipment. They had to experiment with hardier species of cane. They had to buy slaves whenever more were available. They had to arrange for their cane to be quickly and reliably transported to its final destination in Europe or the United States. They had to ensure that their sugar was as good as beet sugar, which was of highest quality.

By 1858, 91 percent of mills were powered by steam, with most of the others still reliant on animals. But steam alone did not engender significant increases in the juice-to-cane ratio. That took huge mills with massive steam engines that rotated slowly. The Arrieta family of Cárdenas imported such machinery from West Point and reported a rise in their juice-to-cane ratio to 72 percent from 52 percent on their Flor-de-Cuba plantation. Mills that invested in modern equipment produced, on average, two and a half times the average of the other steam mills. Vacuum pans, which were closed, also began to replace open pans. The early ones were unreliable but the improved versions saved fuel and produced one-third more sugar than open pans. Planters hoping to replicate the impressive results of their technologically advanced fellows incurred heavy debts to pay for the equipment and expertise as well as the bribes and extortionate taxes exacted by colonial officials. As the sugar industry developed as the driving force of Cuba's economy, indebted planters often lost their plantations to their merchant creditors, usually Spaniards, who then added planting to their other sugar-related businesses.

Meanwhile, the new technology was altering the nature of sugar production. Railroads, introduced into Cuba in 1834, replaced the cumbersome ox-pulled wagons that carried the cane from the fields to the mills and then to the ports. The railroad also transported firewood from distant forests, so planters who had traditionally set aside a quarter of their land as woodlots to supply fuel began to clear and plant on it instead, significantly expanding their operations.

Some small farmers made no attempt to modernize. They maintained their *trapiches*, small, inefficient, animal-powered mills, employed family members and a few workers, and made a living producing the crude muscovado sugar and *raspadura* syrup popular among poorer Cubans.

As modernization increased their capacity to process sugar so that more land had to be freed up to grow cane, planters needed more field hands. At the same time, the issue of emancipation loomed large. The planters argued that freeing their slaves would devastate their sugar operations because Cuba did not have and could not attract the vast numbers of waged workers the sugar industry would require. The mills alone employed 200,000 slaves; 200,000 replacements for them could never be found. Even if freed slaves agreed to work for wages, the planters insisted, the plantations would go bankrupt.

As it was, the planters had difficulty keeping a full complement of slaves. To compensate, they forced slaves to work even longer hours. When the slaves resisted, sabotaging tools and equipment, mutilating farm animals, refusing to work and running away, they were sent off to the cane fields in chains, and given stronger tools that were harder to break. The result was a seething workforce, inferior sugar, lower productivity and standards and a continual dearth of slaves.

To complement their slaves, the Cubans imported Chinese "contract" workers, and the first of them arrived in 1847. In the two decades between 1853 and 1873, more than 150,000 Chinese were brought to Cuba and held captive on the plantations alongside the black slaves. The Cubans also attempted to lure Europeans to the plantations for their supposedly greater skills and above all for their white skins—by 1841, slaves (436,495) and free blacks (152,838) together outnumbered whites (418,291). When these Spaniards, Canary Islanders and famine-plagued Irish arrived, they, too, were treated harshly. Fundamentally, Cuban planters could not imagine producing sugar without coerced labor.

Technological advances also brought additional personnel problems: the lack of skilled workers to operate the new equipment. The slaves, "men who are accustomed to calculating heat on the basis of touch, alkalization from smell, and the point of concentration from sight, cannot measure temperature in tenths of degrees, time in seconds, nor could they understand other industrial processes," historian Moreno Fraginals explains. "The production process is an integral one which includes order of life, culture, social habits and relations, and these factors all influence each other."[470] Nonetheless, research suggests that the most technically advanced Cuban planters successfully relied on slave labor reinforced by a very few waged laborers.[471]

Their inability to function without slaves led Cuban planters to take the extraordinary step of conspiring to join the United States, the great defender of slavery and the principal consumer of Cuban sugar. Since the 1820s, the idea had been discussed at the Havana Club, the planters' social headquarters. From the 1840s until 1855, the planters plotted rather than debated annexation.

Cuba's relationship with Spain was difficult and often adversarial. Colonial officials were corrupt and unsupportive bullies who levied punishingly high taxes. Spanish merchants charged usurious interest rates. Spain was politically chaotic, unresponsive to or contemptuous of Cuba's colonial aspirations, and too weak to provide enough soldiers to defend whites against always-anticipated slave attacks. Lastly, Spain imported only a small percentage of the sugar that had become Cuba's monoculture.

The United States, in contrast, imported more than half of Cuba's sugar; most of the rest came from Louisiana. The United States was a powerful and friendly neighbor even if many Southern planters had designs on Cuba's fertile and abundant land. American slavers defied the law and supplied Cuba with Africans. Annexation to the U.S. would guarantee the preservation of Cuban slavery, and troops to control rebellious Cuban slaves. Spanish, Cuban and American abolitionists seemed remote threats. But after the United States declined the Cuban invitation to annex Cuba, Cuban planters had to find other ways to safeguard their sugar fortunes and ways of life.

The Civil War ended American slavery, and the end of Cuban slavery seemed likely as well. Planters decided to make the best of the situation. They asked Spain to abolish slavery and compensate them at the rate of 450 pesos per slave, money they wanted to maintain and upgrade their operations. They also lobbied for colonial reforms. Spain refused all their requests. The government had no money for compensation and no interest in reform. Instead, it decreed new taxes and trade restrictions.

The planters' frustration and bitterness with Spain's intransigence boiled over. In 1868, Carlos Manuel de Céspedes, owner of La Demajagua plantation, freed his slaves and enlisted them to help him fight for Cuban independence. He also issued a decree on slavery that urged owners to emancipate their slaves but pledged to respect their "property" rights if they did not. His rallying cry was not slavery but Spanish tyranny. "Spain governs Cuba with a bloody, steel hand," he declared, and "denies us all political, civil and religious liberty."[472]

The resulting Ten Years War was confined mainly to the eastern regions of the island, which was split in two by a thick forested area almost seven hundred miles long. The railroad had never reached eastern Cuba and serviced only the regions where the sugarcane industry was concentrated. The war raged for a decade, killing thousands and destroying millions of dollars' worth of property as the rebels, especially slave recruits, burned sugar plantations and houses, razed mills, slaughtered cattle and ravaged the land. The war devastated the eastern provinces' sugar production but scarcely affected it in the western and central provinces.[473]

The Ten Years War ended in 1878, having failed to free Cuba from Spain. But its leaders had freed so many slaves that their war helped free all the others. In 1870, Spain had imposed the Moret Law, emancipating all children born after 1868 and all slaves sixty years of age or older. The rest were freed rotationally from 1881 to 1886, when Cuban slavery ended. The gradualist process of freeing them was designed to alleviate some of the confusion that freeing so many people at once would cause. It was also an expression of Cuba's deep ambivalence about emancipation, and a concession to planters who were losing their slaves without any compensation.

Abolition ended Cuba's traditional world of sugar planting and ushered in labor shortages. Planters in the largest sugar-producing regions responded by forcing landless workers to work for them, to move away or to face punishment under convenient new "vagrancy laws." By 1900 poor Spaniards, Jamaicans, Haitians and other West Indians were filling the gap with seasonal labor.

By the 1860s, Cuba faced a new crisis: competition from sugar beet. By 1862, more beet sugar was produced than Cuban cane, and by 1877 it had such a grip on the European market that Spain and England accounted for a mere 5.7 and 4.4 percent respectively of Cuban sugar sales. By 1880, beet-sugar production nearly equaled the combined output of cane sugar everywhere. Beet sugar was of the highest quality, cheaper to transport to European markets, subsidized by its home government's bounties and virtuously untainted by slave blood and sweat. *El Siglo*, the planters' official newspaper, lamented, "We have neither capital, workers, steel, foundries, fuel, industrial know-how, nor many other major requirements for competing against the forces of beet sugar, which possess all those elements."[474]

Happily for Cuba, the United States removed the sting of Europe's defection by taking a staggering 82 percent of Cuban sugar, and some

Cuban planters sought closer American connections by investing in the U.S. and even becoming American citizens. Cuban sugar brokers sought connections with New England refiners. Increasingly, Cuban and American sugar families established personal relations and even intermarried; the Rionda sugar-planting family's Joaquín became Manhattan commission merchant Lewis Benjamin's partner and married his daughter, Sophie; Manuel Rionda joined his brother in New York City after being schooled in Portland, Maine.

Americans, some of them naturalized Cubans, now controlled the market for Cuban sugar and, increasingly, Cuban production. Some planters lost their plantations to their creditors, including Americans such as Edwin Atkins, whose family had a long involvement with Cuba. Other planters, lacking the means to process their sugar, survived by selling their cane to the *centrales*, the gigantic sugar estates (by 1920, the largest of them would own or lease close to 200,000 acres) that were transforming the Cuban sugar world.

The *centrales* changed the nature of Cuban sugar even more than emancipation had. They introduced a highly industrialized production system that separated agricultural cane growing from industrial processing and in later years transferred ownership from Cubans to Americans. The railroads established in the 1830s to service individual plantations were expanded on a grand scale. The factories that processed the sugar used the most modern equipment and technology. American capital underwrote most of these innovations, but Cubans maintained control of many of the improved mills.

Sugar was king, and like a jealous feudal ruler, eliminated its rivals. It pushed out coffee, so that from 64 million pounds of coffee produced on 2,067 estates in 1833, only five million pounds were produced on only 782 estates in 1862. By the late nineteenth century, Cuba had to import coffee, but by 1894 produced fifty times the amount of sugar Jamaica exported. Between 1815 and 1894, Cuban sugar production tripled, from roughly forty thousand tons to a million.

Sugar monoculture under American direction now defined Cuba's economy and its economic future, and spokesmen for Cuban sugar served American interests in Cuba. The late-nineteenth-century mechanization of milling and refining cane was so intense that it constituted a kind of technical revolution and made mills extraordinarily productive.[475] It also generated an urgent need for engineers, machinists, technicians and chemists, often American; in 1885, an estimated two hundred skilled Bostonians worked on Cuban sugar estates. Ramon O. Williams, the U.S. consul to Havana, reported in a dispatch that "*de facto,* Cuba is already inside the commercial union of the United States. The whole commercial machinery of Cuba depends upon the sugar market of the United States."[476]

In the U.S., Cuban sugar looked to be a sound investment, and American capital gravitated to it. By 1896, direct American investment in Cuba, including sugar, cattle ranching, fruit and tobacco estates, was an estimated $950 million. This included the nineteen Cuban refineries owned by the American Sugar Refining Company, or Sugar Trust, formed in 1888 as the consolidation of twenty-one refining companies in seven U.S. cities.

After 1888, through their American Sugar Refining Company, whose members refined 70 to 90 percent of America's sugar, refiners lobbied hard for low prices and for the raw (and cheap) sugar they wanted to refine in the United States. Its power enabled the ASRC to manage though not set the price of sugar, which plunged from over $100 per ton in 1877 and remained low until World War I wreaked havoc with European beet-sugar exports, causing shortages. American control over Cuba's sugar industry and on Cuba generally was so strong and overt that after the Spanish-American War—in Cuba referred to as the Cuban War of Independence—the U.S. sent troops to occupy Cuba and refashion it in the American image. The 1901 Platt Amendment, incorporated into the Cuban Constitution as a condition for those troops to withdraw, granted the United States the right to intervene in Cuba's affairs and symbolized Cuba's powerlessness.

The 1903 Reciprocity Treaty rewarded Cuba's capitulation by giving Cuban sugar preference in the U.S. market while exploiting it by protecting American products in the Cuban market. The Platt Amendment succeeded in its authors' goals: to make Cuba safe for American investment and business. It was repealed only in 1934 and replaced with a treaty that reflected President Franklin D. Roosevelt's Latin America Good Neighbor Policy. By then, two-thirds of Cuban sugar was produced by North American interests controlled by Big Sugar and such financial institutions as National City Bank, Royal Bank of Canada, Chase National Bank, Guaranty Trust Company and J. and W. Seligman.

Louisiana, Where Sugar Was King

Louisiana, too, sweetened the American people, and was the American market's primary domestic source. Until 1803, Louisiana was North America's bartered bride, batted back and forth between aggrandizing nations (Spain, imperial France, England and Napoleonic France) and American territories. Then Napoleon Bonaparte and President Thomas Jefferson negotiated an extraordinary deal in which France sold the giant territory to the United States for $15 million, nearly doubling its land mass. "Let the Land rejoice, for you have bought Louisiana for a Song," Gen. Horatio Gates congratulated Jefferson.

Louisiana, named for the Sun King, Louis XIV, was one of the thirteen states (or partial states) carved out of the vast territory included in the Louisiana Purchase. Under the French, Jesuits and colonists had made sporadic attempts to cultivate cane, but it was the planters and sugar experts fleeing the Haitian Revolution, and the collapse of Haiti's sugar production, that transformed it into a sugar economy. In 1795, American-born Jean Étienne Boré sparked an agricultural revolution when he applied Haitian sugar maker Antoine Morin's techniques for processing sugar to his crop and produced 100,000 pounds of sugar granules. This earned him $12,000 and the title "savior of Louisiana." Until then, planters had had to be content with making molasses.

By 1812, when Louisiana joined the United States as a slave state, it had seventy-five sugar mills, Anglo-Americans had begun their trek into this new and profitable way of life and Frenchmen and Haitians continued to arrive. These sugar planters faced unique challenges. Louisiana's growing season was very short. The temperature was colder, sometimes icy, and prone to frost that severely damaged uncut cane. Planters had to calculate when the frost would come and harvest their cane just before then to maximize the sugar content, which increases as the cane stands in the ground. They adopted windrowing, cutting and laying the cane out in furrows covered with leaves until the grinding began. They switched from the earlier Creole and Otaheite cane species to larger, faster-maturing and frost-resistant Purple or Black Java and Purple Striped Ribbon Cane, introduced after 1817. Harvesting and processing took six to eight weeks and were always a race against time and frost.

Louisiana planters were plagued as well by drought in summer, swampy, coastal soil that flooded and required levees to keep the water at bay, and the pests, rats and diseases that ravaged their cane fields. The price of sugar soared and plunged, and they were dependent on protective tariffs against competing foreign cane and beet sugar. They were dependent as well on bank loans to modernize and expand their operations as they turned to steam-powered mills, vacuum pans, triple-effect evaporators that controlled steam, centrifugal equipment that spun sugar crystals into raw sugar by removing the syrup, condensers that condensed and controlled the vapor in vacuum pans, and polariscopes that assessed the amount of sucrose in the processed sugar.

The implementation of technological advances and industrialized work rhythms intensified sugar's intrinsically relentless demands. To squeeze the last ounce of work out of their slaves, planters paid wages for "overwork"—that is, hours worked over and above even the usual grueling schedule. To planters, their slaves—125,000 by mid-century—were "sugar machines."[477] Louisiana was, former slaves testified, "a place of slaughter" they dreaded as "de mos' wicked country ... God's son ever died for."[478] "Even in the West Indies," wrote observer Harriet Martineau, the condition of sugar slaves "has never been so dreadful as at present in some parts of Louisiana."[479]

One of Louisiana's "sugar machines" told his tale in *Twelve Years a Slave: Narrative of Solomon Northup, A Citizen of New-York, Kidnapped in Washington City in 1841, and Rescued in 1853.* The kidnapped Northup, free but black, was sold to a cotton planter who then rented him out as part of a jobbing gang to Dr. Hawkins, a cane planter. His description and analysis of his experiences provide penetrating insights into life in mid-nineteenth-century Louisiana's cane fields. Not long after his arrival at Hawkins's plantation, Northup was promoted to the sugar house, given a whip and instructed to use it on idling slaves. "If I failed to obey," he recalled, "there was another one for my own back." He was worked so hard that he could sleep only in brief snatches.

Northup's account of cane production on Bayou Boeuf describes a highly mechanized system. Planting began in January and continued until April; new cane was replanted after two ratoons, unlike the six possible in the West Indies. The field hands worked in three gangs: the first cut and trimmed the cane from the stalk, the second placed the cane in furrows, and the third covered it with three inches of earth. After four weeks the cane began to sprout and grow, and was hoed three times. In mid-September, a portion of the crop was cut and stored as seed. The remainder matured in the field, sweetening as it grew, until the planter gave the order to begin cutting, usually in October.

The field hands used a machete-like cane knife, fifteen inches long and three inches wide in the middle, with a thin blade they had to keep sharpened. In teams of three, they sheared the cane from its stalk and lopped off the top down to where it was green. They had to trim away every unripe part to avoid the risk of souring the sap and ruining the sugar. Once the cane stalk was cleaned, the slaves severed it from the root and placed it on the ground behind them. Younger slaves loaded the cane into a cart and it was hauled to the sugarhouse to be ground. If the planter predicted a frost, the slaves windrowed the cane, which was processed three to four weeks later. In January, the gangs prepared the ground for the next season, burning the dried leaves and debris, cleaning the field and loosening the soil around the roots of the old stubble.

On Hawkins's plantation, as elsewhere, processing sugar was a mechanized operation with an imposing infrastructure, though it did not, as on many Cuban estates, extend to refining; antebellum Louisiana produced little refined sugar. The mill was "an immense" brick building with vast sheds. The boiler was steam-generated. Two giant rollers crushed the cane and were connected by "an endless carrier, made of chain and wood, like leathern belts used in small mills," right through to the exterior of the shed where cane was endlessly loaded from carts "brought from the field as fast as it is cut…. All along the endless carrier are ranged slave children whose business it is to place the cane upon it." Nobody was too young or too old to work. As former slave Ceceil George recalled, "If yo' could carry two or three sugar cane yo' worked."[480]

After the cane was crushed, another conveyor belt removed the *bagasse*, which would otherwise have filled the building. The *bagasse* was then dried and supplemented wood to fuel *bagasse* burners. (Later, in the 1870s and 1880s, burners fueled only by green *bagasse* would enable planters to eliminate the considerable expenses of buying costly wood and paying woodcutters to chop it.)

The cane juice fell into a reservoir from which it was piped through five enormous vats that filtered it through black, pulverized bones that bleached it before it was boiled. Boiling was another complicated process. Pipes carried the syrup to and from each of the pans that clarified it until it could be stashed in coolers on the ground floor. The coolers, wooden boxes with bottoms of fine-mesh wire, acted as giant sieves as the granulating syrup released molasses into a cistern. What remained in the cooler was "white or loaf sugar of the finest kind—clear, clean, and as white as snow,"[481] that was cooled, packed into hogsheads and shipped to a refinery. The molasses was then processed into brown sugar or distilled into rum.

The flow of work in field and factory was relentless, driven by the conveyor belt with its insatiable capacity to feed cane into the heavy, powerful and dangerous machinery. The steam engines demanded an endless supply of wood or, on some plantations, *bagasse*, and three shifts of slaves continuously fueled them. The rhythm of work forced these men and women to push themselves past their biological limits, to toil on despite hunger, debility, boredom, frustration and exhaustion. When they fainted in the field, drivers splashed them with water and ordered them back to work. They worked seven days a week: "Sunday, Monday, it all de same," Ceceil George remembered.[482]

But this was not the whole story, because Louisiana slaves refused to surrender their precious Sundays, when they tended their provision grounds, socialized and slept. At first planters tried to whip them into compliance. Later, they paid for Sunday work and for compulsory, sleep-stealing shifts on the night watch. Some also offered wages if slaves would work during the traditional post-harvest holiday. Over time, they were forced to pay for cutting wood to fuel the voracious steam engines and collecting moss to stuff mattresses, work the slaves dreaded.

Sugar historian Richard Follett shows how, through such arrangements, planters duped their slaves into cooperating in their own oppression, "[strengthening] the regime by working on plantation business in their own time."[483] Yet slaves had no choice, and gouged out a measure of dignity through wages that acknowledged their invaluable labor and enabled them to improve their lives.

The sugar lords controlled every aspect of their slaves' life, even their gender and their height. "They understood the barbarous nature of sugar work and the almost constant need for fresh bodies," and believed that strong, tall men were better suited to it than shorter men or women. For that reason, Follett writes, "men accordingly represented as much as 85 percent of all slaves sold to sugar planters, and those individuals probably stood a full inch taller than most African American slaves."[484] Planters who bought female slaves selected teenagers they hoped were fertile, but as in other sugar regions, those women and girls fell victim to poor and insufficient food, overwork, exhaustion, excessive heat and humidity, and the malaria, yellow fever, diarrhea, ringworm and hookworm, anemia, rheumatism, asthma, fever, pleurisy, intestinal problems, spasms and prolapsed uteruses that were common slave ailments. They conceived and bore fewer babies than other American slaves, and more than half their infants, underweight at birth and undernourished by hungry nursing mothers, died. Mothers, too, often died. "Pa always said they made my ma work too hard," recalled sugar slave Edward De Bieuw of Lafourche Parish. "He said ma was hoein'. She told the driver she was sick; he told her to just hoe right on. Soon, I was born, and my ma die a few minutes after dey brung her to the house."[485] As elsewhere, the Louisiana sugar slaves' birthrate was too low to sustain their numbers.

The slaves' lives revolved around sugar, and "the sugar-house is the capitol of the negro quarters," observed William Howard Russell.[486] Throughout Louisiana, slave quarters were rows of single-storied wooden cottages facing a tree-lined avenue with chicken coops behind them.

The interiors were bare and, on the sugar master's orders, kept clean. Ventilation was primitive, the air hot, humid and mosquito-infested. Outside, wandering pigs, poultry and dogs fouled the ground, and slaves had to use surrounding bushes as toilets.

At night the slaves were crammed together in rooms averaging two hundred square feet, and they slept on plank beds. They had no privacy, even for sexual relations, unless they retreated to a sheltered spot in a nearby field or forest. The shanties provided shelter and storage and little else. But with their "Sunday money" and other wages, the slaves furnished them with at least a few necessities: a knife, a kettle, plates and cutlery. Northup, the "wealthiest 'nigger' on Bayour Boeuf" with $10 in savings, had "visions of cabin furniture, of water pails, of pocket knives, new shoes and coats and hats."[487]

Few sugar slaves had access to provision grounds and had to rely on rations doled out by their masters. The staples were cornmeal, larded pork or bacon, and vegetables or, as former slave Elizabeth Hines recalled, "greens and pickled pork ... pickled pork and corn bread!"[488]

On a post-emancipation plantation, three Louisiana mothers with babes in arms, seven children, one man and two dogs pose in front of their shanties, likely built during slavery.

The average weekly ration was nine liters of corn and 1.4 kilograms of pork, and the quality could be "nauseous and disgusting," Northup recalled. One summer, he said, "worms got into the bacon. Nothing but ravenous hunger could induce us to swallow it." He and his fellows relied on hunting raccoon or opossum "at night, after the day's work is accomplished ... [using] dogs and clubs, slaves not being allowed the use of fire-arms."[489]

Wages, holidays and religion brought the slaves their only relief from the wretchedness of their lives. Money bought the luxury of meat, tobacco, whiskey and cloth markedly different from coarse blue slave garb. During holidays, slaves transformed themselves in joyously flamboyant clothes. "Red—the deep blood red" was the women's favorite color, and they wore "gaudy ribbons, wherewithal to deck their hair in the merry season of the holidays."[490] Dapper men wore rimless hats and shone their shoes with a candle stub. Most slaves were young, and took advantage of holiday leisure and camaraderie to flirt and find a mate. The men, who greatly outnumbered the women, competed among themselves to win a favorite's heart.

At holiday time slaves could get passes to visit friends, relatives, lovers and mates on other plantations. It was also a preferred time to marry, if their owners consented. The owners of female slaves, anticipating the baby slaves likely to result, were usually cooperative. Some planters, fancying themselves as preachers, officiated at their slaves' mock-marriage ceremonies. If the marriage proved unhappy, either partner could end it without formality. If one was sold or ran away alone, the other might take a new mate. As property, slaves had no recourse to Louisiana's marriage laws, but neither were they subject to them. Nonetheless, Ann Patton Malone's *Sweet Chariot: Slave Family and Household Structure in Nineteenth-century Louisiana* finds that an exceedingly high mortality rate ended more marriages on the three plantations she studied than any other cause.

The Christmas holiday was the highlight of the slave's year. Planters chafed at the wasted time but had to accept the ritual. On Northup's plantation the "feasting, and frolicking, and fiddling" lasted three days, and on others could be a week or longer. Slaves from different plantations celebrated together, feasting on chickens, ducks and turkeys, vegetables, flour biscuits, preserves and tarts. Northup noted the large numbers of whites who came to "witness the gastronomical enjoyments."[491] Other whites offered the slaves a drink at the Great House, or allowed them to transform the sugarhouse into a ballroom where they danced to the beat of a drum or the tune of a fiddle.

Religion was the one comfort that was not seasonal. Many Louisiana planters, French Creole Catholic, Anglo-American Episcopalian and Protestant alike, shared the belief that Christianity, properly taught, would keep slaves obedient and satisfied with their lot. Others considered it their moral and paternalistic duty to inculcate Christian truths and values in their slaves. "Sometime, dey make de slaves go to church," William Mathews, a former slave, recalled, describing how whites drove a carriage to each of the slave cabins and rounded up all the slaves for compulsory worship.[492] Some planters transformed mills and boiling houses into chapels; "the sugarhouse is a very fine place for preaching," William Hamilton explained; "there they can enjoy the sweets of various kinds … [and] be constantly nourished by the odouriferous smell of sugar pots and steam engine."[493] Other planters built chapels, hired preachers or appointed slaves to minister to their fellows with instructions to confine themselves to obedience: "obey de massa, obey de overseer, obey dis, obey dat," a former slave recollected.[494] Slave preachers with some autonomy developed their own versions of Christianity, a Christian rite incorporating Afro-American beliefs and, sometimes, the vodun remembered from Haiti. Slaves forbidden to worship or indifferent to their master's rite sneaked off and held secret services. They prayed that "God don't think no different of the blacks and the whites," "that a day would come when Niggers only be slaves of God," and that they might have "all that we wanted to eat" and "shoes that fit our feet."[495]

After the worshippers dispersed, they resumed their lives of drudgery. The grinding season was one of the worst. Then, "the fatigue is so great that nothing but the severest application of the lash can stimulate the human frame to endure it," one planter wrote.[496] Then masters supplemented food rations with calorie-rich hot, sweet coffee and molasses or hot cane juice. To streamline operations and direct every workable minute to processing sugar, a few planters arranged for collective cooking. Often this food service began just before the grinding season opened. On Northup's plantation, drivers distributed corn cake to the field slaves, urging them to gobble it down and return to work.

Paradoxically, in their backbreaking, mind-numbing marathons of toil, sugar slaves were held to industrial standards of precision and punctuality. They worked on assembly-line principles metered out in clanging bells and enforced by drivers with whips. The technology that defined progress demanded more brute labor, more cane and more fuel to make more sugar. The concept of day and night merged into one in a world where mills and boilers never stopped and exhausted slaves were driven to work eighteen to twenty hours at a stretch during the grinding season, fueled by hot sucrose and, when that failed, whipped. Desperate for sleep, working in industrial lockstep, slaves fed unsafe equipment that caught their limbs and tore their flesh.

Planters prided themselves on their grasp of modern methods and of time management. To Bennet H. Barrow of Highland Plantation, "a plantation might be considered a piece of machinery, to operate successfully, all of its parts should be uniform and exact, and the impelling force regular and steady."[497] Alas, complained many planters, their human "sugar machines" were rough and irregular, rendered by their race incapable of skilled mechanical labor. As in Cuba, a few planters taught their slaves to operate, monitor and repair equipment.

Ironically, given the planters' assumptions about the ineptitude of blacks, the inventor of the Rillieux multiple-effect evaporating process, still essential in sugar processing, was a man of color. Norbert Rillieux's mother, Constance Vincent, was the light-skinned slave mistress of white Louisiana planter and engineer-inventor Vincent Rillieux. The story is that Norbert experienced racial discrimination at the hands of Louisiana planters who invited him to redesign their equipment, and installed and appreciated his evaporators, but would not lodge him in their Great Houses.

As elsewhere, Louisiana's sugar slaves engaged in sabotage, passive and active resistance, and running away. Industrial sabotage took many forms: using a blunt knife on the cane, loosening a wheel bolt, maiming

M. NORBERT RILLIEUX

Norbert Rillieux, in 2004 inducted posthumously into the National Inventors' Hall of Fame for automated sugar refining.

mules and oxen, scorching the sugar, letting the fires die, introducing alien objects onto the conveyor belt or into the steam engine. On one estate, a nine-inch steel bolt left on the cane carrier caused the shaft that connects the engine and mill to give way. The most striking example of sabotage was undertaken by Old Pleasant, a slave who shut down Bowdon Plantation's mill by letting the water in the boilers run dry and gouging holes in them.

Resistance ranged from malingering to stealing. Slaves often purloined sugar and molasses and sold them to petty traders. They dismantled sugar-processing equipment and sold that too. They hid and fed fugitives, foiling the slave patrols that planters sponsored to hunt them down with tracking dogs. (One slave described patrollers as "the meanest things in creation … poor, low down white folks, that descended from a French and Spanish mixture.)[498] Some runaways were inspired by their own desperation or news of slave uprisings elsewhere. Others just sought respite from the cane fields and sugar factories.

These Louisiana boys enjoy an unrefined sugar treat.

Despite the frustrations of controlling their obstreperous slaves, Louisiana planters embraced slavery as the best way to produce sugar and old-style plantation culture as the best way to live. Unlike the West Indians and Latin Americans, Louisiana planters were seldom absentees. Even those who owned several plantations visited and personally supervised the properties they did not reside on. Louisiana planters adopted modern technology and business principles and studied scientific reports and sugar-planting manuals. They were generally well informed about their crops, prided themselves on their micromanagement and did not rely on managers. The U.S. commissioner of patents avowed that in no other sugar-growing region had modern improvement been more fairly tested than in Louisiana. Other observers considered Louisiana "far superior to most sugar growing regions ... in the intelligence and skill manifested in both the cultivation and manufacturing of sugar."[499]

In other ways Louisiana sugar culture looked like its models except for its plantocracy's uniquely diverse origins in France, Haiti, the

Anglo-American cotton-growing South and the industrializing North. Louisiana's version of the Creole-European tension pitted Creoles against Americans, but their common interests as planters usually prevailed over their differences. For the most part they valued wealth and its trappings over knowledge and culture, and, in the judgment of Massachusetts-educated Tryphena Fox, the wife of a physician who tended the slaves of wealthy sugar planters, many of them were not "very intellectual or refined."[500] Solomon Northup expressed the same opinion and supported it with examples of outrageous white behavior.

Louisiana planters were also fixated on and often frightened of their slaves, especially as the abolition debate heated up and their slaves got wind of it. The whites on sugar plantations were surrounded by their slaves: 21,000 in 1827; 36,000 in 1830; 56,600 in 1841; 65,000 in 1844; and 125,000 by the 1850s. By the Civil War, the five hundred planters who produced three-quarters of Louisianan sugar each held over a hundred slaves. But although they feared them, it was the planters' ownership of these slaves that defined both their identity and their success in the sugar world.

Part of this identity was the sense of entitlement that prompted planters to acquire—and require—the imposing, pillared Greek Revival and Creole houses with large galleries and magnificent gardens that lined the famed seventy-mile River Road between New Orleans and Baton Rouge. "Plenty of dwellings ... standing so close together, for long distances, that the broad river lying between two rows, becomes a sort of spacious street," Mark Twain enthused.[501] These houses dominated the plantation's village and towered over its tiny slave cabins. They symbolized the planter's power over his slaves, and were daily reminders of the relationship between his world and theirs.

The planter's sense of entitlement defined his material standards: the food-laden table, fully stocked bar, pianos, silver, china and all the accoutrements of the gracious life. It extended to his slaves, especially the women. If the planter did not indulge, his predatory sons often did, stalking the quarters for their sexual experiences. As a free black recalled, "The young masters were criminally intimate with the negro girls; it was their custom."[502] White employees also coerced slave women into sexual relationships. In just two years, overseer S. B. Raby fathered three children with slave women.

Louisiana planters justified sugar slavery on the usual racial grounds and described themselves as benevolent masters caring for childlike and immoral inferiors. They proffered self-congratulatory examples of the great care they took in housing and feeding their slaves and in maintaining order among them. In keeping with their racial views, planters kept slaves separate from white laborers, even the despised Irish and Cajuns who were sometimes hired to dredge the plantation's canals and clear its bayous, because, as one overseer explained, "it was much cheaper to have the Irish to do it, who cost nothing to the planter, if they died, than to use-up good field hands in such severe employment."[503]

The planters' concept of racial order and superiority and their relative isolation on plantations reinforced their belief in individualism and left them indifferent to the need to contribute to the infrastructure of civil society. Even when the legislature proposed matching funds, they preferred to pour their money into their plantations instead of into roads and railroads. They did not support the Agriculturists and Mechanics Association, or the University of Louisiana's sugar-related engineering courses. But when a military academy opened, they sent their sons there to become cadets. And, of course, the planters were united in their support of lobbyists working to maintain the tariff that made it harder for cheap raw Cuban sugar to compete with theirs.

The Civil War brought dramatic change to the Louisiana sugar world. When federal troops captured New Orleans in April 1862, they gained control of the Mississippi River, Louisiana's commercial heartland and the South's financial core. News of their victory precipitated a mass flight of slaves from their plantations to nearby woods, Union camps or New Orleans itself. A few joined together and began to farm land abandoned by panicked Confederate planters.

Many blacks stayed on their plantations but refused to work. "Revolt & Insurrection among the negroes" who beat drums, waved flags and shouted "Abe Lincoln and Freedom," an observer reported.[504] When irate and anxious planters implored or threatened them, their slaves responded that they were now free and had legal rights—although

The Belair Plantation House, Louisiana, photographed after the Civil War.

ironically, the Emancipation Proclamation that formally freed them took effect only in 1865, and Louisiana slaves were among the last to be emancipated. Some returned to work after negotiating reasonable wages and conditions, notably Saturdays off, the dismissal of cruel overseers and, in one case, new shoes. As in the West Indies, they demanded reduced hours for their wives and female relatives, who in any case refused to work as hard as before. Planters were scathing about this new gendered order of things: "[Field women] are idle, impudent, lose a great deal of time by feigning sickness, and some refuse field work entirely," one of them griped.[505]

The Union army's divided command intervened. Gen. Benjamin F. Butler interpreted his orders to mean that slaves of Confederate rebels should be freed but not those of supposed Union loyalists or neutrals such as Appoline Patout, a unilingual French citizen. Those who signed loyalty oaths could hire their soon-to-be emancipated male slaves for 260 hours at $10 a month, plus food and medicine; the rates for women and children were less. Unsurprisingly, many planters signed loyalty oaths, and Butler ordered his troops to help them retrieve runaway slaves and to maintain order on the plantations. Soldiers who refused to do so were threatened with arrest and court-martial.

Butler's colleague Gen. John W. Phelps had a different vision. He aided all slaves who made it to the Union lines he controlled, and launched slave-freeing raids on plantations. He also organized hundreds of blacks into military regiments and drilled them. When Butler objected and assigned the would-be soldiers to tree-cutting duties, Phelps resigned. "I am not willing to become the mere slave-driver which you propose," he wrote, "having no qualifications in that way."[506]

Butler subsequently decided that black troops would solve his two most urgent problems: surging and frightening masses of black refugees, and a shortage of troops. He organized his own black regiments drawn from free blacks and runaway slaves and sent them into battle. In 1864, after seeing two hundred of their corpses on the battlefield, he reflected in a letter to his wife, "They suffered largely … their sable faces made by death a ghastly, tawny blue, with their expressions of determination, which never dies out of brave men's faces who die instantly in a charge, forming a sad sight, which is burnt on my memory as I rode through them as they lay. Poor fellows, they seem to have so little to fight for in this contest, with the weight of prejudice loaded upon them, their lives given to a country which has given them not yet justice, not to say fostering care."[507] (The Confederates, on the other hand, used the Louisiana Native Guards, free black volunteer militiamen, only for propaganda and did not permit them to fight.)

Throughout the war, widows, wives, overseers and those planters who had neither fled nor joined the Confederate army struggled to bring in their crops and make sugar. "There is not a single planter in this department who has not personally suffered through this war," reported Union observer George Hepworth. "Their crops of sugar-cane ... are still standing in February.... Cane is standing now in March, thousands and thousands of acres of it. Thus the crop of the past year is nothing, and that of the coming year will be the same."[508] Even on working plantations, Union soldiers made off with anything they could carry away or consume, including horses, farm animals, poultry, food supplies, sugar, wine, liquor, family silver, pots and pans. To fuel their fires, they dismantled sheds and barns, and even uprooted the fence posts that surrounded pastures for grazing cattle.

RECONSTRUCTING THE SUGAR WORLD, 1865–77

When the Civil War ended in 1865, one-fifth of military-age white men and hundreds of black soldiers were dead, and thousands of both races maimed. The sugar plantations had been abandoned, neglected or laid waste and plundered by Union troops. The countryside was littered with the bones of stolen or abandoned farm animals.

Planters returned and tallied their enormous losses. They had lost the slave workforce that had been as well their greatest capital investment. They had lost their sugar mills and factories, many destroyed and most others severely damaged. From 1861 to 1864, the number of Louisiana's working sugar plantations had been reduced from 1,200 to 231, and their sugar production had plunged from roughly 264,000 tons to a mere 6,000. Once ranked as the second-richest state in per capita wealth, postbellum Louisiana was worth less than half of her former value. Sugar plantations sustained the most crushing losses. Adeline Patout's net worth, for instance, plunged from $140,000 to $20,000.

At the same time, there was a political and social revolution. Louisiana had been exempted from the federal Emancipation Proclamation of January 1863, but in September 1864, the state legislature abolished slavery. Six months later, the federal government set up the Bureau of Refugees, Freedmen and Abandoned Lands, known as the Freedman's Bureau. Hopeful freedman sought its agents' help as they established schools and churches, negotiated labor contracts and set out to locate spouses and children, relatives and friends sold away under slavery.

As the federal will to truly transform the civil state of blacks weakened, and the planters' determination to undermine Reconstruction strengthened, the bureau's financial base and power eroded. But until Reconstruction gave way to Redemption, the bitterly evocative term for the South's reversion to Democratic rule in 1877 that conservatives lauded as a "redemptive" process, blacks fought to establish themelves as political beings. The sugar plantation, home to so many, proved to be prime ground for recruiting, proselytizing and organizing. In sugar parishes, black majorities elected blacks to the state legislature, and blacks served as officials and militiamen.

In other ways, Louisiana sugar's new order did not seem strikingly different from the old. Duncan Kenner, a Confederate official, swore allegiance to the Union and reclaimed his Ashland Plantation from the Freedman's Bureau, which had confiscated it to give to landless freedmen. Appoline Patout swore that she was a neutral foreigner, and remained in full possession of her huge plantation.

Most freedmen were reluctant to return to the cane fields, even for $10 a month. A few planters, such as Appoline Patout, engaged whites instead. A bit later others imported Chinese "coolies," the term for unskilled Asian labor that quickly took on a negative connotation, and later Germans, Dutch, Irish, Spanish, Portuguese and Italians. None of these immigrants accepted the harsh conditions and low pay the planters provided. The Chinese fled the plantations for New Orleans or other urban areas, and the whites broke their contracts and negotiated new ones. Whites "will not come here to be crowded like serfs and harlots into dingy cabins, with a peck of Indian meal and four pounds of pork a week," the *Planters' Banner* concluded.[509]

Freedmen were also unwilling to return to these abysmal conditions. The story of Reconstruction in sugar country is about how they attempted, and sometimes succeeded, in wresting better working conditions for themselves, and made important contributions as new citizens and electors; it is also about how planters tried to reconfigure emancipation to serve their own interests, all the while dealing with the challenges of not only competition from foreign cane and North American sugar beet but also the mighty lobbying power of the sugar refiners, whose priority was cheap sugar from any source.

Like sugar slaves emancipated decades earlier in the British West Indies, Louisiana freedmen yearned for their own land. They wanted their women out of the cane fields. They wanted to choose their own employers. They wanted decent wages paid in full, in cash not scrip, and they rejected the share-cropping arrangement that some had initially favored. If their contracts included meals, they wanted better-quality food. They wanted planters to provide feed for their cows, pigs, chickens and horses. They wanted Saturdays and Sundays off and as much as a month at Christmas. They wanted to vote, form and join political groups and parties, elect officials, participate in and benefit from government. They wanted a measure of respect and refused to tolerate such blatant remnants of slavery as cruel overseers, insults and jeers, and restrictions on their movements.

When planters rejected these demands or fired freedmen unjustly, freedmen learned how and when to strike, for example just when it was time to harvest and process the cane. Political leaders taught the freedmen solidarity, "to act as one man on all plantations" until the planter conceded to them. Sometimes freedmen broke contracts to take up better-paying work, and only very high wages and jiggers of whiskey could induce them to undertake the hated job of levee maintenance. At election time, freedmen gave priority to politics and, in the planters' view, devoted "a little too much time to politics and a little too little to work."[510] At harvest time, when some freedwomen agreed to work in the fields for 75 cents a day, the planters accused them of being insolent and lazy, especially nursing mothers.

For a while, freedmen made good progress. By 1869 they had nego-tiated average annual wages of between $325 and $350, including such benefits as housing and provision grounds, comparable to what non-agricultural workers earned and much better than either waged or share-cropping cotton workers could expect. The freedmen used their wages to upgrade and vary their rations, and enjoyed biscuits, tea, whiskey, gin, wine, brandy, codfish, sardines, salt and pepper, condensed milk, refined sugar and candy. They dressed in better fabrics and accessorized them. They wore eyeglasses, smoked tobacco, used pen and paper, bought mouse- and rattraps for their houses, and treated themselves to a variety of items that made their lives easier and more gracious.

Their dream of owning land was a different story, and only a few achieved it. Over time the Freedman's Bureau was forced to restore all the confiscated plantations that had been their only possible source of land. Those who had tried to save money by investing their savings in the federally chartered Freedmen's Savings and Trust Company lost it all when the bank failed during the financial crisis of 1874.

The freedmen's most formidable opponents in their battle to improve their lives were the incumbent sugar planters staggering under the burden of their ruined property, huge debts, lack of income, uncoopera-tive bankers and competition from domestic beet and foreign cane sugar. They hated having to employ the men and women they had previously owned and, a contemporary concluded, "did not understand ... how men could be induced to work without the whip."[511] New planters from the north and other southern states accommodated more easily, but for a long time the antebellum model cast its dark shadow over postbellum sugar production.

Many planters actively resisted the new order. They conspired behind their workers' backs to keep wages low, to withhold a portion until the sugar season was finished or to deduct or withhold wages on the grounds that freedmen had violated their contracts. They resurrected patrols to keep freedmen from roving between plantations without written permission, effectively denying them their legal right to choose their own employers. Some planters attempted to maintain mastery over freedmen by including pledges of personal conduct—no gambling, drinking or swearing—in labor contracts. Planters lamented the "political flood of fanaticism & anarchy, now sweeping over & desolating the land."[512] They especially hated watching the freedmen register to vote, or leaving the cane fields to attend political meetings, and fired employees they considered politically troublesome. "Instances are daily and hourly coming to my notice, in which Planters are discharging laborers merely for visiting political clubs," a bureau agent reported.[513]

The freedmen retaliated by striking and refusing to sign contracts with unpleasant, dishonest planters. They gained strength from the unity that stemmed from living and working together on huge plantations, from the bureau established to counsel, aid and protect them, and from black politicians who understood the crucial importance of the rural masses. They formed informal militias, mutual aid societies and political clubs called Union Leagues that helped discipline and unify them and, during Reconstruction's violent political struggles and elections, mobilized the black militiamen to provide paramilitary protection. The freedmen made steady progress and forced planters to make concessions. Freedwomen formed their own Republican Party auxiliaries and stiffened their men's resolve by threatening to leave them if they caved in to the planters' pressure to vote Democrat. In at least one instance, women armed themselves with cane-field knives to break up a Democratic meeting. For white men accustomed to dominating them, this forcefulness was unexpected and maddening.

Planters and white Louisianans did not concede gracefully. In May 1867, some of them formed the Knights of the White Camellia, a secret society pledged to restoring and maintaining white supremacy by fighting Reconstruction and black reformist politics. After a Republican newspaper published details of its secrets, the Knights disbanded, and some joined other white supremacist cults dedicated to terrorizing and persecuting ambitious or democratically minded blacks and their white allies. "We will kill the last one of you," a white man threatened freedmen who intended to vote. "The business of negroes is to go into the fields and work."[514] In a precursor to the election violence that would mar Southern politics for over a century, the 1868 electoral campaign in St. Bernard Parish killed sixty people, most of them freedmen.

Fifteen years after the war, planters still had to worry about staying in business. Although between 1860 and 1875 American sugar consumption had skyrocketed 62 percent, Louisiana's contribution had plunged from 27 percent to 8 percent. Bankruptcies and forced sales were rife, and over two in three plantations shut down. To pay their clamorous workers, repair or restore their facilities and buy modern equipment, planters needed credit that was difficult to obtain now that they had lost their primary capital investment: slaves. "The attacks of needy and delinquent Planters today was enough to worry you out of all patience," one factor complained, "they were like a swarm of hornets."[515]

Planters who survived and prospered had to adjust and modernize. New milling methods such as multiple-effect evaporators and vacuum pans that extracted more and better sugar, even when it was frozen, were essential. So were cheaper fuel costs. The widowed Mary Ann Patout, Appoline's daughter-in-law and successor, operating as M. A. Patout and Son—still in operation today and the only mill still run by the original family—switched from coal and wood to fuel oil supplemented with cane *bagasse*. New field equipment such as the row cultivator and mechanical cane loader meant lower costs and relieved reluctant field hands of a particularly onerous task. So did the Patout stubble shaver that shaved off the stubble from cut cane stalks, encouraging them to sprout vegetation-producing eyes that in turn increased their sugar yield. Much later, in the 1920s and 1930s, electricity and then gasoline replaced the steam power that had earlier replaced animals, and manure gave way to chemical fertilizer.

The Louisiana Sugar Planters Association, founded in 1877, created a sugar lobby to influence federal tariff policy-makers. It also helped planters to share research information through association meetings and through its journal, *The Louisiana Sugar Planter*. Unlike earlier generations of planters, these agricultural industrialists were enthusiastic about the research on sugar varieties and technology conducted in Louisiana universities and colleges.

As sugar production modernized, capitalized and increased, mills became so efficient that they outgrew the supply any one plantation could provide. The phenomenon of centralization familiar in other sugar regions began to appear in Louisiana. The more powerful the mills, the more they consolidated; from 1875 to 1905, 732 mills were reduced to 205. These giants were so efficient that productivity skyrocketed and fewer workers produced much more sugar.

REDEMPTION

After years of being battered by discriminatory legislation, economic coercion and physical attacks, black sugar workers were no longer doing well. Reconstruction ended in 1877, when the Republican Party made a Faustian bargain with the white South. In return for the electoral votes that would send Rutherford Hayes to the White House despite his having lost the popular vote, the Hayes government would withdraw federal troops from the South.

Violence and intimidation became the order of the day. In 1883, in Colfax, the paramilitary White League, an unhooded white supremacist successor to the Knights of the White Camellia, killed about one hundred black men gathered at the courthouse, half of them after they had surrendered. Hippolyte Patout, Mary Ann's son, was one of the White League's leaders.

On November 3, 1887, in Thibodaux, the seat of the "sugar bowl" parish of Lafourche, the death knell sounded on eroding black civil, political and economic rights. Freedmen had staged a regional strike, and white planters, led by sugar planter and judge Taylor Beattie, united to crush it. After three days of bloodshed, thirty freedmen died and thousands more were made homeless when planters evicted them from their cabins. Beattie's in-law Mary Pugh confided to her husband, "I think this will settle the question of who is to rule[,] the nigger or the White man? For the next 50 years.... The negroes are as humble as pie today, very different from last week."[516]

The Thibodaux Massacre was the culmination of two decades of struggle between planters and freedmen, between their conflicting versions of how sugar production should operate, between militant employers and militant workers, and between the traditionally privileged and the newly emancipated. "The Thibodeaux Massacre was thus an epilogue to the story of emancipation and a prologue to the saga of Jim Crow and the white lynch mob," historian John C. Rodrigue concludes.[517]

Thibodeaux ushered in an era known as Redemption because the Democratic Party's power had been redeemed. As in Cuba, sugar planting in the South evolved as a system of industrial agriculture that grew cane processed by heavily capitalized and centralized mills. Blacks and a few foreign or poor whites labored long and hard for low wages. Whites again held the whip hand.

The Beet in North America

As the story of sugarcane in Cuba and Louisiana unfolded, sugar beet became an important subplot. At first it was European beet. By the end of the nineteenth century, beet had crossed the Atlantic and rooted in North America, where its sugar supplemented and also challenged cane sugar. At the same time, the cost of producing it had to mirror or best that of cane, which had enormous implications for the men and women out in the beet fields.

Sugar beet thrives in temperate zones blessed with rich soil, sufficient rain and about five months without severe frost. The turnip-like vegetable, long and silvery white, with roots six to ten feet deep, is planted in springtime, in rows at least a foot apart, and paired with wheat, corn, barley, potatoes or rye as the base crop in three- to five-year rotations. It requires deep plowing that increases subsequent grain yields, and frequent hoeing to control or eliminate weeds. Its post-milling leavings of beet tops and pulp feed cattle and fertilize grain crops. Sugar beet is also the temperate zone's highest calorie-yielding field crop.

Many regions of North America are suitable for sugar-beet cultivation, especially the wedge of land that includes part of California and extends east to Michigan and beyond, and in Canada, from British Columbia to Ontario. Yet sugar-beet cultivation had shaky beginnings.

In 1836, a group of would-be sugar farmers formed the Beet Sugar Society of Philadelphia and sent an agent to France to learn the business and acquire seeds, but there is no record of successful planting. Two years later, in Northampton, Massachusetts, a fledgling factory shut down because its beets had a low sugar content.

In 1852, the Mormons attempted to introduce sugar beet into Utah as part of their vision of self-sufficiency in all things. They began with five hundred barrels of beet and processing equipment shipped from France to New Orleans to Fort Leavenworth, Kansas, where it was loaded onto wagons hauled by fifty-two ox teams. Four months later, it arrived in Utah, and the Mormon Church had it installed at Sugar House Ward in Salt Lake City. But the equipment failed to produce crystallized sugar, and in 1855 the factory was shut down.

More beet-sugar operations opened and closed: New York's Germania Beet Sugar Company and plants in Wisconsin, California, Maine, Delaware, Massachusetts and New Jersey. Canada, too, had a string of failed beet-sugar businesses, in Manitoba, Quebec and Ontario. All these endeavors failed because farmers had no experience with beet, the beets were of poor quality, the equipment was faulty and the factories were badly located.

The tide turned in 1890, when, after four failures, E. H. Dyer established a successful beet-sugar business in Alvarado, California. In 1888, Claus Spreckels, experienced in the Hawaiian sugarcane business, set up in Watsonville, California. Brothers Henry, James, Benjamin and Robert Oxnard, scions of a French-American family that had planted cane in Louisiana and refined sugar in Boston and New York, opened beet operations in Grand Island and Norfolk, Nebraska, and at Chino and Oxnard, California. Between 1900 and 1920, beet acreage increased from 135,000 to 872,000, with Colorado and Nebraska most heavily planted. By then the Mormon Church also succeeded in financing an important sugar-beet industry in Utah. By 1902, forty-one factories in the United States produced 2,118,406 tons of sugar. By 1915, seventy-nine factories were in operation, helped by high wartime prices. In Ontario and Alberta, beet operations also began to succeed. In Manitoba, Mennonite farmers and others turned to sugar beet on land farther north than any other North American beet operations.

Once North American sugar beet had become a viable crop, the labor question loomed large. Like cane, sugar beet is a hardscrabble crop, with the beet-thinning process only slightly less onerous than cane holing. "Our knees hurt from thinning," a Manitoba beet worker recalled. "We wrapped feed bags tied with string around them, but once your knees get sore, it's hard to cure them. We tried everything, sitting flat, lying on our sides in the rows. Nothing seemed to help."[518]

Finding people to do such taxing work was a constant challenge, especially since wages had to be kept low to compete with cane. For American growers, Mexico was an obvious source of labor, and many growers initiated recruitment drives there, advertising in Spanish-language pamphlets, posters, calendars and newspapers, and offering transportation. Between 1900 and 1930, more than a million Mexicans arrived in North America

In a scene reminiscent of slave-era sugarcane fields, these infants are cared for in the beet fields by other children. Ordway, Colorado, 1915.

Henry and Hilda, six and three years old respectively, were beet workers. "I don't never git no rest," Henry complained. Wisconsin, 1915.

and many found work as beet workers. Japan also furnished thousands of male agricultural laborers, many previously employed in Hawaii's sugarcane fields.

By 1903, the American Beet Company in Oxnard, California, employed one thousand Mexicans and Japanese who worked their fields, thinned their beets—and initiated the first American farm workers' union strike. Oxnard was a new town whose German, Irish and Jewish whites segregated themselves on the west side and relegated Mexicans and Japanese to the east. "While the east side of town was a rip-roaring slum, the west side was listening to lecture courses, hearing WCTU [Women's Christian Temperance Union] speakers, having gay times at the skating rink in the opera house, putting on minstrel shows," a white resident recalled.[519]

Trouble started when the west-side Western Agricultural Contracting Company was set up to demote Japanese contractors to subcontractors, to force down wages for the hated stoop labor of thinning growing beets

These Canadian-Japanese pose in the beet fields of southern Alberta with smiles as forced as their labor. "It's hard . . . the blade getting dull and mud-caked as I slash . . . and on to the end of the long long row and the next and the next and it will never be done thinning and weeding and weeding and weeding," laments the narrator in Joy Kogawa's Obasan.

Cree women and children labor on a sugar-beet farm in Raymond, Alberta, c. 1910.

Filter presses turning beet into sugar, Greeley, Colorado, 1908.

and to substitute company-store vouchers for cash wages. Mexican and Japanese workers, especially beet thinners, united and formed the Japanese-Mexican Labor Association, and then went on strike. "It is just as necessary … that we get a decent living wage, as it is that the machines in the great sugar factory be properly oiled," a JMLA press release explained.[520]

On March 24, strike-breaking farmer Charles Arnold fired at unarmed unionists, killing one and wounding four others. Despite witnesses to his rampage, an all-Anglo jury acquitted Arnold of all charges. This injustice inflamed the strikers and reinforced their determination to win. On March 30, after tense negotiations, the beet growers conceded most of the union's demands and the strike ended.

The workers' victory had a sad postscript. The JMLA applied for membership in the American Federation of Labor, which agreed to accept the Mexicans but "under no circumstance … any Chinese or Japanese." The JMLA formally denounced these conditions. "We will refuse any … kind of charter, except one which will wipe out race prejudice and recognize our fellow workers as being as good as ourselves."[521]

In years following, the JMLA victory faded, contractors resumed their exploitative practices, Oxnard remained violent and the union eventually disbanded. In 1905, amid anti-Asian prejudice, the Asiatic Exclusion League campaigned to exclude Japanese and Koreans from the United States. But the Oxnard beet workers' strike resonates still as California's first farm workers' union, and the first to transcend racial boundaries.

The Depression exacerbated North American xenophobia that targeted Mexicans and Asians. Some Mexicans left the now-unwelcoming United States to return to Mexico. More than 400,000 were "repatriated" after threats, raids and legal actions. (In January 2006, the California state legislature apologized for these civil rights violations through its Apology Act for the 1930s Mexican Repatriation Program.)

During the Depression, replacing the Mexicans was easy. There were the desperate unemployed who rode the continent's rails and floods of migrants escaping turmoil in their homelands—Russians, Czechs and Poles—and German Mennonites seeking a profitable crop, and German Jews and anti-Nazis fleeing persecution. Employers also hired Native Americans, but they preferred Europeans who had no reserves to take refuge in when the hard work, long hours and low pay became intolerable.

The war ended the bonanza of workers, sucking so many out of the beet fields and into the military that an employment crisis loomed. Both the American and Canadian governments helped their sugar industries by procuring workers from the ranks of conscientious objectors, German prisoners of war and Japanese Americans and Canadians. The Japanese, suddenly classified as "aliens," were wrested from their homes and livelihoods and shipped to detention camps in remote locations.

In 1942, thousands were sent to beet-sugar farms in Oregon, Utah, Idaho, Montana, Alberta and Manitoba, an experience that has become a bitter chapter in their collective memory.

During the war, unreliable and scarce sugarcane imports created a great demand for beet sugar, which, though produced by "enemy aliens" toiling alongside native and new Canadians, was promoted as a "patriotic" commodity. At the end of the war, interned workers were released from the beet fields and new immigrants known as Displaced Peoples replaced them. Beet farms increased in size and adopted new technologies such as chemical weed control, improved seed varieties and precision planting. But the most demanding work, thinning the beets and hoeing, still required armies of field workers. As always, the sugar industry recruited from among migrant and other deprived groups, any local help they could persuade, or any Natives they could coerce. In Canada, various government departments, including the Bureau of Indian Affairs, cooperated to push Natives into the Albertan beet fields.[522]

On the enemy side, sugar beet also had its war stories. Until World War I, Germany led the world in sugar beet exports. (It was also third in total sugar exports, behind only Cuba and Java.) Then its production plunged, and the government intervened to keep sugar affordable for civilians. After the war, despite the government's efforts to resuscitate it, the ailing German industry fought losing battles against dumped foreign sugar and the devastating effects of the Depression.

Help arrived with the Nazis, who made sugar beet the locus of an ideology that idealized *Blut und Boden*—blood and soil. The Nazis praised beet for keeping peasant workers in the countryside (though it kept potential soldiers there too), for supplying Germans with an essential foodstuff and for triumphing over sugarcane that inferior races produced in warmer climes. The Nazis also incorporated sugar beet into their vision of national autarky, or self-sufficiency, although Germany could achieve this only through *Lebensraum*, expanding her territories and acquiring more resources.[523]

Once in office, however, Hitler articulated a less romantic view of sugar beet. He realized, for instance, that the high tax that kept sugar so expensive brought in desperately needed revenue. Instead of lowering the tax, the Nazis encouraged Germans to eat more sugar-laden jam. (They fixed on jam because Frankfurt had recently begun to manufacture pectin, essential to jam making, and as a way of using up poor-quality and damaged fruit.) To encourage sales, they required the sugar-beet industry to subsidize the jam industry and provided state subsidies only in 1938. More and more jam was produced, from 67,200 tons in 1934 to 143,000 tons in 1937, mostly with subsidized sugar.

Besides jam, the Nazis encouraged the manufacture of sugar-beet fodder to reduce animal feed imports while boosting the production of meat and animal fat. The sugar-beet industry was expected to feed both Germany's people and her livestock. With *Lebensraum,* Germany acquired large Austrian and Czechoslovakian sugar-beet areas and entered World War II well sweetened, offering a basic annual per capita ration of 14.56 kilograms of sugar and 5.72 kilograms of jam. The Nazi obsession with sugar beet was so well known that, in 1942, the *Zeitschriften-Dienst,* the Third Reich's confidential weekly instructions to magazine editors, noted: "Do not report on supposed plans to make sugar beet leaves suitable for human consumption."[524]

Sugar had become such an essential element of diet that neither revolution, war nor the demise of slavery could stop its production. Where cane sugar was unavailable, beet sugar sweetened in its place. Even Adolf Hitler knew better than to deprive his people of sugar.

Part 4

The Sweetening World

Chapter 10

The Sugar Diasporas

A Peculiar New Institution Brings Indians to the West Indies

If, today, Christopher Columbus returned to his earthly haunts, he would surely proclaim, as he surveyed the thronged streets of Trinidad and Guyana, "I am vindicated! This *is* the Indies!" In many ways, it is, thanks to post-emancipation sugar planters who reconstructed and recharged their sugar empires by importing hundreds of thousands of Indians and Chinese through a scheme of indentureship scholars describe as "a new system of slavery," historian Hugh Tinker's sadly felicitous phrase.[525] Underlying this new system was the conviction that sugar plantations and free labor were incompatible.

Through indentureship, the British West Indian sugar industry smashed any hope that emancipation would transform the social and economic structure of the sugar colonies. Specifically, indentureship undermined the bargaining power of black workers whose efforts to negotiate fairer wages were stymied by an abundance of cheap imported labor. At the same time, the white, pro-sugar colonial oligarchies squelched the former slaves' longing for farmland by keeping the price of Crown land high and forbidding the sale of smaller lots. The Colonial Office shared the plantocracy's goal of enshrining sugar as a plantation monoculture, and devised fiscal policies that forced the general population, including blacks, to support it.

The new "free" faces of sugar were called coolies, an etymologically obscure word that took on a pejorative tone and came to mean unskilled workers of any race. The first influx, from Madeira and India, died in such numbers that the indenture system was briefly halted and slightly modified before it was relaunched. "The sugar planter had won the war for the soul of the Colonial Office and the humanitarians ... and the Anti-Slavery Society had lost," historian and sugar scholar Alan Adamson writes.[526]

Indentureship was an imperial policy designed and monitored by the British Colonial Office. Its officers, most notably Earl Grey, colonial secretary from 1846 until 1852, and James Stephen, permanent under-secretary until 1847, were reform-minded abolitionists who initially envisioned a labor arrangement freely offered and freely accepted. "The true policy would be to adopt regulations, of which the effect should be, to make it the decided and obvious interest of the immigrants to work steadily and industriously for the same employers for a considerable time," Earl Grey explained.[527] In practice, indenture developed quite differently and, Adamson writes, "remains a notable instance of the easy collapse of liberal ideals before the pressure of [the sugar-planting] special interest."[528]

Indenture evolved as a five-year contract followed by a certificate of "industrial residence," re-indenture or, until 1904, a free trip back to India. At least 25 percent (and later 40 percent) of the coolies had to be female. The indentureship agreement included wage rates, hours of work, unspecified food rations, "suitable dwellings" and medical care, including "comforts," and an agent-cum-immigrant protector. In reality, planters violated most of these provisions but rigorously enforced disciplinary measures, prosecuting coolies for leaving the plantation without a special pass, absence from work, refusal to begin or finish work, vagrancy, failing to obey an order, habitual idleness, using threatening words to authorities and malingering. Indenture "produced a population that was always in the Magistrate's Court," Eric Williams writes.[529]

The British West Indian system became a model for sugar planters worldwide as French and Dutch planters implemented their colonial versions. Indians were the overwhelming majority, though Chinese, Javanese, Japanese, Filipinos, Madeirans and West Africans were also indentured. A statistical overview suggests the demographic impact of Indian indentureship on the Caribbean sugar colonies, Fiji, Mauritius and South Africa: more than 1.2 million indentured Indians emigrated, including over half a million each to the Caribbean and to Africa.

In India, recruiters sought out desperate people rather than experienced sugar workers. Floods, droughts, police trouble, village politics, family quarrels and everyday poverty drove people to sign up. "In most cases the recruiter finds the coolie absolutely on the brink of starvation and he takes him in and feeds him.... Under such conditions, our terms of service are absolute wealth," a colonial emigration agent reported.[530]

Emigrants seldom knew the truth about where they would go and what they would do there. Recruiters hired touts known as *arkatia* who fabricated potential jobs: gardening in Calcutta or sifting sugar in a pleasant colony. After being shepherded to a port city depot, emigrants who had second thoughts discovered that they could return home only after paying the recruiter for transportation and lodging.

The recruiters' documentation was as shoddy as their recruitment techniques. They mislabeled Hindus as Muslims and falsely listed most emigrants as agriculturists, though an 1871 investigative commission reported that on one typical ship, only thirteen were agriculturists and the rest included lime burners, cowherds, peons, sweepers, priests, weavers, scribes, shoemakers and beggars. On another ship, a group of dancing girls and their acolytes "laughed at the idea of becoming agriculturalists."[531]

Many of the women were widowed or abandoned wives who arrived at the depot in rags. Maharani, for instance, was an abused wife who, after spilling boiling milk, ran away to avoid another beating and was recruited to sift sugar in Trinidad. The women often found men to marry them, even across religious barriers. These depot marriages gave women a protector and men a helpmeet.

Until recruiters filled their quotas, they imprisoned recruits in the depot. There, with improvised cooking and washing facilities, the recruit quickly learned that "all his cherished ideas and beliefs about caste and religion would have to be abandoned under sheer compulsion; that he would have to sit and dine in conditions under which," in Hindu nationalist and Gandhi colleague Madan Mohan Malaviya's words, "he would never have consented to dine if he was a free man." Muslims and Hindus of disparate castes, including untouchables, were forced to mingle with each other and, in the first years of indentureship, with the Dhangars, aboriginal agriculturists known as Hill Coolies.

Just before their medical exams, the prospective emigrants were plumped up with goat meat, roti and dahl, and could bathe. A medical officer examined them, usually perfunctorily, even approving the visibly ill, decrepit or old; one would-be laborer was seventy-five. An English medical observer officially condemned the system as "rotten."[532]

The passage from India took twenty-six weeks until the advent of steam halved it. Diarrhea and dysentery, accidents, inadequate food and water, and depression killed many immigrants. In 1856 to 1857, for instance, the mortality rate ranged from just under 6 percent to 31 percent. Upon arrival at destinations often revealed to them just before landing, the Indians were received by planter-employers insensitive to and disrespectful of their culture, religions and needs. Canadian William Sewell, an ailing *New York Times* editor who spent three restorative years in the West Indies, spoke for these planters when he described the Indians as "a set of naked, half-starved, gibbering savages, ready to eat any dead, putrid animal, fish, flesh, or fowl that lay in the path."[533]

Upon arrival, the coolies were processed by a government agent, their supposed protector, and delivered to the plantations. Unlike slaves, they were not seasoned but set to work at once; planters wanted to squeeze every day of their contracted five years out of them. Their suffering was terrible, especially in the relentless grinding season. British absentee Quintin Hogg, visiting his plantation, was horrified to discover his coolies forced to work twenty-two hours a day.[534] Like slaves before them, coolies tried to escape the torment, and the governor, Lord Harris, reported that "scarcely a week passed but reports are sent in from different parts of [Trinidad] *of the skeletons of Coolies being found in the woods and cane-pieces.*"[535]

Arrival Day for these Indians destined for Trinidadian sugar plantations.
In Trinidad and Tobago, May 30 is now celebrated as Arrival Day to commemorate the first Indian arrival.

The infrastructure of most plantations was unchanged from the days of slavery. Indian quarters, still known as "nigger yards," consisted of flimsy, two-storied wood structures with shingled or galvanized-iron roofs. Thin, low partitions separated their very small rooms—about ten feet square. When more women arrived, equally flimsy barracks were built. Families were crammed into a single room, and single workers lived together. Everyone had to share passageways and cook-sheds, anathema to upper castes. The greatest cause of outrage, assaults and complaints to magistrates was the upper-story dwellers' persistent habit of slinging slop out the window or through holes in the floor. The cane fields doubled as toilets. Water was scarce and putrid, and few planters provided iron water tanks. Pigs and cattle roamed freely, and their effluvia added to the general filth.

As in the early days of African slavery, skewed gender ratios changed the nature of male-female relationships. Instead of bringing dowries to their husbands, Indian women demanded bride prices, and some left husbands they disliked for better ones. Sometimes male relatives "sold" girls into marriage. Like sugar workers elsewhere, Indian women had very low birthrates and could not send their children to school; at about ten years of age, children were set to work as well.

White managers and overseers treated Indian women much as they had blacks, reviling them as immoral and coercing them into sexual relationships. They also humiliated Indian men, marching into their rooms and ordering them about even if they were in bed with their wives. Ailing coolies had to go to cheerless plantation hospitals, which the British Guiana Commission of 1871 described as "filthy holes"—in one, for instance, the chief nurse kept a chicken coop on the ward.

Race complicated the despotism of sugar as planters and overseers divided the workers into coolie and Creole gangs they continually compared, encouraging the perception that blacks were stronger but more violent, coolies weaker but more efficient. This strategy worked, as the 1870 Royal Commission learned: "The coolie despises the negro because he considers him ... not so highly civilized as himself, while the negro despises the coolie because he is so immensely inferior to himself in physical strength."[536] Blacks also associated indentureship with slavery and refused to bind themselves to labor contracts as the Indians did. As one black worker explained, "Me fader and me grandfader bin ah slave befoh me, an' me sah neba make contract fo' wo'k pon suga' estate."[537] They resented indentured Indians as impediments in their own struggle to obtain decent wages and working conditions.

These invidious comparisons drove a permanent wedge between the two groups and advanced the planters' goal of using coolies to curb black wages and to forestall any united resistance. "I think the safety of the whites depends very much upon the want of union in the different races," one perceptive manager remarked. The 1870 Royal Commission concurred: "There will never be much danger of seditious disturbances among the East Indian immigrants … so long as large numbers of negroes continue to be employed with them."[538]

The coolies, virtual prisoners on the plantations, communicated in their own language, celebrated traditional festivals, worshipped at Hindu temples and Muslim mosques and focused on saving money to take back to India. Some could not endure the harsh conditions and fled or rebelled, most commonly by malingering. Others sought escape through liquor or marijuana. Most complained ceaselessly that they were not paid the wages promised them, and countless commissions and investigations confirmed this. In 1885, when the legal minimum rate for coolies was twenty-four cents per day, British Guiana's Plantation Turkeyen paid four to eight cents. Trinidadian planters paid an average of a little over eighteen cents for each task, seven less than the legal minimum.

These were not the most egregious cases. Through a task system that penalized workers by paying no wages at all if they did not complete their allotted daily tasks, planters underpaid and cheated their coolies and forced many to work fifteen hours daily to complete these tasks. The first season was the deadliest, and the coolie's worst trials began in the rainy season, as he or she tried to weed in wet and heavy grass and high cane. "The work is hard, monotonous, and in high cane may almost be called solitary; he loses heart, makes a task in double the time in which an experienced hand would make a whole one, returns at a late hour, cold, wet and fatigued, to renew the struggle on the morrow with decreased vitality," the *Trinidad Immigration Report for 1871* noted.[539]

Some planters paid their rookies nothing for an entire year's work yet charged them for rations, keeping them permanently mired in debt. Planters also withheld wages by declaring work stoppages; in British Guiana, these occurred daily. Planters in financial straits put coolies' wages at the top of their nonpayment lists. One planter stopped an entire work gang's wages for three months "to pay for a fork."[540] The difference between wages promised and wages received, writes Tinker, "made all the difference between a decent life and a miserable existence."[541]

Coolies knew they had been cheated, and when possible appealed to magistrates for redress. It was an uphill fight. They had trouble persuading witnesses to testify against vengeful managers. They had to rely on poorly paid and careless translators such as the one who pleaded his client guilty rather than not guilty. The magistrates who went out to the plantations to hear complaints always stayed there as the guests of the manager they were supposed to prosecute. During the hearing, that same manager sat on the bench alongside the magistrate to spare himself the unpleasantness of "standing close-packed among a crowd of Asiatics ... in a crowded, ill-ventilated court room, under a tropical sun."[542] One shining exception to this judicial cronyism was British Guiana's medical inspector Dr. Shier, so sensitive to conflicts of interest that he carried a hammock and slept in police stations or chapels. As the coolies knew and various commissions confirmed, the courts were biased against them. The only way to fight unfairness and injustice was to attack or murder their overseers or managers. The indentured Indian, Eric Williams writes, was "the last victim in the historical sense of the sugar plantation economy."[543]

Despite their low wages, Indian coolies were renowned savers; the British consul in Surinam called them "thrifty to a fault."[544] It is true that they dreamed of the end of their indenture, when they would take their free trip back to India (a feature of indentureship canceled in 1904) to enjoy the sweets of their labor, and white defenders of indentureship made much of Indian savings. Yet the vast majority saved so little that, at indenture's end, planters offering a bounty of between $50 and $60 persuaded tens of thousands to re-indenture for an additional five years. After 1869, Trinidad granted small parcels of land to those who stayed and, in 1873, five acres plus £5 for additional land. Their wives received an additional £5 and took advantage of the opportunity to buy land with it, gaining economic independence, social status, a space to celebrate religious rituals and sometimes the means to abandon an abusive husband. Indian settlements sprang up. In Trinidad, from 1885 to 1895, Indians bought nearly twenty-three thousand acres.

Indenture was only part of the sugar plantocracy's grand plan. Through their influence on policy-makers planters ensured sugar's primacy in the colonial economy and also arranged to have much of the cost of recruiting and transporting indentured workers assumed by blacks and Indians, both indentured and free, through government funds established for the purpose. In British Guiana, underwriting the cost of importing coolies represented 22 to 34 percent of public expenditure. Sir Anthony Musgrave, governor of Jamaica, complained that planters, "like Oliver Twist, were always asking for more."[545]

The planters managed as well to obtain a schedule of duties that cynically catered to their wishes while disregarding the most basic needs of black and Indian workers. Some years, flour, rice, dried fish and salt pork were heavily taxed but diamonds, fresh fish, meat, fruit and vegetables, manure and machinery were tax-exempt. By the mere fact of existing, blacks and immigrants "became involuntary investors in the sugar sector," Adamson writes.[546]

Indentureship struck hard at blacks. It enabled planters to widen the labor pool while rigidly controlling wages, thereby limiting blacks' economic possibilities and keeping their wages low. Blacks sought fairer wages, which planters refused to pay except when they were desperate for workers, and they continued to punish infractions by withholding wages, waiting months before paying or deciding arbitrarily not to pay at all.

The slavery-like restrictions that shored up the indenture system also kept Indians in specific occupational niches and blacks in others. In the sugar industry, some blacks worked as waged laborers, but those eager for better lives went into the cities, where they found jobs on the docks and in transport, the post office and the shops. Some managed to acquire an education and became civil servants and teachers.

By the time indenture ended, Indians found it difficult to penetrate the black-dominated and white-controlled teaching profession, police force and civil service. They turned instead to the retail trade, to growing cane or to cultivating rice, which began to challenge sugar as an important crop.

Although, in the words of Guyanese president Cheddi Jagan, the son of plantation sugar workers, "both our black slave and Indian indentured ancestors watered the sugar-cane with their blood,"[547] the interracial animosity planted and fertilized by the sugar planters survived the end of indentureship and flourishes still, exacerbated by the racialization of trades and professions. As Adamson laments, "Ethnic difference superimposed on class distinction set the subcultures of the oppressed at each others' throats."[548] The mixed-race children of black and Indian struggle for self-identification and are reviled in both communities. In Trinidad and in British Guiana (now Guyana), this implacable hostility and interracial hatred resonate to this day, spawning political impasses and social unrest, and complicating, confusing and poisoning the former sugar colonies.

MAURITIUS

Britain's first attempt to promote the sugar industry on the Indian Ocean island of Mauritius was a fiasco. Indentured Indians arrived in 1829, but within a month began to flee the plantations because planters refused to pay their wages, and Chief of Police John Finiss ordered them repatriated. After emancipation, planter George Arbuthnot of Belle Alliance Sugar Estate resumed the Indian "experiment" by importing thirty-six Dhangar tribesmen on five-year contracts to work alongside Africans. Between 1834 and 1910, Mauritius imported 451,766 more Indians, most for the sugar plantations; by 1872 they had taken the place of the former slaves in the cane fields. By the middle of the nineteenth century, Mauritius produced 9.4 percent of the world's sugar and was a major supplier to Britain.

The Indians endured harsh conditions that included flogging, low or unjustly withheld wages, and imprisonment for running away. To force time-expired Indians to re-indenture, an 1867 law defined anyone not regularly employed as a "vagabond." In 1871, an investigative commission reported that unscrupulous planters did not honor their contracts and permitted overseers to assault the coolies. Police and magistrates, the latter often sugar planters themselves, enforced laws "in such a reckless and indiscreet manner as to cause cruel hardship."[549]

To increase their profits, planters centralized their operations, producing more sugar in fewer factories. Reluctantly, they also sold plots of less productive land to freed Indians who established farms and grew a variety of crops, including sugarcane. More than two-thirds of freed Indians remained in Mauritius, often because of the political machinations of planters who envisioned an agricultural force of freed Indians with no alternative but to work for them. They would no longer have to import large numbers of new Indians and would have experienced workers available during their busiest seasons. But freed Indians shied away from the plantations and, until 1910, planters had to import new indentured workers.

The sugar plantocracy forged a society dominated by a tiny white minority. Until the beginning of the twentieth century, only 6,071 people—one-sixth of 1 percent—could vote. But by independence in 1968, the majority Indian population, the black Creole minority and other minorities had forged a community of interests permitting them to work together for economic growth and other goals, and sugar was the vehicle they chose to achieve these objectives. In 1975, Mauritius negotiated a favorable agreement to provide the European Economic Community with 500,000 tons of sugar annually.

Mauritius is an anomaly in the colonized sugar world. Its minorities, Creole and white, have accepted its Indianness—at 68 percent of the population, it has the largest concentration of Indians outside India—and a succession of Indo-Mauritian leaders have governed. An elite minority speaks English, the country's official language, while everyone else speaks French-derived Creole. Hindu and Muslim holidays are observed, and since 1877, the Mauritian currency has been its rupee. Mauritius's unique circumstances and the dynamics of its society have enabled its people to unite in racial harmony. Ironically, they have embraced sugar as their common denominator.

NATAL, ZULULAND AND MOZAMBIQUE

Nineteenth-century European sugar planters in Natal concluded that they, too, needed to import indentured Indians. The Africans they had corralled onto their plantations were escaping the interminable working hours, terrible conditions and worse pay by running away to their *kraals*, or homesteads. In the 1850s, so much ripe cane was unharvested that some planters went bankrupt, yet they attributed their plight to African laziness and homesickness rather than their own refusal to pay fair wages. Planters complained that they had to hire one hundred Africans to ensure that twenty-five would show up.

The planters tried, unsuccessfully, to attract English farmers and even inmates of Lord Shaftesbury's Homes, where delinquent youngsters from slums learned vocational skills and avoided transshipment to Australia. Finally, British authorities granted them the right to import Indian coolies. The first arrived in 1860 and sugar exports, £3,860 in 1858, soared to £100,000 in 1864. Unlike the planters, the Indians were unhappy and returnees to India complained about brutal treatment. They were often beaten, and forced to work when sick. The Coolie Commission of 1872 reported no evidence of systemic mistreatment but recommended a few measures to mollify the Indians. The planters, by then desperate for more workers, were conciliatory, at least on paper. New laws and regulations granted the Protector of Indian Immigrants more power and a force of Indian immigrant (not coolie) volunteer infantry was established. After a brief interruption in 1872, Indian immigration resumed in 1874.

A series of investigative commissions found that, despite the planters' promises of better treatment, there had been little improvement. Sugar plantation overseers and Indian foremen or drivers known as *sirdars* assaulted and flogged Indian workers with *sjamboks*, cattle prods or whips carved from hippopotamus hide. They underfed, overworked and cheated them of their proper wages. Sick coolies received poor or no medical care, and planters deducted so much money for each sick day that ten days' illness cost the equivalent of three months' wages. Some planters denied rations to women and children. The Protector of Indians failed to protect Indians, and colonial legislation made it so hard for Indians to leave their plantations that they could seek neither help nor redress.

The immigrants lived in abject poverty, housed in shoddy and filthy barracks with no provision for sanitation, privacy or family cohesiveness. They suffered from the dearth of Indian women, the failure of the law to recognize traditional marriage and the *sirdars'* practice of controlling men's contact with their wives (or, if they had none, with prostitutes) to reward or punish them. Many Indians numbed themselves with alcohol or marijuana. Suicide, uncommon in India, was common in Natal.

Many time-expired Indians remained in Natal, leasing land and farming. Planters often waited until their tenants had cleared bush land and then sold it as farmland. Indians struggled to get ahead, inadvertently pioneering sugar's expansion to the north and south.

Natal planters mimicked the racialist, divide-and-rule tactics employed in other sugar colonies and happily set African and Indian at each other's throats. The interracial tensions that resulted eliminated the likelihood that the two groups would ally against their common oppressor. Another feature of this policy was to keep them separate from each other and from whites, making Natal the pioneer of the larger policy of racial segregation, maintained by controlling and restricting mobility through pass laws that ultimately evolved into apartheid.

The colony also assisted the planters by using revenue generated by taxes and levies on African farmers and farming equipment to pay for importing indentured Indians, and granted these planters five years to pay their small share of the charges. The colony itself managed the indenture system and supervised its operation.

These easements helped the white sugar plantocracy to expand, modernize and consolidate into the top ranks of world sugar producers. After the 1897 annexation of Zululand, the pro-sugar Land Board allotted more than two million acres in the form of ninety-nine-year leases to land-hungry planters such as Heaton Nicholls, a Zululand sugar-planting pioneer, who got 73,313 acres. The Land Board also devised a formula, the Zululand Sugar Agreement, to ensure that sugar mills serviced suitably large plantations at prearranged prices. Sugar production became a joint "corporatist" endeavor involving government representatives, the Sugar Millers' Association and the Zululand Planters' Union, all shored up by British imperial military power and capital investment from sugar planters and refiners, including Tate and Lyle, throughout the British sugar colonies.

The Natal government also had to assuage the fears of nonsugar interests. Poor whites worried that time-expired and "passenger" Indians who paid their own way to Natal would swamp them, and white traders and merchants resented the competition from Indians who undersold and outperformed them. In response, Natal imposed harsh regulations on Indians, including an onerous poll tax in 1895 designed to force time-expired Indians to re-indenture or to return to India. Once again, official policies legitimized interracial distinctions and tensions by segregating Indians from whites or removing them from the colony, another example of how Natal adopted segregation to resolve potential problems.

These regulations worked and indentures rose, but so did the deaths of despairing Indian sugar workers. The Protector of Immigrants pointed out but did not prosecute labor law violations by the powerful sugar giant Reynold Brothers. Lewis Reynolds, a member of the Indian Immigrant Trust Board, ensured that the medical officer did not testify about workers' physical conditions. "The institutional mechanism established by the state to oversee the indenture system clearly operated to benefit sugar planters and was easily manipulated by them," writes sugar historian Rick Halpern. "Natal's sugar planters owed their prosperity ... to their imperial connection."[550]

In 1893, twenty-four-year-old Indian lawyer Mohandas Gandhi arrived in Natal to counsel Dada Abdulla Sheth, an Indian Muslim merchant. Gandhi's Natal experiences transformed him. A white man objected to his traveling in a first-class railway car despite his first-class ticket, and railway officials ordered him into the third-class car. Gandhi refused and was ejected from the train. Radicalized, he called on an assembly of Pretoria Indians to revolt against discrimination. The more he learned about the dynamics of Natal society, the clearer it became that Indians of all classes must stand united or the traders and professionals, too, risked being lumped together with the coolies as racial inferiors.

By 1906, Gandhi was articulating the principle of "the great spiritual force" of nonviolence that would later transform India and lead to her independence. He challenged discriminatory legislation and regulations and orchestrated passive resistance in the form of enormous nonviolent marches and strikes, on and off sugar plantations. In 1911, with the support of India's government, indentured immigration to Natal was stopped. Natal intensified its anti-Indian discrimination and Gandhi led the resistance. His reputation soared. In 1913, his wife, Kasturbai, and other women protesting new anti-Indian legislation were arrested, and Gandhi was jailed. He donned the coarse sack uniform of the indentured sugar worker and vowed to eat only once daily until the major issues were resolved. After the Indian Relief Act abolished the poll tax and recognized non-Christian marriages, he suspended resistance and, after twenty years in South Africa, returned to India.

The unlikely catalyst for the movement that ultimately dismantled the British Empire was that imperial creation, the unjust, racialized and greedy South African sugar world. Gandhi sailed into the maelstrom as an ambitious young barrister and sailed out as the founder of a seemingly unstoppable strategy to fight oppression.

As freed Indians left the cane fields for the sugar mills (where they constituted 87 percent of the workforce), planters replaced them with migrant workers from Natal, Zululand and Mozambique. Migrants were easier to control than locals, and too far from home to escape. But the cane fields had to compete with railroads and gold mines on the Rand, both of which paid higher wages. After planters failed to use their political connections to restrict recruitment for mines in Natal and Zululand, they hired workers the mines had rejected on health grounds or because they were under sixteen years of age. Planters also recruited adults loath to work underground, willing to work only six months a year or lured by the promise of an advance on their wages. In 1934, an official contrasted robust mine workers with broken-down sugar workers, coughing and covered with sores.

Officials and others untainted by the sugar interests discovered thousands of children laboring in the cane fields. Many worked alongside their parents, often as part of the new system of labor tenancy by which their labor was pledged as part of a land-lease arrangement, or to fulfill their father's obligations, for instance if he fell sick. Others were rebellious boys eager to escape cattle herding or even school. "I thought I'd be rich in no time if I left school and went to work," one former runaway admitted.[551]

A 1922 photo taken by E. J. Larsen, the railroad station master at Izingolweni, Natal-Zululand, shows a fourteen-year-old African from the Reynolds Brothers sugar plantation. He is emaciated, unsteady on his stick legs and wearing coarse sacking, and he died soon after. Faka's "most ghastly and helpless state" wrung Larsen's heart, and he reported it to the nearest magistrate, who ignored him.

Faka was one of many. "Natives are continually arriving at Izingolweni station from various Sugar Estates in a state of collapse and frequently die within a few hours after arrival," Larsen wrote. Lance Sergeant Schwartz, a policeman, corroborated these deaths. Many more dropped dead in the cane fields and on the roadsides, literally worked to death. The Izingolweni deaths, though exceptionally high, were "symptomatic of a system of employment which persisted for many years afterwards," writes historian William Beinart.[552]

A decade later, planters switched from the Uba cane they had used from the 1880s, hardy, frost- and disease-resistant but low in sucrose, to the faster-growing and higher-yielding Coimbatore variety of cane developed in southern India. They began to pay bonuses for every 100 pounds of cane cut above the minimum standard of 3,000 to 3,500 pounds of Coimbatore. After malaria epidemics decimated their workers and shut down their plants, they took the health department's advice and offered more nutritious food and improved conditions. The state encouraged them by offering price supports and favorable legislation.

FIJI

In 1874, the South Pacific islands of Fiji were ceded to Queen Victoria. Fiji's first British governor, Sir Arthur Hamilton Gordon, formerly governor of Trinidad and of Mauritius, tackled his mission of salvaging the new colony's collapsed economy by creating a plantation sugar industry manned by indentured Indians. To protect Fijians from the fate of other colonized Native peoples, Gordon's policy maintained their traditional way of life under their chieftains and away from the rigors and foreign influences of sugar plantations. Gordon also reserved more than 80 percent of Fiji's land for Fijian ownership.

To establish a sugar industry in Fiji, Gordon invited in Australia's Colonial Sugar Refining Company, known as the CSR. As part of the deal, he negotiated the sale of a thousand acres of land to them and arranged for a workforce of indentured Indians, who began to arrive in 1879. The CSR opened in 1882 and became the most important of Fiji's sugar operations. By 1902, its exports to its New Zealand refinery accounted for nearly three-quarters of Fiji's exports.

In Fiji, the Indian sugar workers' experience, known as the *girmit*, mirrored that of their indentured compatriots in the West Indies, from the trials of recruitment to the difficult sea voyage. Whites belittled the indentured Indians as low-caste coolies and disparaged their religions and cultures. Overseers set tasks most could never complete, and if a worker finished only seven of a ten-chain task, he earned nothing. Poorly paid and therefore poorly fed, the coolie fell victim to myriad diseases and accomplished even fewer tasks. Indian drivers, on the other hand, could amass good sums of money, especially after opening plantation stores—and in one case a gambling hut—they coerced workers into patronizing.

Girmit living conditions were "one of the saddest and most depressing sights, if a man has any soul at all," one missionary lamented.[553] The lack of privacy led to difficult marital relations, and every year, scores of (allegedly) unfaithful women were stabbed to death with cane knives. More indentured Indians committed suicide in Fiji than anywhere else. A repentant overseer, Walter Gill, denounced indenture as "a rotten system ... fathered by Big Business," "five years of slavery in the cane fields of his Britannic Majesty's Crown Colony of Fiji." Gill said the *girmit* contract "contained some of the most pernicious clauses thought up by man," and added, "it was also typical of the era that we white men had no inkling of wrong-doing."[554]

Diarrhea and dysentery killed even more coolies than sexual jealousy, and bronchitis, pneumonia and malnutrition killed about one-fifth of their children. The CSR's grudging maternity leave included neither food nor milk, and infants suckling from undernourished mothers weakened and died. Bad weather and too much sun took their toll on babies lugged out to the cane fields when their mothers had to return to work.

The indentured Indians saw themselves as expatriates rather than immigrants and dreamed of saving money and returning home. As best they could, they lived by Indian standards and, to protest their maltreatment, assaulted brutal overseers, malingered and went on strike. On a plantation whose manager saw them as "simply a nest of rogues and vagabond coolies who are combined for all purposes of illegal conduct," they started a fund to pay the fines continually levied against them for work-related offenses.[555] After their five-year indentureship expired, a small percentage re-indentured. Most of the rest remained in Fiji and leased land; the majority cultivated now-familiar sugarcane. The census of 1921, a year after *girmit* was abolished, listed 84,475 Fijians, 60,634 Indians and 12,117 Europeans, Chinese and others.

That census quantified the legacy of *girmit,* the deep hostility between native Fijians and Indo-Fijians. As elsewhere, sugar planters and the sugar Interest employed divisive racial dynamics with the same hateful results. The Fijians resented the growing numbers of the over-worked, underpaid foreigners who yearned for land; the Indians resented the land-owning natives whom the British protected and favored. Later, Fijians resented them because they had begun to domi-nate commerce and the professions, and feared that further Indian immigration would swamp Fiji demographically and religiously, supplanting Christianity with Hinduism and Islam. Ever since *girmit* ended, Fiji's two major peoples have coexisted with animosity and outbreaks of violence, the familiar legacy of sugarcane culture.

THE "YELLOW TRADE"

China, too, disgorged hundreds of thousands to harvest foreign sugar. Between 1853 and 1884, the British West Indies received 17,904 coolies recruited in Hong Kong and Canton, where British officials supervised the process. Chinese indentureship, which largely ended in 1872, differed from the Indian in two important ways: they were not offered a paid passage home after their indenture, and Chinese women could come only as residents rather than as indentured workers.

The Chinese indenture experience in the British West Indies was plagued by the same abuses as the Indian, and when they were freed, most Chinese fled the plantations to farm or to trade. Planters praised them as more industrious than blacks and stronger than Indians but feared them as violent and cunning. In his 1877 novel, *Lutchmee and Dilloo*, Edward Jenkins portrayed Chin-a-foo, perhaps the only Chinese character in nineteenth-century British West Indian fiction, as "morally and physically repulsive—a very blight on the community within which he lives." Like the Africans and Indians, the Chinese were stereotyped and pitted against other ethnicities in the always-racialized sugar world.

The Chinese coolie trade, run by Chinese warlords and Portuguese and other European merchants, sent 138,000 Chinese to Cuba and 117,000 to Peru; both colonies subjected them to a more grueling indenture than in the British West Indies. It was eight years long, Chinese women were banned, and planters tried to force the coolies to convert to Catholicism. The abuses began in the Portuguese-run colony of Macao, where "crimps," or contractors, recruited even eleven-year-olds from overpopulated and restive Guangdong and Fujian provinces. In Cuba, a fact-finding commission from China heard testimony that at least 80 percent of Chinese workers had been kidnapped, sold as prisoners of war or hoodwinked into signing a contract few could read. "I asked where Havana was, and was told that it was the name of a vessel," Hsu A-fa recalled. "I, in consequence, thought I was being engaged for service on board ship and signed the contract."[556] Other men's signatures were forged.

On the voyage to Cuba or Peru, coolies were "mixed together in a confused heap ... without light, without ventilation ... subjected to miserable food ... thrown into a veritable pigsty and they perish[ed] under the influence of such causes combined." They were flogged for trying to commit suicide and other offenses. The mortality rate was about 20 percent, and survivors disembarked "thin and wan ... mere 'bags of bones.'"[557] After squeezing their biceps and pinching their ribs, sugar planters and their agents made their selections, gave them Spanish names and herded them to the plantations. There the immigrants labored alongside black slaves, rented slave gangs and free black, white and mulatto wage earners paid by the task, the day, the month, the quarter or the year.

Visiting Chinese officials reported that "almost every Chinese met by us was or had been undergoing suffering. The fractured and maimed limbs, blindness, the heads full of sores, the skin and flesh lacerated—proofs of cruelty patent to the eyes of all."[558] When the Chinese demanded their unpaid wages—their contract specified four pesos monthly plus food, lodging and two annual changes of clothes—or more food, the Cubans cut off their pigtails and sent them to work in chains.

Yet their supervisors considered the Chinese very good workers. While slaves cut and loaded cane, the Chinese operated the equipment and, an observer wrote approvingly, were "rapid in their movements, like a conveyor belt, tending to the apparatuses with the mathematical regularity of a pendulum."[559] Eliza Ripley, who fled postbellum Louisiana for a Cuban slave-run plantation, considered her Chinese workers "docile and industrious; they could not stand the same amount of exposure as an African, but they were intelligent and ingenious; within-doors, in the sugar factory, in the carpenter-shop, in the cooper-shop, in driving teams, they were superior."[560]

The Chinese also gained a reputation for slyness and cruelty, and, an American visitor reported, lived "in a state of chronic sullenness."[561] Certainly they were wretched. Many took opium, ran away or committed

A Chinese expatriate's woodcut symbolizes the plight of his indentured compatriots. In a Big House courtyard, drivers bleed trussed Chinese and Indian men as crowds of others await their turn. Boys carry blood-filled swizzle-glasses up to the veranda to fatten up the manager and his attorney while overseers announce wage stoppages. Behind, absentee planters are happy in England. To the right, Chinese weep for their indentured relatives.

suicide: 173 in 1862 alone. "I have seen some 20 men commit suicide," Lin A-pang testified, "by hanging themselves and by jumping into wells and sugar cauldrons."[562] Suicide and death from despair, illness and over-work caused an annual mortality rate planters calculated at 10 percent. The Ch'en Lan Pin Commission estimated that 50 percent died during their first year of indentureship.

Relations between Chinese and blacks were "at times not only hostile but murderous." The Chinese resisted enslavement and saw their wages, however pitiful, as proof of their different status. They also maintained their cultural links to China and refused to renounce Buddhism. Their

Cuban masters encouraged the Chinese-African rift, often providing segregated housing, assigning white rather than black drivers and—as a special concession—not flogging Chinese in the presence of blacks. Sexual tensions also developed when the womanless coolies courted black women.

At the end of eight years, without the money to return to China, most coolies had no means of earning a livelihood except to sign another contract, for one, six or even nine years, or to join a *cuadrilla*, or jobbing gang, headed by a Chinese who contracted out and supervised their labor, food and housing. Sugar mills found *cuadrillas* especially useful at doing the difficult work in the scorchingly hot evaporating rooms.

The Chinese in Peru endured similar conditions on even larger and more isolated plantations; Peru's sugar-growing northern coast extended tens of thousands of acres. As in Cuba, the men worked from dawn to night with an hour's break to cook and eat lunch; after roll call, the men plodded off to work carrying cooking pots and firewood. At night they were packed into crudely constructed, unventilated, unsanitary and usually filthy *galpónes*, or barracks, which strong rains and winds often tore apart. Here they kept their worldly goods: blanket, cooking pot, clothing and sleeping mat. They could not leave the plantation without a pass, and at nightfall, supervisors locked them into the *galpón*.

From avarice and cultural insensitivity, the planters provided the pork-eating coolies with one and a half pounds (or a pannikin) of pebble-strewn rice occasionally supplemented by beef, goat or fish. The coolies spent their tiny wages on pork, lard, tea, bread or fish from the plantation store, and some grew vegetables, sweet potatoes and corn. They ate too little, drank dirty water and were plagued by mosquitoes and disease: typhus, dysentery, typhoid, malaria and influenza. Although some mated with black, *mestizo* and native women, despair and sexual frustration—Peru admitted fifteen Chinese women to 100,000 men—took an additional toll on their community.

Wretched and hopeless, most coolies took opium and often incurred debts to buy it. Others gambled so recklessly that, to stop them from losing a week's or a month's food supplies, planters doled out rice daily.

Coolies ran away from their plantations, committed suicide and, in the 1870s, rebelled and killed overseers. On Cayalti, a coolie hacked his supervisor to death for increasing his allotment of weeding. *El Comercio* newspaper lamented the "feeling of insecurity in Peru from the presence of this great number of desperate men.... Every one goes armed, and every farmhouse is a little armory."[563]

A tiny number of time-expired workers returned to China. The rest remained in Peru as small farmers or traders. Many, hopelessly indebted, continued to work on the sugar estates. Unlike Africans and Indians, who were eventually able to reproduce themselves, the nearly woman-less Chinese made little permanent demographic impact in either Cuba or Peru.

HAWAII BECOMES "KING OF THE SUGAR WORLD"

The story of Hawaiian sugar's Asian indentured laborers (Chinese, Japanese, Korean and Filipino) begins with its American plantocracy's rise to power. In the early nineteenth century, Polynesian Hawaii was evangelized by missionaries sent by the American Board of Foreign Missions. Until then, as the U.S. government acknowledged in 1993 in its official apology to the Hawaiian people, "the Native Hawaiian people lived in a highly organized, self-sufficient, subsistent social system based on communal land tenure with a sophisticated language, culture, and religion."[564]

In 1835, American Ladd and Company leased land on Kauai to grow and mill sugarcane, which became Hawaii's major crop. Many missionaries founded plantations: the Alexanders, Baldwins, Castles, Cookes, Rices and Wilcoxes. "A plantation is a means of civilization," the *Planters' Monthly* proselytized. "It has come in very many instances like a mission of progress into a barbarous region and stamped its character on the neighbourhood for miles around."[565]

Hawaii's *haole*, or foreign, sugar interests depended on land-leases for enormous holdings, cheap labor governed by planter-biased laws, inter-connected and intermarried factors and merchants, and centralized mills. The Big Five mercantile houses—Alexander Baldwin, American

Factors, C. Brewer and Company, Castle and Cooke, and Theo. H. Davies & Company—managed, financed and controlled most plantations.

The land-leases displaced Native Hawaiians from their traditional lands. So did the sugar plantations' intensive irrigation systems, which, by diverting the course of streams, lowered the water table, reducing or drying up the flow of water to small farms and gardens, parching the land and displacing their inhabitants. But instead of resigning themselves to brutish existence as low-waged workers on the sugar plantations, many younger Hawaiians emigrated to California, especially after the 1849 Gold Rush. To try to keep them in Hawaii, the planters pressured the monarchy to require a permit to emigrate.

By the 1860s, Hawaii had twenty-nine flourishing sugar plantations, and Mark Twain dubbed it "the king of the sugar world."[566] But the Native Hawaiians, 85 percent of the plantation workforce, did not satisfy the planters' need for an endless pool of cheap labor. As a result, the planters turned to impoverished Chinese villages for indentured workers. In 1876, when Hawaii signed a reciprocity treaty with the United States exempting Hawaiian sugar from import duties and effectively making it an American economic colony, the planters scrambled to acquire even more Chinese laborers. As elsewhere, they foisted most of the cost onto the state, in this case the monarchy, which paid two-thirds of the total.

Hawaii's coolies were less cruelly treated than elsewhere, though they worked ten-hour days twenty-six days a month, and even more during the harvesting and grinding seasons. They were supervised by *lunas*—overseers—usually Hawaiians or other non-Chinese, and friction between workers and *lunas* was constant. The Chinese also resented that planters hired only Hawaiians as sugar boilers, a skilled job. In 1882, when the Chinese workforce had risen to 49 percent and the Hawaiian had declined to 25 percent, only three out of five thousand sugar boilers were Chinese.

The plantations were isolated, and the coolies were forbidden to leave without passes. Confined there with almost no women, they grew vegetables and raised poultry, gambled and smoked opium. On one plantation, the Chinese cook packed opium into their lunch pails.

In her memoirs, Hawaiian Queen Lili'uokalani recalled innumerable scandals connected with the opium traffic.

At the end of their indenture, many Chinese left Hawaii for opportunities elsewhere. Those who stayed were unwelcome. In 1883 the government restricted Chinese immigration and banned it after 1898.

The planters now turned to Japan for sugar workers. By 1900, Hawaii had 61,111 Japanese, its largest ethnic group. (Much smaller numbers of Portuguese, Norwegians, Germans and South Sea Island sugar workers had also immigrated.) The Japanese had to pay for their passage and their lodgings. Ko Shigeta recalled paying $7 or $8 monthly for "a humble shed—a long ten-foot-wide hallway made of wattle and lined along the sides with a slightly raised floor covered with a grass rug, and two *tatami* mats to be shared among us…. The lives of all the Japanese working on the sugar farms were the same as mine, more or less," he said.[567] A 1900 report described even worse conditions: barracks walls with three to four layers of shelving bunks, their inmates' only private space.

Like the Chinese, the Japanese hated the *lunas*, who were empowered to withhold or deduct their wages and discipline them. They resisted in the usual ways: running away, attacking *lunas* and plantation police, and setting fire to cane fields and sugar mills, even though, after 1892, sugar workers could be sentenced to prison and hard labor for repeated acts of defiance.

As the Japanese produced Hawaii's sugar, the sugar interests intrigued against King Kalakaua. In 1887, the Hawaiian League, a quasi-secret, American-dominated planters' cabal, forced the reluctant king to accept the "bayonet constitution" that transferred most of his power to a cabinet of *haole* Hawaiian Leaguers he could not dismiss. The bayonet constitution also granted voting rights to non-Asian foreigners, in other words white Americans and Europeans, while imposing heavy property qualifications that eliminated most Hawaiian voters.

Four years later, King Kalakaua died of kidney disease and was succeeded by his equally gracious, refined and popular sister, Lili'uokalani. Queen Lili'uokalani responded to her people's outrage against the bayonet constitution by attempting to abolish it, reclaim the royal authority and restore some of the Hawaiian people's "ancient rights." She also hoped to limit the political power of Americans with divided loyalties and asked rhetorically: "Is there another country where a man would be allowed to vote, to seek for office, to hold the most responsible of positions, without becoming naturalized, and reserving to himself the privilege of protection under the guns of a foreign man-of-war at any moment when he should quarrel with the government under which he lived? Yet this is exactly what the quasi Americans do, who call themselves Hawaiians now and Americans when it suits them."[568]

For her pains, Lili'uokalani was overthrown by U.S. marines acting on behalf of the sugar plantocracy and forced to abdicate. (A century later, the United States formally apologized to Hawaii, acknowledging that "the United States Minister assigned to the sovereign and independent

In the final months of her life, Hawaiian Queen Lili'uokalani, deposed by American sugar interests, poses with her little terrier.

Kingdom of Hawaii conspired with a small group of non-Hawaii residents of the Kingdom of Hawaii, including citizens of the United States, to overthrow the indigenous and lawful Government of Hawaii." The apology mentions as well that nearly a year after Lili'uokalani's ouster, in a message to Congress, President Grover Cleveland called the American ambassador "not inconveniently scrupulous" and motivated by "the Hawaiian sugar interests." He styled the coup "an act of war" and declared, "A substantial wrong has thus been done."[569])

Despite having kicked out Hawaii's queen and, as an annexationist American newspaper gloated, "ended the 'Empire of the Calabash,'"[570] the sugar interests remained unsatisfied with Hawaii's status. Like the Cuban sugar planters, they wanted nothing less than free access to the huge American market and believed that only annexation to the United States would achieve it. In 1898, the U.S. annexed Hawaii, and in 1900, it became an American territory. The sugar interests had won an enormous victory in their fight to obtain American federal benefits and favors.

At the same time, the planters had two serious new worries. The first was that annexation brought an end to the indentured-labor system that in postbellum America smacked too strongly of coercion. The second worry was that sugar had reconfigured the face of Hawaii, which, by 1900, looked more Japanese than Hawaiian. Ironically, the very *haole* planters who had imported such large numbers of Japanese were now distressed at the demographic consequences of their handiwork, especially as many Asian sugar workers, freed from indenture, left the plantations. Non-Asian Hawaiians and the United States also reacted strongly, and the 1907 Gentlemen's Agreement between Japan and the U.S. stanched the flow of immigrants, from 14,742 that year to 1,310 in 1909. (As a U.S. territory, Hawaii was also now governed by the American Chinese Exclusion Act of 1882.) Meanwhile, a few thousand Koreans arrived, most destined for the sugar plantations.

The advent of photography introduced a new twist to the story. Unlike their women-deprived Chinese predecessors, many Japanese (and, between 1910 and 1924, Korean) sugar workers found spouses through matchmakers who matched couples using photographs of potential brides and grooms. The arrival of thousands of these Asian "picture brides" transformed Hawaii's cane world. By 1910, women's gangs worked in the cane fields, weeding, hoeing and cleaning cane stalks for wages one-third less than their husbands'. Pregnant field women worked until they gave birth and soon after returned to the cane fields, leaving their babies in nearby lean-tos.

The Japanese women, outnumbered five to one by men, were lonely for female companionship and anxious about frustrated bachelors who propositioned or grabbed them. But the gender imbalance had some benefits. It enabled some women to leave abusive husbands or, as in the lusty Japanese work song that field women composed and sang, to enjoy a lover: "Tomorrow is Sunday, right? / Come over and visit. / My husband will be out / watering cane / And I'll be home alone."

Married workers proved to be more reliable than bachelors, but they needed higher wages to support their families and struck to obtain them. Planters subdued the 1909 strike by mostly Japanese workers and, to counter their solidarity, began to import Filipinos—over 100,000, most males. For decades the two groups lived and organized separately, to the benefit of planters, until 1920, when Filipinos and Japanese acted in solidarity during a sugar strike that cost six major plantations $11.5 million. The angry planters accused the Japanese of wanting "to obtain control of the sugar industry.... They evidently fail to realize that it is one thing to bluff, bulldoze and bamboozle weak oriental peoples and another thing to try to coerce Americans."[571] The planters' solution was to invite Europeans to replace the obstreperous Asians. But when Portuguese and Germans rejected the wages and working conditions on the plantations, the planters comforted themselves with bowdlerized memories of the Chinese indentured workers—how docile they had been! how industrious!—and tried to revive recruitment in China.

As in so much of the sugar world, Hawaii's population and politics reflect its bittersweet past: only one-fifth of its people are descended from Native Hawaiians or Pacific Islanders, while 42 percent are Asian and 44 percent white. Sugar relegated Hawaiians to a minority in their homeland, and *haole* planters kept them almost entirely out of Hawaii's most important economic activity, except as low-paid laborers. The consequences resonate today in Hawaiian society and politics, although sugar is no longer the major commodity.

AUSTRALIAN SUGAR AND INDENTURED MELANESIANS

New South Wales and especially Queensland were important sugar producers even before 1901, when they federated with four other states to form Australia. Sugar competed for workers with other crops and with mining. After a failed attempt to import Indians, Queensland authorized the importation of immigrants from the islands of Melanesia, and before long restricted these Kanakas—the Melanesian word for "man" often used derogatorily in English—to the cane fields and mills.

Unlike indentured workers from complex and densely populated Asian countries, the Kanakas were clansmen bound to the land by social customs and economic constraints that made their communities resistant to change. In the beginning, leaving home to work in white-run Australia was a last resort that only brute force or natural disasters could provoke. White sugar interests provided the brute force; Melanesia, one of the most inhospitable habitats in the world, provided the natural disasters in the form of hurricanes, drought and ecological instability, endemic malaria and often fatal scurvy.

In the early years, recruiters kidnapped or tricked Kanakas onto their ships and coerced them into signing indentures they did not understand. The colloquial term for the process of recruitment—blackbirding—symbolizes the contempt the recruiters and their employers felt for their black victims, mostly young bachelors. One transport ship, the *Daphne*, looked like an African slaver with its cargo of 108 naked Melanesians below deck in a space designed for fifty-eight.[572] An 1885 royal commission called recruitment "one long record of deceit, cruel treachery, deliberate kidnapping and cold-blooded murder,"[573] yet Britain sent only the occasional warship to monitor the situation.

As the sugar industry expanded, Melanesians became familiar with the goods brought home by returning Kanakas. Weapons were in high demand. So were the steel tools, fishing and agricultural implements, and medical supplies that increased clan productivity, the cloth, clothing and household goods popularized by missionaries and the addictive tobacco that the Kanakas even used as currency. Trinkets, too, were much desired: jewelry, rings, umbrellas, tin whistles, musical instruments.

"The trade box system was an example of the way in which colonial capitalism co-opted mechanisms in the pre-capitalist economy to its service," writes economic historian Adrian Graves. "In the process, the growth and development of the Queensland sugar industry was ensured ... [and Melanesia was incorporated] in the web of colonialism.... As long as truck [trade goods] was transformed into gifts in the region, Melanesia remained not the beneficiary, not even the partner of colonial economic development, but its servant."[574]

One commodity in particular obsessed Melanesian bachelors: the "trade box." The first trade boxes were modest-sized lockable wooden boxes full of goods and trinkets. As more Melanesians indentured, their trade boxes were made of pine or imitation oak, standardized to three feet long by eighteen inches wide and deep, with handles and a lock whose key they proudly attached to their belt buckles. Until their triumphal return home with the precious box pressed to their chest, the Kanakas used it to store their treasures and, a contemporary noted, "it is a most exceptional thing for a box to be touched by anyone save the rightful owner."[575]

Back home, senior clan members took charge of the boxes, enriching themselves and using the contents to arrange the returnee's marriage. Because marriage was a man's only way to improve his status in his community, the desire for a trade box kept unhappy workers working, and the debts they incurred played a crucial role in binding them to their employers.

Melanesian indentureship was initially so harsh that, within five years, Queensland passed the 1868 Polynesian Labourers Act to regulate it. The act stipulated three-year contracts, hours to be worked, minimum wages, daily rations, clothing, lodging and medical services. It allowed time-expired workers to either return home or, if they re-indentured, to choose their employer and to bargain over wages, working conditions and even the length of the indenture. Subsequent acts permitted employers to transfer or rent out their workers to other farmers. New South Wales banned indentureship but permitted the hiring of time-expired Kanakas from Queensland.

Kanaka men found the sugar industry's grueling hours and rigid discipline unlike anything they had ever known. Within days of arrival, the unseasoned recruits had to clear, weed and hoe the fields, and cut and cart the cane. During the crushing season, many were worked literally to death. "It must be patent to anyone that young recruits who have never worked and who, in many cases are as soft as females, cannot at once do heavy work in the canefields or at the mills ... new recruits are put to it with often fatal results," concluded Drs. Wray and Thomson in an 1880 report on plantation conditions.[576] The Kanakas were called "boys" and were controlled by white overseers and Kanaka drivers known as "head boys," "boss boys," "trustworthys" or "chiefs." Queensland's Masters and Servants Act established clearly that employers had extensive rights and workers had extensive obligations. The reward for their labor was wages paid at contract's end and usually in goods whose value was marked up at least one-third.

Labor inspectors were in short supply, underpaid and subject to reprisal if they criticized planters who, one observer commented, "treated both the law and the regulations with utter contempt, and appear to assume such an air of superiority that you think sometimes that we can't be in a free country."[577] Until the islanders learned to communicate in "Kanaka English" or pidgin, they had no means of lodging complaints.

A common punishment was deprivation, of medical care, of food and leisure time, and of marital relations: spouses were often separated. Physical punishment was also standard. Rev. James Fussell reported that the islanders felt "the sting of the stockwhip" if they loitered. John Riley, a white plantation laborer, reported that "a nigger-driver named Smith ... did cruelly ill-treat and beat one of the niggers by breaking three of his ribs and shoulders with a hoe in the cane-fields." The worker died of his injuries but Smith went unpunished.[578]

One of the most distressing features of the Kanaka experience was being thrust into work gangs with men from enemy clans or islands. In Melanesia, intervillage warfare was endemic, and the Kanakas perpetuated it on the plantations, where they fought and killed their traditional enemies and raped "enemy" women. The Kanakas also bitterly resented the Chinese whose opium dens, liquor and betting shops and brothels they frequented, and often attacked Chinese plantation owners or employees.

As ever, planters lodged their workers as cheaply as they could, at first in wooden barracks. But the islanders were terrified of sleeping alongside men from hostile clans and built small grass huts where they felt safer. Later, planters provided shanties slapped together with scraps of wood and tin and called them humpies, the name for Aboriginal domed sleeping shelters woven from tree branches and leaves. Sugar-version humpies were sweltering, crowded and filthy, perfect vehicles for spreading lung and intestinal diseases. They also symbolized the islanders' place at the bottom of the social and economic hierarchy just as the planters' fine houses symbolized theirs at the top. The Kanakas' nutrition was as wretched as their housing. The planters provisioned them as cheaply as possible with bulk rations of flour, rice, molasses, yams or potatoes and "Kanaka beef," the often vermin-riddled offal nobody else would eat. They also permitted the Kanakas to grow their own food and to hunt and fish, and did not confine them to their plantations.

The Kanakas suffered such bad health that one in four died, struck down by overwork, psychological and emotional strain, malnutrition or the old diseases that afflicted their homelands—tuberculosis, influenza, pneumonia, bronchitis and dysentery—and the new European diseases such as measles and smallpox. In the last two decades of indentureship, mortality rates declined but remained much higher than among Europeans. Medical care was grudgingly provided, or was withheld because whites objected to sharing facilities with the black workers.

And as ever, to protest their exploitation, the Kanakas feigned illness, disobeyed orders, stole from their employers and each other, torched the cane fields and sometimes attacked their overseers. But few chose to run away, so powerful was their desire to earn a trade box.

Some islanders sought to marry before returning home, but the Australian ratio of about seven or eight islander men to one woman allowed only a tiny minority of men—but 60 percent of women—to do

GROUP OF S. Sea ISLANDERS (CAIRNS) 1890

This cane field gang of South Sea Islanders appear tired and sullen as they pose with their white overseer for this image in a Cairn, Queensland, cane field.

so. For want of culturally acceptable partners, many men contravened the complex and rigid rules that governed Melanesian marriage. They married women outside their clan: islander, European, Asian or Aboriginal, the last of these often kidnapped to avoid paying the bride price. Sometimes even members of enemy clans married.

Islander women often preferred Australia to their homelands, though they could not retreat to their menstrual huts or follow other traditions, and they were vulnerable to rape by enemy islanders and Europeans. But unlike their men, they were seasoned agriculturists and undaunted by doing field work in female work gangs. They were freer in Australia than at home, and by marrying, islander women gained a protector as well as a partner. They spent more time with their husbands than spouses did in the islands. They also responded to Christian missionaries who taught them new and more independent ways of living. Some learned to read and write at mission schools and encouraged their children to become literate.

In the mid-1880s, global sugar prices plunged, sunk by beet sugar dumped onto British and American markets, and they stayed low for two decades. To survive, the Queensland sugar industry had to reinvent itself.

This process, known as reconstruction, transformed a plantation industry reliant on indentured workers into a network of small cane farmers who supplied state-supported central mills. Reconstructed sugar was highly productive and technologically advanced, "the only sugar cane industry in the world to rely on a labor force of European origin … and it pioneered mechanization of field work."[579]

Reconstructed sugar was also the lovechild of white racialism and the growing uneasiness felt by trade unionists, who excluded non-whites from membership, at the increasing numbers of indentured blacks. Beginning in 1890, the importation of Melanesians was banned. Planters found replacement workers among laid-off miners who sought jobs in the sugar industry, even as field hands, and among European immigrants, lured to Australia by a campaign to attract them. As the numbers of white cane cutters increased, blacks had to compete with them for work. The small numbers of Asians in the sugar industry—Chinese and a few Indians— were also targets of white racism. Because of China's international status, her nearness to Australia and her enormous population, whites particularly feared the Chinese and raged against the "yellow agony."

But racist sentiments transformed the sugar industry less profoundly than did rethinking how sugar was produced. Calculations showed that large plantations employed one Kanaka for each five acres, but on a farm of one hundred acres or less, the ratio was one worker, usually the farmer or a family member, for every ten acres. The reason was that wage-earning Europeans or farmers who owned their own land worked harder, longer and better than indentured Melanesians with much less at stake. As a result, small farmers could price their sugar lower to sell to the mills.

This rethinking led to reconstruction, in which large holdings were subdivided and sold, changing the nature of the industry. As cane farmers grew in number, so did their importance to the Liberal Party, which envisioned a society of Liberal cane farmers no longer dominated by Conservative planters. By 1915, as many as 4,300 small farms, all owned by Englishmen and other Europeans, had been carved out of 140 plantations. By 1901, when Queensland joined the Australian federation, its plantation sugar industry had been replaced by thousands of progressive cane farmers.

Meanwhile, new technology—vacuum pans, double and triple crushing, triple-effect evaporators—was making mills more sophisticated and increasing their capacity. In 1885, the Queensland government granted £50,000 for two cooperatively owned central mills, and those mills would accept only sugar produced exclusively by white labor. Subsequent legislation offered a rebate of £2 per ton to white-produced sugar. The following decade, £500,000 was dedicated to establishing eleven new central mills, and sugar production more than doubled. Refining, however, was a virtual monopoly of the Colonial Sugar Refining Company, which, at the invitation of Fiji's governor, had also established Fiji's sugar industry.

In 1901, when Queensland and New South Wales joined the Australian federation, the new parliament got to work cleansing the new nation of its non-white residents and ordered them deported by 1907. A royal commission recommended a few compassionate grounds for staying in Australia: extreme age, physical debility, more than twenty years' residency there, owning land or holding unexpired leaseholds, or having earlier breached tribal law or been targeted by witchcraft or personal vendettas.[580]

Islanders fought hard to stay. Despite its hardships, life in Australia had more possibilities than the unremitting harshness of Melanesia. They petitioned, formed the Pacific Islanders' Association and sought sympathetic European allies. A few bitter islanders set their plantations' cane fields on fire. Others fled and hid out with friends. In the end, however, Australia deported more than four thousand islanders.

Crowds gawking at the departing deportees heard one group shout out: "Goodbye Queensland; Goodbye White Australia; Goodbye Christians."[581] A few deported Kanakas left with an astonishing cornucopia of goods, including sewing machines, kitchen stoves, kerosene lamps, phonographs, bicycles, cricket gear, boxing gloves, spades, hoes and other fancy objects. The bush Kanakas, however, left with a modest trade box or none at all. "White man no more want black man, use him up altogether, chase him away, plenty Kanaka no money go back poor," one empty-handed Kanaka exclaimed bitterly.[582] About 2,500 Kanakas remained in Australia, some illegally, settling in small communities in the main sugar districts.

The campaign for "White Australia" had won. By 1910, whites produced 93 percent of Queensland sugarcane. Racism, vile offspring of the sugar trade, was written right into the law. Queensland was an eager party to it and reaped the benefits: free access for sugar into the Australian market and tariff protection against foreign cane and beet sugar. Shamelessly, Parliament passed laws requiring aliens who wished to lease larger than five-acre plots of land to pass a dictation test in a language of the government's choice; Italians, though belittled for their too-dark skins, were just white enough to be exempted. After 1916, only whites would grow Queensland's sugar.

Other victims were the hundreds of Chinese who had also planted sugar, often on land Europeans rejected as too difficult to clear and cultivate. No trace remains of their contributions to the development of Australia's sugar industry, but historical geographer Peter Griggs calls these Asians the "true pioneers of sugar cultivation."[583]

Australia and its sugar had become white, thanks to the determination of both the government and the trade unions. But unlike other race-driven sugar producers, Australia ended rather than perpetuated the exploitation of non-white sugar workers. Instead, white men toiled in the fields, bringing in profitable cane crops and shattering the myth that the white man is constitutionally unable to do long, hard physical work under the broiling sun. Australia's dismissal of its Kanakas meant that its sugar industry had to be reinvented to accommodate the supposedly greater needs of white workers who would not tolerate the degree of exploitation sugar had hitherto demanded.

Australia's determination to transform and expand its lucrative sugar industry required legislative protection and technological modernization. The government accommodated, regulating and protecting the industry so many whites depended on for their living. The central factories—cooperatives or owned by plantations—streamlined their operations by adopting new technology and building railways. Unlike many cane-producing countries, Australia also exported refined sugar. Its Colonial Sugar Refining Company undertook important research into cultivating and breeding cane. The new varieties introduced have been fundamental to the success of Australia's sugarcane industry.

Chapter 11

Meet and Eat Me in St. Louis!

The World's Fair and the Fast and Sweet Food Revolution

On April 30, 1904, the World's Fair opened in St. Louis, Missouri, and by closing day, seven months later, it had changed how the Western world ate and snacked. The fair celebrated the Louisiana Purchase, was spread across 1,272 acres and featured more than 1,500 buildings. Dozens of "Palaces"—the Palace of Varied Industries, the Palace of Fine Arts, the Palace of Education and Social Economy—were wonderlands of knowledge. Visiting children could play at the Model Playground. Technology such as the newfangled telephone that allowed people to speak to each other from opposite sides of a building thrilled young and old. So did the electricity that lit up the fair at night, such a novelty that Thomas Edison had had to help install it.

President Theodore Roosevelt opened the fair by telegram and later visited in person. His free-spirited seventeen-year-old daughter Alice spent two minutely reported weeks there, smoking cigarettes and enjoying herself. ("I can either run the country or I can control Alice. I cannot possibly do both," the president said.) Scott Joplin, the great ragtime composer, celebrated the fair with his composition "The Cascades," but, because he was black, could not perform it at the Main Picture where white musicians played. Instead, Joplin joined other black entertainers on the Pike, a main thoroughfare that spawned the expression "coming down the pike."

Twenty million visitors gaped at the spectacles, many food-related: Missouri's all-corn Corn Palace, Lot's wife sculpted from salt, Miss Louisiana carved from a five-foot sugar lump, California's almond elephant, Missouri's prune bear, Minnesota's buttery President Roosevelt. Many curiosities were flesh and blood: Juliana de Kol, the world's most prolific cow; Jim Key, the horse that could spell "Hires Root Beer"; and humans on public display, among them Geronimo, the legendary Apache warrior; Nancy Columbia, an Inuit child; Philippine Ogorot boys; tiny African Pygmies and giant Patagonians.

Touring the fair was both exhilarating and exhausting, and propelled hungry and thirsty fairgoers into 130 eateries serving foods from all over the world. One of the most popular was concession no. 66, where much-loved cookbook author Sarah Tyson Rorer presided over a hygienic kitchen applauded for its delicious meals and good coffee. Refreshment stands served tea, coffee, soft drinks, iced tea and other beverages, and finger food. Fairgoers could eat as they strolled: hot dogs, doughnuts, ice-cream cones and cotton candy were favorite choices.

The fair's fast food, packaged to be eaten on the go rather than at a table, saved time and ultimately revolutionized eating. Before then, eating on the run was disdained as vulgar. The fair changed that notion and, explains St. Louis food historian Suzanne Corbett, "really established what we consider fast food or pop-culture food as a part of the mainstay of the American culture."[584] Like the fair's hot dogs, fast food was designed to be easy to consume, tasty and satisfying. When served alongside an energizing drink, it proved a new and wildly popular cuisine.

The most popular of these energizing soft and fruit drinks were orangeade, grape juice, lemonade and apple cider. The fair also introduced Dr. Pepper, Coke, ginger ale and Hires Root Beer. Americans had long enjoyed homemade pennyroyal, sassafras or ginger tea, cranberry, raspberry and elderberry juice and unfermented apple cider. In 1807, Yale chemistry professor Benjamin Silliman began to market a new but bland drink, bottled soda water.

The magic happened when flavors were added—vanilla, sarsaparilla, chocolate, ginger, orange. Sales of soda pop (as it was named in 1861, because of the popping sound as bottles were being uncorked) soared. Orange pop was among the earliest and most popular soft drinks. So was ginger ale, developed in Ireland and first produced in Boston in 1861. In 1876, Charles E. Hires' root beer appeared in Philadelphia. Pharmacist Charles Alderton created the authoritative-sounding Dr. Pepper in 1885 in Waco, Texas. A year later, John Stith Pemberton developed Coca-Cola as a headache and hangover remedy; after Pemberton's death in 1888, Englishman John Matthews invented equipment to manufacture Coca-Cola and popularized it through astute advertising: "Youth as it sips its first soda experiences the sensations which, like the sensations of love, cannot be forgotten." By fair's end, sugared soft drinks were firmly established in the growing lexicon of fast food.

Ice cream, sold at fifty ice-cream stands, made fair history when it was served in cones as portable fast food. "The ice cream melted somewhat and dripped from the hole in the bottom of the cone, but it was delicious," one fairgoer recalled.[585] The ice-cream soda, combining coolness, richness and sweetness, was another favorite. Several men claimed to have invented it, including Philadelphia's Robert Green, whose tombstone proclaimed "The Originator of the Ice-cream Soda."[586]

By the time the fair opened in 1904, the United States already had nearly sixty thousand soda fountains dispensing pop and ice-cream sodas in drugstores, restaurants, candy stores and at roadside stands. The advent of mechanical refrigeration and new kinds of freezers spurred ice-cream production; by the turn of the century, it reached five million gallons. At the same time, popular delight in the ice-cream soda helped to drive the explosive growth of the soda industry.

Fairgoers also enjoyed sweetened fruit frozen inside a tin tube, the precursor to today's popsicle, and iced tea, a refreshing twist on hot tea. The clever owners of Jell-O urged people to sample the jiggly dessert for free, and sent them home with recipes so they could prepare this fastest of fast foods at home. Another sweet, light newcomer was Fairy Floss Candy, pure granulated sugar spun in an electric machine and so resembling cotton that it took the name cotton candy. Fairgoers loved it enough to buy 68,655 small cardboard boxes at 25 cents each, the same price as ever-popular stewed prunes and half the price of admission to the fair.

Fast and Slow Food Before the Fair

The 1904 world's fair was the climax of a century's worth of culinary development. Fast food, most of it sweetened or fatty or both, had precedents in the nineteenth century, when "gobble, gulp and go" prevailed among busy workers who valued speedy food service because it gave them more time to work. In mid-nineteenth-century New York City, for example, a businessman "could hang up his 'Out to Lunch' sign, eat heartily for next to nothing, and be back at work within a quarter of an hour." *Herald Tribune* writer George G. Foster exulted that "it is the culmination, the consummation, the concentration of Americanism; with all its activity, perseverance, energy, and practicality in their highest states of development."[587]

Earlier culinary Americanisms had been quite different. Meals had been grown, plucked, hunted or fished and were generally repetitive and plain. Food historian James E. McWilliams describes the seventeenth-century Cole family tearing meat off its bones, washing it down with apple cider and sharing utensils. In 1744, traveler Dr. Alexander Hamilton declined to join a ferry keeper and his wife's "homely meal of fish without any kind of sauce.... They had no cloth upon the table, and their mess was a dirty, deep, wooden dish which they evacuated with their hands, cramming down skin, scales and all. They used neither knife, fork, spoon, plate, or napkin because, I suppose, they had none to use."[588] A typical Dutch immigrant family made do with endless meals of cornmeal mush and milk. When they could afford to, colonists sweetened their beverages and food, and preserved fruits, with molasses or maple syrup.

By the late eighteenth century, the New World was beginning its slow progress to industrialization and urbanization. Forks and spoons replaced hands, kitchens were equipped with a range of utensils, and cookbooks spread culinary knowledge. Rum, safer than often unpotable water, was a common beverage; so were coffee and tea, taken with pinches of brown sugar. North American lifestyles and tastes in food were increasingly English, although, McWilliams observes, the "conventional [American] narrative rarely acknowledges the power of this attraction" to Anglophilia and its comforts.[589]

American housewives bought so many copies of Englishwoman Hannah Glasse's *The Art of Cookery Made Plain and Easy* that in 1805, an American edition was published. Other English cookbooks also sold well. Among their offerings were puddings and desserts that almost always called for sugar or molasses. *Seventy-five Receipts for Pastry, Cakes, and Sweetmeats*, by "A Lady of Philadelphia"—Eliza Leslie—featured a recipe for molasses stick candy. "Boston" baked beans were heavily sweetened and thickened with molasses. Sweetness was becoming a standard ingredient in everyday meals. Sugar "was incorporated into cakes and fudge, dissolved into sauces, sprinkled on fruits and vegetables, enlisted as the foundation for paste that made sculptures, used as a basis for bonbons, and included as an essential component of ice cream," writes Wendy Woloson in *Refined Tastes*.[590]

By the nineteenth century, as prosperity allowed once self-sufficient colonists more choice in their menus, grocery stores sprang up. One of their standard features was a portable mill to grind lumps of muscovado sugar into granules (until the 1880s, muscovado was cheaper and used much more widely than white sugar). But price alone did not determine usage. As food historian Waverley Root explains, "The rivalry between white and brown sugar provides a chapter in the history of snobbery."[591] As it became more affordable, white sugar also became a status symbol as people served it to guests and relegated brown sugar to the kitchen or for private use. As a measure of snobbery, sugar worked remarkably well, with molasses as its lowest form and refined white sugar its highest, and in between them, many grades of brown and coarser sugar.

The 1858 invention of the Mason jar greatly increased the demand for white sugar. The Mason jar, a reusable, heavy glass container that could be tightly sealed, enabled women to preserve fruits and vegetables they could serve year-round. Because canning required white sugar rather than brown sugar or molasses, it, too, contributed to a large increase in the consumption of white sugar.

ICE CREAM AND SODAS

Ice cream, also sugar laden, was a popular urban treat. In New York City, ice-cream street vendors advertised their wares by bawling, "I scream ice cream."[592] Sold from stands or carts, ice cream was relatively cheap. One observer noted that, by 1847, in Philadelphia, "the stalls of the markets are crowded with it—it is wagoned about the street, and turn where you will, there is ice cream in profusion—cheap but not the less excellent on that account."[593] The wealthier and more sophisticated also appreciated ice cream. In so-called pleasure gardens, like "Ice Cream City" in Philadelphia's Vauxhall Garden, they gathered to listen to music and enjoy such delicacies as concoctions of fruit and ice cream—about two tablespoons' worth—served in delicate glassware.

Increasingly, ice cream was identified with women, just as candy was, and women could satisfy their cravings in Ladies' Ice-Cream Rooms, saloons or parlors, as some were called. These were extravagantly decorated

Interior of McCutcheon and McGill drugstore, Calgary, Alberta, 1907–08.
The chairs and tables are for customers to enjoy their ice cream.

palaces of cool pleasure, decent and safe. In New York, two majestic ice-cream saloons catered to "women who would rather starve to death than enter a restaurant alone."[594] Of course, men could also enjoy ice cream in public places. A New York opera house had an ice-cream saloon on its ground floor. Hotel confectioners created enchanting ice-cream dishes. In mid-nineteenth-century New York City, "in the sultry summer evenings, every one of these fashionable Ice-cream Saloons is crowded with throngs of well-dressed men and women, belonging for the most part to the great middle classes."[595]

Ice-cream lovers also made their treat at home, a laborious and imprecise process of beating the cream with a spoon until it was stiff and then cooling the ingredients in a container surrounded by ice mixed with salt. Then New Jersey's Nancy Johnson invented a hand-cranked freezer in 1846, and William Young patented it as the Johnson Patent Ice-Cream Freezer. With rotary paddles that replaced aching arms and with mechanical refrigeration, these freezers democratized ice

A little girl happily helps make ice cream, Chestermere Lake, Alberta, 1940.

cream, making it universally available. The more ice cream that was produced, the greater the demand for sugar.

Ice cream became so ubiquitous that in 1850, the widely read *Godey's Magazine and Lady's Book* pronounced it one of life's "necessary luxuries. A party without it would be like a breakfast without bread or a dinner without a roast."[596] By then, improved technology made ice cream cheap enough for the middle classes to enjoy regularly. (Poet and philosopher Ralph Waldo Emerson did not approve: "We dare not trust our wit for making our house pleasant to our friend so we buy ice cream."[597])

The new freezers also meant that ice cream need not be made where it was consumed but could be produced near sources of fruit and cream, then transported to distant markets. In 1851, Baltimore milk dealer Jacob Fussell opened a factory where he made ice cream from surplus cream and sold it at 25 cents a quart instead of the usual 65 cents. He did so well that, in 1885, he began to open ice-cream factories, first in Washington and later in Boston, New York, Cincinnati, Chicago and St. Louis, and earned the title Father of the Ice-cream Industry. In 1893 in Toronto, milk producer William Neilson, his wife and five children hand-cranked three freezers, producing 3,750 gallons of ice cream. By 1900, steam boilers and gasoline-powered engines did the work instead. The 1880s saw the appearance of an even sugarier version of ice cream— the sundae. The name stems either from a syrup-on-ice-cream concoction served only on Sundays or from the fact that when bars shut down on Sundays, their deprived clients comforted themselves with rich and sweet ice cream—the sunday or sundae.

Before long, sundaes were fantastical creations in which ice cream and syrup were topped by fruits, nuts, marshmallows, whipped cream and candy and given such grandiose names as Heavenly Twins or Buffalo Tip. Even the president's children were susceptible. An indulgent Theodore Roosevelt wrote, "Mother went off for three days to New York and Mame and Quentin took instant advantage of her absence to fall sick. Quentin's sickness was surely due to a riot in candy and ice-cream with chocolate sauce."[598]

The ice-cream soda, a happy union of favorites, became more popular than the too-rich sundae. It spawned its own vocabulary—black and white, for instance, meant chocolate soda with vanilla ice cream. As the range of ice cream and soft drinks widened, so did the possibilities of the ice-cream soda. Root beer with vanilla ice cream was immensely popular, but young people could express their individuality with other combinations: Dr. Pepper with chocolate ice cream, Coke with cherry ice cream.

A culture developed around the soda, plain or enriched with ice cream: soda fountains. Until the bottling process matured and individual bottles of pop were distributed in large quantities, pop was served at soda fountains. Like ice-cream saloons and parlors, soda fountains increasingly attracted female customers. True soda fountains were specially manufactured, usually of marble, tastefully decorated and kept spotlessly clean. Everything gleamed: countertops, work area, faucets, ornate silver-plated serving dishes, polished mirrors and the glistening ice cream and sparkling pop at the heart of the operation.

Soda fountains were often set up in department stores or pharmacies and served to revive shoppers and as safe and pleasant meeting places. At the same time, they provided stools that encouraged or at least assumed shorter stays than more comfortable chairs would have. Soda fountains attracted fashionable women, whose tastes set the standards for the aspiring lower classes. Decor was specifically chosen to echo the jewelry and sophistication of female patrons. The servers were young, wholesome yet winsome and gleaming. Some of the males were "stunning." All were instructed to be friendly but not seductively so. One manual advised soda-fountain operators to "place a handsome young man behind the counter. He'll draw the best trade in a city if he strictly minds his own business and dresses neatly and fashionably."[599]

CANDY

Children, too, enjoyed ice cream and soda, and accompanied their mothers and fathers to ice-cream saloons and soda fountains. But there was something even better than sugar-laced ice cream and sweet-and-tart pop: candy, special designed-for-children candy, candy a child could choose and buy, candy that would train that child to become an adult consumer for whom purchasing it would be an enjoyable habit tinged with nostalgia. As a mid-nineteenth-century London "sweet-stuff man" told interviewer Henry Mayhew, "Boys and girls are my best customers, sir, and mostly the smallest of them."[600]

This candy would also help children to plan and to budget their money, important life skills. It had to appeal greatly but cost little—one penny—so children could afford it. Penny candy transformed the confectioner's from an emporium of luxury sweets including sweetmeats, biscuits, cakes, syrups and candied fruit into a candy store that "became a venue for the children of early American capitalism."[601] Penny candies were jewel-like, boiled hard, brilliantly colored, deliciously flavored and intriguingly shaped. They were meant for children, and children yearned for them.

Images of children with noses pressed to store windows, wistfully surveying the array of goods inside, reflected reality. The child with a penny could enter, but the penniless could only stare from outside. The glass display case and the gorgeously arranged windows were early examples of successful marketing strategy. After their close scrutiny of the goods, children could exchange their penny for a special candy. By the time of the Civil War, the confectioner relied more on children than adults for his customer base.

Many children earned their own pennies, selling newspapers, flowers or candy, running errands or, when they could find no work, begging. The candy-store owner welcomed these youngsters and did not rush them to decide. "You would feast your eyes from left to right, from right to left, from front to back, and even diagonally," one American man recalled.[602] The selection was vast: sourballs, mint sticks, gumdrops, jellybeans, lollipops, maple sugar penny cakes, jawbreakers, marshmallows, lemon drops and Tootsie Rolls (the first individually wrapped penny candy) were a few of many. Canadian children, with similar choices, were especially fond of candy sticks and Ganong's All-Day Suckers, hard candy on a stick.

Poorer adults were also drawn to candy stores. "Our shop windows are a kindergarten for grown-up people, as well as little ones," one trade journal noted.[603] The London "sweet-stuff man" also had older customers: "Some of them's fifty, aye, turned fifty; Lor' love you. An old fellow, that hasn't a stump of a tooth, why, he'll stop and buy ... and he'll

Noses against the window, the children look longingly at the penny sweets in a shop in this British photo.

say, 'I've a deal of the boy left about me still.'"[604] In North America as in England, modern techniques, more disposable income and a national sweet tooth stimulated candy production and democratized its consumption. Not all candy cost a penny; more elaborate and bigger pieces, or several packaged together—Life Savers, for instance—cost more, but poor adults could sometimes indulge. Candy was also regional. Pralines—caramelized almonds or hazelnuts—were Southern specialties so popular in New Orleans that their Creole vendors were known as pralinieres. In the northeast, maple candy was popular.

As North America's sweetness commerce grew, women were targeted as candy buyers and eaters. They were "known" to have an intrinsic weakness for sweets, part of their delightful nature but also a reminder of their need to guard against self-indulgence. Women bought candy for their families and, as a tradition of giving candy as gifts was encouraged, received it in turn. In the late nineteenth century, store catalogs directed to rural communities began to appear: in the United States, Montgomery Ward's was the first, in 1872, followed in Canada by the T. Eaton catalogue, the "Prairie Bible," in 1884, and, again in the States, the Sears, Roebuck catalogue, in 1886. These wondrous compendia offered a richness of wares that included prepackaged food and candy. Even farm women without access to stores could now indulge.

For variety and to stimulate sales, candy was tailored to seasons until no holiday could pass without celebratory candy: Christmas, Halloween, Thanksgiving, Washington's birthday, Mother's Day, Father's Day, Valentine's Day and Easter. Courtship, weddings and graduations were also targeted, as were children's celebrations, especially birthdays.

Chocolates, and their feminization, played a crucial role in these celebrations. Until the mid-nineteenth century, chocolate was known mainly as a beverage, heavy, rich and laden with sugar and spice, or, among the elite, as a gourmet bonbon. Then, in 1828, Dutch chemist Coenraad Van Houten invented a hand-operated cocoa press that removed two-thirds of the cocoa butter, leaving a chocolate mass he could crush into the fine powder we know as cocoa. In 1875, Daniel Peter of the Swiss General

Chocolate Company and Henri Nestlé united to produce Nestlé's milk chocolate, the happy fix for pure chocolate's extraordinary bitterness.

As the public embraced milk chocolate, rivalrous and secretive European *chocolatiers* spied on each other and produced quite different-tasting chocolate: caramelized Cadbury for the British, milk Toblerone and Lindt for the Swiss, dark Baci for Italians. Snobbery and nationalism merged in the battle to define "true" chocolate: to many Europeans, British and North American chocolate was (and still is) too sugary and milky. By 1897, Britain consumed 36 million pounds of chocolate, other Europeans 100 million pounds and the United States 26 million pounds.

Until the latter part of the nineteenth century, North Americans imported much of their chocolate candy from Britain, where the Frys of Bristol, the Cadburys of Birmingham and the Rowntrees of York, all Quakers, were the industry giants. In 1761, pharmacist Dr. Joseph Fry took over Bristol-based Dr. Charles Churchman's chocolate business and produced sugar-sweetened chocolate tablets that, boiled in hot water and sweetened with a fine moist sugar and a little cream or milk, made cocoa. In 1776, one pound of Fry's Bristol chocolate sold for nearly as much as an average agricultural worker earned in a week. But chocolate had become popular with the Bristol elite, and Fry's business thrived.

When Joseph died in 1787, his wife, Anna, renamed the business Anna Fry & Sons and ran it with their third son, Joseph Storrs Fry, who at the age of twenty married Elizabeth, later famous as a prison reformer. An 1800 ad shows that chocolate was still seen as a medicinal substance: "This Cocoa is recommended by the most eminent of Faculty, in Preference to every other kind of Breakfast, to such who have Tender Habits, decayed Health, weak lungs, or scorbutis tendencies, being easy of Digestion, affording a fine and light nourishment, and greatly correcting the sharp Humours of the Constitution." But unless it was heavily sugared, chocolate was intolerably bitter, as nineteenth-century salesman David Jones learned after presenting samples of it to grocers to taste "only to watch their faces lose their customary shape, as if they had taken vinegar or woodworm."[605]

In 1789, Fry introduced England's first steam-driven cocoa-bean grinder into his chocolate factory, a revolutionary development, according to confectionery historian Tim Richardson.[606] Later, railroads replaced horse-drawn wagons to deliver Fry's chocolate throughout England. British cocoa consumption was growing: from 122 tons in 1822 to 176 tons in 1830 to 910 tons in 1840.[607]

In 1847, Fry produced the first "eating" as opposed to drinking chocolate after developing a way to make a paste of blended cocoa powder, sugar and melted cocoa butter. This led, in 1853, to the first factory-made chocolate: chocolate-covered cream sticks. Yet making chocolate remained a laborious, hand-dipping process followed by improvised cooling. "Oh, the job we had to cool the work!" chocolate worker Bertha Fackrell recalled. "I remember once we girls putting our work on to the window sill to cool when someone accidentally knocked the whole lot down into the yard below."[608] The earliest chocolate bars

Bars of Fry's Five Boys' Milk Chocolate, an all-time favorite from 1885 to 1976, sold in the millions. The five boys are all Lindsay Poulton, the photographer's son, whose Desperation pose was provoked by an odiferous rag his father soaked in ammonia and then held up to his nose.

were too acrid to be popular, but by 1885, Fry's Five Boys' Milk Chocolate, much tastier and milkier, became a great success.

From the early nineteenth century, Fry's was challenged by Cadbury and Rowntree. After brothers George and Richard Cadbury took over their father's failing business, Richard designed splendid images for Cadbury chocolate: a winsome blue-eyed six-year-old cradling a cat; a mother and child. In 1868, Cadbury mass-produced the first boxed chocolates, and in 1875, the chocolate Easter egg, a chocolate shell filled with sugar-coated nuts. By the end of the nineteenth century, Cadbury offered more than two hundred types of boxed chocolates, employed 2,685 people and had a worldwide market. In 1905, the Dairy Milk chocolate bar was a spectacular success, much creamier and sweeter than the darker milk chocolate it "pushed into obscurity," in the words of Lawrence Cadbury, and beautifully packaged in lavender wrapping with gold and black print.

Rowntree, the third of the major British candy makers, was begun in the 1860s by brothers Henry Isaac and Joseph Rowntree. Rock Cocoa was their primary product, though they also produced Chocolate Drops, Chocolate Creams, halfpenny and penny Balls and many other chocolate items. The staff was seven strong, and took turns "grinding, roasting, rubbing, and fetching in the sugar."[609] By 1881, Rowntree's Crystallized Gum Pastilles, at a penny an ounce, were a smashing success.

The Quaker trio had British challengers, among them Terry's, founded in 1886, while Switzerland's Lindt and Tobler, Italy's Caffarel and other European companies forged strong markets with their own kinds of chocolate. Rudolphe Lindt's 1879 invention of conching—a kind of chocolate kneading machine—revolutionized the industry. It produced very fine and rich chocolate and, by the late nineteenth century, won Switzerland its reputation as the world's most respected source of chocolate. French chocolate, too, earned a reputation for fine quality.

Candy making was increasingly internationalized. British firms in particular exported huge quantities of chocolate bars to North America and the empire. North Americans entered the contest toward the end of the nineteenth century, when Mennonite Milton Snavely Hershey, who as a little-educated teenaged apprentice confectioner had learned the candy business well enough to make his own milk-based caramels that his mother and sister hand-wrapped in tissue paper. After a happy encounter with an Englishman who agreed to import his caramels, and a banker who agreed to lend him money, Hershey established his Lancaster Caramel Company, whose four factories soon employed fifteen hundred people.

In 1893, at Chicago's Columbian Exposition, Hershey was struck by J. M. Lehmann's sophisticated chocolate-manufacturing equipment, which roasted, hulled and ground chocolate beans into chocolate liquor. After it was blended with sugar, vanilla and cocoa butter and churned, the mixture was poured into square molds and hardened as chocolate bars. Hershey bought the equipment and staked his future on chocolate. He began intensive experiments to add milk to his chocolate as he had to his caramel. He observed his dairy herd's 4:30 A.M. milking, switched from Jersey cows to Holstein and, to the horror of European connoisseurs, processed the milk until it was slightly soured. The result was revolutionary: North America's first milk chocolate, and cheap to produce.

In 1900 Hershey sold his caramel factory to focus on chocolate—"it is more than just a sweet, it is a food," he declared. By 1915, he was producing more than 100,000 pounds a day of more than a hundred varieties, most selling for only five cents each. The most popular were Hershey Kisses, introduced in 1907. The most elegant were distinguished by French names, such as *Le Chat Noir* (the black cat) and *Le Roi de Chocolat* (the king of chocolate), and gorgeous wrappings. As Joël Glenn Brenner notes in *The Emperors of Chocolate*, "A fancy ribbon turned any item into a De Luxe."[610] Much of Hershey's milky, sugary chocolate, shaped and priced like penny candy, appealed to children. Even Kisses were advertised with images of a boy and girl exchanging an innocent kiss. Hershey and his competitors targeted young boys with chocolate cigarettes and cigars, delicious, mock manly and a way to identify with dad and the future delights of smoking.

Young Frank Mars became the most important of Hershey's thousands of competitors. Crippled by polio and unable to play with other boys, Mars learned candy making in his mother's kitchen. He later made penny candies, but his business failed and with it, his marriage. After several more bitter attempts at candy making, Mars invented the Milky Way. His son, Forrest, describes the process: "It's a chocolate malted drink. He put some caramel on top of it, and some chocolate around it—not very good chocolate, he was buying cheap chocolate—but that damn thing sold."[611] At five cents, with its filling making it bigger than Hershey's solid-chocolate bars, the Milky Way seemed a good buy.

Canadians also loved chocolate, imported and domestic. The New Brunswick Ganong Brothers' Chicken Bones, developed in 1885, pink cinnamon candy with a bitter chocolate center in the shape of a chicken bone, were favorites, and in 1900 Ganong introduced North America's first five-cent chocolate nut bar. Their boxed chocolate was graced by an image of the Acadian heroine Evangeline, the epitome of "purity, excellence, constancy, romance, and sweetness."

Moirs, Viau, Cowan, Lowney and many others chocolate makers catered to Canadians' very sweet tastes. Forrest Mars, raised by his maternal grandparents in North Battleford, Saskatchewan, after his parents' divorce, wanted to expand into Canada. Ice-cream manufacturer William Neilson gambled on making boxed chocolates and, by 1914, was selling 563,000 pounds annually in Canada. Under his son, Morden Neilson, the company became the British Empire's largest ice-cream manufacturer and Canada's largest chocolate manufacturer.

Canada's most resourceful *chocolatier*, Frank O'Connor, named his company Laura Secord Chocolates after the heroic soldier's wife who, during the War of 1812, tramped through swamp and bush to warn the British of an impending American attack. He sold his chocolate in a distinctive box imprinted with an idealized cameo of Laura Secord. In 1919, O'Connor expanded to New York, where he prudently renamed his brand of chocolates after the much-loved cookbook author Fanny Farmer, whose cameo graced the American boxes.

On both sides of the border, milk chocolate, a combination of cocoa products, milk and sugar bound with an emulsifier, was an easy sell. Unlike the more familiar Baker's Chocolate, suitable for baking, milk chocolate contains less of the non-fat part of the cocoa bean and much more milk fat. It is also so heavily sugared that half its calories come from sugar and half from fat, a combination that is, one nutrition researcher says, "pure heaven to our brains. Chemically speaking, chocolate really is the world's perfect food."[612]

Chocolate is so delicious that legions of aficionados claim to be "addicted" to it. Women seem particularly prone to chocolate cravings, though there is no scientific evidence of any physiological cause. What is certain is that since milk chocolate appeared, women were assumed to yearn for it, and, despite or perhaps because of chocolate's alleged power to stimulate erotic desires, it was marketed to them.

Sweets for All Seasons

In the battle to sell as much chocolate to as many people as possible, packaging and presentation were almost as important as the chocolate inside. In its earlier, expensive incarnation, chocolate had conjured up images of France, romance and women. Although Baker's Chocolate made unsweetened and semisweet chocolate, its marketing strategy harked back to French bonbons, and, in 1877, Walter Baker adopted one poignant image: *La Belle Chocolatière*, the elegant portrait of Anna Baltauf as Prince Dietrichstein first saw her on a wintry afternoon in 1745, when she served him a delicate mug of hot chocolate in a Viennese chocolate shop. The prince fell in love with and married the lovely young *chocolatière*, and commissioned her portrait to commemorate their "love at first sight" or romance by chocolate. Dutch chocolate makers Droste, DeJong and Van Houten and England's Rowntree knew a good image when they saw one, and adapted it for their own cocoas.

Even before chocolate, courtship by candy was common and the meaning of sweet exchanges was clearly understood. A young man could give his sweetheart French Secrets, hard candy wrapped in tissue and accompanied by a romantic verse, or other luxuriously packaged sweets. By the 1870s, romance had more choice of expression as hard candies lost ground to "dipped walnuts, dipped caramels, nougats, Italian cream bonbons, cream patties, chocolate drops, etc.," confectioner George J. Hazlitt recalled. "Very nearly if not quite half of the stock generally carried by jobbers is fine chocolate goods."[613] Chocolates were swiftly replacing soft bonbons and hard candy as the language of love.

Unlike hard candy, soft bonbons and chocolates had to be boxed— and you *could* tell a sweet by the gorgeousness of its cover. Indeed, to present a beloved with a plain-Jane box was a social gaffe of the highest order. In 1861, Cadbury offered the first heart-shaped Valentine's Day candy box. The race was on to mass-produce boxes that were both beautiful and distinctive to the occasion.

Valentine's Day used to mean card-giving—Saint Valentine sent the first one, a loving note signed "From Your Valentine," from prison. His crime, for which he was beheaded, was having defied the Emperor Claudius II by officiating at the marriages of Roman soldiers the emperor had decreed must remain celibate. Thanks largely to enterprising candy makers, Valentine's Day evolved into a candy-giving event.

Christmas also became a prime occasion for giving and consuming candy. Christmas candy canes began in Europe as straight and white sticks, later bent to resemble shepherd's crooks. Candy canes soothed cranky children during reenactments of the Nativity, a custom that spread throughout Europe and later to North America. The more recent tradition of white and red stripes may represent the purity of Christ and his shed blood.

Easter eggs and rabbits are linked to pagan festivals that early Christians incorporated into their own rituals. Traditional Easter egg hunts involved real eggs, often decorated and supposedly delivered by the Easter Bunny. Children's participation in these rituals made transforming real eggs to candy easy and popular. Cadbury first made chocolate eggs filled with fondant or marshmallow in 1923. Non-candied Easter eggs and bunnies were also produced, strengthening the connection between Easter and candy giving.

Mother's Day in its present incarnation dates from the early twentieth century and was so instantly commercialized that its chief promoter, American Anna Jarvis, denounced it: "I wanted it to be a day of sentiment, not profit," she declared. But Mother's Day and its associated merchandise—candy and chocolates in particular—have been unstoppable.

Thanksgiving, the Fourth of July, birthdays, anniversaries and ubiquitous "special occasions" ranging from graduations to visits successfully received similar attention; by the twentieth century, candy, preferably chocolate, became the common currency of celebration and gratitude. In 1912,

Whitman's Chocolate launched its pretty yellow Whitman's Samplers, a selection of its soft-centered chocolates in a traditional, faux-embroidered sampler box, suitable for all special occasions. The Sampler was graciously homey, suitable for a sweetheart, a grandmother or even a family.

Even war presented opportunities for candy manufacturers and vendors. Candy represents comfort, childhood and home; it is also tasty, satisfying and energizing. Candy from home reassures soldiers that they are not forgotten, and reminds them of what they are fighting for. Queen Victoria understood this, and during the Boer War she requested special Christmas tins of Cadbury chocolate to send to British troops. At first George Cadbury declined, on the grounds that he was a pacifist. The queen was not amused, and her request became an order. Cadbury and his Quaker competitors Fry and Rowntree complied, together producing 100,000 tins—minus their brand names. During World War I, Canada's Neilson Company exported enormous quantities of the plain-chocolate Soldier Bar to allied troops overseas. Soldiers' families often sent chocolates as gifts. "A box of Ganong's Chocolates makes it seem almost like being home again," a Canadian soldier wrote on Christmas Day 1917.[614] American soldiers dug mind and body into Whitman's Service Chocolates—Sweets with a Book, one pound of chocolate with an abridged classic.

Many military commanders disdained chocolate and other sweets as effeminate and unworthy of fighting men, and recommended hard liquor instead. But during World War II, as the USS *Lexington* was sinking, sailors salvaged ice cream from the hold and devoured it until they took to the lifeboats.[615] During the Korean War, the Pentagon sent American soldiers ice cream three times a week. American soldiers continue to dole out chocolates to civilians in conquered or liberated territories.

Weddings evolved into occasions to provide massive amounts of sugar in the form of elaborately iced and decorated wedding cakes. The fancily sugared wedding cake was born after bakers who fled to England from revolutionary France began selling stacked buns covered with icing. Queen Victoria, wed in 1840, had a cake nearly ten feet in circumference, and her children's were even grander. Princess Vicky's was a magnificent construction of layers of iced round cakes stacked

Montrealer Hope Simpson, serving with the American Red Cross, offers candy and cigarettes to American soldiers in London, 1943.

one on the other, all but the bottom one pure sugar, while all the layers of Prince Leopold's were cake. Princess Louise's cake was a person-sized miniature temple.

The next "advancement" in wedding cakes was the use of pillars to support and separate each layer so they no longer rested on top of each other; in England, richly decorated, tiered wedding cakes date from the late nineteenth century. Their increasing complexity was directly related to the commercialization of "special events," with bakers replacing homemakers who lacked the skills to produce the complicated confections that had become the new standard. In energetic, enterprising America, *The Art of Confectionery*, published in 1866, decreed that the art of molding sugar into "quaint and fanciful forms ... should form a part of every lady's education."[616]

In America, fancily designed wedding cakes were common by the early nineteenth century, and *Godey's Lady's Book* likened their sugar-frosted non-cake components to marital duplicities: "The sugar was only a covering to the carbonized surface, the eating of which discovered itself in the honied terms of 'my love,' and 'my dear,' that are first all sweetness, but soon discover the crusty humour beneath."[617] By the 1870s, wondrous, sometimes monstrous cakes were popular and set the standard for wedding feasts. The tradition of offering guests a slice to take home also took root.

More ordinary cakes, those not associated with weddings, were centuries old, and by the mid-seventeenth century, Europeans who could afford the sugar baked round cakes and iced them. The birthday cake as a cultural institution dates from the nineteenth century, when increasing numbers of people could afford the ingredients and had the ovens and fuel to bake with. North Americans took enthusiastically to birthday cakes, and children, especially, could expect a cake such as Fanny Farmer's recommended Angel or Sunshine Birthday Cake with a White Mountain Frosting made with one cup of sugar, two egg whites and boiling water flavored with vanilla or lemon juice. The birthday cake evolved as a cake layered with jam or icing and decorated with icing. After the Civil War, when sugar was a staple rather than a luxury, the icing grew more elaborate, and personalized messages in icing script— Many Happy Returns of the Day, Amelia!—finished a finely iced cake.

Home Sweetest Home

By the late nineteenth century, sugar was a fact of daily life as well as of special occasions. As an early-nineteenth-century American folk song exulted, "Sugar in the gourd and honey in the horn, / I never was so happy since the hour I was born." Sugared products were increasing in number, availability and popularity. Proliferating women's magazines and advertisements for cake, cookies, candy, jam and ice cream set standards for homemakers. Technology, even simple improvements in pots and pans and cooking utensils, made home baking easier. Recipe book authors—notably Sarah Tyson Rorer and Fanny Merritt Farmer—spelled out what to make and how to make it.

Fanny Farmer, author of the 1896 *Boston Cooking School Cook Book*, later renamed *The Fanny Farmer Cookbook*, was immensely helpful, and revolutionized home cooking by providing precise measurements: instead of estimates such as "a pinch of," "a piece of" or "a cup full," Farmer called for "one teaspoonful" or "one-third of a cup" and also defined what she meant by these terms. In her long section on cakes, Farmer also underscored the importance of sugar and warned against skimping on it: "It is essential to the balance of flavor in a good cake. If you begin to reduce the sugar you lose some of the essential texture and the result is bound to disappoint anyone who loves cake.... If you are going to bake a cake, make it a good one."[618] Farmer also had remedies to salvage the inevitable failures such as the sunken or burnt cake. Real women with real problems could safely turn to Farmer, Rorer or a host of other authors for help in sweetening their homes. Woloson emphasizes just how important it was for homemakers to be gifted as well as generous in their sweet offerings: "Homemade confections were not merely tasteful dainties but, more important, crucial morsels that defined and determined social standing and degree of refinement: how you were with sweets indicated how sweet you were yourself."[619]

Cakes, pastries and confections were elegant ways to provide sweets, but not all women had the time to devote to producing them. Happily for them, along came Jell-O. By the second half of the nineteenth century, with ice-cream-making established as a middle-class ritual, advertisements for Jell-O praised it as an easy and fail-safe alternative and a treat "that more or less critical feminine company will discuss favourably." As instant gelatin, Jell-O also permitted all social classes to produce desserts once limited to the elite. Jell-O's campaign to advertise itself as a stylish dessert was consistent with social standards that distinguished between kinds of sweets, as people used sugar "as a potent social communicator in the guise of an innocent dietary flavoring."[620]

Sugar was also the unpretentious preserver of fruit that, slathered on toast, transformed breakfast or tea into a sweet, substantial and—because of the fruit—not entirely unhealthful meal. People had long preserved fruits with honey, maple syrup or molasses and apple-peel pectin, but as safer canning techniques developed, commercially produced jam and jelly became common as well. Sugar-heavy, fruit-light jam was already a British household staple by the 1870s, and until the late nineteenth century, Britain exported jam to North America. At the end of the nineteenth century, North Americans began to produce their own. Jerome M. Smucker made apple butter. Canada's E. D. Smith opened a factory where plum, grape and apple jams were cooked in open kettles. In 1918, Paul Welch developed a grape jam called Grapelade, popularized during World War I when the U.S. army shipped it to American troops in France who loved it so much they sought it out when they returned home. And so sugar in yet another form found a permanent place in the average home's pantry.

Thanks to the growing demand for and availability of tea, coffee, cocoa, cake, pastries, ice cream, soda pop, candy, chocolates and jam, thanks to technology that made mass production and distribution possible, thanks to sweeter taste requirements and recipes that called for sugar even in savory dishes like soups and stews, thanks to social standards that used sugar as a measure of status and hospitality, thanks to increasing prosperity and thanks to the historical anomaly that during the nineteenth century, sugar was the one foodstuff that plummeted in price and remained cheaper, sugar consumption in the Western world rose steadily and sometimes astronomically. In the United States, it went from 8.4 pounds per person in 1801 to 70.6 pounds in 1905.[621]

THE FEMINIZATION OF SUGAR

As Wendy Woloson so ably demonstrates in *Refined Tastes*, when sugar was largely restricted to the wealthy, it was associated with male economic power. As its price declined and the less privileged began to incorporate it into their daily meals as well as their treats, the nature of sugar changed. "Its economic devaluation coincided with its cultural demotion," she explains. By the end of the nineteenth century, when refined sugar was acknowledged as an essential foodstuff, "consumer and consumed had become entirely conflated: sweets had been feminized, and women were sweet."[622]

A now-classic nursery rhyme—"What Are Little Boys Made Of?"—encapsulated this idea, declaring that little boys are made of "snips and snails, and puppy dogs' tails," while little girls are made of "sugar and spice and all things nice." Like sugar, girls were innately sweet; also like sugar, which lacked nutritional value, girls were frivolous and impractical. And just as the way to a man's heart was through his stomach, the way to a woman's heart was through the sweetness of candy. Sugar-related retail businesses, heavily reinforced by advertising, encouraged and depended on the public's acceptance of these cultural connotations.

Women were also one of Coca-Cola's first targets. In 1907, ads called Coke "the shoppers' panacea" and featured a Mrs. Cheerful's "wonderful secret" of successful shopping. "When I start out I get a glass of Coca-Cola; that keeps my nerves quiet. On the way home I get another. This relieves that headachy feeling and I return home as fresh as when I started out."

Sugar's feminization objectified women and, like cheap abundant sugar, undervalued them. "It also made them saccharine—nonessential, decorative, sweet, ethereal, and generally lacking in substance," Woloson concludes. "This encouraged women's relegation to a separate sphere by associating them with the commodities they purchased. It also constituted a clearly articulated and naturalized way of seeing women as essentially different from and inferior to men."[623]

Culturally, sugar as feminine had virulent detractors who denounced it as insubstantial and seductive, a temptress to be avoided. In the era of the moral purity movement that emerged in North America and western Europe early in the nineteenth century, and faded away a century later, sugar and its sweet confections and cakes were demoralizing and emasculating enemies to be resisted. As if that weren't enough, sugar was unhealthy and caused dental decay.

Even children were susceptible to sugar-as-sin. Through candy, poor children especially would be led into "intemperance, gluttony, and debauchery," *The Friend* newspaper warned. *The Colored American*, the most influential African-American newspaper from its inception in 1836 to its demise in 1841, denounced candy shops as "hot beds of disease," "filled with putrid rottenness."[624] Childhood addiction to candy could easily, perhaps inevitably, evolve into adult alcoholism. Even the sensible Mrs. Rorer weighed in against sugar and the women who shoveled it into their mouths, sickening themselves. And by polluting cereal and other food with excessive sugar, mothers caused their children's sugar cravings.

PHILANTHROPY IN MILK CHOCOLATE

After abolition, the suffering of the sugar workers who replaced the slaves attracted little attention, and sugar production ceased to be a primary target for reformers. But sugar was not entirely off the hook: critics took aim at the self-indulgence of its consumers and at its dire medical consequences. In curious irony, although chocolate makers relied on sugar to make their products palatable, they largely escaped the wrath of the anti-sugar concerns, and several among them were notable philanthropists, Milton Hershey spectacularly so.

The chocolate makers' philanthropy was not driven by guilt or even uneasiness, and a comment by Joseph Rowntree biographer Anne Vernon almost certainly applies to them all: "His father had seen nothing incongruous in mentioning his stocks of sugar and the Holy Spirit in the same paragraph of a letter, and it would never have occurred to Joseph that there might be a code of ethics applicable only to commerce."[625]

In England, the trio of Fry, Cadbury and Rowntree tried to apply Quaker precepts to every aspect of their lives. Every day Joseph Fry opened his factory with a compulsory Bible reading, a hymn and a prayer. The family members who ran the company invented the phrase "Happiness in Industry," instituted good working conditions and provided youth clubs, sports, health and sickness benefits and pensions.

Joseph's wife, Elizabeth Fry, was instrumental in achieving English prison reform. She also campaigned for the homeless, mental patients and workhouse inmates and vigorously opposed capital punishment. Queen Victoria donated money to her causes and noted in her journal that Elizabeth Fry was a "very superior person." Her work was unconnected to the family business but reflected favorably on it.

The Cadbury brothers were enlightened employers, and George Cadbury built a model "factory in a garden" and a company town at Bournville, Birmingham, with spacious houses for workers, schools, a library and a hospital. They also sponsored many sports and recreational activities. "It seemed to me to be all holiday and a sort of fairyland factory," one former employee recalled.[626] In 1901, Cadbury donated the village to the Bournville Village Trust; to this day it houses twenty-five thousand people.

The Rowntrees, too, were concerned employers who finally rectified difficult work conditions in their old factory—gloomy work areas, few washrooms or facilities to make hot meals or even tea—by building a new factory. Under Seebohm Rowntree's guidance, the company established a workers' pension plan, a five-day work week and benefits. Another Rowntree project was New Earswick, a 150-acre project of houses "artistic in appearance, sanitary, well-built" but affordable to even low-paid workers.

The Rowntrees were distinguished by their research into the root causes of poverty and related issues. Joseph founded three Rowntree Trusts to fund research into the causes of poverty and published seminal studies about alcoholism and poverty. His son Seebohm's *Poverty: A Study of Town Life* remains a classic.

In the United States, Milton Hershey used his chocolate fortune to build an idyllic factory town, Hershey, Pennsylvania, with such street names as Chocolate and Cocoa. Hershey was a haven of fine homes and parks, schools, churches, a hotel, a free junior college, sports and recreation facilities and an impressive community center with a theater. "We had everything they had in the big city—maybe more," one resident recalled.[627] To keep it perfect, Hershey hired investigators to report unmowed lawns, trash and illicit drinking. Like virtue, Hershey was its own reward. People flocked to it to enjoy its wonders and made the name Hershey synonymous with excitement and gracious living. Hershey, too, provided health and accident insurance, a retirement plan and death benefits for his workers. He also established a school for poor orphans, explaining, "Well, I have no heirs; so I decided to make the orphan boys of the United States my heirs."[628]

In 1916, Hershey duplicated Hershey, Pennsylvania, in Cuba, where he bought more than 100,000 acres of sugarcane to ensure his supply during World War I rationing and built the world's largest refinery, employing twelve thousand. (Root beer maker Charles Hire Company also bought Cuban sugar factories.) Central Hershey was electrified and featured an electric railroad, running water, physicians and dentists, teachers, a baseball diamond, a golf course, a racetrack and a country club. As he had in the United States, Hershey founded a school for orphans. The man known as the Chocolate Czar was "a magnificent ambassador," gushed Cuban president Gerardo Machado.[629]

DEMON RUM AND TEMPERANCE

In alcohol-rich North America, the average colonist consumed more than double the amount of alcohol of today's average American, much of it in the form of rum. Rum eased colicky New England infants, stiffened the resolve of exam-shy students, heartened workers during breaks and soothed old-timers' aches and pains. Rum also influenced elections as politicians plied their voters with alcohol: in 1758, George Washington's were awash in twenty-eight gallons of rum and fifty more of rum punch.

Americans drank so much rum that by 1770 there were 141 distilleries and twenty-four associated sugar distilleries that produced the molasses needed to make rum. Sugar and rum distilleries were so lucrative and such economic stimulants in the northeastern colonies that, food historian McWilliams opines, through this commerce "all in the name of demon rum ... did merchants begin to pull the disparate regions of colonial American into something of a well-tied knot."[630]

In the literal sense, distilled sugar was integral to intemperate drinking and alcoholism, but, sensibly, temperance advocates preferred to praise its sweetness, which made tea, coffee, cocoa and more recently soda pop agreeable alternatives to beer and hard liquor: Coke, for instance, was promoted as "the Intellectual Beverage and Temperance Drink." (Its detractors, however, claimed that its cocaine content was transforming Coke-swigging blacks into dope fiends who terrorized whites, though a single hit of cocaine would have been the equivalent of thirty gulped glasses of Coke. By the early twentieth century, all traces of cocaine had been removed from Coca-Cola.)

Happily for its producers, sugar sales were excellent whether it was destined to make rum or to sweeten food or drink.

Chapter 12

Sugar's Legacies and Prospects

Around the Globe: Sugar Comes Full Circle

By the twentieth century, sugarcane had circled the globe, traveling north and west from New Guinea then back again to the Pacific, and its legacies mark its global passage even where it is no longer grown, especially in the Caribbean. In the Caribbean, where King Sugar is now expiring as a major industry (Guyana, the Dominican Republic and Cuba are exceptions) and where most former colonies have become independent, political and commercial unions remain skewed along historical lines. Sugar culture is at the root of why Afro- and Indo-Trinidadians and Guyanese are mired in political enmity, why Hawaii and Fiji endure perpetual conflict between their Native and their Asian populations and why the official currency of Mauritius, off the coast of Africa, is the rupee and its population is primarily Indian.

In Asia, where sugar is now a giant industry, its legacies are just as firmly entrenched. In India, Pakistan and China in particular, they are quite different from those of the Caribbean's plantation-style, metropolitan-directed sugar trade. In India, the sugar industry grew to become the nation's second-largest agro-industry, and modern twentieth-century factories were built to supply the refined white sugar desired by expatriates and people in cities. But the majority of Indians preferred traditional kinds of sugar; the coarse khandsari, and the gur, or jaggery, they considered more nutritious than refined white sugar and better for candy making. As well, the less refined molasses and even raw cane were in great demand to feed horses, dairy cows and the majestic elephants owned by the state.

The most interesting of sugar's legacies in India is that the industry there is not plantation based. Most cane comes from small peasant holdings and is processed in mills owned either by private capitalists or, in western India, by peasant cooperatives; sugarcane farmers number about fifty million and employ millions of laborers. Unlike so many other sugar-producing colonies and countries that adopted the plantation system, India was not a new territory open to settlers and offering vast expanses of cheap land. Furthermore, its peasants could not be forced off their land to be transformed into low-paid workers on newly created plantations, as happened in Java and Latin America. The Indian Sugar Committee, appointed in 1920 to advise the government on a national sugar policy, denounced the forced land purchases and other coercive measures that would be required to create an Indian plantation sugar industry: "We cannot contemplate with equanimity the establishment of factories in the midst of an aggrieved and sullen peasantry ... the inevitable outcome."[631]

China's sugar legacy is unique because, unlike almost all other peoples, the Chinese have never used sugar as food and, in consequence, it is still not an item of mass consumption there. The Chinese chew cane stalks and drink heated cane juice, use it as a medicine and as a condiment, preserve fruit and vegetables with it, bake it in moon cakes and such treats as decorative animal-shaped candy and ferment cane juice and molasses into wine. But they drink tea without sugar and, until the advent of soft drinks and candy, sweetened their food sparingly or not at all.

Like India, China also developed a nonplantation sugar culture, described by China scholar Christian Daniels in his magisterial *Agro-Industries: Sugarcane Technology*. Peasants grew cane as one of several crops and, unless they had access to one of the larger sugar mill cooperatives, hired itinerant sugar-bakers to crush their sugar. The bakers used a structure of bamboo mats containing a large iron cauldron, a fireplace and rollers, "a small apparatus sufficient for their purpose, but which a

West India planter would consider as inefficacious and contemptible," a British observer noted in 1797. The quality of the processed sugar was uneven—brown, semi-refined and the hardened crystals known as rock—but satisfied the local market. Traveling merchants and traders bought it up and shipped it to Chinese destinations. These men also kept foreigners out of China's sugar industry. Today China is the world's fourth-largest producer of sugar, able to supply its more than one billion citizens with their modest annual twenty pounds per capita.

Trash Talk: Sugarcane's Environmental Legacy

Sugarcane (but not sugar beet) has irreversibly altered the environment and, the World Wildlife Fund reports, has likely "caused a greater loss of biodiversity on the planet than any other single crop, due to its destruction of habitat to make way for plantations, its intensive use of water for irrigation, its heavy use of agricultural chemicals, and the polluted wastewater that is routinely discharged in the sugar production process."[632]

In his monumental *The West Indies: Patterns of Development, Culture and Environmental Change Since 1492*, historical geographer David Watts describes how, in Barbados, planters almost entirely destroyed "a complete, natural island ecosystem" and replaced it with sugarcane and other foreign species such as coconut trees, creating "an attractive, but ecologically and environmentally unstable landscape."[633] In the seventeenth century, the island's forests, including rain forests, were razed; the unprotected soil was eroded and compacted, and its fertility decreased. The loss of tree canopy interfered with the process by which evapotranspiration cooled the air but intensified the trade wind effect and the amount of sea salt deposited on land. Weeds choked the denuded earth. Some planters attempted to offset the destruction and restore nutrients to the soil by ordering slaves to spread manure on the fields and to carry topsoil sediment back up to the bare slopes the rain had washed it off. Even so, by the 1830s, "most of the major agriculturally induced modifications of the environment ... may be categorized under two headings: further deforestation and its biological consequences, and additional soil erosion," Watts concludes.[634]

A burning cane field in Guanica, Puerto Rico, January 1942. "They burn the leaves to process the cane. A controlled burn. Think of that, when you put sugar in your coffee," says a character in Vincent Lam's Bloodletting & Miraculous Cures.

Where water is in short supply, cane also competes with people for water. In the drought-prone Indian province of Maharashtra, for instance, cane accounts for only 4 percent of cultivated land but swallows half of the irrigation supply, forcing people to travel long distances to find potable water.

Cane culture also decimated or eliminated millions of animals and plants. Monkeys and birds lost their homes in tree branches and canopies. At least sixteen kinds of parrots have disappeared, captured as pets or dinner or killed by cats whose ancestors were brought over from Europe. In India and elsewhere, the liquid and solid waste from sugar mills contaminates nearby streams or coastal waters and kills off marine life. A sugar factory crushing 1,250 tons of cane daily uses forty thousand gallons of water an hour and discharges anywhere from eight thousand to twenty thousand gallons per hour of liquid waste as well as solid and gaseous waste and other contaminants.[635]

In Australia, an annual 15 million tons of sugarcane-industry sediment contaminated by 7,700 tons of nitrogen and 11,000 tons of phosphorus have eroded the coral of the Great Barrier Reef, a World Heritage Site extending 1,200 miles and the only living organism visible from space. Coral reefs take centuries to grow a few feet yet can be destroyed in just a few years.

Rats, a foreign species that became the bane of the cane fields, also wreaked havoc on native species, killing and eating slow-moving ground animals including the iguana hatchlings that disseminate the seeds of native plants. To control the rats, planters in the West Indies, British Guiana, Surinam, Colombia, Hawaii and Fiji happily imported the Indian mongoose to control them. Too late, they realized that the voracious, prolific and adaptable mongoose also preyed on domestic poultry, wild birds and even more of the small animals targeted by rats.

In Australia, the cane toad (Bufo Marinus) *is an acknowledged enemy.*

In Jamaica, for instance, the mongoose is responsible for the extinction of the giant galliwasp lizard, the black racer snake, the Jamaican rice rat, the Jamaican poor-will and the Jamaican petrel.

Nonetheless, in 1934, failing to grasp the dangers of introducing foreign species, sugar planters in Hawaii and in Australia introduced the now infamous Central and South American cane toads onto their sugar plantations. The toads were expected to ravage the sugarcane beetle and its larvae, which kill or stunt cane by munching on its roots. But, planters soon learned, although cane toads do not jump high enough to catch beetles clinging to the upper stalks of cane plants, their toxins kill frogs, goannas, crocodiles, tiger snakes, red-bellied black snakes, death adders, dingoes, kangaroos, western quolls, dogs and cats, even honey bees. Furthermore, they have no natural predators, are prolific and grow as large as dinner plates. In Australia, where they are perhaps 100 million strong, cane toads are now a recognized enemy.

The Refined and Unrefined Politics of Sugar

The art of lobbying is one of sugar's enduring legacies and the model for other special interests. To this day, the sugar lobby, whether representing cane, beet or both, remains extraordinarily powerful. In Europe, when the first Napoleonic sugar loaves redefined continental sugar interests, pitting them against other European nations and against colonial cane sugar, governments responded to powerful lobbies with their usual strategies of trade policy, tariffs and bounties to establish or maintain supremacy. Beet and cane interests benefited as well from the traditional "right" of citizens to enjoy abundant amounts of sugar at cheap prices, something even Napoleon and Hitler accommodated.

Within the sugar industry, refiners have emerged to replace producers as power brokers, and many dominate production as well. In the United States, refiners process both cane and beet sugar. In the U.K., refiners have divided the spoils, giving British Sugar's six factories the job of processing beet, and leaving Tate & Lyle's Silvertown refinery in East London, the world's largest, about 70 percent of the raw cane sugar imported into the U.K. annually. This happy division of product produces 1.4 million tons of beet-derived white sugar and 1.1 million tons of cane-derived white sugar annually. Whether they deal in cane, beet or both, today's power brokers walk in the footsteps of their powerful predecessors.

In the United States, Big Sugar contributes millions of dollars yearly to political candidates and parties to preserve the sugar program that has, since 1934, protected cane- and beet-sugar producers, millers and refiners from operating losses. Other agricultural supports involve direct government grants, but the sugar program operates differently. It maintains a high minimum price for domestic sugar by controlling how much is produced through marketing allotments, by preferential price support loans and by limiting imports of foreign sugar through the Tariff-Rate Quota. This quota levies a prohibitive tariff that essentially knocks foreign sugar out of competition in the U.S. market.

The quota's opponents argue that by embittering sugar growers such as India, Brazil, Chile, Thailand, the Philippines, Colombia, Costa Rica, El Salvador, Guatemala, Honduras, Nicaragua and Panama—countries that Oxfam estimates lose $1.68 billion annually through lack of access to the U.S. market—the U.S. sugar program invites retaliatory high tariffs against other American crops. "Every nation has its sensitive commodities, and sugar is plainly one of ours," says Ira S. Shapiro of the Coalition for Sugar Reform.[636]

Big Sugar has devised ways to avoid transgressing U.S. anti-trust laws, primarily by marketing through cooperatives. Sugar growers have managed to win exemption from some labor regulations, notably the obligation to pay overtime wages. No matter how long their work day, beet workers average $5.15 to $7.50 an hour, cane workers about $6.00. Growers also lobbied successfully to exempt sugar workers from the Reagan administration's 1986 temporary amnesty for seasonal agricultural workers, depriving them of a chance for a green card and legal status in the United States.

Florida's cane fields have a separate labor history. Until 1942, cane growers recruited and sometimes kidnapped African-Americans from southern states to harvest their cane, promising them free transportation to the work site and $6.00 daily wages. In Florida, the men learned the truth: $1.80 daily wages minus room and board, $8.00 for the crammed bus or truck ride and 90 cents for the cane knife. If they tried to run away, said one elderly cane cutter, "They comed and get you and chained you to the bed at night. I saw people locked to the beds.... I saw some men get a beating. They whopped you with a cane knife."[637]

By 1942, the abuse of cane cutters was so egregious and widespread that the federal government indicted U.S. Sugar Corporation for peonage, involuntary servitude based on a peon's—or worker's—indebtedness to his creditor, specifically prohibited by the Thirteenth Amendment. The case was dismissed, but the indictment had made it clear that Americans could not be enslaved. Accordingly, Big Sugar began to recruit West Indians, who could be controlled by the threat of deportation. (Puerto Ricans, who could not be deported, were not welcome.) The federal government helpfully negotiated the contracts and assumed the cost of transporting the workers into and out of the country.

By 1986, this arrangement was breaking down, and West Indian cane cutters engaged by the Fanjul family, Big Sugar's most prominent members, stopped work to protest being cheated of their wages. The Fanjuls sent in Palm Beach County police in riot gear and used attack dogs to force all the cutters and other plantation employees, rebellious or not, onto Miami-bound buses. During what became known as the "Dog War," the West Indians had to leave all their belongings behind; some were "repatriated" in their underwear. The Fanjuls' Okeelanta Corporation eventually paid each deportee $1,000 for lost possessions, and Alfonso Fanjul admitted, "We mishandled the Dog War and I am sorry that it was handled that way."[638]

Alfonso "Alfy" Fanjul and his brothers, José "Pepe," Andres and Alexander, are Big Sugar incarnate. Scions of Cuban sugar-planting families uprooted by the revolution, they re-created their sugar world in the United States, where their company Florida Crystals owns about 180,000 acres and grows, mills and refines sugar. Once, to experience field work, Alfy tried cutting cane but found it "so brutal I couldn't last 20 minutes.... I thought I was going to have a heart attack."[639]

The Fanjuls make large and strategic political contributions—Alfy to the Democrats, José to the Republicans—and pay lobbyists to maintain or improve their favored economic status. Fanjul intimates include highly placed members of whatever administration is in power, of Congress and of Florida's political elite. The celebrities they host at their lavish seven-thousand-acre Casa de Campo in the Dominican Republic have included Henry Kissinger, Rothschild family members, Sean "Puff Daddy" Combs, even Lisa Marie Presley and Michael Jackson, who married there in 1994.

Monica Lewinsky, testifying to the Starr Commission, recalled that while she was in President Bill Clinton's office learning that their sexual relationship was over, Alfy Fanjul telephoned; telephone records show that he and the president spoke for twenty-two minutes. Observes novelist and *Miami Herald* columnist Carl Hiaasen, "That tells you all you need to know about [the Fanjuls'] influence."[640] So does their nickname—the First Family of Corporate Welfare—a reference to the fact that the Fanjuls benefit hugely from the sugar program.

In 1989, in a class action suit on behalf of twenty thousand Jamaican cane cutters, Bernard Bygrave sued Atlantic Sugar Association, Florida Crystals' subsidiary Okeelanta, U.S. Sugar, Osceola Farms and the Sugar Growers Cooperative of Florida for back wages totaling millions of dollars earned between 1987 and 1991. Despite working ten- to twelve-hour days, the cutters made at most $40 to $45 and often only $15, but had been too terrified of losing their jobs or being blacklisted to complain. They also knew all about the "Dog War."

The Bygrave lawsuit did not result in fairer working conditions. Instead, most of the cutters lost their jobs as the Fanjuls, U.S. Sugar and other growers mechanized their fields with cane-cutting machines. U.S. Sugar eventually settled with the cane cutters for $5.7 million. The Fanjuls preferred to proceed in court, knowing the cane cutters have minimal resources. The case has now been divided into separate lawsuits against each sugar-growing plaintiff, and Marie Brenner's 2001 *Vanity Fair* exposé about it, "In the Kingdom of Big Sugar," has inspired the movie *Sugar Kings*, starring Jodie Foster and Robert De Niro.

Nowhere are the politics of sugar more catastrophic than in south Florida's Everglades. Once the Everglades was a "river of grass," 120 miles long by fifty feet wide and shallow enough to sustain a marshy subtropical wetland and a complex and fragile ecosystem unique in the world. A multitude of plants, birds and animals lived there, including the rare and endangered American crocodile, Florida panther and West Indian manatee. In 1947, Marjory Stoneman Douglas's book *Everglades: River of Grass* focused attention on how relentless settlement and agriculture were destroying the ecosystem and diverting and draining its water. President Harry Truman responded with an executive order that protected over two million acres of the Everglades National Park, including 20 percent of the original wetlands.

Then Big Sugar arrived, and the devastation escalated. The notoriously thirsty crop gobbles water from the Everglades, diverts its flow and spews phosphorus from its runoffs into ground and surface water. Phosphorus saturates topsoil, which then dries out and washes away. It also nourishes cattails that choke other flora and destroy tens of thousands of acres of underwater sea grass. Wading birds—wood storks, white ibises, great egrets—can no longer land, eat or nest.

Big Sugar scoffs at its environmental critics. Here, for example, is U.S. Sugar spokesman Otis Wragg III: "One hundred years ago we called this place a swamp, and we drained it. Now we call it a fragile ecosystem."[641] Between 1990 and 1998, Big Sugar spent $13 million on presidential and congressional electoral campaigns, millions more on local ones and at least $26 million in Florida to subvert attempts to require sugar growers to pay for the cleanup. One beneficiary was Jeb Bush, elected governor in 1998.

This connection brings us back to President Clinton's phone call from Alfy Fanjul, who was even more distraught than Monica Lewinsky that day because Vice-President Al Gore wanted to protect the Everglades through a "polluter's tax" and reconversion of 100,000 acres of sugarcane into swampland. "Alfy felt betrayed," a lobbyist said. "He'd campaigned for Clinton, delivered a lot of votes, and here was Gore paying him back with a tax. Alfy was actually bitching [Clinton] out, just yelling."[642]

Yelling paid off. Clinton capitulated to his urgent desire not to lose Florida to the Republicans. The subsequent Everglades restoration plan spared the sugar farms even though scientists at the Everglades National

Park cited "substantial, credible and compelling evidence" that the new "restoration" would not regenerate the wounded ecosystem.[643] Alfy Fanjul praised Clinton as "a great president."

The administration of George W. Bush further emasculated the restoration project and effectively delayed the cleanup for ten years. When Jeb Bush signed the project into law as the Everglades Restoration Act, Pepe Fanjul was at his side. Big Sugar had outgunned and outspent the friends of the Everglades, investing millions of dollars in strategic donations, in hiring legions of lobbyists and lawyers and scientists they called as expert witnesses, and in wining and dining, manipulating and convincing.

In the Dominican Republic, where the Fanjuls are also Sugar Kings, the politics of sugar are as unrefined as cane stalks. The country's history helps explain its peculiar obsessions. In the nineteenth century, the Dominican Republic was batted back and forth between France, Spain and independence; from 1822 to 1844 it was occupied by Haiti and then, independent again, racked by dictatorships, anarchy, chaos and corruption. In 1865, the United States declined an invitation to annex it, just as it had Cuba. By the turn of the twentieth century, however, growing American interest led to an active role in Dominican administration, and in 1916, the U.S. sent its marines, already in control of neighboring Haiti, to occupy it.

By then the Dominican Republic had a burgeoning sugar industry that was also the country's largest employer. Cubans fleeing the Ten Years' War had begun the sugar business, but in the 1870s and 1880s, Americans, Europeans and Canadians had taken it over. The newcomers modernized the mills, built sugarcane railroads, increased production and exported sugar to the U.K., France and Canada. The American occupation, which lasted until 1924, consolidated these trends, bringing improved infrastructure, including railways and roads, and foreign investment. But as the sugar industry grew, British West Indians, or Cocolos, replaced Dominicans in the cane fields. Then in the 1920s, as the Cocolos moved into more skilled jobs in sugar mills, Haitians replaced them in the cane fields. A potentially dangerous situation was thus created: in a poor agricultural country, foreigners owned the most important industry and employed few Dominicans. The Haitians over-running the cane fields were still hated and feared as former occupiers and as revolutionary troublemakers who fought relentlessly against the American occupation of Haiti.

Conditions on the *bateys* deteriorated; in 1926 the American consul in Santo Domingo described them as "primitive in the extreme." Most Haitians sought work elsewhere, and those who stayed on the planta-tions resisted in traditional ways: setting fire to cane fields; sabotaging property, equipment and tools; stealing and working carelessly and slowly. They also protested against the reduction of their pay rates, halved in 1930, and against being cheated at the cane-weighing scales. The Haitian government did not intervene. The revenue generated from the licenses recruits had to buy if they wished to cut Dominican cane was Haiti's most important source of revenue.

In 1930, Dominican dictator Rafael Trujillo took power. Trujillo hated and scapegoated Haitians as a menace to the Dominican "race" and culture, which he characterized as Hispanic rather than African, lighter-skinned rather than black, and Christian rather than vodunesque. He fed Dominicans' fears that armies of Haitians would Haitianize the republic, and he orchestrated campaigns to import Europeans to inter-marry with and lighten Dominicans' skin color. He devised a system of identity cards still used today, identifying Dominicans as "Indio"—a fictional Taino-Spanish ancestry that ignores their African roots—or "white," alongside a cursed minority "black."

In October 1937, on Trujillo's orders, the national guard rounded up as many as twenty thousand Haitian men, women and children and bludgeoned, bayoneted and drowned them, reddening the Massacre River with their blood, a tragedy memorialized in Edwidge Danticat's novel *The Farming of Bones*. The massacre was an expression of ethno-racial hatred and also a political move calculated to distract Dominicans suffering from the miseries of the Depression. Most of the victims lived near the Haiti-Dominican border, but Trujillo spared Haitians on Dominican sugar plantations. From then on, Haitians understood that the Dominican Republic would tolerate them only as cane cutters.

Later, after driving out foreign sugar interests and taking over their properties to become the prime producer of Dominican sugar, Trujillo acknowledged that even he needed Haitians to cut his cane. The Dominican government bribed Haiti's usually dictatorial presidents to supply Haitian *braceros*; Papa Doc Duvalier got $1 million and enlisted his civilian militia, the dreaded Tonton Macoutes, to fill the quota. These shameful arrangements ended only in 1986, after Haitian dictator Jean-Claude Duvalier, or Baby Doc, was expelled from Haiti. Since then, if enough Haitians cannot be recruited, corrupt soldiers and thugs snatch people from the streets of border towns, transport them to Dominican depots, then distribute them to the *bateys*.

Today, hundreds of thousands of Haitians cut Dominican cane. Almost all are considered "illegals," including the half a million born

The author met these Haitians, most in their first season as cane cutters, in the Dominican Republic. Here they stand in front of the cement barracks where they live six to a tiny room, without toilets or access to running water. The upright cane stalks, cut into pieces, are their only breakfast.

in the Dominican Republic; they have few or no civil rights and can be deported at will in sporadic raids that terrorize the *bateys* and remind their residents that they are officially despised. Cane cutters work from dawn to dusk, earning 55 pesos (US$1.20) per ton, with free housing in shared shanties without water, toilets or cooking facilities. Most are forbidden to garden and must buy their food from *batey* stores. Despite reports by foreign investigators and human rights groups deploring the Haitians' plight, sugar's legacy of racism, brutality and coerced labor lives on.

In 1985, the Fanjul family bought nearly a quarter of a million verdant acres in the province of La Romana from American conglomerate Gulf and Western and now produces half the Dominican Republic's sugar. (The state-run Consejo Estatal de Azúcar, owner of many former Trujillo properties, and the family-owned Casa Vicini produce most of the rest.) The Fanjuls' Dominican sugar empire benefits enormously from the American

These Haitians, from Jérémie, are cooking a collective meal in the coal pot.
Each tosses in whatever foodstuffs he can. The twenty-two-year-old
on the left was badly injured when he was loading cane onto a railway car pulled
by oxen into the cane field.

John and Walson, rookie cutters from Jéremie, Haiti, look younger than the fifteen years they claim to be. They told the author the work was hard and they missed their families.

quota system, which permits their American-based companies to import half the Dominican sugar quota free of punishing tariffs.[644]

The Fanjuls employ nearly twenty thousand hard-worked and under-paid Haitians in their cane fields. Unlike Florida cane cutters, the Haitians are not equipped with metal arm and shin guards, and their flesh bears the scars and gouges of their dangerous profession. They are also hungry and complain that on Fanjul *bateys*, vegetable gardening or keeping poultry is forbidden, a modern-day twist on slavery's provision-grounds policies. The 2005 Canadian documentary *Big Sugar* juxtaposed images of interviews with these cane cutters with Pepe Fanjul sipping wine at a high-society function in Florida, denying the abysmal conditions on the family's *bateys* and calling them "progressive." The 2007 American documentary *The Sugar Babies: The Plight of the Children of Agricultural Workers in the Sugar Industry of the Dominican Republic*,

This retired cane cutter left Haiti for the Dominican Republic as a teenager. She lives in a hovel and depends on family and friends for sustenance. Today, only 5 percent of cane cutters are women.

This Haitian cuts cane much as his ancestors did, and lives in similar conditions.

narrated by Edwidge Danticat, focused on the plight of the cane cutters' children, especially in La Romana. Angry Dominican officials tried to bribe Dominican journalists to give the film bad reviews. *The Price of Sugar*, Bill Haney's documentary narrated by Paul Newman, focuses on the plight of Haittans in Dominican cane fields. The film shadows cane workers on *Bateys*, owned by the Vicini family, a dynasty of sugar barons.

The Fanjuls are the twenty-first-century counterparts of the West Indian sugar planters whom British society mocked yet sought out as marriage and business partners. Society pages photograph them and detail their marital flounderings, infidelities, legal escapades and charities. These last are modest, for like old-style sugar planters, the Fanjuls opt for conspicuous personal consumption over philanthropy.

In nearby Cuba, Fidel Castro and his comrades transformed the 1959 revolution into an extraordinary story about the power of sugar. The new government first challenged Big Sugar by increasing the minimum wage for cane cutters and, through the Agrarian Reform Law, expropriating sugar plantations and mills. This hit American interests, owners of one-quarter of Cuba's best land, hard, and the United States retaliated by reallocating 95 percent of its sugar import quota. Because sugar accounted for 82 percent of Cuba's exports and, for four decades, half of it had gone to the States, Cuba's economic survival was at stake.

Enter the Soviet Union. In 1960, the Soviets signed the first of many agreements about sugar exports and oil imports. Cuba continued to nationalize U.S. properties and harass U.S. businesses. In November 1960, the United States launched an economic embargo of Cuba, and one of President Dwight Eisenhower's last official acts was to break off diplomatic relations. Months later, the Bay of Pigs fiasco enabled Castro to push Cuba into the Communist economic community's embrace.

Cuba decided to focus on sugar and not to break up large holdings. As Minister of Industry Che Guevara explained, "The entire economic history of Cuba has demonstrated that no other agricultural activity would give such returns as those yielded by the cultivation of the sugar-cane. At the outset of the Revolution many of us were not aware of this basic economic fact, because a fetishistic idea connected sugar with our dependence on imperialism and with the misery in the rural areas, without analysing the real causes: the relation to the unequal balance of trade."[645] Sugar prices were high and, thanks to favorable arrangements with East European nations, stable. But the revolutionaries had inherited a structurally flawed sugar industry, which they further undermined through inexperience and ignorance.

In 1962, confiscated plantations became state farms and their workers were guaranteed permanent employment, a goal of the revolution and an anomaly in the sugar business. To free workers from "the worship of the god called money," moral incentives replaced material ones. But workers with job security and no tangible rewards were disinclined to work long, hard hours and worry about productivity. Many drifted off to easier, equally secure jobs. Foreign idealists and mostly reluctant Cubans replaced them with such disastrous results that, in 1968, the harvest was militarized. Castro himself went into the cane fields, chopped vigorously, preached and praised, and signed his co-workers' machetes. Despite his efforts, productivity remained low.

Sugar managers and technicians were also in short supply. Many had fled Cuba and others were disqualified for being insufficiently revolutionary. Later, Castro admitted that "sometimes, the neighborhood fool was named sugar mill administrator ... begging the fool's pardon."[646] Poor organization and planning added to the sugar industry's personnel, technical and administrative woes. Attempts to transform Cuba's sugar industry into the world's most highly automated failed, because of inexperience and because the Cubans' Eastern European advisers had expertise in sugar beet, not cane.

Nonetheless, Castro decided to stake everything on the Ten Million Ton sugar harvest of 1970 as "a fundamental economic challenge to our country ... [to] strengthen foreign confidence in our people."[647] The harvest was 90 percent better than in 1969, the Year of the Decisive Effort, and 1.3 million tons better than the record 1952 harvest of 7.2 million tons. But its 8.5 million tons fell short of Castro's goal, and he publicly offered to resign but was easily persuaded to remain in power.

Post-harvest, Castro vowed to "bravely correct any idealistic errors we may have made." The government scrapped moral incentives and instead offered television sets, new houses, cars and other benefits. Soon sugar workers, who with their families constitute one-sixth of the Cuban population, were enjoying demonstrably better standards of living. Management was decentralized, leading to better decision-making. At considerable cost and at the expense of other industries, the sugar industry was modernized. In 1971, only 2.4 percent of the cane was cut by machines. This rose to 25 percent in 1975 and later to 66 percent. Because of its sweetheart agreements with the Soviet Union, sugar prices were high enough for Cuba to pay for its imports. Castro boasted in 1973, "Severed from the fluctuations in the world market, Cuban sugar has guaranteed demand in the Soviet Union and all other social countries. Moreover, this industry which continues to be the most important in the nation, is also the most economical one."[648]

For two decades Cuba made sugar the economic motor of its revolution, empowering once-exploited sugar workers, borrowing foreign techniques and relying on foreign markets to pay high prices for Cuban cane. Then the Soviet Union crumbled and with it, Cuba's sugar-based economy, 85 percent dependent on Soviet markets. Cuba struggled to pay for fuel to operate its heavily mechanized sugar industry. Production plummeted. Cuban sugar now commanded lower prices, causing scarcities in almost every sector. Severe oil shortages forced Cubans to use bicycles and oxen instead of cars and tractors, and to endure blackouts, interminable waits for public transportation, strict food rationing and a scarcity of imported medicine, spare parts and clothing. (In the early 1990s, in the city of Trinidad, the author visited an ice-cream parlor that had no ice cream and a state clothing store stocked mainly with large-cupped bras.)

Over the years, seventy-one of Cuba's 156 sugar mills have closed and 60 percent of its cane fields have been converted to vegetable farms or cattle ranches. One hundred thousand cane workers have been retrained. But with the advent of ethanol, sugar is suddenly resurging. Distilleries are being modernized and new ones opened in the rush to quintuple current ethanol production, pumping sweet energy into Cuba's tired electricity grid.

BIG SUGAR'S CHALLENGES

As in the days of empire, globalization continually challenges cane and beet Big Sugar. A recurrent worry is the competitive edge of less developed sugar-growing countries with very different conditions, in particular more felicitous climates and more exploitative labor cultures, to produce cheap sugar. Even child labor, for instance, is rampant in much of the sugar world, though legally prohibited. Adolescent (and some younger) Haitians continue to work in Dominican cane fields, some alongside their fathers. Child labor is widespread in El Salvador, where sugar became an important crop only after World War II, and in Brazil's northeast Bahia region, where the legacy of four centuries of cane culture is illiteracy, poor health standards and high child mortality rates. In adulthood, cane workers remain underpaid, overworked and indifferently treated.

Fears about irreconcilably different labor conditions and other issues pit beet against cane grower, ex-colony against ex-colony, and the entire developing, less and least developed world against former imperialists. Rival ideologies of free trade, liberalized trade and protectionism enter the fray as they vie for recognition, as do consumer advocates clamoring for cheaper prices and social justice advocates demanding fair trade. A series of international agreements formalize these changes in traditional sugar trade relationships. The Central American Free Trade Agreement, for instance, nudges American sugar producers into competition with five Central American nations plus the Dominican Republic, though just 1 percent of U.S. production is involved.

Sugar faces serious challenges from nontraditional sweeteners. Intense sweeteners, synthetic, non-nutritive and many times sweeter than sugar—aspartame, saccharin, acesulfame and cyclamates—are low calorie or calorie-free, and although they sweeten without energizing, they do so without fattening. They have won many sweet-toothed converts and will likely continue to make inroads on the sugar market. In the face of fashion standards that idealize thinness, many consumers choose to abandon sugar in favor of pure water or artificially sweetened beverages. Soda-pop and food manufacturers respond by creating low-calorie products.

High fructose corn syrup (HFCS), produced by converting corn to fructose, is a more difficult rival to combat because it has the same sweet taste as sugar but is cheaper to produce and transport. Already HFCS has wrested the enormous U.S. soft-drink market away from beet and cane, and it sweetens such well-known or classic items as Newman's Own Pink Lemonade; Ocean Spray Cranberry Juice; Starbucks' Frappuccino; Pepperidge Farms line of 100 percent whole-grain breads; Sara Lee Heart Healthy Whole Grain Bread; Wonderbread; dozens of Kellogg's breakfast cereals; Eggo Pancakes; Life Savers; Heinz Ketchup, Hunt's Catsup and Miracle Whip; Nabisco Fig Newtons and Grandma's Homestyle Peanut Butter Cookies; cough syrups such as Robitussin, Dimetapp and Vicks; Nabisco Ritz crackers; Cool Whip; Claussen Bread and Butter pickles; Ben & Jerry's and Dreyer's ice creams; jams, jellies and syrups; pastries such as Jell-O No-Bake Oreo and Pepperidge Farm's puff pastry sheets; sauces such as A.1. Steak Sauce Cajun, Chicago and Teriyaki marinades; Kraft Philadelphia Cream Cheese Strawberry Cheesecake Bar; Oscar Mayer Lunchables; and Campbell's vegetable microwaveable soup.

Anxious sugar producers fight back hard, emphasizing the differences between sugar and HFCS, reminding consumers that a teaspoon of sugar contains only about fifteen calories, is all natural, is fat-free and satiates hunger. They argue that HFCS may, on the other hand, "go straight to fat," in beet executive Jim Horvath's words.[649]

As well as these new challenges, the industry faces the fury of sugar's traditional health-related adversaries. Sugar is still targeted as the main cause of dental decay, although flossing and brushing might counter its effects. Sugar stands accused as well of complicity in contributing to obesity and hence the terrible duo of type 2 diabetes and heart disease that obesity triggers. It does this in delicious but dangerous combination with fats such as butter or carbohydrates like flour and cereal, creating chocolate bars, breakfast cereals and other instruments of obesity. It also does this through soft drinks, nicknamed liquid sugar, and the locus of much of the anti-sugar battle.

The soft drink is the world's primary source of sugary calories, and Coca-Cola alone accounts for one billion of a calculated forty-seven billion beverage servings human beings consume daily, fulfillment of the hope expressed in its classic 1971 commercial, "I'd like to buy the world a Coke, and keep it company." (A story as classic as Coke tells how, in 1945, a guard asked a group of German prisoners of war just arrived in Hoboken, New Jersey, why they suddenly seemed so excited. A prisoner replied, "We are surprised that you have Coca-Cola here too.") HFCS now sweetens most North American pop, but the rest of the fattening world still sweetens mainly with sugar.

As obesity rates soar, so does the type 2 diabetes it so often sets off. Medical experts identify sugar as an accessory; it contributes to obesity, although sugar itself causes neither diabetes nor heart disease. It also has disturbing social implications in that the consumption of sugar and junk food, and the resulting obesity, is higher among less advantaged classes. Sugar remains cheap—in the United States, for instance, it takes only 1.4 minutes of work to buy a pound of it, while in cane-producing India, it takes more than forty-five minutes. Its accessibility coupled with its deliciousness—not to mention its ubiquity—make trying to persuade overindulgers to cut back their consumption very difficult.

Sugar-laden junk food is particularly seductive to children, the newest victims of diabetes.

Worldwide, an estimated 30 million people had diabetes in 1985. By 2000 this number had risen to 171 million, and the World Health Organization expects this to double to at least 366 million by 2030; many diabetes researchers are predicting an even steeper increase. Diabetes is incurable and progressive, and if not well managed it destroys organs and limbs and leads to a plethora of medical complications including amputation and blindness. Raging diabetes will burden health care systems, erode the labor force, hobble military enlistment and transform the families of unwell diabetics. New York endocrinologist Daniel Lorber makes a stark prediction: "The work force 50 years from now is going to look fat, one-legged, blind, a diminution of able-bodied workers at every level."[650]

The Anti-Sugar Wars

Sugar and its foes fight an ongoing media war as magazines, newspapers, television and radio routinely feature cautionary stories linking excessive sugar consumption with various ailments, from obesity and diabetes to heart disease and attention deficit disorder. (But they also carry many ads extolling candies and chocolates, cookies and cake, and they feature sugared recipes.) Michael Jacobson, who in 1971 founded the Center for Science in the Public Interest, a nonprofit health-advocacy organization, coined the phrases "junk food" and "empty calories" and attacked the candy industry so effectively that candy consumption temporarily plunged 25 percent. A stream of cookbooks tout sugarless or sugar-reduced recipes.

William Dufty's bestselling *Sugar Blues*, published in 1976 and reissued in 1993, condemned refined white sugar and denounced the iconic Fannie Farmer as the queen of "American sugar-pushing people killers.… For she was the one—if not the—originator of the deadly idea of adding sugar to practically everything: Bread, vegetables, salads, and their dressings."[651] In England, John Yudkin's 1978 *Sweet and Dangerous* carried similar messages.

The sugar industry and its allies fight back, their most persuasive weapons Snickers! Chocolate bars! Chocolate cake! Bubble gum! Sweetened tea! Double-double coffee! Confusion is rife. As American writer Hilary Liftin muses in *Candy and Me (A Love Story)*, "On the one hand, candy is evil. It is bright, pretty, and sweet, and it is a quicksand lover. Once it has you in its grasp, it pulls you deeper and deeper into trouble. On the other hand, candy is a simple joy. It's a fun, tasty snack reminiscent of childhood. For me, candy has been the complex flavour of doubt, fear, guilt, hope, and love."[652]

The sugar industry feels no such ambivalence and focuses on fighting back. One strategy has been to try to influence the WHO and government food guidelines to declare that significant amounts of sugar are permissible in a healthful diet. The stakes are high. Government guidelines influence food labeling, government dietary education and even school lunch programs. Millions of people the world over depend for some or all of their meals on NGOs that base their menus on WHO guidelines. Food and nutrition writers cite them as references.

Behind-the-scenes revelations paint a picture of coerced compromises and of policy-makers pressured by the sugar lobbyists, with cane, beet and HFCS setting aside rivalry to work together in their common interest. Dr. Aubrey Sheiham, a British dental public health professor who wrote the sugar part of the 2000 Eurodiet, a European Community guideline, recalls how the "sugar people" bullied him and his colleagues, threatening to block the report "if the 10% [limit] was in.... We went into a huddle with various people and some of the diplomats, and we were meeting in people's bedrooms and saying, how can we work around this?" Their clever solution was to recommend that sugar be eaten no more than four times a day, which was actually equivalent to the now unmentioned 10 percent.[653]

The 2005 U.S. Department of Agriculture guidelines broke with twenty-five years of advising against "too much sugar" and instead praised the health benefits of carbohydrates and natural sugars, noting only that "added sugars supply calories but few or no nutrients. Consequently, it is important to choose carbohydrates wisely." As an editorial in *The New York Times* observed, "It strains the imagination to believe that the sugar industry did not have undue influence this time around. [The government should] fulfill its mission to promote health—not the sugar lobby—by rewriting the advice on sugar."[654]

The sugar lobby was less successful with the WHO guidelines to healthy eating. The issue was huge: the WHO advised that a healthy diet consists of no more than 10 percent sugar, while the Sugar Association, whose members include the U.S.'s major cane- and beet-sugar companies, demanded an outrageous 25 percent and accused WHO of relying on "misguided, non-science-based reports which do not add to the health and well-being of Americans, much less the rest of the world."[655] The association also threatened to exert pressure to have American funding for WHO withdrawn unless WHO withdrew the guidelines. But the 10 percent guideline remained, defended by Director-General Gro Harlem Brundtland as "the foundation for a global policy response to ... the great surge we have seen in the incidence of chronic diseases."[656]

Whether consumed as unadulterated candy or to sweeten beverages or other foodstuffs, sugar in all its seductive deliciousness has become a lightning rod for those concerned with public health. Their battle with the powerful sugar lobby resembles nothing so much as the struggle of the abolitionists against the same interests.

SUGAR'S NEW POWER

Stunningly, a new chapter, one of hope and possible redemption, is being added to sugar's relentlessly sad and bad story. The best place to start telling it is Brazil, the political handiwork of a distant pope and the exploited colony of a distant European nation. Brazil today is the world's largest sugarcane producer and, during the oil shortages and price rises of the 1970s, processed its vast cane crop into fuel as well as sugar.

This was a brilliant move because sugarcane, immensely versatile and sustainable, is the only renewable source of carbon. It is "the world's finest living collector of sunlight, storing the energy in huge quantities as biomass in the form of fiber (lignocellulose) and fermentable sugars," sustainability experts Pincas Jawetz and George Samuels explain.[657] The Brazilian government enforced its new policy, including mixing cane-derived ethanol with gasoline, through Proalcool, its national alcohol program. (This practice is increasingly common. In the United States, Canada, China and Australia, for example, gas is now 10 to 15 percent ethanol.) Government incentives encouraged Brazilians to buy alcohol-fueled cars. By 1988, more than 90 percent of all cars sold in Brazil were alcohol fueled.

Brazil's is not, however, a linear story with a fairytale ending, but rather a real-life tale replete with downturns and obstacles to overcome. When the price of gas declined, so did the sale of alcohol-fueled cars; by the end of the 1990s, they amounted to less than 1 percent of total automobile sales. To protect themselves against changes in sugar and gas prices, exchange rates and government policies, Brazilians have turned to flex-fueled vehicles such as Fiat, Chevrolet, Ford, Renault and Peugeot cars, the

These men are likely prouder of their Model T's sporty style after its conversion from a roundabout body than they are of its flex-fuel capacity—it can use either gas or ethanol as fuel, c. 1910.

Volkswagen TotalFlex Golf and the Saab biofueled car. (A century ago, Henry Ford introduced the Model T, the first flex-fueled car: it ran on either gas or ethanol.)

Brazil's sugar industry is both efficient and exploitative, relying on streamlined technology and underpaid cane workers to produce cane cheaply. Cane sugar employs over a million Brazilians and accounts for more than a tenth of the country's agriculture. It can be planted more cheaply than crops such as citrus fruit or than pastureland and, historically, has a better rate of investment return. At the same time, Brazil's oil production is another factor in government fuel policy. Requiring that gas contain at least 25 percent ethanol ensures a regular and affordable fuel supply and supports the huge sugar industry; about half of Brazilian sugar is transformed into ethanol, and most of the rest is exported, making Brazil the world's largest sugar exporter, ahead of the European Union.

In a world where "development" implies the right to a car, the automotive and fuel industries are a married couple that must find ways to coexist. In Brazil, their common interests are facilitated by having flex-fuel and uni-fuel cars cost the same, and consumer confidence in the future availability of ethanol raises the resale value of flexcars. Although fueling a car requires significantly more ethanol than gas, ethanol's cheaper price makes it the better buy.

Brazil's successful embrace of cane-derived ethanol fuel has much more than economic benefits to commend it. Although Brazilian cane production is notoriously destructive to the environment, cane-derived fuel is precisely the opposite. It is much cleaner than fossil fuels and contains no contaminants such as sulfur dioxide. It emits much less carbon dioxide and protects the climate by vastly reducing carbon emissions, hence reducing pollution. It is sustainable. It yields 8.3 times as much energy as that expended to make it and, as new cane varieties are developed, will yield even more. Even its by-products are valuable, and Brazilian mills process them into electricity for their own use and to sell to the national grid. Other countries that produce ethanol and electricity from cane include India, Australia, Mauritius, Reunion, Guadeloupe, Hawaii, Guatemala, Colombia, Thailand, Venezuela, Peru and Ecuador.

Cane-based ethanol is the twenty-first century's miracle-in-waiting, the natural substance that can drastically alter international economic and diplomatic relationships by ending or at least reducing dependence on fundamentalist Middle Eastern oil-rich regimes that now supply much of the carbon-emitting fuel that perpetuates global warming and exacerbates natural disasters from the Gulf Coast to the Indian Ocean. The existence of a quickly producible (it takes three days to transform sugarcane into ethanol) and in most ways superior alternative fuel may have political and diplomatic consequences as important as historic sugar's. An obvious one is that the availability of ethanol will encourage formerly oil-needy nations to end their complicity in supporting unsavory government-sanctioned behavior such as human rights abuses in many oil-rich regimes.

Fueling themselves with ethanol will enable developing and many less developed sugarcane-producing nations to move toward self-sufficiency. In one of his first announcements after his 2006 election, Haiti's president René Préval outlined his plan to resuscitate the country's sugar industry and, with Brazil's help, to produce ethanol to fuel cars and generate electricity. Haiti is not alone; Brazil is advising Jamaica and Guatemala, among other cane growers, on ethanol production, and Haiti's neighbor, the Dominican Republic, is building ethanol distilleries. "In the next 10 to 15 years," Antonio Japa, general manager of the national Dominican sugar cooperative, predicts, "ethanol will be the king of fuels."[658]

Ethanol and the electricity that is one of its by-products can be produced from beet sugar as well as from cane, and from other crops such as corn and grain. In the U.K., for instance, British Sugar is producing bioethanol to mix with gas. But European interest in beet-derived ethanol is tempered by the fact that beet is costlier to produce than wheat, its bio-energy rival, a situation paralleled in the United States by cheaper corn. In 2004, the European Union diverted only 0.8 percent, or one million tons, of its 131 million tons of sugar beets to ethanol (in contrast to only 0.4 percent of its 138 tons of wheat).

Yet this is counterintuitive and pits immediate economies against long-term environmental costs. Although wheat and corn are cheaper to grow, they have much lower energy yields than sugar beet and cane. Beet sugar uses only 100.5 energy units to produce 150 energy units compared with wheat's 136.5, though wheat is superior to gasoline, which requires 184.5 energy units. Translated into greenhouse gas (GHG) emissions, sugar-beet and wheat-based ethanol create respective GHG reductions of 35 to 56 percent and 19 to 49 percent per kilometer compared with gas-fueled vehicles. In the United States, corn yields a ratio of only 1.3 of energy produced against energy expended, whereas sugar beet has an impressive energy yield ratio of 8.3.

In the narrative of sugar's story, its biofuel derivatives have a redemptive quality. They undermine the seductive power of oil-rich tyrannies and encourage moral political stances. They put needy former colonies on the road to self-sufficiency. They are clean rivals to fossil fuels that poison the atmosphere with carbon, contribute to global warming and exacerbate natural disasters. They transform the nature of sugarcane from luxury and much-loved foodstuff to a versatile crop that is now an energy source as well as food. A classically happy ending would be to describe the enshrinement of sugar biofuel as the ideal energy source for most of the world.

But the story of sugar as bioenergy has complex subtexts. One is the shortsighted tradition that permits immediate cost factors and special interests to outweigh long-term environmental consequences. In beet-growing Europe, political will could overcome this reluctance to mass-produce and popularize beet-derived energy. European lawmakers could modify their sugar market regulations to make sugar beet an affordable energy source, blended or alone, with Germany, France, Belgium and Austria likely the most competitive producers.

Another subplot to the cane-ethanol business is the age-old disregard of the environment that poisons cane culture. In Brazil, for example, as cane growers push to expand their thriving operations, they compete with food producers and move into former pastureland and ecologically sensitive wetlands. The dislocated cattle ranchers then seek new pastures, and deforestation follows in their wake; today, even the Amazon is at risk. In Australia, Florida and elsewhere, the runoff and emission of contaminants into water and air remain critical problems.

The temptation to forge ahead as cheaply as possible usually overpowers these concerns, and Big Sugar has the political clout to beat down environmental objections.

Yet solutions exist. China's traditional sugarcane did not degrade the environment. Neither, today, does the plantation sugar culture of Cuba—an unlikely model given its record of human rights abuses and faulty economic planning, but a planned economy has replaced its dissolving sugar industry with tourism, including eco-tourism. Cuba has promoted forestry and conservation of natural resources, created impressive nature reserves and has Latin America's lowest rates of deforestation. The director of the government-run National Industry for the Protection of Flora and Fauna, Guillermo García Frías, speaks passionately about the "fight for life on the planet," adding that "Nature is grateful, and she will reward you with a better world." Unable to purchase pesticides, herbicides and fertilizers, Cuba improvised its own version of organic sugar farming and intense recycling, generating electricity, cattle feed, even furniture from cane *bagasse*. "In the face of economic challenges," Mike Garvey of WWF-Canada opines, "Cuba has become known for its conservation efforts."659

Just as the environment has benefited from Cuban sugar's decline, it could benefit from its renewal. Biodiversity ecologist Eduardo Santana has explained how the United States could again import vast quantities of organically produced Cuban sugar to replace that now grown in Florida's wounded Everglades. A bilateral trade agreement would include environmental issues such as conserving migratory birds and hemispheric biological diversity.660

Whether or not Cuban sugar is reborn, all cane sugar should be organically grown on suitable land, not carved out of wetlands and other environmentally sensitive land. Brazil, an egregious offender, must be persuaded to adhere to new international standards. So must all sugarbeet producers. Sugar residues, though massively reduced and less toxic, must be kept out of nearby water sources. The highest internationally accepted environmental standards should govern sugar's production and conversion to biofuel, so that clean energy is cleanly produced. Clean sugarcane will seem costlier to produce only because standard economic analyses fail to factor in the economic consequences of environmental degradation. When they are included, clean sugar and biofuel will prove cheaper.

Sugar beet's superiority remains a subtext in the beet-versus-cane discussion. Environmental studies confirm that, mated with diverse winter grains, sugar beet indirectly aids the survival of at-risk species of birds. It also nurtures such animals as hawks and owls, and some species of endangered snakes, by sheltering the small rodents they prey on. Because it is a rotational crop, beet and crops planted with it require little fertilizer or pesticide. Beet does not contaminate the soil and only minimally erodes it; and the soil coating the harvested beets can be recycled rather than discarded. Beet *bagasse* is used to fatten cattle. Its molasses leavings are processed into potassium-rich "raffinate" for use as fertilizer. The lime used to extract sugar from beet is reused to neutralize and prepare farmland.

Whether in beet or cane fields, the sugar labor force must be fairly treated. Equitably paid workers committed to organic, environment-friendly farming will support the sustainable development that is one of sugar's—and its biofuel's—most extraordinary advantages.

Big (Better) Sugar will still confront rivals—corn in the New World, wheat in the old—and drastically changing political priorities. In the United States, a growing revulsion against the political and environmental consequences of dependence on (or addiction to) oil has sparked a rush to ethanol and federal tax credits for its production. The urgency and incentives to mass-produce ethanol have created serious new issues. One is that low production costs of corn and other grains trump sugar's superior energy efficiency; though self-sufficiency is achieved, significant reduction of fossil fuel is not. Another issue is that, as in Brazil, crops destined for conversion to ethanol will compete with food crops and many growers will succumb to the temptation to expand their farming operations to fragile, marginal or otherwise unsuitable land.

Until better alternatives to sugar ethanol become available—cellulosic ethanol, processed from agricultural waste or *bagasse*, shows potential—fairly traded, environmentally sound and renewable sugarcane and beet should lead the ethanol revolution. Although it will continue to delight and comfort, and to be the handmaiden of celebration, sugar will no longer need to rely on promoting grotesquely unhealthy consumption to stay in business. Research is already developing sugar's potential in other areas, such as plastics. Sugar as medicine, transformed by biomedical research into dissolvable surgical plates, for instance, may be another of its new narratives. One day, the meaning of sugar may become as sweet as the storied sugar of metaphor.

Notes

INTRODUCTION

1. I owe this scenario to Sidney Mintz's *Sweetness and Power*, which refers to such a farm laborer's woman.

CHAPTER 1

2. Hobhouse, *Seeds of Change*, p. 45.

3. Judith Miller and Jeff Gerth, "Trade in Honey Is Said to Provide Money and Cover," *The New York Times*, Oct. 11, 2001.

4. Flannigan, *Antigua and the Antiguans*, vol. 1, p. 173.

5. Quoted in Mintz, *Sweetness and Power*, pp. 105 and 41.

6. Mintz, *Sweetness and Power*, p. 25.

7. Galloway, *The Sugar Cane Industry*, p. 25.

8. Deerr, *The History of Sugar*, vol. 1, p. 74.

9. Albert van Aachen, who recorded the experiences of First Crusade veterans, quoted in Mintz, *Sweetness and Power*, p. 28.

10. Davidson, *Black Mother*, p. 54.

11. Ibid., p. 57.

12. Galloway, *The Sugar Cane Industry*, p. 42.

13. Ibid., p. 37.

14. Quoted in Deerr, *The History of Sugar*, vol. 1, p. 78.

15. Galloway, *The Sugar Cane Industry*, p. 32.

16. Day, *Royal Sugar Sculpture*, p. 7.

17. Mintz, *Sweetness and Power*, p. 89. Ivan Day's *Royal Sugar Sculpture: 600 Years of Splendour* is an excellent and comprehensive study of sugar sculpture technique and models. The Amsterdams Historisch Museum's publication *Suiker/Sugar* includes illustrations of Dutch sugar sculptures. By 1700, Amsterdam had almost a hundred sugar bakeries producing elaborate sugar sculptures.

18. Mintz, *Sweetness and Power*, pp. 243–44, n. 52.

19. Ibid., p. 90.

20. Ibid., quoting the 1968 reprint of William Harrison's 1587 *The Description of England*, p. 129.

21. Galloway, *The Sugar Cane Industry*, p. 42.

22. "King Ferdinand's letter to the Taino/Arawak Indians," provided by Bob Corbett, www.hartford-hwp.com/archives/41/038.html.

23. Deerr, *The History of Sugar*, vol. 1, p. 117.

24. Quoted in ibid., p. 122.

25. Sale, "What Columbus Discovered," pp. 444–46.

26. James Hamilton, "New Report Slams Sugar Industry for Environmental Destruction," *Sunday Herald*, Nov. 14, 2004.

27. Quoted in Sale, *The Conquest of Paradise*, pp. 96, 197.

28. Quoted in ibid., pp. 313–14.

29. This contentious issue remains unresolved. David Watts, *The West Indies*, tends toward the conservative figure of three million. Sale, *The Conquest of Paradise*, argues convincingly for nearly eight million, as does David E. Stannard in *American Holocaust.*

30. E. Williams, *From Columbus to Castro*, p. 37.

31. Patterson, *The Sociology of Slavery*, p. 15.

32. Quoted in Kolbert, "The Lost Mariner," *The New Yorker*, Oct. 14, 2002.

33. "The Legend of Hatuey," written and compiled by J. A. Sierra, www. historyofcuba.com/history/oriente/hatuey.htm. See also Allahar, *Class, Politics, and Sugar in Colonial Cuba*, p. 48: "Once again, let me remind you that the god that these tyrants adore is the gold which is hidden in the entrails of our land. This is their lord. That is what they serve."

34. Clifford Krauss, "A Historic Figure Is Still Hated by Many in Mexico," *The New York Times*, March 26, 1997.

35. Ibid.

36. Sanderlin, *Bartolomé de Las Casas*, pp. 80–81.

37. Bonar Ludwig Hernandez, "The Las Casas-Sepúlveda Controversy, 1550–1551," www.sfsu.edu/~epf/2001/hernandez.html.

38. Carrozza, "Bartolomé de Las Casas," www.lascasas.org/carrozo.htm.

39. Ibid.

40. Quoted in Sanderlin, *Bartolomé de Las Casas*, pp. 183–85.

41. Davidson, *Black Mother*, p. 66.

42. Sanderlin, *Bartolomé de Las Casas*, p. 102.

43. E. Williams, *From Columbus to Castro*, p. 43.

44. Las Casas, *Obras Escogidas*, vol. II, 487–88, quoted in Sanderlin, *Bartolomé de Las Casas*, pp. 100–102.

45. E. Williams, *From Columbus to Castro*, p. 43.

46. Herrara, *History of the Indies*, quoted in Williams, *From Columbus to Castro*, p. 43.

47. Beckles, *White Servitude and Slavery in Barbados*, p. 5.

48. E. Williams, *From Columbus to Castro*, p. 96.

49. William Dickson, LL.D., *Mitigation of Slavery, In Two Parts. Part I: Letters and Papers of The Late Hon. Joshua Steele*, www.yale.edu/glc/archive/1162.htm.

50. E. Williams, *From Columbus to Castro*, p. 103.

51. Ibid.

52. Ibid.

53. Ibid., p. 110.

54. David Watts, *The West Indies*, p. 119.

55. E. Williams, *Capitalism and Slavery*, p. 24.

CHAPTER 2

56. Strong, *Feast*, p. 199. The descriptions of sugar collations are taken from Roy.

57. K. Hall, "Culinary Spaces, Colonial Spaces," p. 173.

58. Ibid., p. 178.

59. Quoted in ibid., p. 175.

60. Nineteenth-century British historian William B. Rye, quoted in Mintz, *Sweetness and Power*, p. 135.

61. Ayrton, *The Cookery of England*, p. 429.

62. Ibid., p. 430.

63. Ibid., pp. 463–64.

64. Quoted in Powell, *Cool*, p. xiii.

65. Root and de Rochemont, *Eating in America*, p. 425.

66. Ibid.

67. Ibid., p. 426.

68. A good source on Canadian ice cream is Prof. Douglas Goff's project, the Dairy Technology Education Series. See in particular "Ice Cream History and Folklore," at www.foodsci.uoguelph.ca/dairyedu/icecream.html.

69. Mintz, *Sweetness and Power*, p. 110.

70. Quoted in ibid., p. 111.

71. "The Character of a Coffee-House, 1673," www.fordham.edu/halsall/mod/1670coffee.html.

72. Cited in Botsford, *English Society in the Eighteenth Century*, p. 69.

73. Quoted in Mintz, *Sweetness and Power*, p. 106.

74. Mintz, *Tasting Food, Tasting Freedom*, p. 71.

75. Woloson, *Refined Tastes*, p. 113.

76. P. Morton Shand, *A Book of Food*, 1927, quoted in Mintz, *Sweetness and Power*, p. 141.

77. Mintz, *Sweetness and Power*, p. 39.

78. Smith, "From Coffeehouse to Parlour," p. 159.

79. Ibid., p. 161.

80. P. Morton Shand, *A Book of Food*, p. 39, quoted in Mintz, *Sweetness and Power*, pp. 141–42.

81. Landes, *The Unbound Prometheus*, p. 41.

82. Gaskell, *The Manufacturing Population of England*, p. 185.

83. Quoted in Edward Royle, *Modern Britain: A Social History 1750–1997*, p. 169.

84. Shammas, "Food Expenditures and Economic Well-Being in Early Modern England," p. 90.

85. These statistics are taken from Mintz, *Sweetness and Power*, p. 67.

86. Deerr, *The History of Sugar*, vol. 2, p. 532.

87. Shammas, "Food Expenditures and Economic Well-Being in Early Modern England," p. 99.

88. Davies, *The Case of Labourers in Husbandry Stated and Considered*, 1795, p. 21, quoted in Oddy, "Food, Drink and Nutrition," p. 255.

89. Shuttleworth, "The Moral and Physical Condition of the Working Classes of Manchester."

90. Oddy, "Food, Drink and Nutrition," pp. 269–70.

91. Burnett, *Plenty and Want*, pp. 14–15, features a chart of sugar consumption from 1801 to 1850, showing how per capita annual consumption "fluctuated in direct relation to price": the lower the price, the higher the consumption.

92. *6th Report of the Medical Officer of the Privy Council, PP 1864*, 28, p. 249, quoted in Oddy, "Food, Drink and Nutrition," p. 44.

93. Thompson, *The Making of the English Working Class*, p. 316.

94. Quoted in Oddy, "Food, Drink and Nutrition," p. 271.

95. Rowntree, *Poverty: A Study of Town Life*, p. 135, n. 1, quoted in Oddy, "Food, Drink and Nutrition," pp. 272–73.

96. Mintz, *Sweetness and Power*, pp. 64, 61.

97. Bayne-Powell, *English Country Life in the Eighteenth Century*, p. 207.

98. Duncan Forbes in 1744, quoted in Pettigrew, *A Social History of Tea*, p. 52.

99. Smith, "From Coffeehouse to Parlour," p. 161.

100. Mintz, *Sweetness and Power*, p. 141.

101. Ibid., p. 165.

102. Richardson, *Sweets*, p. 316.

103. Mintz, *Sweetness and Power*, p. 172.

104. Ibid., p. 186.

105. The Nepal Distilleries, www.khukrirum.com/history.htm.

106. Rutz, "Salt Horse and Ship's Biscuit."

107. Toussaint-Samat, *A History of Food*, p. 560.

CHAPTER 3

108. Chapter 10 deals with indentured labor, a form of bondage planters returned to after slavery was abolished. In the early years of settlement, indentured whites worked alongside the black slaves; in Brazil, so did natives.

109. These figures have been the subject of intense research and debate, summed up in Hugh Thomas's *The Slave Trade*, pp. 861–62. The statistics I have used are widely though not universally accepted; a few historians argue that a few million more, or less, would be more accurate.

110. Thistlewood's journal, Aug. 12, 1776, quoted in Hall, *In Miserable Slavery*, p. 178.

111. Quoted in Thomas, *The Slave Trade*, pp. 395, 396.

112. Equiano, *The Life of Olaudah Equiano*, p. 33.

113. Ferguson, *Empire*, p. 82, calculates that from 1662 until 1807, one out of seven Africans died on British slavers, and before that, the mortality rate was one out of four.

114. Quoted in Augier et al., *The Making of the West Indies*, p. 73.

115. Quoted in Richardson, "Shipboard Revolts," p. 3.

116. Patterson, *The Sociology of Slavery*, p. 151.

117. A statement made in the Antigua Legislature, 1788, quoted in Goveia, *Slave Society in the British Leeward Islands*, p. 121.

118. Higman, *Slave Population and Economy in Jamaica*, p. 188, citing Edwin Lascelles, *Instructions for the Management of a Plantation in Barbados, and for the Treatment of Negroes &c*, 1786.

119. "The Professional Planter" advised that a working five-year-old could earn his keep. Patterson, *The Sociology of Slavery*, p. 156.

120. Higman, *Slave Population and Economy in Jamaica*, p. 192.

121. Beckles, *Natural Rebels*, p. 31.

122. Quoted in Braithwaite, *The Development of Creole Society in Jamaica*, p. 155.

123. D. Hall, *In Miserable Slavery*, p. 234.

124. Scottish visitor Janet Schaw, quoted in Goveia, *Slave Society in the British Leeward Islands*, p. 131.

125. Tomlich, *Slavery in the Circuit of Sugar*, p. 146, notes that in the nineteenth century in the French islands, spoiled codfish, dried cattle blood and the entrails discarded by the North Atlantic fishery made excellent though often expensive fertilizer.

126. Ibid.

127. Klein, *African Slavery in Latin America and the Caribbean*, p. 55.

128. Quoted in Dyde *A History of Antigua*, p. 112.

129. Both taken from Patterson, *The Sociology of Slavery*, pp. 255–57.

130. William Henry Hurlbert, *Gan-Eden; or, Picture of Cuba*, quoted in Perez, *Slaves, Sugar, and Colonial Society*, p. 111.

131. Richard Henry Dana Jr., *To Cuba and Back: A Vacation Voyage*, quoted in Perez, *Slaves, Sugar, and Colonial Society*, p. 62.

132. Quoted in Fick, *The Making of Haiti*, p. 28.

133. Lewis, *Journal of a West India Proprietor*, pp. 65–66.

134. Quoted in Higman, *Slave Population and Economy in Jamaica*, p. 124.

135. C. Williams, *Tour Through Jamaica*, 1826, pp. 13–14, quoted in Patterson, *The Sociology of Slavery*, p. 155.

136. Beckles, *Natural Rebels*, p. 37.

137. Seventeenth-century account by Richard Ligon, quoted in Beckles, *Afro-Caribbean Women and Resistance to Slavery*, p. 23.

138. Julia M. Woodruff (writing as W. M. L. Jay), *My Winter in Cuba*, 1871, quoted in Perez, *Slaves, Sugar, and Colonial Society*, p. 73, 72.

139. Samuel Hazard, *Cuba with Pen and Pencil*, 1871, quoted in Perez, *Slaves, Sugar, and Colonial Society*, p. 76.

140. Quoted in Beckles, *Natural Rebels*, p. 39.

141. William Drysdale, *In Sunny Lands*, 1885, quoted in Perez, *Slaves, Sugar, and Colonial Society*, p. 92.

142. D. Hall, *In Miserable Slavery*, p. 125.

143. Quoted in Scarano, *Sugar and Slavery in Puerto Rico*, p. 29.

144. Quoted in Forster and Forster, *Sugar and Slavery, Family and Race*, p. 17.

145. Fredrika Bremer, *The Homes of the New World: Impressions of America*, 1853, quoted in Perez, *Slaves, Sugar, and Colonial Society*, p. 117.

146. Julia Ward Howe, *A Trip to Cuba*, 1860, quoted in Perez, *Slaves, Sugar, and Colonial Society*, p. 122.

147. Fick, *The Making of Haiti*, p. 34, quotes Baron de Wimpffen, who noted this "with a sense of incredulity."

148. Quoted in Goveia, *Slave Society in the British Leeward Islands*, p. 131.

149. Prince, *The History of Mary Prince, a West Indian Slave*, pp. 18, 23.

150. Quoted in Walvin, *Black Ivory*, p. 241.

151. Forster and Forster, *Sugar and Slavery, Family and Race*, p. 17.

152. D. Hall, *In Miserable Slavery*, p. 47.

153. Prince, *The History of Mary Prince, a West Indian Slave*, p. 17.

154. Goveia, *Slave Society in the British Leeward Islands*, p. 117, quoting the late-eighteenth-century testimony of James Ramsay, *An Essay on the Treatment and Conversion of African Slaves in the British Sugar Colonies*, 1784, pp. 69–70.

155. Quoted in Goveia, *Slave Society in the British Leeward Islands*, p. 29.

156. Quoted in ibid., p. 118.

157. Quoted in ibid., p. 119.

158. Quoted in ibid., p. 222.

159. Henry T. De La Beche, *Notes on the Present Condition of the Negroes in Jamaica*, 1825, p. 7, quoted in Patterson, *The Sociology of Slavery*, p. 156.

160. Frederick T. Townshend, *Wild Life in Florida with a Visit to Cuba*, 1875, quoted in Perez, *Slaves, Sugar, and Colonial Society*, p. 86.

161. Poyen de Sainte-Marie, quoted in Moitt, *Women and Slavery in the French Antilles*, p. 43.

162. D. Hall, *In Miserable Slavery*, p. 154.

163. Jamaican free-born black anti-slavery advocate William Dickson, *Letters on Slavery*, quoted in Beckles, *Natural Rebels*, p. 51.

164. Patterson, *The Sociology of Slavery*, p. 159.

165. D. Hall, *In Miserable Slavery*, p. 50.

166. Quoted in Patterson, *The Sociology of Slavery*, p. 58.

167. Quoted in Goveia, *Slave Society in the British Leeward Islands*, p. 150.

168. Quoted in ibid., p. 141.

169. Quoted in Braithwaite, *The Development of Creole Society in Jamaica*, p. 142.

170. Quoted in Pares, *A West-India Fortune*, p. 58.

171. Quoted in Forster and Forster, *Sugar and Slavery, Family and Race*, pp. 60, 73.

172. Quoted in D. Hall, *In Miserable Slavery*, pp. 118, 128.

173. Quoted in ibid., p. 72.

174. Quoted in ibid., pp. 282, 283, 293, 72–73.

175. Quoted in Forster and Forster, *Sugar and Slavery, Family and Race*, p. 167.

176. Quoted in D. Hall, *In Miserable Slavery*, p. 46.

177. Quoted in Goveia, *Slave Society in the British Leeward Islands*, p. 242.

178. Patterson, *The Sociology of Slavery*, p. 9.

179. Donoghue, *Black Women/White Men*, p. 134.

180. Miguel Barnet, *Biography of a Runaway Slave*, quoted in Chomsky et al., *The Cuba Reader*, pp. 58–59.

181. Woodruff, *My Winter in Cuba*, quoted in Perez, *Slaves, Sugar, and Colonial Society*, p. 71.

182. Schwartz, *Sugar Plantations in the Formation of Brazilian Society*, p. 137.

183. Quoted in Fick, *Haiti in the Making*, p. 33.

184. William Dickson, quoted in Beckles, *Natural Rebels*, p. 45.

185. Barnet, *Biography of a Runaway Slave*, p. 59.

186. Quoted in Beckles, *Natural Rebels*, p. 79. This is why slaves sold their Guinea-corn to buy other foodstuffs.

187. Quoted in E. Williams, *Capitalism and Slavery*, p. 59.

188. Quoted in Beckles, *Natural Rebels*, p. 48.

189. Schwartz, *Sugar Plantations in the Formation of Brazilian Society*, p. 138.

190. Tomlich, *Slavery in the Circuit of Sugar*, pp. 259–60.

191. Quoted in Goveia, *Slave Society in the British Leeward Islands*, p. 238.

192. Quoted in Bush, *Slave Women in Caribbean Society*, p. 93.

193. Fick, *The Making of Haiti*, p. 31.

194. See Higman, *Slave Population and Economy in Jamaica*, for a long discussion of living arrangements.

195. Howe, *A Trip to Cuba*, quoted in Perez, *Slaves, Sugar, and Colonial Society*, p. 124.

196. Quoted in Bush, *Slave Women in Caribbean Society*, p. 101.

197. Quoted in Forster and Forster, *Sugar and Slavery, Family and Race*, p. 46.

198. Quoted in ibid., p. 47.

199. Quoted in Moitt, *Women and Slavery in the French Antilles*, p. 80.

200. Quoted in Schwartz, *Sugar Plantations in the Formation of Brazilian Society*, p. 384.

201. Quoted in D. Hall, *In Miserable Slavery*, pp. 77, 189.

202. Beckles, *Natural Rebels*, p. 94.

203. Quoted in Schwartz, *Sugar Plantations in the Formation of Brazilian Society*, p. 354.

204. Quoted in Forster and Forster, *Sugar and Slavery, Family and Race*, p. 117.

205. Quoted in D. Hall, *In Miserable Slavery*, pp. 184, 186.

206. Schwartz, *Sugar Plantations in the Formation of Brazilian Society*, p. 370.

207. Woodruff, *My Winter in Cuba*, quoted in Perez, *Slaves, Sugar, and Colonial Society*, p. 73.

208. This situation was so common that, in 1810, Antigua's Assembly decided that physicians had to possess "a certificate from the Surgeons' Hall, or from one of the universities in Great Britain shewing his admittance in them." Dyde, *A History of Antigua*, p. 112.

209. Quoted in Fick, *Haiti in the Making*, p. 39.

210. Quoted in Forster and Forster, *Sugar and Slavery, Family and Race*, p. 136.

211. Quoted in Goveia, *Slave Society in the British Leeward Islands*, p. 139.

212. Quoted in Moitt, *Women and Slavery in the French Antilles*, p. 74.

CHAPTER 4

213. Charles Leslie, *New History of Jamaica*, 1740, quoted in Matthew Mulcahy, "Weathering the Storms: Hurricanes and Plantation Agriculture in the British Greater Caribbean," www.librarycompany.org/Economics/PDF%20Files/C2002-mulcahy.pdf.

214. Ibid.

215. Lewis, *Journal of a West India Proprietor*, p. 43.

216. Nugent, *Lady Nugent's Journal*, p. 103.

217. Ibid., p. 98.

218. Ibid., p. 108.

219. Quoted in Braithwaite, *The Cultural Politics of Sugar*, p. 111.

220. John Shipman, a Methodist missionary, quoted in Braithwaite, *The Development of Creole Society in Jamaica*, p. 299.

221. Quoted in McDonald, *Between Slavery and Freedom*, p. 104.

222. Nugent, *Lady Nugent's Journal*, p. 66.

223. Lewis, *Journal of a West India Proprietor*, pp. 81, 209, 82.

224. Ibid., p. 55.

225. Quoted in Braithwaite, *The Development of Creole Society in Jamaica*, p. 105.

226. Haitian sugar planter St. Foäche's instructions to his estates' managers, quoted in Fick, *The Making of Haiti*, p. 37.

227. Quoted in Forster and Forster, *Sugar and Slavery, Family and Race*, p. 111.

228. Quoted in ibid., p. 42.

229. Lewis, *Journal of a West India Proprietor*, p. 111.

230. Quoted in D. Hall, *In Miserable Slavery*, p. 46.

231. Nugent, *Lady Nugent's Journal*, p. 226.

232. Quoted in D. Hall, *In Miserable Slavery*, p. 69.

233. Quoted in Burnard, *Mastery, Tyranny, and Desire*, pp. 237–38.

234. Quoted in Beckles, *Natural Rebels*, p. 136.

235. Quoted in Braithwaite, *The Development of Creole Society in Jamaica*, p. 191.

236. Quoted in D. Hall, *In Miserable Slavery*, p. 19.

237. Quoted in Forster and Forster, *Sugar and Slavery, Family and Race*, p. 112.

238. Koster, *Travels in Brazil*, p. 144.

239. Nugent, *Lady Nugent's Journal*, pp. 32, 162.

240. Patterson, *The Sociology of Slavery*, p. 129.

241. Quoted in Mulcahy, "Weathering the Storms."

242. Quoted in Beckles, *Natural Rebels*, p. 69.

243. Quoted in ibid., p. 24.

244. Quoted in Forster and Forster, *Sugar and Slavery, Family and Race*, p. 189.

245. Richard Ligon, 1647, quoted in Galenson, *Traders, Planters, and Slaves*, p. 137.

246. Burnard, *Mastery, Tyranny, and Desire*, p. 17; see also John, *The Plantation Slaves of Trinidad*, p. 104.

247. Patterson, *The Sociology of Slavery*, p. 33.

248. Quoted in Goveia, *Slave Society in the British Leeward Islands*, p. 208.

249. Drax, 1680, quoted in Galenson, *Traders, Planters and Slaves*, p. 139.

250. Richard Robert Madden, *The Island of Cuba*, quoted in Perez, *Slaves, Sugar, and Colonial Society*, p. 50.

251. D. Hall, *In Miserable Slavery*, p. 72.

252. Nugent, *Lady Nugent's Journal*, pp. 118, 46.

253. Forster and Forster, *Sugar and Slavery, Family and Race*, p. 253.

254. Elizabeth Fenwick, quoted in Beckles, *Natural Rebels*, p. 65.

255. Freyre, *The Masters and the Slaves*, p. 305.

256. Quoted in Burnard, *Mastery, Tyranny, and Desire*, p. 309.

257. Lewis, *Journal of a West India Proprietor*, p. 146.

258. Quoted in Braithwaite, *The Development of Creole Society in Jamaica*, p. 158.

259. Lewis, *Journal of a West India Proprietor*, p. 105.

260. Long, *History of Jamaica*, vol. 2, p. 332.

261. Lewis, *Journal of a West India Proprietor*, p. 52.

262. Goveia, *Slave Society in the British Leeward Islands*, p. 318.

263. Quoted in ibid., pp. 232–33.

264. Nugent, *Lady Nugent's Journal*, p. 132.

265. Quoted in Patterson, *The Sociology of Slavery*, p. 171.

266. Freyre, *The Masters and the Slaves*, p. 347.

267. Nugent, *Lady Nugent's Journal*, pp. 107, 193.

268. Beckles, *Black Rebellion in Barbados*, p. 121.

269. Quoted in D. Hall, *In Miserable Slavery*, p. 94.

270. Burnard, *Mastery, Tyranny, and Desire*, p. 233.

271. Burnard, in *Mastery, Tyranny, and Desire*, tabulated Thistlewood's journals and calculated his sexual relations. See, for example, p. 238.

272. Quoted in D. Hall, *In Miserable Slavery*, p. 67.

273. Quoted in ibid., pp. 79, 80.

274. Quoted in Burnard, *Mastery, Tyranny, and Desire*, p. 309.

275. Burnard, *Mastery, Tyranny, and Desire*, p. 237.

276. Quoted in ibid., p. 238.

277. The source for this section is Guédé, *Monsieur de Saint-George*.

278. The source for this section is Forster and Forster, *Sugar and Slavery, Family and Race*, pp. 11, 92–98, 149.

279. Forster and Forster, *Sugar and Slavery, Family and Race*, p. 11.

CHAPTER 5

280. Quoted in Duffy, *Soldiers, Sugar, and Seapower*, p. 6.

281. E. Willliams, *Capitalism and Slavery*, p. 65.

282. Ibid., p. 105.

283. Ibid., pp. 52–53.

284. Butler's excellent *Economics of Emancipation* details where the money went. "Very little of the 'monstrous sum' found its way to the West India colonies. It was paid for the most part, to mortgagees, in or about, the small circle of Threadneedle Street" (p. 141). Threadneedle Street was the home of the Bank of England.

285. Quoted in E. Williams, *Capitalism and Slavery*, p. 61.

286. G. Williams, *History of the Liverpool Privateers*, p. 477.

287. E. Williams, *Capitalism and Slavery*, p. 37.

288. Quoted in G. Williams, *History of the Liverpool Privateers*, p. 594.

289. Dalby, *Historical Account of the Rise of the West-India Colonies* (1690), quoted in Matthew Mulcahy, "Weathering the Storms."

290. Galloway, *The Sugar Cane Industry*, pp. 88–90.

291. Mulcahy, "Weathering the Storms."

292. From *The West Indian*, by Richard Cumberland, www.joensuu.fi/fld/english/meaney/playtexts/wi/west_indian_2v.html.

293. From James Boswell's *Life of Johnson*, p. 3, www.public-domain-content.com/books/Johnson/C14P3.shtml.

294. Gregson Davis, "Jane Austen's *Mansfield Park*: The Antigua Connection," presented at the Antigua and Barbuda Country Conference, Nov. 13–15, 2003, www.uwichill.edu.bb/bnccde/antigua/conference/paperdex.html.

295. E. Williams, *Capitalism and Slavery*, p. 87.

296. Quoted in Pares, *A West-India Fortune*, p. 65.

297. Quoted in ibid., p. 69.

298. Pares, *A West-India Fortune*, p. 80.

299. Quoted in ibid., pp. 101–2.

300. Quoted in ibid., p. 196.

301. Quoted in ibid.

302. Pares, *A West-India Fortune*, p. 198.

303. Quoted in ibid.

304. E. Williams, *Capitalism and Slavery*, p. 95.

305. Quoted in E. Williams, *From Columbus to Castro*, p. 130.

306. Quoted in Ragatz, *The Fall of the Planter Class*, p. 150.

307. Quoted in Duffy, *Soldiers, Sugar, and Seapower*, p. 385.

308. Ragatz, *The Fall of the Planter Class*, p. 206.

309. By 1787, Britain's share of the continental sugar trade had risen to 65.7 percent, and by 1800–2, the U.S.'s share had risen from zero to 18.2 percent (Duffy, *Soldiers, Sugar, and Seapower*, p. 384).

310. Quoted in Ragatz, *The Fall of the Planter Class*, p. 306.

311. Quoted in ibid., p. 307.

312. Medford, "Oil without Vinegar, and Dignity without Pride," Philadelphia, 1807, online resource #392198, University of Toronto Library.

313. Quoted in Ragatz, *The Fall of the Planter Class*, p. 375.

314. Quoted in ibid., p. 383.

315. This is expressed in terms of unrefined sugar. They ate it refined, and hence consumed much less poundage per person.

316. Duffy, *Soldiers, Sugar, and Seapower*, pp. 7, 13.

317. Quoted in Stein, *The French Sugar Business in the Eighteenth Century*, p. 78.

318. Stein, *The French Sugar Business in the Eighteenth Century*, p. 108.

319. Ibid., p. 120.

320. Ibid., p. 126.

321. Robertson, *Sugar Farmers of Manitoba*, p. 17.

322. Harris, *The Sugar-Beet in America*, pp. 11–12.

323. Inikori, *Forced Migration*, p. 54.

CHAPTER 6

324. E. Williams, *Capitalism and Slavery*, p. 7.

325. Goveia, in *Slave Society in the British Leeward Islands*, describes how slavery spread into other areas.

326. Lewis, *Journal of a West India Proprietor*, p. 68.

327. Goveia, *Slave Society in the British Leeward Islands*, p. 319.

328. Koster, *Travels in Brazil*, p. 174.

329. Dunn, *Sugar and Slaves*, pp. 254–55.

330. Goveia, *Slave Society in the British Leeward Islands*, p. 167.

331. Dunn, *Sugar and Slaves*, p. 256.

332. Alexander von Humboldt, *The Island of Cuba*, quoted in Perez, *Slaves, Sugar, and Colonial Society*, p. 98.

333. In the last decade of slavery, the American South averaged 20.6 slaves to one white. Schwartz, *Sugar Plantations in the Formation of Brazilian Society,* p. 462.

334. Quoted in Goveia, *Slave Society in the British Leeward Islands,* p. 174.

335. Goveia, *Slave Society in the British Leeward Islands,* p. 191.

336. A contemporary abolitionist, quoted in John, *The Plantation Slaves of Trinidad,* p. 122.

337. Quoted in Goveia, *Slave Society in the British Leeward Islands,* pp. 190–91.

338. Quoted in Forster and Forster, *Sugar and Slavery, Family and Race,* p. 66.

339. Quoted in Fick, *The Making of Haiti,* p. 46.

340. Quoted in Forster and Forster, *Sugar and Slavery, Family and Race,* pp. 55, 143, 145.

341. Lewis, *Journal of a West India Proprietor,* pp. 77–78.

342. Schwartz, *Sugar Plantations in the Formation of Brazilian Society,* p. 403.

343. Lewis, *Journal of a West India Proprietor,* p. 72.

344. Ibid., pp. 87, 89.

345. Beckles, *Natural Rebels,* pp. 157–58.

346. Vallentine Morris, quoted in Gaspar, *Bondsmen and Rebels,* p. 220.

347. Quoted in McDonald, *Between Slavery and Freedom,* p. 119.

348. Beckles, *Natural Rebels,* pp. 66–68, 159.

349. Quoted in Beckles, *Black Rebellion in Barbados,* p. 75.

350. Nugent, *Lady Nugent's Journal,* pp. 161–62.

351. Phillip, "Producers, Reproducers, and Rebels."

352. Quoted in Patterson, *The Sociology of Slavery,* p. 178.

353. Koster, *Travels in Brazil,* p. 182.

354. Lewis, *Journal of a West India Proprietor,* p. 127.

355. Charles Campbell's 1828 memoirs, quoted in Braithwaite, *The Development of Creole Society in Jamaica,* pp. 207–8.

356. Goveia, *Slave Society in the British Leeward Islands,* p. 180.

357. Ibid., p. 163.

358. Quoted in Hall, *In Miserable Slavery,* p. 176.

359. Quoted in James, *The Black Jacobins,* p. 15.

360. Beckles, *Natural Rebels,* p. 159.

361. Lewis, *Journal of a West India Proprietor,* p. 63.

362. John, *The Plantation Slaves of Trinidad,* p. 159.

363. Quoted in Phillip, "Producers, Reproducers, and Rebels."

364. Quoted in Beckles, *Natural Rebels,* p. 120.

365. D. Hall, *In Miserable Slavery,* pp. 54–55. Thistlewood laid assault charges against Congo Sam and sent him to jail to await trial. However, the slave London refused to testify, and Congo Sam was acquitted. See Paton, "Punishments, Crime, and the Bodies of Slaves."

366. Quoted in Goveia, *Slave Society in the British Leeward Islands,* p. 154.

367. Fick, *The Making of Haiti*, pp. 7–8, discusses the meaning and implications of marronage, including its meaning as "an integral and active part of the dynamics of slavery and slave resistance and a form of resistance that facilitated others, including insurrectionary activities within the revolution" (p. 10).

368. Campbell, *The Maroons of Jamaica*, pp. 3–4.

369. McFarlane, *Cudjoe of Jamaica*, p. 29.

370. Quoted in Campbell, *The Maroons of Jamaica*, p. 80.

371. Campbell, *The Maroons of Jamaica*, p. 6.

372. Ibid., p. 46, and D. Hall, *In Miserable Slavery*, p. 110.

373. Quoted in Hall, *In Miserable Slavery*, p. 14.

374. Quoted in Campbell, *The Maroons of Jamaica*, p. 115.

375. Ibid., p. 229.

376. Quoted in Miguel Barnet et al., "Fleeing Slavery," in Chomsky et al., *The Cuba Reader*, p. 67.

377. Quoted in Beckles, *Black Rebellion in Barbados*, p. 75.

378. An anonymous essay, quoted in Burnard, *Mastery, Tyranny, and Desire*, p. 140.

379. Edward Long, *History*, quoted in Burnard, *Mastery, Tyranny, and Desire*, p. 171.

380. Quoted in D. Hall, *In Miserable Slavery*, p. 97.

381. Quoted in ibid.

382. Quoted in Paton, "Punishments, Crime, and the Bodies of Slaves."

383. James, *The Black Jacobins*, p. 88.

384. Quoted in Fick, *The Making of Haiti*, p. 110.

385. Fick, *The Making of Haiti*, p. 110.

386. Ibid., p. 201.

387. Nugent, *Lady Nugent's Journal*, pp. 82, 182, 222, 175.

388. Dubois, *Avengers of the New World*, p. 277, cites the officer's words without identifying him.

389. Quoted in James, *The Black Jacobins*, p. 364.

390. Dubois, *Avengers of the New World*, pp. 298–99.

391. Harking back to Dessalines, the word "neg" in Haitian Creole still means man and gives no hint of origins; to specify race, Creole requires "nwa" or "blan" as well. And, because "blan" also means foreigner, an African-American visitor becomes a "blanc nwa."

CHAPTER 7

392. An 1826 abolitionist pamphlet, *What Does Your Sugar Cost?* quoted in Charlotte Sussman, "Women and the Politics of Sugar, 1792," *Representations*, no. 48 (Autumn 1994), p. 57.

393. Wise, *Though the Heavens May Fall*, p. xiv. (Italics in original.) This is a comprehensive and dramatic account and analysis of Granville Sharp's legal battle on behalf of English slaves.

394. Quoted in Wise, *Though the Heavens May Fall*, p. 209.

395. Quoted in ibid., p. 194.

396. Shyllon, *Black Slaves in Britain*, p. 188.

397. Quoted in Anstey, *The Atlantic Slave Trade and British Abolition*, p. 103.

398. Ibid., pp. 114–15.

399. Ibid., p. 127.

400. Codrington College now serves as the religion department of the University of West Indies and an internationally recognized Anglican divinity school.

401. Quoted in Goveia, *Slave Society in the British Leeward Islands*, p. 268.

402. Quoted in Michael Craton, "Slave Culture, Resistance and the Achievement of Emancipation in the British West Indies, 1783–1838," in Walvin, *Slavery and British Society*, p. 109. See also Goveia, *Slave Society in the British Leeward Islands*, pp. 284–85, 305.

403. Quoted in Northcott, *Slavery's Martyr*, p. 106.

404. Hurwitz, *Politics and the Public Conscience*, p. 88.

405. The "Ladies of Lyme Regis" petition to the House of Lords for the abolition of slavery, quoted in Hurwitz, *Politics and the Public Conscience*, p. 89.

406. Quoted in E. Wilson, *Thomas Clarkson*, p. 24.

407. Wesley, quoted by Brycchan Carey, "British Abolitionists: John Wesley," www.brycchancarey.com/abolition/wesley.htm.

408. Quoted at Christian History Institute, chi.gospelcom.net/DAILYF/2002/06/daily-06-30-2002.shtml.

409. Samuel Coleridge, Clarkson's friend, quoted in Wilson, *Thomas Clarkson*, p. 1.

410. E. Wilson, *Thomas Clarkson*, pp. 61, 31.

411. Carey et al., *Discourses*, p. 85.

412. Hochschild, "Against All Odds," p. 10.

413. Cugoano, *Narrative of the Enslavement of a Native of Africa*.

414. "Valuable Articles for the Slave Trade," unknown date, www.discoveringbristol.org.uk/showImageDetails.php?sit_id=1&img_id=716.

415. James Gillray, 1792, "Barbarities in the West Indies," www.discoveringbristol.org.uk/showImageDetails.php?sit_id=1&img_id=2388.

416. Quoted in Anstey, *The Atlantic Slave Trade and British Abolition*, p. 289.

417. Quoted in Hochschild, "Against All Odds," p. 10.

418. Anonymous, *Remarkable Extracts and Observations on the Slave Trade with Some Considerations on the Consumption of West India Produce*, 1792, quoted in Williams, *Capitalism and Slavery*, p. 183.

419. Quoted in Kitson, "'The Eucharist of Hell.'"

420. From "London Debates: 1792," *London Debating Societies 1776–1799* (1994), pp. 318–21, British History Online, www.british-history.ac.uk/report.asp?compid=38856.

421. Quoted in Midgley, *Women Against Slavery*, p. 39.

422. Brycchan Carey's scholarly website is an excellent source for abolitionist poetry: www.brycchancarey.com/slavery/cowperpoems.htm.

423. Quoted in Warner, *William Wilberforce*, p. 55.

424. Quoted in Walvin, *Slavery and British Society*, p. 124.

425. Quoted in Warner, *William Wilberforce*, p. 139.

426. Quoted in Drescher, "Whose Abolition?"

427. Wilberforce to William Hey, Feb. 28, 1807, quoted in Brycchan Carey, "William Wilberforce," www.brycchancarey.com/abolition/wilberforce.htm.

CHAPTER 8

428. Drescher, "Whose Abolition?"

429. Quoted in Northcott, *Slavery's Martyr*, p. 27.

430. Quoted in Matthews, "The Rumour Syndrome."

431. Quoted in Northcott, *Slavery's Martyr*, pp. 32, 46.

432. Ibid., p. 119.

433. Quoted in "Records relating to the Birmingham Ladies' Society for the Relief of British Negro Slaves, 1825–1919, in the Birmingham Reference Library," http://dydo1.lib.unimelb.edu.au/index.php?view=html; docid=1837;groupid=

434. Heyrick, *Immediate, Not Gradual, Abolition*, p. 9.

435. Quoted in Sussman, *Consuming Anxieties*, p. 139.

436. Heyrick, *Immediate, Not Gradual, Abolition*, p. 4.

437. *Reasons for Using East India Sugar*, 1828, printed for the Peckham Ladies' African and Anti-Slavery Association.

438. Quoted in Sussman, *Consuming Anxieties*, p. 122.

439. Heyrick, *Immediate, Not Gradual, Abolition*, p. 24.

440. Midgley, *Women Against Slavery*, p. 62.

441. Third edition of *The History of Mary Prince*, docsouth.unc.edu/neh/prince/prince.html.

442. Quoted in C. Hall, "Civilising Subjects."

443. Quoted in Alan Jackson, "William Knibb, 1803–1845, Jamaican Missionary and Slaves' Friend," *The Victorian Web*, www.victorianweb.org/history/knibb/knibb.html.

444. Quoted in E. Williams, *From Columbus to Castro*, p. 325.

445. Butler, *The Economics of Emancipation*, p. 19.

446. Sussman, *Consuming Anxieties*, p. 191.

447. Butler, *The Economics of Emancipation*, p. 141.

448. Mrs. A. C. Carmichael, 1834, quoted in Craton, "Slave Culture, Resistance and the Achievement of Emancipation in the British West Indies," p. 100.

449. E. Williams, *Capitalism and Slavery*, p. 158.

450. Quoted in Dyde, *A History of Antigua*, p. 132.

451. All quotations from J. Williams are taken from Williams, *A Narrative of Events*.

452. Altink, "To Wed or Not to Wed?" p. 98.

453. Quoted in Sturge's postscript to J. Williams's *A Narrative of Events*.

454. Altink, "To Wed or Not to Wed?" p. 97.

455. Sheller, "Quasheba, Mother, Queen."

456. Quoted in Boa, "Experiences of Women Estate Workers."

457. Quoted in C. Hall, *Civilising Subjects*, p. 118.

458. Quoted in ibid.

459. Quoted in ibid., p. 127.

460. Knibb, quoted in ibid.

461. Knibb, quoted in ibid., p. 165.

CHAPTER 9

462. Quoted in E. Williams, *From Columbus to Castro*, p. 319.

463. Quoted in *The Making of the West Indies*, p. 211.

464. Allahar, *Class, Politics, and Sugar in Colonial Cuba*, p. 63.

465. Quoted in ibid., p. 87.

466. Rachel Wilson Moore, *The Journal of Rachel Wilson Moore*, quoted in Perez, *Slaves, Sugar, and Colonial Society*, p. 127.

467. Robert Paquette, in *Sugar Is Made with Blood*, explores the hypothesis that the conspiracy never existed, and that it was invented by authorities to legitimize repression.

468. Fredrika Bremer, *The Homes of the New World: Impressions of America*, quoted in Perez, *Slaves, Sugar, and Colonial Society*, p. 117.

469. Calatrava, quoted in Allahar, *Class, Politics, and Sugar in Colonial Cuba*, p. 87.

470. Moreno Fraginals, quoted in Perez, *Slaves, Sugar, and Colonial Society*, p. 109.

471. Dye, *Cuban Sugar in the Age of Mass Production*, discusses this on pp. 74–75, citing studies by Laird Bergad, Rebecca Scott and others.

472. Quoted in Allahar, *Class, Politics, and Sugar in Colonial Cuba*, p. 161.

473. Perez, *Slaves, Sugar and Colonial Society*, claims that only 207 mills out of 1,100 survived the war. In *Cuban Sugar in the Age of Mass Production*, Alan Dye suggests that many of these mills were antiquated and that their destruction was a weeding-out process that helped the Cuban sugar industry modernize.

474. Quoted in Allahar, *Class, Politics, and Sugar in Colonial Cuba*, p. 158.

475. Dye outlines these new technologies in *Cuban Sugar in the Age of Mass Production*; see for instance pp. 78–82.

476. Dec. 28, 1886, quoted in Perez, *Slaves, Sugar and Colonial* Society, p. xvii.

477. Quoted in Richard Follett, "On the Edge of Modernity: Louisiana's Landed Elites in the Nineteenth-Century Sugar Country," in Del Lago and Halpern, *The American South and the Italian Mezzogiorno*, p. 76.

478. Quoted in Follett, "Heat, Sex, and Sugar," pp. 511, 510.

479. Martineau, *Society in America*.

480. Quoted in Follett, *The Sugar Masters*, p. 46.

481. Northup, *Twelve Years a Slave*, p. 213.

482. Quoted in Follett, *The Sugar Masters*, p. 46.

483. Follett, *The Sugar Masters*, p. 140. See also Follett, "On the Edge of Modernity," pp. 88–89.

484. Follett, *The Sugar Masters*, p. 50.

485. Quoted in Follett, "Heat, Sex, and Sugar," p. 528.

486. Quoted in Follett, *The Sugar Masters*, p. 180.

487. Northup, *Twelve Years a Slave*, p. 196.

488. Quoted in Follett, *The Sugar Masters*, p. 161.

489. Northup, *Twelve Years a Slave*, p. 200.

490. Ibid., pp. 214, 196.

491. Ibid., p. 215.

492. Quoted in Malone, *Sweet Chariot*, p. 245.

493. Quoted in Follett, *The Sugar Masters*, p. 231.

494. Quoted in Malone, *Sweet Chariot*, p. 246.

495. Quoted in ibid., p. 149.

496. Quoted in Follett, "On the Edge of Modernity," p. 86.

497. Quoted in Follett, *The Sugar Masters*, p. 115.

498. Albert, *The House of Bondage*, p. 106.

499. Quoted in Follett, "On the Edge of Modernity," p. 80.

500. Quoted in King, *A Northern Woman in the Plantation South*, p. 10.

501. Quoted in "Louisiana Tourist Guide," www.louisianatourguide.com/aariverroad.htm.

502. Quoted in Follett, *The Sugar Masters*, p. 68.

503. Quoted in ibid., p. 85.

504. Quoted in Rodrigue, *Reconstruction in the Cane Fields*, p. 36.

505. Quoted in ibid., p. 48.

506. Quoted in Mayhew, America's Civil War, July 2004, The History Net, www.thehistorynet.com.

507. Quoted in Mayhew, America's Civil War, July 2004.

508. Quoted in Wade, *Sugar Dynasty*, p. 73.

509. Quoted in ibid., p. 88.

510. Quoted in Rodrigue, *Reconstruction in the Cane Fields*, p. 95.

511. Quoted in ibid., p. 64.

512. Planter William T. Palfrey, quoted in ibid., p. 81.

513. Quoted in ibid., p. 95.

514. Quoted in ibid., p. 100.

515. Quoted in ibid., p. 107.

516. Quoted in ibid., p. 183.

517. Rodrigue, *Reconstruction in the Cane Fields*, p. 191.

518. Quoted in Robertson, *Sugar Farmers of Manitoba*, p. 79.

519. Vera Bloom, "Oxnard: A Social History of the Early Years," *Ventura County*

Historical Society Quarterly 4 (Feb. 1956), p. 19, quoted in Tomás Almaguer, "Racial Domination and Class Conflict in Capitalist Agriculture: The Oxnard Sugar Beet Workers' Strike of 1903," in *Working People of California*, edited by Daniel Conford (Berkeley: University of California Press, 1995).

520. JMLA press release, quoted in Prof. G. Amatsu's Class Web Magazine, www.sscnet.ucla.edu/aasc/classweb/winter02/aas197a/apaplabo_fp.html, accessed Sept. 15, 2003.

521. Murray, "A Foretaste of the Orient."

522. An excellent scholarly exposé of their situation is found in Laliberte and Satzewich, "Native Migrant Labour in the Southern Alberta Sugar Beet Industry."

523. Perkins, "Nazi Autarchic Aspirations and the Beet-Sugar Industry," pp. 497–518.

524. Quoted in Randall L. Bytwerk, *German Propaganda Archive*, www.calvin.edu/academic/cas/gpa/zd3.htm.

CHAPTER 10

525. This is the title of a leading source on indentured labor. See Tinker, *A New System of Slavery*.

526. Adamson, "Immigration into British Guiana," in Saunders, *Indentured Labour in the British Empire*, p. 45.

527. Quoted in Adamson, *Sugar without Slaves*, p. 51.

528. Adamson, *Sugar without Slaves*, p. 51.

529. E. Williams, *History of the People of Trinidad and Tobago*, p. 108.

530. Quoted in Tinker, *A New System of Slavery*, p. 119.

531. Quoted in ibid., p. 52.

532. Jenkins, *The Coolie*, p. 194.

533. Sewell, *The Ordeal of Free Labor in the West Indies*, pp. 123–24.

534. Jenkins, *The Coolie*, p. 388.

535. Quoted in ibid., p. 424. (Italics in original.)

536. Quoted in Adamson, "The Impact of Indentured Immigration on the Political Economy of British Guiana," in Saunders, *Indentured Labour in the British Empire*, p. 49.

537. Quoted in Adamson, *Sugar without Slaves*, p. 147.

538. Both quotations in Adamson, "The Impact of Indentured Immigration," p. 49.

539. Quoted in Tinker, *A New System of Slavery*, p. 182.

540. Tinker, *A New System of Slavery*, p. 187.

541. Ibid., p. 184.

542. Quoted in Adamson, *Sugar without Slaves*, p. 117.

543. E. Williams, *History of the People of Trinidad and Tobago*, p. 121.

544. Quoted in Tinker, *A New System of Slavery*, p. 215.

545. Quoted in E. Williams, *History of the People of Trinidad and Tobago*, p. 100.

546. Adamson, "The Impact of Indentured Immigration," p. 50.

547. Jagan, "Indo-Caribbean Political Leadership," in Birbalsingh, *Indenture and Exile*, p. 24.

548. Adamson, *Sugar without Slaves*, p. 266.

549. Deerr, *The History of Sugar*, p. 394.

550. Halpern, "Solving the 'Labour Problem,'" pp. 9, 10.

551. Quoted in Beinart, "Transkeian Migrant Workers," p. 58.

552. Faka's story is described by Beinart in "Transkeian Migrant Workers," p. 44.

553. Quoted in Lal, *Bittersweet*, p. 15.

554. Walter Gill, "Turn North-East at the Tombstone," quoted in Ali, "Girmit—The Indenture Experience in Fiji."

555. William Mune of the Rewa Sugar Co. to Colonial Secretary Office, Fiji, 1887, quoted in Ali, "Girmit—The Indenture Experience in Fiji."

556. The Cuba Commission Report, p. 42.

557. The *South Pacific Times*, Sept. 11, 1873, quoted in Stewart, *Chinese Bondage in Peru*, p. 68.

558. Quoted in Augier et al., *Making of the West Indies*, p. 202.

559. De Sagra, quoted in Perez, *Slaves, Sugar, and Colonial Society*, p. 112.

560. Quoted in Guterl, "After Slavery."

561. Julia Woodruff, My Winter in Cuba, quoted in Perez, *Slaves, Sugar, and Colonial Society*, p. 69.

562. Quoted in Guterl, "After Slavery."

563. Quoted in Gonzales, *Plantation Agriculture and Social Control in Northern Peru*, p. 121.

564. Public Law 103–150, the "Apology Resolution" to Native Hawaiians, November 23, 1993, www.hawaii-nation.org/publawsum.html.

565. Quoted in Okihiro, *Cane Fires*, p. 39.

566. Mark Twain, "The High Chief of Sugardom," in *The Sacramento Daily Union*, Sept. 26, 1866, wrote about the Hawaii sugar industry: "Its importance to America, surpasses them all. A land which produces six, eight, ten, twelve, yea, even thirteen thousand pounds of sugar to the acre on unmanured soil! ... This country is the king of the sugar world, as far as astonishing productiveness is concerned. Heretofore the Mauritius has held this high place." Found at www.twainquotes.com.

567. Quoted in Okihiro, *Cane Fires*, p. 28.

568. Liliuokalani, *Hawaii's Story by Hawaii's Queen*, pp. 237–38.

569. Grover, quoted at www.hawaii-nation.org/cleveland.html.

570. Quoted in R. Wilson, "Exporting Christian Transcendentalism, Importing Hawaiian Sugar," p. 19.

571. *The Advertiser*, quoted in Okihiro, *Cane Fires*, p. 79.

572. Docker, *The Blackbirders*, p. 61.

573. Saunders, *Exclusion, Exploitation and Extermination*, p. 161.

574. Adrian Graves, "Truck and Gifts: Melanesian Immigrants and the Trade Box System in Colonial Queensland," *Past and Present*, no. 101 (Nov. 1983) pp. 123–24.

575. H. I. Blake, "The Kanaka. A Character Sketch," *The Antipodean*, 1882, quoted in Saunders, *Exclusion, Exploitation and Extermination*, p. 394.

576. Quoted in Saunders, *Exclusion, Exploitation and Extermination*, p. 183.

577. Quoted in ibid., p. 196.

578. Quoted in ibid., pp. 173, 197.

579. Galloway, *The Sugar Cane Industry*, p. 229.

580. Docker, *The Blackbirders*, pp. 263–64.

581. Mercer, *White Australia Defied*, p. 98.

582. Quoted in Docker, *The Blackbirders*, p. 165.

583. Peter Griggs, "Alien Agriculturalists: Non-European Small Farmers in the Australian Sugar Industry, 1880–1920," in Ahluwalia et al., *White and Deadly*, p. 155.

CHAPTER 11

584. Quoted in Shawn McCarthy, "Hot Dog! A Century of Fast Food Is Relished," *The Globe and Mail*, Dec. 27, 2003.

585. Quoted in Vaccaro, *Beyond the Ice Cream Cone*, p. 127.

586. Powell, *Cool*, p. 202.

587. Batterberry, *On the Town in New York*, pp. 69–70.

588. Quoted in McWilliams, *A Revolution in Eating*, p. 179.

589. McWilliams, *A Revolution in Eating*, p. 211.

590. Woloson, *Refined Tastes*, p. 10.

591. Root, *Food*, p. 293.

592. Powell, *Cool*, p. 162.

593. Quoted in Woloson, *Refined Tastes*, p. 102.

594. Batterberry, *On the Town in New York*, p. 92.

595. Quoted in Woloson, *Refined Tastes*, p. 83.

596. Quoted in Root and de Rochemont, *Eating in America*, p. 427.

597. Quoted in ibid.

598. Theodore Roosevelt to Kermit, Feb. 7, 1904, quoted in Theodore Roosevelt, *Letters to His Children*, New York: Charles Scribner, 1919, The Project Gutenberg Ebook of *Letters to His Children*, edited by Joseph Bucklin Bishop, www.gutenberg.org.

599. Quoted in Woloson, *Refined Tastes*, p. 94.

600. Mayhew, *London Labour and the London Poor*, quoted in Richardson, *Sweets*, dedication page.

601. Woloson, *Refined Tastes*, p. 33.

602. Quoted in ibid., p. 40.

603. Quoted in ibid., p. 39.

604. Mayhew, *London Labour and the London Poor*, quoted in Richardson, *Sweets*, dedication page.

605. Quoted in Chinn, *The Cadbury Story*, p. 18.

606. Richardson, *Sweets*, p. 225.

607. Chinn, *The Cadbury Story*, p. 7.

608. Quoted in ibid., p. 16.

609. Vernon, *A Quaker Business Man*, p. 82, quoting an old employee.

610. Brenner, *The Emperors of Chocolate*, p. 73.

611. Ibid., p. 54.

612. Michael Levine, quoted in ibid., p. 97.

613. Quoted in Woloson, *Refined Tastes*, pp. 151–52.

614. Quoted in Folster, *The Chocolate Ganongs of St. Stephen, New Brunswick*, p. 78.

615. Visser, *Much Depends on Dinner*, p. 312.

616. Quoted in Woloson, *Refined Tastes*, p. 211.

617. Quoted in ibid., p. 169.

618. Farmer, *The Fanny Farmer Cookbook* (New York, Toronto: Bantam Books, 1994), p. 784. The book was revised in 1990 without one word of the original being omitted.

619. Woloson, *Refined Tastes*, p. 197.

620. Ibid., p. 221.

621. Ibid., p. 194.

622. Ibid., p. 3. I am indebted to Woloson for this interpretation.

623. Ibid., p. 226.

624. Quoted in ibid., p. 35.

625. Vernon, *A Quaker Business Man*, p. 197.

626. Quoted in Richardson, *Sweets*, p. 258.

627. Monroe Stover, quoted in Brenner, *The Emperors of Chocolate*, p. 117.

628. Quoted in ibid., p. 117.

629. Quoted in ibid., p. 138.

630. McWilliams, *A Revolution in Eating*, p. 266.

CHAPTER 12

631. Quoted in Attwood, *Raising Cane,* p. 71.

632. World Wildlife Fund, "Sugar and the Environment: Encouraging Better Management Practices in Sugar Production and Processing," www.panda.org.

633. Watts, *The West Indies*, p. 231.

634. Ibid., p. 434.

635. Singh and Solomon (eds.), *Sugarcane*, p. 419.

636. Shapiro, on behalf of the Coalition for Sugar Reform, before the U.S. Senate Committee on Agriculture, July 26, 2000.

637. Unnamed cane cutter quoted in Wilkinson, *Big Sugar*, p. 82.

638. Quoted in Brenner, "In the Kingdom of Big Sugar," *Vanity Fair*, Feb. 2001.

639. Quoted in ibid.

640. Hiassen, quoted in Brenner, "In the Kingdom of Big Sugar," *Vanity Fair*, Feb. 2001.

641. Quoted in Daniel Glick, "Big Sugar vs. the Everglades," *Rolling Stone*, May 2, 1996.

642. Roberts, "The Sweet Hereafter," *Harper's Magazine*, Nov. 1999.

643. Ibid.

644. At least 10 percent of sugar consumed in the U.S. comes from the Dominican Republic.

645. Quoted in Pollitt and Hagelberg, "The Cuban Sugar Economy in the Soviet Era and After," *Cambridge Journal of Economics*, vol. 18 (Dec. 1994), p. 558.

646. Quoted in Roca, *Cuban Economic Policy and Ideology*, p. 61.

647. Quoted in ibid., p. 7.

648. Speeches in 1979 and 1985, quoted in Perez-Lopez, "Sugar and Structural Change in the Cuban Economy," in *World Development*, vol. 17, no. 10 (1989), p. 1628.

649. James Horvath, "Changes and Challenges in the Sugar Industry Today," lecture given at North Dakota State University, April 7, 2004, www.ag.ndsu. nodak.edu/qbcc/BloomquistLectures/2004.

650. Quoted in N. R. Kleinfield, "Diabetes and Its Awful Toll Quietly Emerge as a Crisis," *The New York Times*, Jan. 9, 2006.

651. Dufty, *Sugar Blues*, p. 221.

652. Liftin, *Candy and Me*, p. 186.

653. Sarah Bosely, "Sugar Industry Threatens to Scupper WHO," *The Guardian*, April 21, 2003.

654. "The Food Pyramid Scheme," *The New York Times*, Sept. 1, 2004.

655. "Sugar Lobbyists Sour on Study," *CBS News*, April 23, 2003.

656. "FAO/WHO launch expert report on diet, nutrition and prevention of chronic diseases," WHO press release, April 23, 2003, www.who.int/hpr/gs_comments/ sugar_research.pdf.

657. Quoted in F. Joseph Demetrius, "Ethanol as Fuel: An Old Idea in New Tanks," in Scott B. MacDonald and Georges A. Fauriol (eds.), *The Politics of the Caribbean Basin Sugar Trade*, p. 149.

658. Quoted in "Ethanol Fuels Hope for Sugar Industry," *Dominican Today*, June 2, 2006.

659. Quoted in Ralf Kircher, "The Changing Face of Cuba," *Naples Daily News*, Dec. 2, 2003.

660. Santana, "Saving Tax $$, the Everglades and Birds … Using Cuban Sugar," *Progreso Weekly*, Nov. 1, 2003, www.progresoweekly.com/2003/11Nov/ 04week/Santana.htm.

Select Bibliography

BOOKS

Alan Adamson, *Sugar without Slaves: The Political Economy of British Guiana*, 1838–1904. New Haven: Yale University Press, 1972.

Pal Ahluwalia, Bill Ashcroft and Roger Knight (eds.), *White and Deadly: Sugar and Colonialism*. Commack, N.Y.: Nova Science Publishers, 1999.

Bill Albert and Adrian Graves (eds.), *The World Sugar Economy in War and Depression, 1914–1940*. New York: Routledge, Chapman and Hall, 1988.

Octavia V. Rogers Albert, *The House of Bondage or Charlotte Brooks and Other Slaves, Original and Life-like, as They Appeared in Their Old Plantation and City Slave Life; Together with Pen-pictures of the Peculiar Institution, with Sights and Insights into Their new Relations as Freedmen, Freemen, and Citizens*. New York: 1890, http://docsouth.unc.edu/neh/albert/albert.html.

Anton Allahar, *Class, Politics, and Sugar in Colonial Cuba*. Lewiston, N.Y.: Edwin Mellon Press, 1990.

Roger Anstey, *The Atlantic Slave Trade and British Abolition, 1760–1810*. London: Macmillan, 1975.

Donald W. Attwood, *Raising Cane: The Political Economy of Sugar in Western India*. Toronto: HarperCollins, 1991.

F. R. Augier et al., *The Making of the West Indies*. London, Trinidad and Tobago: Longman, 1976.

Elisabeth Ayrton, *The Cookery of England*. Harmondsworth, Middlesex: Penguin, 1977.

Michael Batterberry and Ariane Ruskin Batterberry, *On the Town in New York*. New York: Scribner, 1973.

Rosamond Bayne-Powell, *English Country Life in the Eighteenth Century*. London: J. Murray, 1935.

R. W. Beachey, *The British West Indies Sugar Industry in the Late 19th Century*. Oxford: Basil Blackwell, 1957.

Hilary Beckles, *Afro-Caribbean Women and Resistance to Slavery in Barbados*. London: Karnak House, 1988.

—*Black Rebellion in Barbados*. Bridgetown, Barbados: Carib Research and Publications, 1987.

—*Natural Rebels: A Social History of Enslaved Black Women in Barbados*. New Brunswick, N.J.: Rutgers University Press, 1989.

—*White Servitude and Slavery in Barbados, 1627–1715*. Knoxville: University of Tennessee Press, 1989.

Frank Birbalsingh (ed.), *Indenture and Exile: The Indo-Caribbean Experience*. Toronto: TSAR, 1989.

Jay Barrett Botsford, *English Society in the Eighteenth Century as Influenced from Oversea*. New York: Macmillan, 1924.

Kamau Braithwaite, *The Development of Creole Society in Jamaica, 1770–1820*. Oxford: Clarendon Press, 1971.

Joël Glenn Brenner, *The Emperors of Chocolate: Inside the Secret World of Hershey and Mars*. New York: Random House, 1999.

Trevor Burnard, *Mastery, Tyranny, and Desire: Thomas Thistlewood and His Slaves in the Anglo-Jamaican World*. Chapel Hill: University of North Carolina Press, 2004.

John Burnett, *Plenty and Want: A Social History of Diet in England from 1815 to the Present Day*. London: Scholar Press, 1979.

Barbara Bush, *Slave Women in Caribbean Society, 1650–1838*. Kingston, Jamaica: Heinemann; Bloomington: Indiana University Press; London: J. Currey, 1990.

Kathleen Mary Butler, *The Economics of Emancipation: Jamaica and Barbados, 1823–1843*. Chapel Hill and London: University of North Carolina Press, 1995.

Mavis Christine Campbell, *The Maroons of Jamaica, 1655–1796: A History of Resistance, Collaboration and Betrayal*. Granby, Mass.: Bergin, Garvey, 1988.

Brycchan Carey, Ellis Markman and Sarah Salih (eds.), *Discourses of Slavery and Abolition: Britain and Its Colonies, 1760–1838*. Basingstoke: Palgrave Macmillan, 2004.

Selwyn H. Carrington, *The Sugar Industry and the Abolition of the Slave Trade, 1775–1810*. Gainesville: University Press of Florida, 2002.

Carl Chinn, *The Cadbury Story*. Studley, Warwickshire: Brewin Books, 1998.

Aviva Chomsky, Barry Carr and Pamela Maria Smorkaloff (eds.), *The Cuba Reader: History, Culture, Politics*. Durham, N.C., and London: Duke University Press, 2003.

Belinda Coote, *The Hunger Crop: Poverty and the Sugar Industry*. London: Oxfam, 1987.

The Cuba Commission Report: *A Hidden History of the Chinese in Cuba: The Original English-language Text of 1876*. Baltimore and London: Johns Hopkins University Press, 1994.

Ottobah Cugoano, *Narrative of the Enslavement of a Native of Africa … 1787*, docsouth.unc.edu/neh/cugoano/menu.html.

Richard Cumberland, *The West Indian*, www.joensuu.fi/fld/english/meaney/ playtexts/wi/west_indian_2v.html.

Christian Daniels, "Agro-Industries: Sugarcane Technology," in Joseph Needham, *Science and Civilisation in China*, vol. 6, part 3. Cambridge: Cambridge University Press, 1996.

Basil Davidson, *Black Mother: Africa and the Atlantic Slave Trade*. Harmondsworth, Middlesex: Penguin Books, 1980.

Ivan Day, *Royal Sugar Sculpture: 600 Years of Splendour*. Barnard Castle: The Bowes Museum, 2002.

Noel Deerr, *The History of Sugar*, 2 vols. London: Chapman and Hall, 1949–50.

Enrico Del Lago and Rick Halpern (eds.), *The American South and the Italian Mezzogiorno: Essays in Comparative History*.

David Denslow, *Sugar Production in Northeastern Brazil and Cuba*. New York: Garland, 1987.

William Dickson and Joshua Steele, *Mitigation of Slavery, In Two Parts*. Westport, Conn.: Negro Universities Press, 1970, www.yale.edu/glc/ archive/1162.htm.

Edward Wybergh Docker, *The Blackbirders*. London and Sydney: Angus and Robertson, 1981.

Eddie Donoghue, *Black Women/White Men: The Sexual Exploitation of Female Slaves in the Danish West Indies*. Trenton, N.J.: Africa World Press, 2002.

Laurent Dubois, *Avengers of the New World*. Cambridge, Mass., and London: Harvard University Press, 2004.

Michael Duffy, *Soldiers, Sugar, and Seapower: The British Expeditions to the West Indies and the War against Revolutionary France.* Oxford: Clarendon Press; New York: Oxford University Press, 1987.

William Dufty, *Sugar Blues.* New York: Warner, 1993.

Richard Dunn, *Sugar and Slaves: The Rise of the Planter Class in the English West Indies.* New York: Norton, 1973.

Brian Dyde, *A History of Antigua: The Unsuspected Isle.* London: Macmillan Caribbean, 2000.

Alan Dye, *Cuban Sugar in the Age of Mass Production: Technology and the Economics of the Sugar Central, 1899–1929.* Stanford: Stanford University Press, 1998.

Oscar A. Echevarría (ed.), *Captains of Industry, Builders of Wealth: Miguel Angel Falla: The Cuban Sugar Industry.* Washington, D.C.: New House Pub., 2002.

P. C. Emmer (ed.), Colonialism and Migration: *Indentured Labour Before and After Slavery.* Higham, Mass.; Dordrecht: Nijhoff, 1986.

Olaudah Equiano, *The Life of Olaudah Equiano, or Gustavus Vassa, the African.* Mineola, N.Y.: Dover Publications, 1999.

Raymond Evans, Kay Saunders and Kathryn Cronin, *Exclusion, Exploitation and Extermination: Race Relations in Colonial Queensland.* Sydney: Australia and New Zealand Book Co., 1975.

Fanny Farmer, *Fanny Farmer Cookbook,* edited by Marion Cunningham; revised 1990. Formerly *The Boston Cooking School Book.* New York, Toronto: Bantam Books, 1994.

Niall Ferguson, *Empire: The Rise and Demise of the British World Order and the Lessons for Global Power.* New York: Basic Books, 2002.

Jose D. Fermin, *1904 World's Fair: The Filipino Experience.* Hawaii: University of Hawaii Press, 2005.

Carolyn Fick, *The Making of Haiti: The Saint Domingue Revolution from Below.* Knoxville: University of Tennessee Press, 2000.

Mrs. Flannigan, *Antigua and the Antiguans,* 2 vols. London: 1884; reprinted by Elibron Classics, no date.

Richard J. Follett, *The Sugar Masters: Planters and Slaves in Louisiana's Cane World, 1820–1860.* Baton Rouge: Louisiana State University Press, 2005.

David Folster, *The Chocolate Ganongs of St. Stephen, New Brunswick.* St. Stephen, N.B.: Ganongs, 1999.

Elborg Forster and Robert Forster (eds.), *Sugar and Slavery, Family and Race: The Letters and Diary of Pierre Dessalles, Planter in Martinique, 1808–1856.* Baltimore: Johns Hopkins University Press, 1996.

Tryphena Blanche Holder Fox, *A Northern Woman in the Plantation South: Letters of Tryphena Blanche Holder, 1834–1912.* Edited by Wilma King. Columbia: University of South Carolina Press, 1993.

Gilberto Freyre, *The Masters and the Slaves: A Study in the Development of Brazilian Civilization.* New York: Alfred A. Knopf, 1967.

David Galenson, *Traders, Planters, and Slaves.* Cambridge, and New York: Cambridge University Press, 1986.

Jock H. Galloway, *The Sugar Cane Industry: An Historical Geography from Its Origins to 1914.* Cambridge: Cambridge University Press, 1989.

P. Gaskell, *The Manufacturing Population of England: Its Moral, Social, and Physical Conditions, and the Changes Which Have Arisen from the Use of Steam Machinery; with an Examination of Infant Labour.* London: 1833.

David Barry Gaspar, *Bondsmen and Rebels: A Study of Master-Slave Relations in Antigua*. Durham, N.C.: Duke University Press, 1993.

Carol Gistitin, *Quite a Colony: South Sea Islanders in Central Queensland, 1867 to 1993*. Brisbane: AEBIS Publishing, 1995.

Michael Gonzales, *Plantation Agriculture and Social Control in Northern Peru, 1875–1933*. Austin: University of Texas Press, 1985.

Elsa V. Goveia, *Slave Society in the British Leeward Islands at the End of the Eighteenth Century*. New Haven and London: Yale University Press, 1965.

Alain Guédé, *Monsieur de Saint-George: Virtuoso, Swordsman, Revolutionary: A Legendary Life Rediscovered*. New York: Picador, 2003.

Catherine Hall, *Civilising Subjects: Metropole and Colony in the English Imagination 1830–1867*. Chicago and London: University of Chicago Press and Polity Press, 2002.

Douglas Hall, *In Miserable Slavery: Thomas Thistlewood in Jamaica, 1750–86*. Jamaica: University of the West Indies Press, 1999.

Kim F. Hall, "Culinary Spaces, Colonial Spaces: The Gendering of Sugar in the Seventeenth Century," in Valerie Traub, M. Lindsay Kaplan and Dympna Callaghan (eds.), *Feminist Readings of Early Modern Culture: Emerging Subjects*. Cambridge: Cambridge University Press, 1996.

Franklin Stewart Harris, *The Sugar-Beet in America*. New York: Macmillan, 1919.

Elizabeth Heyrick, *Immediate, Not Gradual, Abolition; or, an Inquiry into the Shortest, Safest, and Most Effectual Means of Getting Rid of West Indian Slavery*. London: 1824. Cornell University Library, Division of Rare and Manuscript Collections, Samuel J. May Anti-Slavery Collection, http://dlxs.library.cornell.edu/m/mayantislavery/index.htm.

Barry Higman, *Slave Population and Economy in Jamaica, 1807–1834*. Cambridge: Cambridge University Press, 1979.

Henry Hobhouse, *Seeds of Change: Five Plants That Transformed Mankind*. New York: Harper and Row, 1986.

Adam Hochschild, *Bury the Chains: Prophets and Rebels in the Fight to Free an Empire's Slaves*. Boston: Houghton Mifflin, 2005.

Edith F. Hurwitz, *Politics and the Public Conscience: Slave Emancipation and the Abolitionist Movement in Britain*. London: Allen and Unwin; New York: Barnes and Noble Books, 1973.

Joseph Inikori, *Forced Migration: The Impact of the Export Slave Trade on African Societies*. New York: Africana Publishing, 1982.

C. L. R. James, *The Black Jacobins*. London: Allison and Busby, 1980.

John Edward Jenkins, *The Coolie: His Rights and Wrongs*. New York: 1871.

Meredith John, *The Plantation Slaves of Trinidad, 1783–1816*. Cambridge: Cambridge University Press, 1988.

Sir James Kay-Shuttleworth, "The Moral and Physical Condition of the Working Classes of Manchester in 1832," www.historyhome.co.uk/peel/p-health/mterkay.htm.

Herbert S. Klein, *African Slavery in Latin America and the Caribbean*. Oxford: Oxford University Press, 1986.

Henry Koster, *Travels in Brazil*. Carbondale: Southern Illinois University Press, 1966.

Brij V. Lal, *Bittersweet: An Indo-Fijian Experience*. Canberra: Pandanus, 2004.

David S. Landes, *The Unbound Prometheus: Technological Change and Industrial Development in Western Europe from 1560 to the Present*. Cambridge: Cambridge University Press, 2003.

Matthew Lewis, *Journal of a West India Proprietor: Kept during a Residence in the Island of Jamaica*, edited by Judith Terry. Oxford: Oxford University Press, 1999.

Hilary Liftin, *Candy and Me (A Love Story)*. New York: Free Press, 2003.

Liliuokalani, *Queen of Hawaii, Hawaii's Story by Hawaii's Queen*. Rutland, Vt.: Charles E. Tuttle, 1990.

Ann Patton Malone, *Sweet Chariot: Slave Family and Household Structure in Nineteenth-century Louisiana*. Chapel Hill: University of North Carolina Press, 1992.

Teresita Martinez-Vergne, *Capitalism in Colonial Puerto Rico: Central San Vincente in the Late Nineteenth Century*. Gainesville: University Press of Florida, 1992.

Roderick A. McDonald, *Between Slavery and Freedom: Special Magistrate John Anderson's Journal of St. Vincent during the Apprenticeship*. Philadelphia: University of Pennsylvania Press, 2001.

Milton C. McFarlane, *Cudjoe of Jamaica: Pioneer for Black Freedom in the New World*. Short Hills, N.J.: R. Enslow, 1977.

James E. McWilliams, *A Revolution in Eating: How the Quest for Food Shaped America*. New York: Columbia University Press, 2005.

Patricia Mercer, *White Australia Defied: Pacific Islander Settlement in North Queensland*. Townsville, Queensland: Dept. of History and Politics, James Cook University, 1995.

Clare Midgley, *Women Against Slavery: The British Campaigns, 1780–1870*. London, New York: Routledge, 1992.

Sidney W. Mintz, *Sweetness and Power: The Place of Sugar in Modern History*. New York: Penguin, 1986.

— *Tasting Food, Tasting Freedom*. Boston: Beacon Press, 1996.

Bernard Moitt, *Women and Slavery in the French Antilles, 1635–1848*. Bloomington: Indiana University Press, 2001.

Roy Moxham, *Tea: Addiction, Exploitation, and Empire*. New York: Carroll and Graf, 2003.

Cecil Northcott, *Slavery's Martyr: John Smith of Demerara and the Emancipation Movement, 1817–1824*. London: Epworth Press, 1976.

Solomon Northup, *Twelve Years a Slave: Narrative of Solomon Northup, a Citizen of New-York, Kidnapped in Washington City in 1841, and Rescued in 1853*. Auburn, N.Y.: 1853; docsouth.unc.edu/fpn/northup/menu.html.

Maria Nugent, *Lady Nugent's Journal of her Residence in Jamaica from 1801 to 1805*. 4th edition. Kingston: Institute of Jamaica, 1966.

D. J. Oddy, "Food, Drink and Nutrition," in *The Cambridge Social History of Britain 1750–1950*, vol. 2, edited by F. L. M. Thompson. Cambridge: Cambridge University Press, 1993.

Gary Y. Okihiro, *Cane Fires: The Anti-Japanese Movement in Hawaii, 1865–1945*. Philadelphia: Temple University Press, 1991.

Robert L. Paquette, *Sugar Is Made with Blood: The Conspiracy of La Escalera and the Conflict between Empires over Slavery in Cuba*. Middletown, Conn.: Wesleyan University Press, 1988.

Richard Pares, *A West-India Fortune*. London: Longmans, Green, 1950.

Orlando Patterson, *The Sociology of Slavery*. Jamaica: Granada Publishing, 1973.

Mark Pendergrast, *For God, Country and Coca-Cola: The Unauthorized History of the Great American Soft Drink and the Company That Makes It*. New York: Scribner, 1993.

Louis A. Perez, *Slaves, Sugar, and Colonial Society: Travel Accounts of Cuba, 1801–1899*. Wilmington, Del.: Scholarly Resources, 1992.

Jane Pettigrew, *A Social History of Tea*. London: National Trust, 2001.

Marilyn Powell, *Cool: The Story of Ice Cream*. Toronto: Penguin, 2005.

Mary Prince, *The History of Mary Prince, a West Indian Slave. Related by Herself.* London: 1831. Electronic edition, University of North Carolina at Chapel Hill, Academic Affairs Library, 2000, docsouth.unc.edu/neh/prince/prince.html.

Lowell Ragatz, *The Fall of the Planter Class in the British Caribbean, 1763–1833: A Study in Social and Economic History*. New York: Octagon Books, 1963.

Ron Ramdin, *Arising from Bondage: A History of the Indo-Caribbean People*. New York: New York University Press, 2000.

Tim Richardson, *Sweets*. Bloomsbury, N.Y.: Bloomsbury, 2002.

Heather Robertson, *Sugar Farmers of Manitoba: The Manitoba Sugar Beet Industry in Story and Picture*. Altona: Manitoba Beet Growers Association, 1968.

Sergio Roca, *Cuban Economic Policy and Ideology: The Ten Million Ton Sugar Harvest*. Beverly Hills, Calif.: Sage Publications, 1976.

John C. Rodrigue, *Reconstruction in the Cane Fields: From Slavery to Free Labor in Louisiana's Sugar Parishes, 1862–1880*. Baton Rouge: Louisiana State University Press, 2001.

Waverley Lewis Root, *Food: An Authoritative and Visual History and Dictionary of the Foods of the World*. New York: Simon and Schuster, 1980.

Waverley Lewis Root and Richard de Rochemont, *Eating in America: A History*. New York: Morrow, 1976.

Edward Royle, *Modern Britain: A Social History, 1750–1985*. London, Baltimore: Edward Arnold, 1987.

Kirkpatrick Sale, *The Conquest of Paradise: Christopher Columbus and the Columbian Legacy*. New York: Plume, 1991.

George Sanderlin (ed.), *Bartolomé de Las Casas: A Selection of His Writings*. New York: Alfred A. Knopf, 1975.

Keith Albert Sandiford, *The Cultural Politics of Sugar: Caribbean Slavery and Narratives of Colonialism*. Cambridge, New York: Cambridge University Press, 2000.

Kay Saunders, *Indentured Labour in the British Empire, 1834–1920*. London: Croom Helm, 1984.

Francisco A. Scarano, *Sugar and Slavery in Puerto Rico*. Madison: University of Wisconsin Press, 1984.

Stuart B. Schwartz, *Sugar Plantations in the Formation of Brazilian Society*. Cambridge, New York: Cambridge University Press, 1985.

Rebecca J. Scott, *Slave Emancipation in Cuba: The Transition to Free Labor, 1860–1899*. Princeton: Princeton University Press, 1985.

William Grant Sewell, *The Ordeal of Free Labor in the West Indies*. New York: A. M. Kelley, 1968.

Folarin O. Shyllon, *Black Slaves in Britain, 1555–1833*. Oxford: Oxford University Press, 1977.

Folarin O. Shyllon and James Ramsay, *The Unknown Abolitionist*. Edinburgh: Canongate, 1977.

G. B. Singh and S. Solomon (eds.), *Sugarcane: Agro-Industrial Alternatives*. New Delhi: Oxford and IBH Publishing, 1995.

Woodruff D. Smith, "From Coffeehouse to Parlour: The Consumption of Coffee, Tea and Sugar in North-western Europe in the Seventeenth and Eighteenth

Centuries," in *Consuming Habits: Drugs in History and Anthropology*, edited by Jordan Goodman et al. New York: Routledge, 1995.

David E. Stannard, *American Holocaust: Columbus and the Conquest of the New World*. Oxford: Oxford University Press, 1992.

Robert Louis Stein, *The French Sugar Business in the Eighteenth Century*. Baton Rouge: Louisiana State University Press, 1988.

Watt Stewart, *Chinese Bondage in Peru*. Durham, N.C.: Duke University Press, 1951.

Roy C. Strong, *Feast: A History of Grand Eating*. Orlando, Fla.: Harcourt, 2002.

Suiker/Sugar. Amsterdam: Amsterdams Historisch Museum, 2006.

Charlotte Sussman, *Consuming Anxieties: Consumer Protest, Gender, and British Slavery, 1713–1833*. Stanford: Stanford University Press, 2000.

Kit Sims Taylor, *Sugar and the Underdevelopment of Northeastern Brazil, 1500–1970*. Gainesville: University Press of Florida, 1978.

E. P. Thompson, *The Making of the English Working Class*. London: Gollancz, 1980.

Mary Elizabeth Thurston, *The Lost History of the Canine Race*. Kansas City: Andrews and McMeel, 1996.

Hugh Tinker, *A New System of Slavery*. London, New York: Institute of Race Relations, Oxford University Press, 1974.

Dale W. Tomlich, *Slavery in the Circuit of Sugar: Martinique and the World Economy, 1830–1848*. Baltimore: Johns Hopkins University Press, 1990.

Maguelonne Toussaint-Samat, *A History of Food* (translated by Anthea Bell). Cambridge, Mass.: Blackwell, 1992.

Pamela J. Vaccaro, *Beyond the Ice Cream Cone: The Whole Scoop on Food at the 1904 World's Fair*. St. Louis: Enid Press, 2004.

Anne Vernon, *A Quaker Business Man: The Life of Joseph Rowntree, 1836–1925*. London: Allen and Unwin, 1958.

Margaret Visser, *Much Depends on Dinner*. Toronto: McClelland and Stewart, 1987.

Michael G. Wade, *Sugar Dynasty: M. A. Patout & Son, 1791–1993*. Lafayette: Center for Louisiana Studies, University of Southwestern Louisiana, 1995.

James Walvin, *Black Ivory: Slavery in the British Empire*. Oxford: Blackwell, 2001.

—*Slavery and British Society, 1776–1846*. Baton Rouge: Louisiana State University Press, 1982.

Oliver Warner, *William Wilberforce and His Times*. London: Batsford, 1962.

David Watts, *The West Indies: Patterns of Development, Culture and Environmental Change Since 1492*. Cambridge: Cambridge University Press, 1987.

Alec Wilkinson, *Big Sugar: Seasons in the Cane Fields of Florida*. New York: Alfred A. Knopf, 1989.

Eric Williams, *Capitalism and Slavery*. London: Andre Deutsch, 1964.

—*From Columbus to Castro: The History of the Caribbean, 1492–1969*. London: Andre Deutsch, 1983.

—*History of the People of Trinidad and Tobago*. London: Andre Deutsch, 1982.

Gomer Williams, *History of the Liverpool Privateers and Letters of Marque, with an Account of the Liverpool Slave Trade*. New York: A. M. Kelley, 1966.

Andrew R. Wilson, *The Chinese in the Caribbean*. Princeton, N.J.: M. Wiener Publishers, 2004.

Ellen Gibson Wilson, *Thomas Clarkson: A Biography*. New York: St. Martin's Press, 1990.

Stephen M. Wise, *Though the Heavens May Fall.* Cambridge, Mass.: Da Capo Press, 2005.

Wendy Woloson, *Refined Tastes: Sugar, Confectionery, and Consumers in Nineteenth-century America.* Baltimore: Johns Hopkins University Press, 2002.

ARTICLES

Ahmed Ali, "Girmit—The Indenture Experience in Fiji," *Bulletin of the Fiji Museum*, no. 5 (1979), www.fijigirmit.org/a_girmit_an_introduction.htm.

Tomás Almaguer, "Racial Domination and Class Conflict in Capitalist Agriculture: The Oxnard Sugar Beet Workers' Strike of 1903," in *Working People of California*, edited by Daniel Conford. Berkeley: University of California Press, 1995.

Henrice Altink, "To Wed or Not to Wed? The Struggle to Define Afro-Jamaican Relationships, 1834–1838," *Journal of Social History*, vol. 38, no. 1 (2004), pp. 81–111.

B. J. Barickman, "Persistence and Decline: Slave Labour and Sugar Production in the Bahian Reconcavo, 1850–1888," *Journal of Latin American Studies*, vol. 28 (Oct. 1996), pp. 581–633.

W. Beinart, "Transkeian Migrant Workers and Youth Labour on the Natal Sugar Estates, 1918–1948," *Journal of African History*, vol. 32 (1991), pp. 41–63.

Sheena Boa, "Experiences of Women Estate Workers during the Apprenticeship Period in St. Vincent, 1834–38: The Transition from Slavery to Freedom," *Women's History Review*, vol. 10, no. 3 (2001), pp. 381–408.

Marie Brenner, "In the Kingdom of Big Sugar," *Vanity Fair*, Feb. 2001.

Paolo Carrozza, "Bartolomé de Las Casas, the Midwife of Modern Human Rights Talk," in "From Conquest to Constitutions: Retrieving a Latin American Tradition of the Idea of Human Rights," www.lascasas.org/carrozo.htm.

T. Carroll and B. Carroll, "Accommodating Ethnic Diversity in a Modernizing Democratic State: Theory and Practice in the Case of Mauritius," *Ethnic and Racial Studies*, vol. 23, no. 1 (Jan. 2000), pp. 120–42.

—"Trouble in Paradise: Ethnic Conflict in Mauritius," *Journal of Commonwealth and Comparative Politics*, vol. 38, no. 2 (July 2000), pp. 25–50.

Center for Responsive Politics, "The Politics of Sugar: Sugar's First Family," www.opensecrets.org/pubs/cashingin_sugar/sugar08.html.

"The Character of a Coffee-House, 1673," pterodactylcoffee.com/fyi/coffee_info_coffeehouse.htm.

Bob Corbett (ed.), "King Ferdinand's letter to the Taino/Arawak Indians," www.hartford-hwp.com/archives/41/038.html.

Gregson Davis, "Jane Austen's Mansfield Park: The Antigua Connection," presented at the Antigua and Barbuda Country Conference, Nov. 13–15, 2003, www.uwichill.edu.bb/bnccde/antigua/conference/paperdex.html.

Seymour Drescher, "Whose Abolition? Popular Pressure and the Ending of the British Slave Trade," in *Past and Present*, May 1994, findarticles.com/p/articles/mi_m2279/is_n143/ai_15646034.

Richard Follett, "Heat, Sex, and Sugar: Pregnancy and Childbearing in the Slave Quarters," *Journal of Family History*, vol. 28, no. 4 (2003), pp. 510–39.

Daniel Glick, "Big Sugar vs. the Everglades," *Rolling Stone*, May 2, 1996.

Douglas Goff, "Ice Cream History and Folklore," www.foodsci.uoguelph.ca/dairyedu/ichist.html.

George Grantham, "Agricultural Supply During the Industrial Revolution: French Evidence and European Implications," *Journal of Economic History*, vol. 49, no. 1 (March 1989), pp. 43–72.

Peter Griggs, "The Origins and Early Development of the Small Cane Farming System in Queensland, 1870–1915," *Journal of Historical Geography*, vol. 23 (Jan. 1997), pp. 46–61.

Matthew Pratt Guterl, "After Slavery: Asian Labor, the American South, and the Age of Emancipation," *Journal of World History*, vol. 14, no. 2 (2003); www.historycooperative.org/journals/jwh/14.2/guterl.html.

Rick Halpern, "Solving the 'Labour Problem': Race, Work and the State in the Sugar Industries of Louisiana and Natal, 1870–1910," *Journal of Southern African Studies*, vol. 30, no. 1 (March 2004), pp. 19–40.

Bonar Ludwig Hernandez, "The Las Casas–Sepúlveda Controversy, 1550–1551, http://userwww.sfsu.edu/~epf/2001/hernandez.html.

Adam Hochschild, "Against All Odds," *Mother Jones*, Jan/Feb. 2004, p. 10.

Shaheeda Hosain, "A Space of Their Own: Indian Women and Land Ownership in Trinidad 1870–1945." *Caribbean Review of Gender Studies,* issue no. 1 (April 2007), pp. 1–17, www.sta.uwi.edu/crgs/cfp.pdf.

Joseph Inikori, "The 'Wonders of Africa' and the Trans-Atlantic Slave Trade," *West Africa Review* (2000), condor.depaul.edu/~diaspora/html/community/ inikori1.html.

Peter J. Kitson, "'The Eucharist of Hell'; or, Eating People Is Right: Romantic Representations of Cannibalism," Romanticism on the Net, no. 17 (Feb. 2000), www.erudit.org/revue/ron/2000/v/n17/005892ar.html.

Elizabeth Kolbert, "The Lost Mariner," *The New Yorker*, Oct. 14, 2002.

Ron Laliberte and Vic Satzewich, "Native Migrant Labour in the Southern Alberta Sugar Beet Industry: Coercion and Paternalism in the Recruitment of Labour," *Canadian Review of Sociology and Anthropology*, vol. 36, no. 1 (Feb. 1999), pp. 65–85.

Christian Leuprecht, "Comparing Demographic Policy, Change, and Ethnic Relations in Mauritius and Fiji," May 2005, www.cpsa-acsp.ca/papers-2005/Leuprecht,%20 Christian.pdf.

Alex Lichtenstein, "The Roots of Black Nationalism?" *American Quarterly*, vol. 57, no. 1 (2005), pp. 261–69.

"London Debates: 1792," *London Debating Societies 1776–1799* (1994), pp. 318–21, www.british-history.ac.uk/report.asp?compid=38856.

Harriet Martineau, "Agriculture," in *Society in America*, vol. 2. London: 1837; www2.pfeiffer.edu/~lridener/DSS/Martineau/v2p2c1.html.

Samuel Martinez, "From Hidden Hand to Heavy Hand: Sugar, the State, and Migrant Labor in Haiti and the Dominican Republic," *Latin American Research Review*, vol. 34, no. 1 (1999), pp. 57–84.

Gelien Matthews, "The Rumour Syndrome, Sectarian Missionaries and Nineteenth Century Slave Rebels of the British West Indies," The Society for Caribbean Studies Annual Conference Papers, vol. 2 (2001), www.scsonline.freeserve.co.uk/olvol2.html.

David R. Mayhew, letter, America's Civil War, July 2004, The History Net, www.thehistorynet.com/acw/letters_07_04/.

Doug Munro, "Indenture, Deportation, Survival: Recent Books on Australian South Sea Islanders," *Journal of Social History* (Summer 1998).

John Murray, "A Foretaste of the Orient," *International Socialist Review*, vol. 4 (Aug. 1903), pp. 72–79; historymatters.gmu.edu/d/5564.

Diana Paton, "Punishments, Crime, and the Bodies of Slaves in Eighteenth-century Jamaica," *Journal of Social History* (Summer 2001), p. 8; www.findarticles.com/p/articles/mi_m2005/is_4_34/ai_7671303.

Jorge F. Perez-Lopez, "Sugar and Structural Change in the Cuban Economy," *World Development*, vol. 17, no. 10 (1989), pp. 1627–46.

John Perkins, "Nazi Autarchic Aspirations and the Beet-Sugar Industry, 1933–9," *European History Quarterly*, vol. 20 (1990), pp. 497–518.

Nicole Phillip, "Producers, Reproducers, and Rebels: Grenadian Slave Women, 1783–1833," presented at the Grenada Country Conference, January 2002, www.cavehill.uwi.edu/bnccde/grenada/conference/ papers/phillip.html.

Steven Pincus, "Coffee Politicians Does Create: Coffeehouses and Restoration Political Culture," *Journal of Modern History*, vol. 67, no. 4 (Dec. 1995), pp. 807–34.

Brian H. Pollitt and G. B. Hagelberg, "The Cuban Sugar Economy in the Soviet Era and After," *Cambridge Journal of Economics*, vol. 18 (Dec. 1994), pp. 547–69.

David Richardson, "Shipboard Revolts, African Authority, and the Atlantic Trade," *William and Mary Quarterly*, vol. 58 (Jan. 2001), pp. 69–92.

Paul Roberts, "The Sweet Hereafter: Our Craving for Sugar Starves the Everglades and Fattens Politicians," *Harper's Magazine*, Nov. 1999, www.saveoureverglades.org/news/articles/news_after.html.

Meryl Rutz, "Salt Horse and Ship's Biscuit: A Short Essay on the Diet of the Royal Navy Seaman During the American Revolution," www.navyandmarine.org/ondeck/1776salthorse.htm.

Kirkpatrick Sale, "What Columbus Discovered," *The Nation*, Oct. 22, 1990.

Eduardo Santana, "Saving Tax $$, the Everglades and Birds … Using Cuban Sugar," *Progreso Weekly*, Nov. 1, 2003, www.progresoweekly.com/2003/11Nov/04week/Santana.htm.

Carole Shammas, "Food Expenditures and Economic Well-Being in Early Modern England," *Journal of Economic History*, vol. 43, no. 1, pp. 89–100.

Mimi Sheller, "Quasheba, Mother, Queen: Black Women's Public Leadership and Political Protest in Post-emancipation Jamaica, 1834–1865," Department of Sociology, Lancaster University, www.comp.lancs.ac.uk/sociology/papers/Sheller-Quasheba-Mother-Queen.pdf.

J. A. Sierra, "The Legend of Hatuey," www.historyofcuba.com/history/oriente/hatuey.htm.

Woodruff D. Smith, "Complications of the Commonplace: Tea, Sugar, and Imperialism," *Journal of Interdisciplinary History*, vol. 23, no. 2 (Autumn 1992), pp. 259–78.

Michael Tadman, "The Demographic Cost of Sugar: Debates on Slave Societies and Natural Increase in the Americas," *The American Historical Review*, vol. 105, no. 5, pp. 1534–75.

James Williams, "A Narrative of Events, Since the First of August, 1834," docsouth.unc.edu/neh/williamsjames/williams.html.

Rob Wilson, "Exporting Christian Transcendentalism, Importing Hawaiian Sugar: The Trans-Americanization of Hawai'i," *American Literature*, vol. 72, no. 3 (Sept. 2000), pp. 521–52.

Index

Credits

Page 2: 10462564 Emile Frechon/Royal Photographic Society/Science & Society Picture Library.

Page 3: Courtesy of the author. Photographer: Heather Conway.

Page 4: Courtesy of Phillip Abbott.

Page 5: Jean-Max Benjamin.

Page 14: Library of Congress, Prints and Photographs Division, LC-USZ62-65546. Public domain.

Page 26: Public domain.

Page 38: Public domain.

Page 43: Courtesy of Bowes Museum, Barnard Castle, County Durham, UK.

Page 45: Jupiterimages Unlimited.

Page 52: Daumier print DR Number 453, LD number 453, HD number 1088, Daumier Register Digital Work Catalogue, www.daumier.org. Public domain.

Page 59: Archives, Stanstead Historical Society.

Page 60: Photograph attributed to James Ballantyne/Library and Archives Canada/PA-131929.

Page 61: Robert Redord/Library and Archives Canada/C-060817.

Page 65: www.gutenberg.org. From *Real Life in London . . . Illustrated with a Series of Coloured Prints, Designed and Engraved by Messrs. Heath, Aiken, Dighton, Brooke, Rowlandson, etc.* Volume II, Part 1. London: Methuen & CO. London.

Page 76: Photographer: Dave Ley, Wiki Media Commons, http://common. wikimedia.org/.

Page 78: Wiki Media Commons, http://common.wikimedia.org/. Public domain.

Pages 85-86: William Clark, *Ten Views in the Island of Antigua, in which are Represented the Process of Sugar Making, and the Employment of the Negroes, in the Field, Boiling-House, and Distillery.* From drawings made by William Clark, during a residence of three years in the West Indies, upon the estates of Admiral Tallemach.

London: Thomas Clay, Ludgate-Hill, 1823. Public domain.

Page 90: Wiki Media Commons, http://common.wikimedia.org/. Public domain.

Page 109: Library of Congress, LC-USZ62-65530. Public domain.

Page 118: Public domain.

Page 125: Library of Congress, LC-USZ62-97233. Public domain.

Page 126: National Library of Australia, Canberra, NLA. PIC-an282264.

Page 131: Library of Congress LC-DIG-ppmsca-07200 (digital file from original print). Public domain.

Page 135: Illustration by Thomas Rowlandson, published in London by William Holland, 1796. Public domain.

Page 144: Wiki Media Commons, http://common.wikimedia.org/. Public domain.

Page 158: Public domain.

Page 164: (top) www.gutenberg.org. *From Real Life in London . . . Illustrated*

with a Series of Coloured Prints,
Designed and Engraved by Messrs.
Heath, Aiken, Dighton, Brooke,
Rowlandson, etc. Volume II, Part 1.
London: Methuen & CO. London.

Page 164: (bottom): Public domain.

Page 184: Public domain.

Page 191: Public domain.

Page 192 (top): Public domain.

Page 192 (bottom): Public domain.

Page 213: *Burning of the Plaine du Cap,
Haiti*, 1794 (painter unknown).
Public domain.

Page 235: Library of Congress, Prints
and Photographs Division, LC-
USZC-4-6204. Public domain.

Page 237: Library of Congress, Prints
and Photographs Division, LC-
USZ62-30930. Public domain.

Page 240: Public domain.

Page 244: Library of Congress, Prints
and Photographs Division, LC-
USZc4-8775. Public domain.

Page 254: Courtesy National Library of
Jamaica.

Page 261: Richard Bridgens, *West India
scenery with illustrations of Negro character, the process of making sugar, &c.
from sketches taken during a voyage to
and residence of seven years in, the
island of Trinidad.* London, R.
Jennings [1836?]. Public domain.

Page 264: Library of Congress, Prints
and Photographs Division, LC-
USZ62-117226. Public domain.

Page 267: Library of Congress Stereo,
"Two pretty girls I met in a cane field
in St. Kitts," 1903. Public domain.

Page 285: Louisiana Division/City
Archives, New Orleans Public Library.

Page 289: National Inventors Hall of
Fame.

Page 290: Louisiana Division/City
Archives, New Orleans Public Library.

Page 293: Louisiana Division/City
Archives, New Orleans Public Library.

Page 304: Library of Congress, Prints and
Photographs Division, LC-DIG-
nclc-00260. Public domain.

Page 305: Library of Congress, Prints and
Photographs Division, LC-DIG-
nclc-00280. Public domain.

Page 306 (top): Glenbow Museum-
NA-3369

Page 306 (bottom): Library and Archives
Canada, C-007819.

Page 307: Library of Congress, Prints
and Photographs Division, LC-
USZ62-121292. Public domain.

Page 317: Wiki Media Commons,
http://common.wikimedia.org/.
Public domain.

Page 333: Illustration from Edward Jenkins,
*The Coolie: His Rights and Wrongs:
notes of a journey to British Guiana,
with a review of the system and of the
recent commission of inquiry.* London:
Strahan, 1871. Public domain.

Page 338: Library of Congress Prints and
Photographs Division, LC-USZ62-
105894. Public domain.

Page 345: John Oxley Library, State
Library of Queensland Image
#60623.

Page 354: Glenbow Museum, NA-4026-3.

Page 355: Glenbow Museum, NA-4159-
14.

Page 359: Courtesy of Bowes Museum
Barnard Castle, County Durham,
UK, Accession Number
1973/43/ARC.

Page 362: Public domain.

Page 369: Library of Congress, Prints
and Photographs Division, LC-
USW33-042520. Public domain.

Page 380: Library of Congress, Prints
and Photographs Division, LC-
USF35-440. Public domain.

Page 381: Wiki Media Commons,
    http://common.wikimedia.org/.
    Public domain.

Page 389: Photographer: Matthew Casey.

Page 390: Photographer: Anna Peters.

Page 391: Photographer: Matthew Casey.

Page 392: Photographer: Anna Peters.

Page 393: Photographer: Anna Peters.

Page 402: Glenbow Museum,
    NA-2316-7.